the ballets russes and its world

yale university press

new haven and london

The Ballets Russes

and Its World

afola and Nancy Van Norman Baer

Illustrations, title pages: André Derain, costume designs for
the ballerinas from *Jack-in-the-Box.* Wadsworth
Atheneum, Hartford. The Ella Gallup Sumner and
Mary Catlin Sumner Collection Fund, 1933.465 and
1933.468.

Designed by Sonia Scanlon and set in Monotype
Joanna by Running Feet Books, Morrisville, N.C.
Printed in Italy by Eurographica S.p.A.

Library of Congress Cataloging-in-Publication Data
The Ballets russes and its world / edited by Lynn
Garafola and Nancy Van Norman Baer.
p.   cm.
Includes bibliographical references and index.
ISBN 0–300–06176–5 (alk. paper)
1. Ballets russes—History.   2. Diaghilev, Serge,
1872–1929.   I. Garafola, Lynn.   II. Baer, Nancy Van
Norman.
GV1786.B355B35   1999
792.8'0947—dc21   98–51002
                              CIP
A catalogue record for this book is available from the
British Library.
The paper in this book meets the guidelines for
permanence and durability of the Committee on
Production Guidelines for Book Longevity of the
Council on Library Resources.

10 9 8 7 6 5 4 3 2 1

contents

acknowledgments

We are deeply grateful to the many individuals who helped bring this project to fruition. These include Pierre Alechinsky; Xoán Carreira; Ruth Eagleton-Grocott, Vogue House, London; Mary Edsel and Annette Fern, Harvard Theatre Collection, Cambridge, Massachusetts; Francesca Franchi, Royal Opera House Archives, London; Howard B. Gotlieb, Special Collections, Mugar Memorial Library, Boston University; Linda Hardberger, Marion Koogler McNay Art Museum, San Antonio, Texas; Audrey Harman, Royal Ballet School, London; Mary Haas, Fine Arts Museums of San Francisco; Brigitte Hédel-Samson, Fernand Léger Museum, Biot, France; Millicent Hodson; Barbara Horgan, The George Balanchine Trust, New York; Claudia Jeschke; Deborah Koolish, New York City Ballet; Nancy Lassalle and Lynn Foster, Ballet Society, New York; George Platt Lynes II, Bloomfield College, Bloomfield, New Jersey; Frederick Maddox; Ulrich Mosch and Johanna Blask, Paul Sacher Foundation, Basel; Monica Moseley and Charles Perrier, Dance Collection, New York Public Library for the Performing Arts; Katy Naquin, Société des Bains de Mer, Monte Carlo; Erik Naslund and Thomas Skalm, Dansmuseet, Stockholm; Margaret Norton, San Francisco Performing Arts Library and Museum; Marianne Olivieri; Marilyn Palmeri, Pierpont Morgan Library, New York; Jean-Pierre Pastori; Jane Pritchard, Rambert Dance Company Archives, London; Lisa D. Roush, Jane Voorhees Zimmerli Art Museum, Rutgers University, New Brunswick, New Jersey; José Sasportes; Inger Schoelkopf, Yale Center for British Art, New Haven, Connecticut; Thomas W. Schoff, School of American Ballet, New York City; Herbert Schimmel; Jerry L. Thompson, Armenia, New York; Douglas Blair Turnbaugh; Patrizia Veroli; Sarah C. Woodcock, Theatre Museum, London; Vicky Wulff, Music Division, Library of Congress, Washington, D.C. We are also grateful to the Archivo de Compositores Vascos, Rentería, Spain; Artists Rights Society (ARS), New York City; Bakhrushin State Central Theatrical Museum, Moscow; Bancroft Library, University of California, Berkeley; Central State Archive of Cinema and Photo Documents, St. Petersburg; King's College, Cambridge; Prints and Photographs Division, Library of Congress, Washington, D.C.; The Museum of Modern Art, New York City; State Russian Museum, St. Petersburg; and Victor Gollancz, London. A special thanks to Syracuse University Library, Department of Special Collections, Syracuse, New York, for waiving its usual permissions fees.

To the authors and translators who have contributed to this book, we are indebted for their patience and good cheer under sometimes trying circumstances. We are deeply grateful to Elizabeth Souritz for her unstinting help with the Russian material; Alan R. Dodge for his assistance with permissions; and Tirza True Latimer, Research Assistant, Theatre and Dance Department, Fine Arts Museums of San Francisco, for her invaluable assistance. We are grateful to our editor, Harry Haskell, for his belief in the project from the start, and to Susan Laity of Yale University Press for treating the manuscript with exemplary care. Their contributions have made the book much the richer.

To the late N. V. N. B. from her friend and collaborator Lynn Garafola

introduction

The Legacy of Diaghilev's Ballets Russes

Lynn Garafola

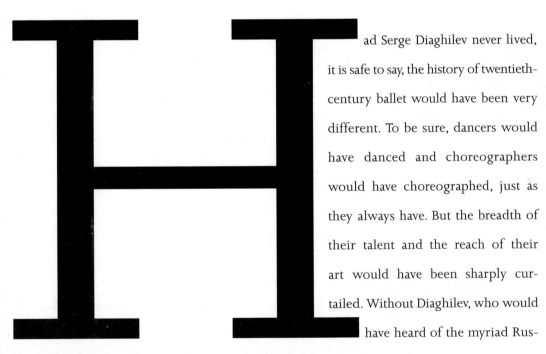ad Serge Diaghilev never lived, it is safe to say, the history of twentieth-century ballet would have been very different. To be sure, dancers would have danced and choreographers would have choreographed, just as they always have. But the breadth of their talent and the reach of their art would have been sharply curtailed. Without Diaghilev, who would have heard of the myriad Russians who joined the vast ballet exodus set in motion by his company? Without Diaghilev, would Stravinsky have composed *Le Sacre du Printemps* or Ravel *Daphnis and Chloé?* Would Nijinsky have choreographed *L'Après-midi d'un Faune*—or any ballet, for that matter? Would Balanchine have found his true path with *Apollo?* Would Picasso or Matisse have designed for the stage?

Were it not for Diaghilev, would ballet during the twenty years his company existed—from 1909 to 1929—have become the most exciting of the era's performing arts, a magnet for artists of genius and meeting ground for a sophisticated, international elite? To raise these questions is involuntarily to know the answer: probably not.

To be sure, winds of change were blowing in Western theater dance in 1909, when Diaghilev presented his first thrilling season of Russian ballet in Paris. The city, home for years to Isadora Duncan and a host of classic, exotic, eurhythmic, and lapsed ballet dancers, was glittering with dance wares, even if opera house ballet was in the doldrums and music hall ballet in decline. In fact, it seemed only a matter of time before the new breed of female soloists would triumph on both the commercial and the elite dance stage. Elsewhere, dance was also changing. In Central Europe, as George Jackson has pointed out, "balanced programs of one-act ballets were perfected . . . well before Diaghilev."[1] Meanwhile, at London's Alhambra Theatre, Loie Fuller imitators from America and apache dancers from Paris jostled with performers of more traditional numbers in the divertissements of many ballets. Even if the occasional Russian—Olga Preobrajenska, say, or Nijinsky's father—turned up from time to time in London, Paris, or Monte Carlo, ballet itself was regarded as a French or Italian art. Thus, on the eve of World War I, when Mrs. Lilith Stannus cast about for a name for her stagebound daughter Edris, she chose to emphasize the family's putative French connection; so the aspiring dancer became Ninette de Valois. Ten years later, she would have gone Russian. What caused this shift in the public perception of ballet's national identity was the impact of Diaghilev's dancers.

Audiences went wild over them. Even in Paris, where ballerinas like Carlotta Zambelli enjoyed something akin to cult status, they came and conquered. They did so not only because they were magnificent dancers, but also because they were tantalizingly exotic, with a perfume of forbidden pleasure; imagine Ida Rubinstein, glimpsed for the first time in *Cléopâtre*, raven-haired, with the lineaments of an ibex and the mystery of all the East, as it seemed to Comte Robert de Montesquiou. And there was pleasure. Diaghilev once described himself as "an incorrigible sensualist." His ballets delighted both the ear and the eye. Born in 1872, in his youth he had aspired to be a composer but gave up that ambition when Rimsky-Korsakov pronounced his music "absurd." Too proud to be third-rate, he turned to writing. He became an art critic and a historian, discovered forgotten painters, and published a book, his only full-length work, on the eighteenth-century Russian portraitist Dmitry Levitsky.[2]

Full of vigor, with an energy as boundless as Russia itself, Diaghilev was an empire builder. He founded *Mir iskusstva* (World of art), a journal comparable in sensibility to *La Revue blanche* or *The Yellow Book* that championed symbolism, neonationalism, *décadence*, and other new artistic currents, ushering in Russia's Silver Age. He organized numerous art exhibitions, including the mammoth Exhibition of Historic Russian Portraits of 1905, which brought thousands to the Tauride Palace despite the political unrest of the time and prompted Diaghilev's aunt to write to his stepmother, "I have been to the exhibition at the Tauride Palace, and you cannot imagine . . . the superhuman grandeur of what I saw. I was transported into a world that seems infinitely nearer than our own."[3] For a time, he worked as an assistant to the director of the Imperial Theaters, editing its yearbook and doing the spadework for a production of *Sylvia* that was never realized but anticipated the collaborative method of his future ballet enterprise and involved its key designers. He has been called a dilettante and an amateur because he abjured the practice of music and ceased to write criticism. In fact, he was a thoroughgoing professional, an editor of genius, an Ur-artist whose great creation, which ended with his death in 1929, was the Ballets Russes.

Although most of the works produced by his company have gone out of repertory, ballet remains profoundly indebted to Diaghilev. He transformed the character of ballet music, putting the final nail in the coffin of the specialist tradition exemplified by such composers as Ludwig Minkus and Cesare Pugni. With Diaghilev as midwife, ballet acquired a remarkable body of new music, equally at home in the concert hall and in the theater. He plucked Stravinsky from obscurity and through this first son, as he called the composer of *Firebird, Petrouchka, Le Sacre du Printemps, Pulcinella, Les Noces,* and *Apollon Musagète,* al-

Diaghilev's death mask,

1929

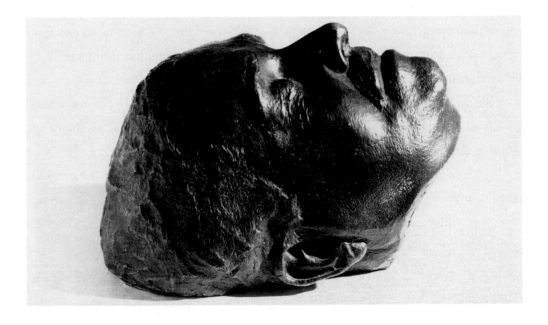

tered the course of twentieth-century music. Although none were as important to the Ballets Russes as Stravinsky, many composers enjoyed Diaghilev's largess, including Prokofiev (*Prodigal Son*), Debussy (*Jeux*), Ravel (*Daphnis and Chloé*), Richard Strauss (*Legend of Joseph*), Falla (*Le Tricorne*), Satie (*Parade*), Poulenc (*Les Biches*), Milhaud (*Le Train Bleu*), and Sauguet (*La Chatte*). Not all of Diaghilev's music was new. Even when dealing with pre-existing material, however, he tended to avoid program music: the score for *The Good-Humoured Ladies* was pieced together from a half-dozen Scarlatti sonatas. Thus, the "fit" between dance and music ceased to be explicitly based on narrative but relied instead on a general sense of congruity. If ballet music today is infinitely more varied and sophisticated than in 1900, it is largely because of Diaghilev.

As much as Diaghilev's ballets delighted the ear, they were also a feast for the eye. Just as he abjured "ballet music," so he rejected the specialist tradition of ballet scene and costume design. Beginning with Léon Bakst and Alexandre Benois, he commissioned designs for both scenery and costumes from easel painters, bypassing the in-house craftsmen who typically supplied them. Although some of those scene painters had created marvels, as artisans they operated within a set of highly limiting conventions; indeed, at the Maryinsky Theater, according to Vladimir Telyakovsky (the last director of the Imperial Theaters), they "were divided according to their painting specialties: architectural, forest, marine, and other types of décor." Scene painters never did costumes (or props), and several frequently contributed to a multi-act work, making it "impossible," as Telyakovsky noted, "to gain a coherent impression from the entire production."[4]

Artistic coherence early became a Diaghilev trademark. Typically, only one artist was assigned to a production. But even in cases where a second or even a third was involved, their contributions worked together harmoniously. Diversity was another Diaghilev trademark. Ballets Russes designers spanned the stylistic gamut, from Bakst, the virtuoso colorist of fin-de-siècle fantasies, to Picasso, whose magnificent designs for *Parade* announced Diaghilev's conversion to modernism. Diaghilev did not invent a school of design or a formula to be applied universally (as some of his British acolytes seemed to believe). Rather, he treated design as a creative element, a way of making the imagination of the visual artist palpable.

He thought of movement in a similar way. Diaghilev never abjured the academic dance—or *danse d'école*—as a system of training: indeed, after transforming his troupe into a permanent ensemble in 1911, he engaged Enrico Cecchetti, one of the great teachers of the age, to travel with the company and conduct daily class. The danse d'école also remained a stylistic baseline: even in such overtly antiballetic works as *Faune, Sacre,* and *Parade,* it could be discerned like a palimpsest through successive statements of modernism.

Although it can easily seem otherwise, the classical dance is not a language writ in stone but an idiom in constant evolution. Steps have been added, elaborated, or put on pointe; jumps have gotten bigger, extensions higher, and turns more complicated; even something as basic as turnout has changed over time. Such nuances contextualize a step: they locate it in a time and place, linking it to a prevailing style or artistic tradition. They differentiate a Kirov arabesque from a New York City Ballet one, a nineteenth-century Italian *attitude* from its contemporary French counterpart.

Diaghilev came to adulthood during the culminating era of Marius Petipa's dominion over St. Petersburg's Imperial Ballet. He saw *The Sleeping Beauty* and most of Petipa's other ballets, including his last realized work, *The Magic Mirror* (1903), a four-act retelling of "Snow White and the Seven Dwarfs" that the future impresario described in a letter to the *Peterburgskaia gazeta* as "boring, long, complicated, and pretentious."[5] Within a year of the premiere Petipa retired. He was eighty-five and had ruled the Imperial Ballet for forty years. His legacy was enormous, as was the burden of that legacy. Diaghilev did not shun it (indeed, his 1921 production of *Beauty,* renamed *The Sleeping Princess,* at London's Alhambra Theatre introduced Petipa's masterwork to the Western repertory), but for the most part he preferred to ignore it. This was certainly the case with *Sacre,* which, amazingly, came to the stage a mere ten years after *The Magic Mirror.* Unlike today's breed of artistic directors, Diaghilev both knew what he wanted and was prepared to bring it about, no matter what the cost and regardless of the consequences.

In varying degrees, the works that Diaghilev chose to produce broke with the dramaturgical and choreographic conventions associated with Petipa. He adopted the one-act ballet as his company's basic format, emphasized dramatic and formal consistency, and focused attention on the male dancer. He insisted that the movement style of a work reflect the subject, rather than the other way around, thus implicitly rejecting the notion of the danse d'école as an all-purpose Ur-language. In most instances he eschewed Petipa's highly structured pas de deux, with its opening supported adagio, solo variations, and razzle-dazzle coda. He rejected the conventions of the bravura dance, along with showstopping steps like fouetté turns and double *tours en l'air.* And although his dancers continued to perform their daily exercises with full turnout (or what was considered full turnout at the time), all his choreographers, beginning with Michel Fokine, experimented with modifying this most defining element of ballet technique and with the parallel positions that were typically regarded as its antithesis. This was true even of Balanchine, whose later teaching emphasized and significantly extended the use of turnout. In *Apollo* and *Prodigal Son*, his two surviving ballets from the Diaghilev period, parallel positions abound, not only in the choreography for what might be called the "character" dancers—Apollo's mother, Leto, and the Prodigal's Drinking Companions—but also in the variations and pas de deux for the principals. A similar phenomenon can be observed in Bronislava Nijinska's *Les Noces* and *Les Biches*, also survivors from the Diaghilev period, in which anticlassical elements, so to speak, coexist with bona fide classical ones, such as pointe.[6]

Although this incipient neoclassicism certainly had something to do with Petipa —both Nijinska and Balanchine, after all, were Maryinsky graduates—it was hardly a carbon copy of the master's style. In fact, it was only distantly related to it, more like a grandchild than a son or daughter—something recollected from the past rather than lived in the here and now. Indeed, by the late 1920s, even Diaghilev, that most clearsighted and unsentimental of men, seems to have succumbed to nostalgia, contemplating a revival of *Giselle*, a ballet that Petipa had made a staple of the Imperial Ballet repertory through his recension of the 1880s.

Diaghilev did not live to revive the ballet (he died several months before the intended opening), but this idea of returning to the past, a past now so distant—so irrevocably gone—that it could be savored like a Victorian collectible, suggests how complete was the break with Petipa. For unlike the English of the 1920s, whose acquaintance with Petipa was pretty much limited to what Diaghilev had shown them, Russians of Nijinska's generation could only reclaim the master's legacy from across the divide of modernism. Even if in later years Balanchine "stole" an idea or two from Petipa or his assistant Lev Ivanov (the hoop dance for the Candy Canes in *The Nutcracker* was one such borrowing), his classicism—unlike Ninette de Valois's productions of Maryinsky classics at Sadler's Wells during the 1930s—was never imitation. Rather, it expressed an act of memory that was also an act of forgetfulness, a homage from the diaspora to a vanished homeland of the ideal.

Diaghilev's troupe existed for only twenty years, but it was the seedbed for the extraordinary renaissance of ballet in the twentieth century. Few companies, including the major Soviet ones (at least during the régime's early years), proved impervious to its influence. Even the Paris Opéra, that bastion of French chauvinism, found a place for some of Diaghilev's Russians, including Bakst, who designed *Artémis Troublée*, *Frivolant*, and other ballets in the early 1920s; Benois, who in 1924 designed the first French production of *Giselle* since the 1860s; Olga Spessivtzeva, a sometime Diaghilev ballerina who danced the title role in the 1924 revival; and Serge Lifar, Diaghilev's last leading man, who became the director of the Opéra company after Diaghilev's death.

But the impact of the Ballets Russes went far beyond established troupes. As a company, the Ballets Russes was unique. Affiliated with neither an opera house or commercial theater (many of which had ballet troupes in the late nineteenth century) nor with a particular star (as was the case of Anna Pavlova's company), it was defined by its artistic identity and a commitment to ballet as a fine art. Beginning in the late 1910s and continuing well into the 1950s, a host of companies came into being whose existence, directly or indirectly, was indebted to the Ballets Russes. Some, including Rolf de Maré's Ballets Suédois and Comte Etienne de Beaumont's Soirées de Paris, were closely modeled on the Diaghilev enterprise, sharing a similar aesthetic and even some of the same personnel. Others, such as Adolph Bolm's Ballet Intime, Marie Rambert's Ballet Rambert, Ninette de Valois's Vic-Wells (later Sadler's Wells) company, and Lincoln Kirstein's Ballet Caravan, sought to transplant elements of the Diaghilev aesthetic to other climes, while calling on a very different set of artists. Finally, in companies like England's Royal Ballet (a direct descendant of the Vic-Wells) and the New York City Ballet (a Balanchine-Kirstein enterprise) one finds the institutionalization of certain aspects of the Ballets Russes—the Gesamtkunstwerk idea in the case of the Royal, the experimentalist impulse in that of the New York City Ballet—as well as the presence of major Diaghilev works in the repertory.

The void created by Diaghilev's death was largely filled in the 1930s by the various Ballet Russe (as the name came to be Americanized) companies that had inherited his repertory and most of his personnel. By the 1940s, however, the émigré world that had nourished those companies had lost its vitality, and by 1961 the last of them had collapsed. Nevertheless, Diaghilev's memory did not fade. If anything, the 1950s brought him back to public view, most spectacularly with Richard Buckle's 1954 Diaghilev Exhibition, which proved so popular at the Edinburgh Festival where it opened that it subsequently moved to London and prompted the first of Buckle's books about the impresario, *In Search of Diaghilev*. In the 1960s, along with several highly publicized sales of Ballets Russes material through Sotheby's, there were revivals by the Royal Ballet of Nijinska's *Les Noces* and *Les Biches*, both of which were filmed and notated, and two BBC programs by John Drummond, *Diaghilev: The Years Abroad* and *Diaghilev: The Years in Exile*.[7] Meanwhile, in the

United States, Robert Joffrey, who had studied at one point with Ballets Russes alumna Marie Rambert, was about to produce *Le Tricorne*, the first of several Diaghilev-era works that would eventually become one of the glories of his company's repertory. (Among the others were *Petrouchka, Parade, Faune, Les Noces*, and the Millicent Hodson–Kenneth Archer reconstruction of *Sacre*.) In the 1970s, too, defector superstars Rudolf Nureyev and Mikhail Baryshnikov tried their hand at various Diaghilev roles, especially those created for Nijinsky, thus linking their fame with his. With the publication of Buckle's 1971 biography of Nijinsky, which roughly coincided with the birth of the gay liberation movement, the dancer's sexual relationship with Diaghilev, whispered in the dance world but never mentioned in print, finally came out the closet. And in the late 1980s the end of the Cold War and the growing sophistication of dance scholarship brought new sources and a new set of perspectives—some of which are reflected in this book—to bear on key aspects of Diaghilev's life and career.

Veterans of the Ballets Russes seeded ballet on several continents. For a time it seemed they were everywhere, dancing, teaching, choreographing, not just for the Ballets Russes and the émigré companies that were its immediate descendants but in Hollywood and the West End, on Broadway and the Lower East Side, in Chicago, Buenos Aires, and the Baltic. Wherever they scattered, they set up studios or found their way to academies where they passed on their inheritance. At the New York City Ballet's affiliated School of American Ballet, the Diaghilev veterans over the years included Alexandra Danilova, Felia Doubrovska and her husband, Pierre Vladimirov, Anatole Oboukhoff, and, of course, Balanchine, although what Balanchine came to prize most, especially in later years, was their Maryinsky schooling rather than their Ballets Russes experience.

Finally, there remains the legacy of the Ballets Russes works. Even today, nearly a century after Diaghilev led his first troupe of dancers to Paris, there is hardly a company with a twentieth-century repertory that does not perform at least one Diaghilev ballet. These works have become part of ballet's great tradition: they belong to the interregnum between the age of Petipa and the age of Balanchine, late nineteenth-century Russian classicism and twentieth-century Western neoclassicism. Diaghilev, the iconoclast, was also a passionate believer in high art. It was this faith, not unmixed with a certain snobbery, that rescued ballet from the ghetto of triviality and insignificance in which it had languished in the West for several decades. The renaissance of ballet as an art capable of the highest form of human expression may well be Diaghilev's greatest and most enduring legacy.

Serge de Diaghileffs

I Diaghilev

In the late 1980s I visited Perm. There wasn't a shred of parsley in the entire city, nothing,

the soup was like water, the factories were rusting, a trip abroad was only a fantasy. And

there, amid the desolation, I met an old woman, Evgenia Egorova, who was born in the

shadow of the Diaghilev estate in Bikbarda; when she was a child there was still something

left of the house, and she had played in the apple orchard. She told me about this magical place

and the extraordinary clan who had made music to gladden the soul . . .

—L. G.

one **The Diaghilev Family in Perm**

Evgenia Egorova

Throughout his childhood and early youth Sergei Pavlovich Diaghilev lived in the home of his paternal grandfather, Pavel Dmitrievich Diaghilev, in Perm. The Diaghilevs occupied a special place in the history of pre-revolutionary Perm, where they had been social, cultural, and charitable benefactors for nearly a century.

Diaghilev's great-grandfather Dmitry Vasilievich Diaghilev (1773–1823) was the son of the *Berggeschvoren* Vasily Pavlovich, the manager of an Ekaterinburg factory, and Tatiana Stepanovna Nechaeva, the daughter of a merchant from Solikamsk, a city on the Kama River north of Perm. Dmitry Vasilievich was an educated and talented man—musician, artist, collector, bibliophile, and man of letters. In his youth he published fables and verses in the first Ural-Siberian journal, *Irtysh Turning into Hippocrene*. [The Irtysh River lies to the southeast of Omsk.] Later he developed a passion for music, and at the end of his life for painting. In the list of property left after his death are two violins, a viola, and forty pictures he had painted.[1]

Church of Mary Magdalene

Old Siberian Gate

The administration building of the Ural Railroad Lines

These photographs of Perm, commissioned by Nicholas II as part of a vast scheme to record the heritage and notable sights of the entire Russian empire, were taken in 1909 by Sergei Mikhailovich Prokudin-Gorskii. Prokudin-Gorskii made several journeys across Russia in the years before World War I, amassing the collection of nearly 2,000 glass-plate negatives that now resides in the Prints and Photographs Division of the Library of Congress.

Located on the western slopes of the Ural Mountains about halfway down the Kama River, a tributary of the Volga, Perm stood on the divide between Europe and Asia. The city's early wealth came from copper. Later, as the capital of the Perm oblast, or province, the city became an important administrative center, a distant outpost of the tsarist government. Finally, it was a flourishing trade and transport center, the gateway to Siberia. Rafts covered with timber or loaded with potash, chemicals, and precious stones floated down the river to Kazan and the Volga. By the late nineteenth century there were railroad tracks along the Kama and in the less attractive parts of town; and sitting proudly on a hill overlooking the port was the administration building of the Ural Railroad Lines, a veritable mansion. Although Diaghilev left Perm nearly twenty years before these pictures were taken, they convey—far better than the rust-belt survivor of today—the prosperous, well-appointed city of his childhood.

General view of Perm from the city hills

Summer quarters of the Exchange

Dmitry Vasilievich moved to Perm in 1793 shortly after the decree that created the *gubernia* (province) embracing Perm and its surrounding region. He began his career as clerk of the city council, then became the district and city treasurer. In 1800 he married Maria Ivanovna Zhmaeva, daughter of the merchant Ivan Romanovich Zhmaev (1743–1807).[2] Zhmaev's home stood at the corner of Siberia and Petropavlovsk Streets and according to contemporary accounts was one of the most beautiful and richest houses of the city.[3] The property occupied the entire block from Petropavlovsk to Commerce Streets, and it was entered by a stone gateway with pillars decorated with cast-iron vases. A stone orangerie with a circular gallery stood out among the adjoining buildings, which included a coach house and several outhouses and storehouses. The walls and ceilings of the orangerie were painted with flowers and cupids; exotic fruits ripened there in the winter.[4] Zhmaev bequeathed all his property, including a factory in the Bikbardinsky region, to his daughter, son-in-law, and their children "Vanyusha" and "Tanyusha."[5]

In 1805 Dmitry Vasilievich was raised to the rank of collegiate assessor, the civil-service equivalent of a major in the army. According to the Senate decree of 1791, this rank gave an official the right to be added to the nobility. But in the newly founded gubernia of Perm an assembly of the nobility did not yet exist. So Dmitry Vasilievich applied to "the Moscow nobility, the marshal and deputies of the district nobility charged with compiling the noble genealogical book" and requested that he be admitted to the city's nobility. On 23 January 1806, he was entered in the third section of the noble genealogical book for the Moscow region, along with his children—present and future.[6]

After the death of his wife in 1814, Dmitry Vasilievich was left with three sons and two daughters to rear. The boys were sent off with tutors to St. Petersburg, where Ivan became a boarding student at the lycée in Tsarskoe Selo and Viacheslav and Pavel entered the Cadet Corps. The girls were educated at home.[7]

After Dmitry Vasilievich died in 1823, the trustees restored the Bikbardinsky factory, which had fallen into disrepair. In 1829, when his property was divided among his heirs, the factory passed to his son Pavel Dmitrievich, the future impresario's grandfather.[8]

After completing the course at the Chief Engineering College, Pavel Dmitrievich (1808–1882) joined an engineering battalion. In 1828–1829 he served in the Russo-Turkish War with the rank of major, retiring to enter state service in the Ministry of State Property and on a special committee for horse breeding.[9]

Thanks to the efforts of the trustees, the Bikbardinsky factory now yielded an income that allowed Pavel Dmitrievich to acquire a house in St. Petersburg and marry Anna Ivanovna Sulmeneva, the daughter of Admiral Sulmenev. Their children—four sons and four daughters—all received excellent educations.

In 1850 Pavel Dmitrievich retired and settled in Bikbarda. In 1862 he moved to Perm. Here, little by little, he was joined by his sons, with their wives and children. In the summer the clan gathered on the beautiful estate of Bikbarda. There was a pond and a large, comfortable house, leisure for all, diversions, music. "Along the southern facade of this one-story wooden house," recalled Elena Valerianovna Diaghileva (1853–1919), Diaghilev's stepmother, "there was a balcony that ended in a large rotunda . . . at the road, which ran along a ravine. Beyond the ravine was the factory, pond, village, and forest, as boundless as the sea. Usually, the family drank evening tea in the rotunda, watching the sunset. The great trees of the garden came up to the balcony. A broad avenue, covered with sand and planted with flowers, led to the north entrance of the church."[10] When no general outing was planned, everyone did as they pleased.

"Now, from the hall," Elena Valerianovna continued, "came the sound of the piano. The talk, laughter, and bustle died down; everyone hurried to find a place; even the children moved on tiptoe and sat quietly down. Silence reigned: everyone was now listening. The family music making, where even little boys whistled a quintet by Schumann or a symphony by Beethoven, approached a religious rite."[11] In the special room built under the direction of Diaghilev's uncle Ivan Pavlovich, concerts were often given—sometimes even entire opera productions. There were also pantomimes, in which the future ballet reformer played the roles of Tom Thumb, the Prince in *Sleeping Beauty*, and Little Red Riding Hood. All these performances brought joy. As Diaghilev wrote in one of his first letters from Bikbarda to Elena Valerianovna: "We had theater; it gave us great pleasure."[12] But equally they enjoyed a swim in the pond, a walk in the forest or in the fields of wild strawberries, an excursion along the beautiful forest road that led to the Nikolaevsky factory. The young Diaghilev spent almost every summer in Bikbarda, enjoying the companionship of his large, warm family.

His grandfather's home in Perm was on Siberia Street. It was built in the middle of the nineteenth century by the architect R. I. Karvovsky in the classical revival style with an inner courtyard garden and balcony whose dimensions amazed the boy. There was a piano in the sitting room. The walls were covered with the paintings Dmitry Vasilievich had collected years ago; here, too, were portraits of the patriarch, his son Pavel

Dmitrievich, his father-in-law, Ivan Zhmaev, and K. F. Moderakh, one of Perm's first governors. No list of the Diaghilev family collection survives, but we can assume that among the paintings and portraits were works by Pavel Dmitrievich's great-nephews Alexander and Pavel Svedomsky, who were graduates of the Düsseldorf Academy of Arts. Cabinets with books and albums of engravings of pictures by well-known artists graced Pavel Dmitrievich's study and the long corridors, whose windows looked out on the inner courtyard. Here one could gaze for hours and dream of visiting the celebrated picture galleries of Italy, France, and Germany to see the originals. Diaghilev's grandfather was a devout man and had a small collection of icons as well. He prized the icons painted by his father as well as those given to him by the bishops of Kiev and Perm. In the 1870s icons for the church at Bikbarda were commissioned from V. P. Vereshchagin, a professor at the Academy of Arts and a native of Perm.

From the beginning, the Diaghilev home was full of people. All were welcome, and for rich and poor alike there was a kind word and a helping hand. Charity was a Diaghilev family tradition. In the 1810s and early 1820s Dmitry Vasilievich supported a hospital for the poor;[13] Pavel Dmitrievich donated money not only to support alms-houses, churches, and monasteries but also to build schools and a municipal theater; and Diaghilev's father belonged to many charitable societies while his stepmother served on the women's board of guardians for the poor and the care of the blind.

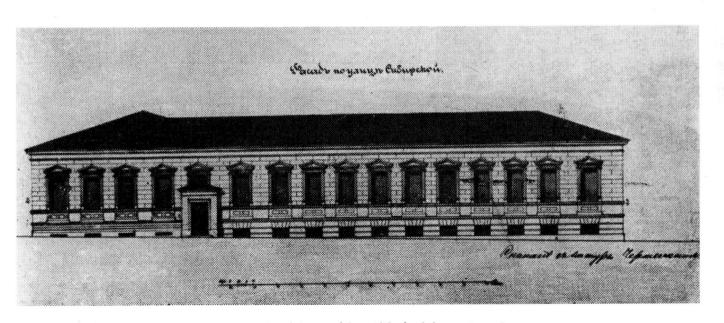

Architect's drawing of the Diaghilev family home in Perm, 1854

Every Thursday during Diaghilev's youth a large formal party was held at the house. Friends of the family attended these receptions, along with teachers, doctors, and engineers, and members of Perm's musical circle, which played an important part in Diaghilev's education, as well as in that of many Perm citizens. The organizer of the circle and one of its senior members was Diaghilev's uncle Ivan Pavlovich (1838–1906). He had received a brilliant musical education: he played the cello and the piano and accompanied nearly all the group concerts. His brother, Pavel Pavlovich (1848–1914), Diaghilev's father, had taken singing lessons in his youth with the well-known teacher Rotkovsky and loved to perform romances and arias from operas; Elena Valerianovna, Pavel's second wife, both sang and recited with success.

The circle's musical repertory was varied. Romances, folk songs, and arias were all performed, as well as scenes from the operas *Eugene Onegin, Russalka, Il Trovatore,* and *Ernani.* Glinka's opera *A Life for the Tsar* was given more than fifty times in concert form, sometimes with the addition of professional artists. The string quartet, directed by M. P. Norin, a tax board official, also took part in the concerts, as did the student choruses of the two secondary schools (male and female) under the direction of Eduard Eduardovich Danemark. Often the concerts at the Diaghilev home, like the musical society's concerts at the Assembly of the Nobility, ended with tableaux vivants on themes of paintings by Russian artists or with opera scenes.

In summer 1876 Diaghilev's parents went to Italy. On the return journey they stopped in Paris. Here, in the salon of Pauline Viardot, with whom Elena Valerianovna's sister Alexandra was then studying, they met the novelist Ivan Turgenev and the fashionable painter Konstantin Makovsky. His painting *In the Tower of the Boyar's Wife,* as well as his scenes from the works of Alexander Pushkin, were often the subjects of the tableaux vivants performed in the Diaghilev home.

From childhood, young Sergei loved Russian literature and music. The Diaghilevs made a cult of Pushkin, Glinka, and Tchaikovsky—a distant relation whom everyone in the family called "Uncle Petya."[14] Elena Valerianovna often told the children of meeting Turgenev and the writer Nikolai Nekrasov, who had both frequented her father's home and read aloud from their works. Nekrasov's celebrated poem "Russian Women" made a deep impression on the young boy. During his secondary school years Diaghilev was a great reader, and in his letters to Elena Valerianovna he shared his impressions of the books he had read.

In 1883 Diaghilev was admitted into the second class of the men's gymnasium, or classical high school. Learning came easily to him, and he devoted much of his time to music. He had mastered the rudiments of musical notation from Elena Valerianovna and various governesses, and now he began more serious study as a student of Danemark. Diaghilev also received private lessons from his father and his aunt Alexandra Panaeva-Kartseva (1853–1943), a professional singer.

Diaghilev's high school years were a time for testing his strengths and choosing his future profession. He dreamed of being an artist and took part in school concerts: he played the piano, sang, and was praised for his interpretation of Neschastlivtsev in Alexander Ostrovsky's play *The Forest*. He also tried his hand at composing various kinds of music. At the age of fifteen, for instance, he wrote a romance to the words of Alexei (Konstantinovich) Tolstoy's "Do you remember, Maria?" on the occasion of his parents' anniversary. The score still survives.

Beginning in the 1870s professional people in Perm had sought to awaken local interest in music, theater, and regional history. As an administrative, economic, and cultural center, Perm developed much later than other Ural cities like Cherdyn, Solikamsk, Usolye, and Kungur. In the second half of the nineteenth century Perm was still provincial, far from the nation's center, and cultural life was confined to a small intelligentsia. But thanks to the efforts of local doctors, teachers, zemstvo (village council) officials, and engineers, by the end of the nineteenth century Perm had forged ahead of other Russian provincial capitals in many cultural arenas. The city became an outstanding theatrical center, where Russian opera flourished. This flowering had been preceded, however, by more than thirty years of activity by the Perm musical circle (which broke up when the Diaghilevs left in the 1890s) and by the opening in 1886 of a private music academy directed by E. Cabella, a graduate of the Milan conservatory. Whether Diaghilev took music lessons from Cabella is unknown, but we do know that Cabella frequented the Diaghilev home and took part in the concerts of the Perm musical circle. Members of the circle participated in the concerts he organized.

In 1875 the artist Afrikan Sidorovich Shanin, a graduate of the Academy of Arts who taught drawing and calligraphy in the high schools, organized an art school in his home.[15] In 1888 the Perm Academy of Arts took the school under its wing, supplying it with plaster of Paris and engraving plates and approving the creation of a formal curriculum. Shanin now rented new premises. We have no information about whether Diaghilev studied at Shanin's school, but we can assume that he took a strong interest in its work and even consulted the teacher about the drawings he was doing. In the exhibition

"Serge Diaghilev and Russian Artistic Culture of the Nineteenth and Twentieth Centuries" held in Perm in 1989 were two drawings attributed to Diaghilev—a portrait of Nikolai Pavlovich Diaghilev and a landscape inscribed "To Konstantinovich."

In June 1887 Perm was in a state of excitement because Grand Duke Mikhail Alexandrovich, president of the Ural-Siberian science and industry fair due to open in Ekaterinburg on 14 June, would be visiting the city. From 10 to 12 June the city wore a festive air, with greenery, flags, and banners. Students from the high schools met the grand duke at the pier, and the fair exhibits were transported through Perm. Local craft and factory wares were represented at the fair as well, and the library of Diaghilev's high school sent its unique collection of rare old books.

The regional movement—and Perm's, it has been said, was "among the strongest and most impressive of provincial Russia"—played an important role in the city's cultural life.[16] One A. A. Dmitriev, a teacher of Diaghilev's at the gymnasium, made a significant contribution to the study of Urals history, publishing 140 scholarly works. By the 1890s the regional movement had taken shape in various commissions and societies. Especially noteworthy were the activities of the Perm branch of the Urals Natural History Society and the Perm Regional Archive Commission, of which Diaghilev's father was a member. Both these organizations began collecting exhibits for a science and industry museum that opened in Perm in November 1890. The chairman of the board was the physician Pavel Nikolaevich Serebrennikov, who had taken part in the concerts of the Perm musical circle. Some years later, he appealed to Diaghilev, as the editor of *Mir iskusstva* (World of art), "on behalf of the people of Perm and all those to whom the history of our country is dear, to make a donation of the [journal's] materials to the Perm museum."

The rich cultural and social life of Perm in these years exerted an unquestionable influence on the formation of Diaghilev's character and the choice of his ultimate sphere of activity. He never forgot the city or the teachers and students at the gymnasium or the beautiful Kama River and boundless expanses of forest that surrounded it. He even remembered the local fairy tales.

At the end of his life, like his grandfather and great-grandfather before him, he became an ardent bibliophile. His passion for collecting Russian books and manuscripts led him to hunt down more than two thousand rare editions, eleven Pushkin letters, four letters of Lermontov, letters by Gogol, Viazemsky, and Zhukovsky, and autographs of Glinka, Delvig, Derzhavin, Karamzin, and Turgenev. Throughout his travels the memory of Russia—and Perm—never left him.

—Translated by Irene Huntoon

Serge Diaghilev, Old Castle, late 1880s. Signed "S. Diaghilev" and inscribed "To Konstantinovich."

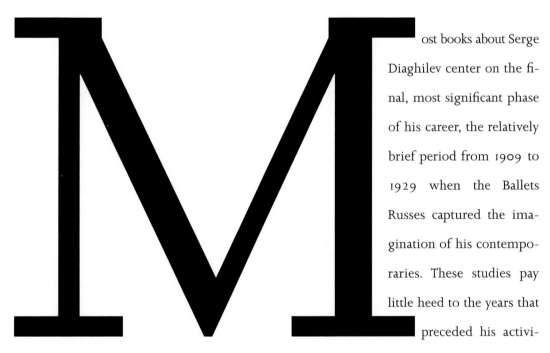

two   Diaghilev's Musical Education

Israel Nesteev

Most books about Serge Diaghilev center on the final, most significant phase of his career, the relatively brief period from 1909 to 1929 when the Ballets Russes captured the imagination of his contemporaries. These studies pay little heed to the years that preceded his activities as a theatrical producer, when his tastes were formed—often in battle with the artistic opponents of his aesthetic program—and when he gathered the knowledge that allowed him to reign as *arbiter arbitrorum* among the greatest masters of contemporary art.

It is unnecessary here to give a detailed account of Diaghilev's life, already described in a shelfful of books. In this connection, let us recall Diaghilev's own memorable opinion,

Léon Bakst, portrait of Diaghilev's nanny, Avdotia Andrianovna, 1901

cited in one of his biographies: "I, personally, can be of no interest to anyone: it is not my life that is interesting, but my work."[1]

Outwardly, nothing special distinguished the first twenty years of Diaghilev's life, which was typical for a young, well-born Russian in the last quarter of the nineteenth century.[2] His was the happy childhood of a nobleman's son, raised in a prosperous, highly cultured family. His father was an army officer, an amateur singer, and a favorite with the provincial aristocrats who formed his circle. His mother died in childbirth, leaving little Seriozha (as he was called) in the care of his nanny, Avdotia Andrianovna, whom Léon Bakst later depicted in his celebrated portrait of the young Diaghilev (pl. 1). After two years of widowerhood, Diaghilev's father remarried. His bride, Elena Valerianovna Panaeva, became the teacher of the man who would found the Ballets Russes. The correspondence between the young man and his active, intelligent stepmother contains much valuable information about Diaghilev's life. In later years, he would confess that there was no better woman in the world. It seems likely that no one exerted so strong an influence on his spiritual growth as this remarkable woman.

The Panaev family entered the history of Russian cultural life thanks to the activities of Elena Valerianovna's father, who founded his own private theater in St. Petersburg (known as the Panaevsky Theater), and her younger sister, Alexandra Valerianovna Panaeva-Kartseva (1853–1941). "Aunt Tatusia," as Panaeva-Kartseva was familiarly known, was an outstanding singer, who remained active as a teacher up to the beginning of the Second World War. She received an excellent musical education in St. Petersburg, first with Natalia Iretskaia, then with Henriette Nissen-Saloman. Her patron was Ivan Turgenev, who persuaded her father—a great enthusiast of Italian opera—to send her to France, where for two years she honed her skills under the tutelage of the celebrated Pauline Viardot. Upon returning to her native land, Alexandra Valerianovna sang in numerous concerts and, at the invitation of Anton Rubinstein, in the composer's own jubilee performance. In 1877 she made the acquaintance of Tchaikovsky, who held the talented young singer in high esteem. In January 1879 she took part in the first concert performance of *Eugene Onegin*, singing the role of Tatiana to Elizaveta Lavrovskaia's Olga, and Peter Lody's Lensky.[3] The celebrated composer dedicated his song cycle, op. 47 (then widely known as "Does the Day Reign?"), to her, and he repeatedly entrusted the performance of new works to her.

Diaghilev's paternal aunt Anna Pavlovna Filosofova also played an important role in his life. Indeed, it was in her home that the celebrated "Mir iskusstva," or World of Art, group was born. The Diaghilevs, Panaevs, and Filosofovs shared a deep love and appreciation of the arts—not only music, but also painting and theater. In this favorable environment the aesthetic aspirations of the future leader of the World of Art took shape.

His biographers tell of the unforgettable journey that took the ten-year-old Serge Diaghilev from St. Petersburg to Perm, especially the four-day steamer trip down the Volga to Kazan and, from there, up to Perm along the Kama. The impressions of the beautiful Volga landscapes and Urals foothills were etched into the boy's consciousness for the rest of his life, strengthening his love of Russia.

During his school days in Perm, Diaghilev stood out for his erudition and knowledge of art, which far surpassed that of the other students. The old-fashioned traditions of the gymnasium alternately irritated and amused him. "He knew things of which his schoolmates had no notion, such as Russian and foreign literature, the theater, and music," recalled one of his classmates, O. Vasiliev, in a memoir.[4] Frequently Diaghilev did not bother to

The young Diaghilev with his stepmother, Elena Valerianovna

prepare his lessons, relying instead on "prompting" from the others. He had a hot temper, and early on displayed an imperious, high-handed manner.

In the Diaghilev family, there reigned an atmosphere of passionate admiration for art. Their spacious town house on Siberia Street was known as "the Athens of Perm." There was constant music making: Diaghilev's father and stepmother were both excellent singers, while his father's brother Ivan Pavlovich ("Uncle Vanya") played the cello and conducted an amateur orchestra. Two or three times a year, the Diaghilevs arranged charity concerts at gatherings of the local nobility. Every Thursday they held a musical evening at home, where symphonies by Haydn, Mozart, and Beethoven, transposed into four-hand piano arrangements, were given, as well as virtually complete scenes from operas. Dmitry Filosofov recalled hearing a quartet from *Rigoletto* or Glinka's *A Life for the Tsar* "executed," as he put it, "by family forces."[5] Among the Perm music lovers who attended these "Thursdays" was Eduard Eduardovich Danemark, who not only taught German but was also Diaghilev's first piano teacher.

During the summer the whole enormous clan—as many as fifty, including servants—assembled at the family estate, Bikbarda, where the arts flourished with grace and exuberance. Diaghilev's grandfather Pavel Dmitrievich Diaghilev was extremely musical: he played the piano well and recalled with pride that he had once taken lessons from the celebrated composer John Field. Bikbarda had its own little organ and an old Flügel

The corner ballroom that served as the family music room in the Diaghilev home in Perm, 1880

piano. Everyone breathed classical music, Elena Valerianovna later wrote; even the little boys, out for a walk, whistled melodies from a Schumann quintet or a Beethoven symphony.[6] At Bikbarda, too, one could hear the region's old folk songs, which Ivan Pavlovich performed masterfully.

The cult of Russian classical music reigned supreme in the Diaghilev home, and Glinka, above all, was worshiped. "Glinka was a god to them," Diaghilev's friend Walter Nouvel later wrote, "and they all knew his opera *Ruslan and Ludmila* nearly by heart." Nouvel also relates that Diaghilev's piano lessons in Perm "did not especially interest him," although "the natural dexterity of his fingers permitted him to overcome his technical difficulties."[7] Among the works Diaghilev and Nouvel performed together was Schumann's Piano Concerto in E Minor. A program still survives in Perm for a children's literary and music evening given on 7 February 1890 at the Maryinsky Gymnasium for Girls. The first number, the Allegro from this Schumann concerto, was performed by "the student Diaghilev," who later in the evening accompanied the school chorus in a fragment from Dargomizhsky's *Russalka*. An account of the performance, published in the *Permskie gubernskie vedomosti* (Perm provincial gazette) on 10 February 1890, commended the young performer for his success.

Diaghilev sight-read easily, a skill that considerably enriched his knowledge of musical literature, both classical and contemporary. In addition, he endeavored to compose. To the Perm period belongs the song he wrote when he was fifteen, "Do you remember, Maria?" to verses by Alexei Tolstoy. Composed for a family concert that took place on 14 October 1887, this is the only original musical manuscript by Diaghilev that has come down to us.

The letters Diaghilev wrote to Elena Valerianovna during his schooldays are full of references to musical activities, domestic concerts, and amateur performances. "You can't imagine what enormous pleasure I received from the music you sent. . . . I have already studied four things and want to play them for you when you come," he wrote in 1884. On 28 July 1885 he announced: "Yesterday we arranged a concert for grandmother. We played the four-hand arrangement of the Gala March, then the 'Songs Without Words' of Mendelssohn. They applauded everything wildly." And two years later he wrote: "I spend all my time playing the piano and reading. . . . I am awfully sorry that I won't hear the opera, which will certainly be in Perm for several days (you know how much I love it)."[8]

Diaghilev's artistic interests were notably eclectic: he was fascinated not only by

the symphonies of Beethoven, which he played in four-hand arrangements with his Aunt Tatusia, but also by literature (Walter Scott's *Ivanhoe* and Alexei Tolstoy's *Prince Serebrianyi* were among his favorite books), theater rehearsals and outings, and trips to the circus. In addition, he took an interest in the art books he encountered at home. The collection included albums of reproductions, with old engravings of works by Rembrandt, Raphael, and Rubens, as well as deluxe publications from museums in Munich and Florence. The future impresario absorbed all this with enthusiasm, in a cultured and intellectual atmosphere.

In summer 1890 Diaghilev completed his gymnasium studies in Perm and traveled to St. Petersburg to enroll at the university. Within a few years, however, severe financial reverses forced the family to abandon Perm. It now fell to Diaghilev to make his own way in life, and for a time he even assumed responsibility for educating his younger half-brothers Valentin and Yury.

Nevertheless, his first years in St. Petersburg were singularly rich. While a student

Diaghilev as a young man in St. Petersburg, 1890s

at the university (from 1890 to 1896), he joined a small circle of friends who met for the purpose of broadening their education in the arts. The circle consisted of former students of the May Academy—a private institution on Vasilievsky Island renowned for its outstanding education in the humanities—including Alexandre Benois, Walter Nouvel, Léon Bakst, and Dmitry Filosofov.

During this period, Diaghilev's life was divided. On the one hand, there were his studies at the university law school, which Benois, Nouvel, and Filosofov also attended—studies that he neither worked hard at nor enjoyed. On the other hand, there was his intensive self-education in music, theater, and the fine arts. "I never leave the theater," he wrote his stepmother. "I have made the following decisions: to attend my classes at the university punctually, to listen attentively to the teachers, and afterward . . . to play and read. And to spend all my money on operas and concerts."

The memoirs of Benois, Filosofov, and Nouvel make it clear that Diaghilev's new friends in St. Petersburg—more knowledgeable than he in matters of art—received him into their circle with hauteur, as befitted residents of the capital. Admitted to their refined company only because he was Filosofov's cousin, he appeared to them provincial, indifferent to the complex aesthetic problems that were discussed at their gatherings. According to Benois, the young Diaghilev was not very keen on "lofty subjects" and for a long time lagged behind his classmates in his appreciation of the fine arts. The self-assured Petersburgers even attempted to examine their new friend "to see how well he would 'fit in,' and whether he wasn't too hopelessly far behind us."[9]

On the other hand, in musical matters, Diaghilev at once occupied a prominent position in the group. He was not only a connoisseur but also a talented singer and pi-

The Nevsky Prospect, St. Petersburg, at the turn of the century

The Hermitage, St. Petersburg, at the turn of the century

anist, who often played four-hand duets with Nouvel. "His interests were chiefly musical," recalled Filosofov. "Tchaikovsky and Borodin were his favorites. For hours at a stretch he would sing arias from *Prince Igor* and other operas. Though his voice was completely unschooled, he sang with great taste, since he was raised in a professional musical environment, under the wing of such a wonderful singer as Alexandra Valerianovna Panaeva-Kartseva."[10] Of course, Diaghilev could not avoid fierce arguments: his companions regarded his affection for broad melodies and for the elegiac lyrics of Tchaikovsky as a sign of "provincialism."[11] At that time they preferred the more complex musical ideas of Wagner, with his emphasis on continuous symphonic evolution and "endless melody," while in Tchaikovsky they chiefly esteemed the dramatic episodes rendered in symphonic style, such as the bedroom scene in *The Queen of Spades*. "Though at first [Diaghilev] was enthusiastic about Wagner," Benois recalled, "he could remain indifferent to the storm scene in *Die Walküre* and to 'The Forest Murmurs' in *Siegfried*. Above all he esteemed the 'Hymn to Venus' and 'Winterstürme wichen.' Because of this [his friends] accused him of retarded development and of possessing 'the basest instincts.' "[12] In all probability, this was less a matter of "inadequate education" than hostility toward every kind of philosophical speculation and dilettantish theorizing. In spite of these disagreements, Diaghilev learned a great deal from his companions, especially Benois, whom he considered his mentor and intellectual guardian, above all with regard to the fine arts (pl. 2).

It is astonishing that neither Diaghilev nor his cousin Filosofov took the slightest interest in the various political problems that so excited students of those times. They considered themselves neither leftists nor rightists, and if, in later years, they aspired to "épater les bourgeois," this was solely in the field of aesthetics.

Visits to the Bogdanovskoe estate (in the province of Pskov) where the Filosofovs spent their summers also played a large role in Diaghilev's intellectual development. This was a genuinely cultured aristocratic nest, ruled over Diaghilev's aunt Anna Pavlovna Filosofova, one of the most prominent activists of the Russian women's movement. Like all the Diaghilevs, she was very fond of music, often played four-hand duets, and continually attended concerts and the opera. Among the writers who frequented her St. Petersburg salon were Dostoevsky, Turgenev, Yakov Polonsky, Mikhail Saltykov-Shchedrin, and the poet Apollon Maikov. She was friends with the family of Dmitry Stasov and was considered one of the bright women of the 1860s, a partisan of democratic reforms and a supporter of education for the common people. Dostoevsky called her a "wise heart," while Alexander Blok portrayed her as Anna Vrevskaia in his poem "Retribution."

Diaghilev was charmed by many things at Bogdanovskoe, including the baronial garden and shady avenues lined with ancient lime trees. Not far from the estate were many places connected with the life of Pushkin: Mikhailovskoe, Trigorskoe, Golubovo, Vrevo, the Sviatye (Holy) Mountains. In Trigorskoe there still lived a close acquaintance of Pushkin's, Maria Ossipova. Not surprisingly, these sojourns at Bogdanovskoe instilled in the young Diaghilev a veritable "cult of Pushkin." After a visit to the Sviatogorsk monastery on 19 July 1893 he wrote to his stepmother: "I stopped at Pushkin's grave and paid my respects. I even tore off a few small leaves, which I will send to you. . . . An extraordinary feeling of reverence envelops one in this humble monastery on a hill, where a simple gravestone covers such a great man!" Pushkin's son, Grigory Alexandrovich, frequented Bogdanovskoe, and the evenings were filled with conversation about bygone days in Russia. As Filosofov later recalled: "We children, just dying of ecstasy, listened to the endless tales of old times that to them seemed recent, . . . the legends of the twenties and thirties."[13]

At Bogdanovskoe music was heard continuously. "It's very pleasant here," Diaghilev wrote to his stepmother in 1892. "And sometimes it even reminds me of our dear

Bikbarda. . . . I sing a great deal here, and am popular. Just wait, and I'll show you! In St. Petersburg I will take lessons in everything. I have so many, many plans."

Anna Pavlovna encouraged the young people, who even then were contemplating large-scale, artistic enterprises such as exhibitions and the publication of a magazine. Brought up at the height of the Russian populist movement, she herself remained adamantly opposed to the idea of art for art's sake, an art severed from all connection with the social order. At the same time, she did all she could to support their endeavors, sensing the enormous potential of their ideas. "Mir iskusstva"—the art magazine Diaghilev founded in 1898 and edited until 1904—"was conceived in our home," she recalled with a certain pride. "For me, a woman of the 1860s, it was all so ridiculous, that it was difficult for me to contain my indignation. . . . Nevertheless, after I recovered from the initial shock, I became interested in their vision of the world, and I must say that frankly there was much that captivated me. The phony atmosphere dissipated, . . . and a single, unquestionably great idea remained, seeking and giving birth to beauty."[14]

Anna Pavlovna expressed serious doubts about her nephew's proposed matriculation at the conservatory; it would distract him, she felt, from more important social concerns. "She says that this is egotistical," Diaghilev reported to his stepmother on 28 August 1894 from Bogdanovskoe, "that we don't need people who will lose themselves in abstract theories or compose symphonies, but people who will help the common man." Later, when Diaghilev's vast undertakings began to unfold, Anna Pavlovna toned down her criticism somewhat. "If Seriozha had created nothing more than Mir iskusstva," she wrote sometime after the magazine's demise, "he would still have merited a permanent place in history." She was profoundly distressed by the fact that the magazine born at Bogdanovskoe had ceased publication.

During his student years at the university, Diaghilev made several trips abroad. The first, during the summer of 1890, was in the company of his cousin Filosofov and included visits to Warsaw, Vienna, Trieste, Venice, Padua, Verona, Milan, Geneva, and various cities in Germany. "We traveled extremely modestly, in third class," Filosofov later wrote, "only taking berths in second class to cover long distances. In Berlin . . . we ate only once a day, in some kind of beer hall, preferring to save our money for the opera. We attended the theater zealously, since we were both inveterate theater-goers, especially in Vienna, Frankfurt, and Berlin." In a letter written in 1892, Diaghilev summed up the purpose of the trip: "I traveled with a musical goal, and in order to study Wagner, and . . . I clarified my thoughts a great deal."

Attending the *Ring* cycle of Wagner operas at Bayreuth made a truly indelible impression on him. But as his letters to Elena Valerianovna attest, there was a host of vivid impressions. He wrote from Venice: "In the evening, we turned our steps to the opera. They performed *Mignon*, but we didn't like it. In the first place, the theater was nasty, and in the second, it was impossible to listen to anyone, except for two or three singers." In a letter from Padua, he described coming by accident upon a Mass at the cathedral: "Lord, what a delight! . . . It was a High Mass with a huge orchestra that included four organs (in honor of the feast of St. Francis). I was positively dumbfounded. So far everything has been grand." And writing from Verona, he related his dash to the small town of Recoaro: "At the train station I read a poster saying that the next day in the town of Recoaro the *illustro baritono* Antonio Cotogni would give a concert. Put yourself in my place; how could I fail to set off for Recoaro, which is six hours from Verona? . . . I flew to Recoaro and just barely got a ticket to the concert. Cotogni sang so amazingly well that I came close to throwing myself at him and embracing him. I positively cannot understand how a man sixty years old can sing so beautifully."

There were just as many things to see and do in St. Petersburg. "[Adelina] Patti is still here concertizing," he wrote on 17 October 1890. "I simply don't have the strength for it all! There are too many temptations. Medea Figner is singing; they're offering a subscription to [Marcella] Sembrich and Cotogni; and on top of that there are the first performances of *Prince Igor*. . . . Imagine what an effect all this has on a poor, country boy from Perm!"

Early in 1892, Diaghilev and Filosofov spent two weeks in Moscow, where they eagerly examined historical monuments, attended the theater, and visited museums. "For whole days we dragged ourselves through monasteries, the Kremlin, picture galleries, etc.," Diaghilev reported home. "We inspected Moscow in the most minute detail." His interest was especially aroused by performances at the Maly Theater in which Marya Yermolova, Glikeriya Fedotova, and Alexander Yuzhin took part. But the most significant event of the trip proved to be a visit to the home of Lev Nikolaevich Tolstoy. In a letter home Diaghilev recorded their conversation with the famous writer almost verbatim.[15] Tolstoy's outward appearance sent him into raptures ("he wears peasant clothing but has a certain gentlemanly way of carrying himself and speaking"), while the writer's "touching figure" seemed a personification of "primal truth and nature." The young men handed Tolstoy a small sum of money as a contribution to a relief fund for starving peasants. During the long conversation, Tolstoy spoke half-jestingly of student days as a "brief moment of repose," when a young person, his opinions still unset, could figure out "what [he] should be doing," the "path [he should] follow." Diaghilev was deeply stirred by the meeting with Tolstoy: "There was something unimaginably sincere, something touching and saintly in the very being of this great man. . . . Seeing him, I understood that the man who walks a path toward absolute perfection acquires moral sanctity. . . . I learned that even in our day there can be holy warriors who seek to discover and preach the truth." The following day the young Petersburger received a photograph of the writer inscribed "To Serge Diaghilev. Lev Tolstoy, 17 January 1892."[16] A correspondence between the two now began in which the delighted young man asked the writer a series of philosophical questions about the meaning of life. One of the answers was signed, "Thinking of you with love, L. Tolstoy."

Diaghilev's next trips abroad, in 1892–1893 and 1895–1896, spread new artistic treasures before him. The scope of his musical interests grew broader. He visited Johannes Brahms at his summer home in the little Austrian village of Ischl and listened to music of Mozart in Nuremberg, where he was staggered by the city's historic architecture. He spent exciting evenings in Bayreuth, attending performances of Wagner's operatic masterpieces. The 1895 journey was marked by an enthusiasm for historical and contemporary painting that was new to him. He visited the studios of prominent German, French, and Swiss artists, and acquired a number of pictures for his own collection, which he dreamed of converting into a Serge Diaghilev Art Museum.

In a letter to his stepmother dated 16 August 1892, Diaghilev related: "During the past few days abroad, I again had the pleasure of listening to music. I heard the whole *Nibelungenlied* and went to the final performance of *Parsifal*. . . . Of course, the conversations about Wagner never end." A first encounter with *Die Meistersinger* and *Tristan und Isolde* deeply affected the young enthusiast. On 14 July the overture of *Die Meistersinger* prompted this romantic outpouring:

> The sound grew and transformed itself into a storm. There were more and more sounds, whirlwinds of sound, more, and more, and more, heavenly thunderclaps, floods, a whole forest of sounds. Blackness! And then suddenly paradise, with the Muse of Melody plucking her lyre. It has everything—pettiness, intrigue, grief, wrath, love, jealousy, endearments, and groans. All of this congeals and in the end comes together to engender life, the same life that flows through each of us. But true beauty triumphs over all.

Richard Wagner

To Russian music lovers of those distant times brought up on Mozart and Italian opera, Wagner's music was not only strange but even "decadent." This explains the response to Diaghilev's transports of his acquaintance Platon Vaksel, who wrote for the newspaper *Journal de St. Petersbourg*. "He is horrified by my opinion," wrote Diaghilev on 14 July 1892 to his stepmother, "and assures me that he can't stand me because I, 'with my poetic soul,' am mad about Wagner and Zola—'those coarse realists.'" At the same time Diaghilev begged Elena Valerianovna not to show his enthusiastic letters about Wagner to her elderly father, known for his passion for Italian opera and deep distaste for Wagner: "Don't read grandfather the parts about Wagner's music, or he will cease to love me!"

Today it seems incredible that Diaghilev, a friend of Stravinsky and Picasso, met Brahms and Verdi, Zola and Chabrier. Each of his trips abroad in the early and mid-1890s was marked by meetings with famous composers, writers, and painters. "He visited a series of artists," wrote Benois in 1930, "just as Nikolai Karamzin, another Russian traveler, had done a hundred years before. For this we accused him of being an egregious sycophant. . . . However, I now believe that he was not motivated in the slightest either by vanity or idle curiosity but rather by some kind of astonishing compulsion to make personal contact with such people, by an eccentric desire 'to get a feel for the man.'"[17]

Diaghilev's letter of 14 July 1892 to Elena Valerianovna gave a colorful account of his visit to the sixty-year-old Brahms:

> I traveled to Ischl, in order to see the famous Brahms, who lives there. . . .
> Brahms turned out to be a small, nimble German, who didn't speak any
> French. He at once complied with my request for an autograph, writing on
> a small card. I sat with him for a quarter of an hour, but our conversation
> was rendered difficult by the fact that we barely understood each other. At
> everything I said, for example that I had come to Ischl to visit him, he fid-

geted and blushed. For some reason he's awfully kept down in Germany. His apartment is like an old hovel. Such a talent and in such surroundings! So, you think, Beethoven was also a poor German, and deaf besides. It's better to imagine them than it is to see them for oneself. But I'm happy, in any case, that I could press his hand with heartfelt goodwill.

In a letter from Rome, Diaghilev announced that he was going to Genoa in order "to interview Verdi, who lives there." He described this visit in a letter from Nice on 17 January 1894: "By the way, I was at Verdi's house in Genoa, but I have nothing interesting to report since, in the first place, he is too old to be interesting, and, in the second place, I found him about to leave for the opera. . . . You will understand how I risked impoliteness by staring at him through my lorgnette."

The impetuous energy shown by this student in his early twenties to meet the most eminent foreign composers, win their confidence, and obtain admission to their rehearsals can be startling. In December 1893, while visiting Paris, he struck up a friendship with Chabrier:

> At first I wanted to leave after three days, but on Saturday at the Opera they were performing *Die Walküre*, so I remained until Sunday. . . . Then I got bogged down further because of the premiere of *Gwendoline* by Chabrier. . . . Suddenly I learned that it would be performed the following Wednesday, and that the *répétition générale* would be on Sunday. . . . I set in motion all the intrigues in the world, wrote letters to Chabrier, wrote to his wife, flew to the box office and shook hands with all the clerks in a friendly way . . . in order to obtain a pass for the rehearsal. Yesterday morning I appeared in person at the composer's house to get a definitive answer. I was met by a little old man, who on the spot locked me in an embrace. He took me to an

office, to a gallery, gave me a wonderful seat at the rehearsal, and I sat with him for no less than three-quarters of an hour. . . . He entreated me to come dine at his home and promised to introduce me to several famous people.

Thus the young Petersburger realized his fondest wish: he attended the répétition générale of *Gwendoline*. Near him were the most illustrious people of Paris: "Just imagine, in the box were Monsieur and Madame Zola, and with them the famous young composer Alfred Bruneau (who wrote the operas *Le Rêve* and *L'Attaque du moulin*). In addition, there was the family of Victor Hugo, Massenet with his family, Chabrier with the young composer Vincent d'Indy (who wrote *Wallenstein*), and the famous conductor Charles Lamoureux, while in a seat not far from me was Alexandre Dumas. . . . All of this is much more interesting than Paris itself."

Encounters like these were not simply occasions for youthful braggadocio but also a learning experience. "My acquaintance with Chabrier and with Dagnan, about whom I wrote to you and with whom I continue to correspond, will help me a great deal to understand the essence of the new trends, both in painting and in music," Diaghilev asserted in a letter from Nice on 17 January 1894.[18]

During the same Paris trip Diaghilev paid a call on Emile Zola, the most important living French writer of the time:

A few days ago, I went to visit Zola and sat with him for an hour. We spoke a great deal about such interesting topics as the anarchists, Tolstoy, ideals, and art. I naturally took care to write all of this down and will read it to you. Toward the end I asked him to write something for me on a little card, and he wrote the nice phrase: "The production of art is indeed a part of nature, filtered through the temperament of the artist." Although I don't agree with this at all, it is quite interesting nonetheless.

In the West, Diaghilev eagerly studied the artistry of the most prominent actors and actresses. He went into raptures over Sarah Bernhardt. He saw her Italian rival Eleonora Duse and attended performances by Jean Mounet-Sully (whose "affected howling" displeased him). One of his letters described a popular festival on the streets of Venice, where the famous baritone Francesco Tamagno sang for the Italian crowds.

It was an enormous celebration, the night of the Festa di Predentove. All night long the whole of Venice rode in gondolas; there were bonfires, fireworks, and barge music. In short, it was like a fairy tale. . . . Right near us an enormous company, with Tamagno at its head, stationed itself. Ah, what a night it was! Tamagno sang accompanied by a piano, which had been placed in a gondola. He sang all night! The moon was up; there were the palaces, canals—all the adornments of Venice—and then the sound of that preternatural voice carried across the water. He sang *Il Trovatore*, *Otello*, and *Andrea Chénier* and some song about the milk of human kindness. Everyone was moved, and when he fell silent, they yelled to him from the barge: "Tamagno, your public calls."

Elsewhere in the letter are Diaghilev's delighted impressions of a concert given by Tamagno, Giuseppe Kaschmann, Romano Nanetti, and other Italian singers at the Venetian theater La Fenice:

What Tamagno was up to in the duet from *Polinto* it is impossible to say. But here they barely let him sing. In the very first aria of *Andrea Chénier*, as soon as he sang, "in tutto firmamento," and on the C flat spread open his hands—the whole theater cried out, rumbled, screamed, and jumped to its feet. And from that moment on it was impossible to hear anything, because everyone sang along with him, and they made such a ruckus, that it was truly like the days of the Roman circus.

Once Diaghilev returned to St. Petersburg, his correspondence with his step-mother began to contain reports of the music studies that were increasingly supplanting his limited interest in the law. He writes about his singing lessons and his growing eagerness to become a composer. Here are a few excerpts:

I am in the habit of visiting Aunt Tatusia about twice a week. On Thursdays I stay for dinner and take a singing lesson. Just imagine, Auntie has helped me to discover that I have a very fine voice (undated, 1890).

I continue to take singing lessons with Aunt Tatusia, and this month I begin to study music theory to prepare myself for the conservatory, which I hope to enter next year without fail (16 November 1890).

I am terribly busy with my voice and have already had some success, although thus far only among my friends (21 September 1891).

By autumn 1892, Diaghilev had his own apartment in St. Petersburg and took great pleasure in playing his excellent Bechstein, which he had arranged to have sent from Perm. "My piano is magnificent," he wrote on 14 October, "so that Wagner is in full bloom. It's already been two weeks since I began to take singing lessons from [Stanislav]

Gabel, a professor at the conservatory. I spent a long time asking for advice about whom I should study with, and a great many people agreed on Gabel. He is very pleased with me. . . . This week I begin lessons in music theory with [Nikolai] Soloviev. It's time to take this matter seriously, otherwise the years go by, and it's easy to waste them."

A little later, in autumn 1894, he sought out the eminent Italian singer Antonio Cotogni, who had been invited to conduct a singing class at the St. Petersburg Conservatory. Diaghilev's brother Yury related the incident to Elena Valerianovna: "Seriozha returned from his lesson with Cotogni. Cotogni was delighted with Seriozha's voice, and he was particularly pleased with his mezzo voce. . . . He said that he had never heard this kind of mezzo baritono, even among Italian singers."

Diaghilev's correspondence describes evenings at his home when masterpieces of classical music were played. In a note to Benois on 24 September 1893, Diaghilev wrote: "If you aren't busy tomorrow evening, . . . why don't you drop by my place around eight o'clock. I will have music. The program is expected to include the Trio in B Major of Beethoven, the Schumann and Tchaikovsky trios, and the cello sonata of Rubinstein. There won't be more than ten or twelve people, including the instrumentalists." On 4 November 1891 he reported to his stepmother that he had been "invited Saturday evening to the Cossack barracks to accompany a whole evening of [Nikolai] Figner and [Leonid] Yakovlev." He was "terribly anxious," he added, "but . . . didn't have the strength to refuse such a pleasure." In a letter to Benois on 30 July 1893, Filosofov described a difficult concert program sung by the Diaghilev during one of the evenings at Bogdanovskoe—"The Dew Glistens," by [Anton] Rubinstein, "Don't Cry, My Child," from *The Demon*, and the monologue from *Parsifal*. On the same program Diaghilev also performed his own "Melody" and the songs "The Maiden and the Sun" and "The Psalmodist of David."

Diaghilev was received in the most distinguished musical circles of St. Petersburg. Besides the home of critic Platon Vaksel he frequented the salon of the singer Alexandra Molas, Rimsky-Korsakov's sister-in-law and an ardent propagandist for the Mighty Five [Rimsky-Korsakov, Cui, Balakirev, Mussorgsky, and Borodin]. "I often stop by the home of Molas," he wrote on 11 October 1893. "Rimsky-Korsakov, Cui, Balakirev, and other composers are there constantly. It's very interesting."

Increasingly, one encounters mentions of chamber works and songs he had completed. Sometimes he referred sarcastically to these freshly minted works, acknowledging their lack of originality and "old-fashioned" style: "In my activities as a composer I have progressed, creating yet another immortal work—a romance for cello and piano that is an example of gross and vile salon music, although it has some very pretty little melodies" (11 August 1893). "I have nearly finished the first part of my violin sonata, which seems to me to be very successful," he reported two months later.

> My sonata, though it may be indifferently composed, is at least thoroughly sincere and has the right tone. It is in an unrelieved, macabre minor key, and if I were to give it a name, then it would be something like 'The Death of Tchaikovsky and Death Always.' . . . Of course, the sonata does not illustrate this phrase (because in order to illustrate this it would be necessary to write something more within my powers), but my mood, especially in the second part, which was written on the day Tchaikovsky died, is exactly like that.[19]

Among Diaghilev's own essays in composition was a sonata for cello and piano, a vocal setting of some poetry by Baudelaire, and a series of romances. From Benois we know that in 1894 Diaghilev was composing an opera, *Boris Godunov*, after the tragedy by Pushkin, and that he completed the Fountain Scene, which he performed for friends. (For the occasion Diaghilev himself sang the part of the Impostor, to Panaeva-Kartseva's Marina.) These operatic fragments met with little enthusiasm. Benois, for instance, dismissed them as highly virtuosic, with an outpouring of "broad melodies" combining "elements of Mussorgsky with reminders of Tchaikovsky."[20]

With whom Diaghilev studied musical theory or composition remains a fairly tangled question in his biographies. Among those mentioned are Rimsky-Korsakov, Anatol Liadov, Nikolai Sokolov, Vasily Kalafati, and Nikolai Soloviev, although Diaghilev himself, in his "Autobiographical Notes," identifies only Sokolov and Liadov as his teachers.[21] In his letters to Elena Valerianovna he speaks of taking lessons from Massenet and Saint-Saëns, of consulting Chabrier. But these were idle dreams, never to be realized. His studies at the university coupled with his boundless enthusiasm for exhibitions, concerts, and opera first nights kept him, it seems, from concentrating in earnest on composition.

In 1894 Diaghilev's musical ambitions suffered a serious setback. "On Wednesday, Seriozha will show his things to Rimsky-Korsakov," Yury informed Elena Valerianovna on 18 September. Among the compositions Rimsky was destined to see four days later were a violin sonata, the song "King David," and, possibly, the first part of a cello sonata. An account of the visit, so humiliating to the young man, appears in the memoirs of Vasily Yastrebtsev:

Nikolai Andreyevich gave an account of a curious visit he had from some young man named Diaghilev, who fancies himself a great composer but, nevertheless, would like to study music theory with Nikolai Andreyevich. His compositions proved to be absurd, and Nikolai Andreyevich told him so bluntly, whereupon he became offended and, on leaving, declared arrogantly that nevertheless he believes in himself and his gifts; that he will never forget this day and that some day Rimsky-Korsakov's opinion will occupy a shameful place in his (Rimsky-Korsakov's) biography and make him regret his rash words, but then it will be too late.[22]

Typically, Yastrebtsev and Rimsky-Korsakov went on to comment about "a certain type of deranged person who, though undoubtedly gifted, never creates anything that is not bizarre, inane, and even downright stupid." To illustrate the point Rimsky-Korsakov suggested that his friend "listen to a number of strange works by the composer [Vincent] d'Indy . . . who is well known in the West and has the approval of such people as the young Belgian composer [Paul] Gilson." " 'I'm inclined to think,' added Nikolai Andreyevich, 'that either he has no ear whatsoever or he's decided to make fun of us.' "[23] But if the "stupidity" and "bizarreness" of Diaghilev's works were on the same level as those of d'Indy, a composer much esteemed in France, one may well ask if Rimsky-Korsakov's judgment was a fair one or instead a display of his well-known peevishness. Were Diaghilev's compositions really so "absurd"? In other quarters, his creations met with a very different response: Benois, for instance, considered them marked by an excessive traditionalism and stylistic timidity. And some listeners, including Alexandra Panaeva-Kartseva, found definite artistic merit in his works. As she wrote to her sister Elena Valerianovna: "Seriozha . . . tells me all the details of his visits to musical people. . . . Their indignation at Seriozha's work convinces me that I am not mistaken in recognizing its outstanding talent."

Nevertheless, Rimsky-Korsakov's uncompromising opinion played its fatal role in Diaghilev's musical biography. With his work categorically rejected by one of Russia's most important musicians, he understood that as a composer, he was not in his natural element and must therefore seek another outlet for his dynamic, creative nature. Thus, in 1894–1895, partly influenced by his close association with Benois and Bakst, Diaghilev's artistic interests began to incline toward painting.

In September 1896, however, soon after passing his final law school examinations, Diaghilev again attempted to enroll at the conservatory, this time in the voice department. His application, which survives in the archives of the St. Petersburg Conservatory, reads: "To His Excellency, the Director of the St. Petersburg Conservatory, from Serge Pavlovich Diaghilev, Esq., A Petition. I humbly request Your Excellency to accept me as an auditor in the St. Petersburg Conservatory, in the singing class of Professor Cotogni. S. P. Diaghilev, Esq., 16 September 1896. Liteinyi St. 45."[24] The Diaghilev file contains no response to this petition, nor does it include any examination papers or other documents. So it remains unknown whether he became an auditor and studied with the celebrated Cotogni, a singer who was indeed a professor at the St. Petersburg Conservatory from 1894 to 1898 (at which time he returned to Italy to teach at the Liceo Santa Cecilia in Rome).

We can assume, however, that even if Diaghilev did attend a certain number of classes with Cotogni, it is unlikely that he poured his efforts into a systematic course of study. A new period of his creative life was now opening, one marked by an enthusiasm for the fine arts and the start of his activities as an art critic.

Nevertheless, Diaghilev's study of composition and voice and his various trips abroad left indelible marks on his aesthetic development. He could read a score, analyze a complicated musical manuscript on his own, accompany singers (including such titans as Fedor Chaliapin and Nikolai Figner). He played duets on the piano often and with pleasure. Indeed, his enthusiasm for them was so great that Igor Stravinsky later dedicated to him—along with *Les Noces*—one of his Three Easy Pieces for Piano Duet. In later years Diaghilev's thorough grounding in music would add special distinction to his activities as a producer, while giving him the knowledge to demand revisions from composers of the stature of Stravinsky, Prokofiev, Ravel, and Falla, and even to reject scores that he felt were unsuitable for ballet.

To his musical talent were added his gifts as a writer, critic, and stylist. These gifts, revealed in his letters and in his first published essays, make the brilliance of his literary talent obvious. Benois, in fact, asserted that if Diaghilev had continued to write, he would almost certainly have occupied an important place in the history of Russian art criticism. But Diaghilev answered a different call: not only to comment upon and appraise the creations of his contemporaries but also to have a hand in their birth, to strive for their perfect realization and for their acceptance by society. Indeed, it was Diaghilev's education and personal experience as a musician that allowed him to become the leader of a new artistic movement.

—Translated by Robert Johnson

three Early Writings of Serge Diaghilev

Edited, translated, and with an introduction

by John E. Bowlt

The writings of Serge Diaghilev, especially of the pre-Paris period, bring into relief a creative talent that has remained largely unrecognized in Western scholarship of Diaghilev and the Ballets Russes. In 1982 the imbalance was somewhat rectified by the appearance of the two-volume anthology of Diaghilev's writings in Russian, compiled by Ilya Zilbershtein and Vladimir Samkov.[1] The fruit of a long and painstaking examination of archival and periodical sources, this remarkable epistolary and critical legacy, and the comprehensive commentary that accompanies it, has yet to be translated. This is unfortunate, for it is a vital source that can expand our knowledge not only of Diaghilev's biography but also of the rich mosaic of Russia's Silver Age. The intricate network of cultural references in Diaghilev's writings emphasizes once again that Russia's fin de siècle was, indeed, a time of artistic synthesis, when painters, poets, musicians, and philosophers aspired to integrate the separate arts into a single pantheon, mysterium or, more appropriately, World of Art.

The eager correspondence that Diaghilev maintained with friends and foes, artists and patrons in the 1890s and early 1900s, as well as the numerous reviews and articles he published in both moderate and radical journals and newspapers of the time, reveal a perspicacious mind, a sophisticated wit, an unfailing distinction between the elevated and the vulgar, and a broad diapason of cultural concerns that encompassed literature, painting, industrial design, and museology, as well as opera and the ballet. Indeed, the early writings remind us that Diaghilev was an art critic and a magazine editor, an art administrator and an exhibition organizer well before he achieved international prestige as the impresario of the Ballets Russes. Diaghilev was able to grapple with complex questions in the various arts thanks to his own exposure to a variety of disciplines: he trained as a musician; he was a student of law; he was an avid collector of paintings, engravings, and books; he spoke Russian, French, German, and English; and he wrote "charming fairy stories."[2] Certainly, Diaghilev's critical views owed much to Alexandre Benois, in the 1890s his mentor, and his sensitive antennae received messages from numerous sources, Eastern and Western. But Diaghilev had a remarkable knack for distinguishing the essential in a new artifact or aesthetic discourse and for detecting permanence and value. This talent to see and recognize helped Diaghilev to expand his interests and evolve his own taste over the years from symbolism to constructivism, as is clear from a comparison of his aesthetic preferences and cultural activities in the 1890s and the 1920s.

Diaghilev's publications of the late 1890s and early 1900s are striking in their abrupt departure from the kind of criticism that dominated Russian art appreciation in the nineteenth century. Diaghilev stressed the importance of individual expression and formal measure rather than extrinsic or narrative value. Of course, originality of vision had to be accompanied by technical competence, but the cult of technique for its own sake, like the cult of technology, was of little concern to Diaghilev because "a scientific attitude toward art . . . will never resolve the question of the relative value of creative talent."[3] Consequently, while always looking ahead, Diaghilev also acknowledged achievements of the past, both recent and remote. He nurtured an unfailing passion for eighteenth-century Russian portraits, compiling a survey of Dmitry Levitsky's portraits in 1902 and organizing the enormous Exhibition of Historic Russian Portraits for the Tauride Palace, St. Petersburg, in 1905.[4] Diaghilev even found some praise for the painting of the realists (the *peredvizhniki*), admiring them for their protest against the moribund academy. Still, Diaghilev was perturbed by the average taste of his contemporary public, which could not discern the difference between the mastery of Velázquez and the derivative style of Genrikh

Semiradsky or between the majesty of *Die Nibelungen* and the sentimentalism of *Pagliacci*. Diaghilev mounted a fierce attack against his detractors by arguing that they, not he, were the real decadents and that Russia's cultural renaissance depended precisely on the new, the strange, and the excessive. In turn, this attitude encouraged his interest in experiment and transgression whether in the decorative arts, in the ballet—or in personal relationships.

Like many of his generation, Diaghilev was fluent in French, and he scattered French words liberally throughout his Russian letters. But he also loved the Russian language, especially unusual words and idioms, some of which, presumably, he assimilated from his old nanny (a colloquy implied in Léon Bakst's 1906 double portrait of them [pl. 1] and in Diaghilev's own reference to the "elderly nannies" who still "remember those fables" in his 1905 speech in Moscow at the Metropole Hotel). The analogy with Alexander Pushkin and his nanny is inviting and may have stimulated Diaghilev's lifelong enthusiasm for the poetry and prose of the great writer.

The small sampling below cannot do full justice to Diaghilev's gifts as a writer and polemicist, and important letters and essays concerning many people and subjects, especially in the realm of music and the theater, are not included. But within the limitations of space, my primary goal in this compilation is to emphasize the multifarious interests of the early Diaghilev (before his virtual emigration to the West in 1906) and the forthrightness of expression and clarity of style with which he wrote and spoke, whether in the intimacy of a letter to his stepmother or in the formality of a published review. Nonetheless, although Diaghilev's letters and essays should reinforce our admiration of his intellectual acumen, good taste, and entrepreneurship, we still recognize the same obdurateness and manipulativeness that enabled this "rather adventuristic operator" to establish and control the greatest ballet company of all time.[5] Whether as protagonist of the new or antagonist of the old, Diaghilev did not hesitate to voice his opinion, a habit that often elicited anger, indignation, and condemnation (as he admitted in his letter to Benois of April 1897). Diaghilev's censure of the Academy of Arts and the Imperial Theaters extends his intolerance of bureaucratic structures, while his appreciation of the *style russe* and modern Scandinavian art illustrates his enthusiasm for fresh experiment; his praise of Tolstoy and Chekhov indicates that he supported the traditions of realism while advocating the aesthetic of decadence and symbolism; and his dramatic description of the effects of the 1905 revolution in St. Petersburg reveals an apocalyptic Diaghilev, poignantly concerned with the fate of his country.

The time frame of the selection is 1892–1905. In 1892 Diaghilev had just moved permanently from Perm to St. Petersburg and, as a student at the university, was already a member of the Nevsky Pickwickians led by Alexandre Benois. The year 1905 signaled the finale of Diaghilev's exclusive advocacy of Russian culture in Russia, marked by his Exhibition of Historic Russian Portraits. Thereafter, Diaghilev shifted his activities increasingly to the West, particularly Paris. In 1906 he organized the Russian section for the Salon d'Automne; in 1907 he presented concerts of Russian music; in 1908 he produced *Boris Godunov*; and in 1909 he presented the Ballets Russes. But as we can see from the selection below, the Ballets Russes, however different in scope and composition, extended many of the aesthetic principles that Diaghilev had outlined in his early pronouncements. Study of this legacy helps us to understand the tensions, rifts, and curious continuity of Diaghilev's Ballets Russes.

Excerpt from a letter from Serge Diaghilev to his stepmother, Elena Valerianovna Diaghileva, 18 February 1892, St. Petersburg

After saying hello, [Tolstoy] turned to us and asked: "How can I help you?"[6] Confused, I responded with a sentence that I had prepared in advance: "Well, Lev Nikolaevich, we are Petersburg students and wanted to send you our modest contributions, but when we found out that you were in Moscow, we decided to give them to you in person."[7]

Tolstoy: "Fine. But how did you end up here?"

(Dima decided to venture a white lie, since it would have been terribly awkward to confess that we had come to Moscow just to have fun, so we answered:)

Dima: "We're here on business."

T.: "Ah, for the university . . ."

D.: "No, my father sent me."

T.: "I see. Are you here for long?"

D.: "No. We're thinking of leaving tomorrow or the day after."

T.: "Well, which departments are you in? Which courses are you taking?"

I: "We're both in second year law school."

T.: "You mean, you're not doing anything?"

(At these words we smiled and I answered:)

I: "Actually, that's quite true."

T.: "Well, there's nothing wrong with that."

(We smiled again.)

Tolstoy at Yasnaya Polyana, 1908

T.: "I'm not joking, you know, I mean it seriously. That brief moment of repose is very beneficial—when you don't know what you should be doing or which path to follow or when you still lack your own convictions. Indeed, what convictions can you have when you're young? This gives you time to think things over. When my son thought of leaving the university, I told him not to do so, and just for that reason."

I: "Yes, one or two people work in our department, but in other departments people do work and often hard."

T.: "Well, I don't know, maybe doctors and mathematicians, but generally speaking, university teaching is totally useless. Of course, that's my personal opinion. What are your names?"

D. and I: "Diaghilev and Filosofov . . ."

I: "Lev Nikolaevich, are you here for long?"

T.: "Until the 20th, I think. You know, after sitting around here, once again I feel this ennui, a kind of melancholy. I wonder what's going on down there during these cold spells. It's so good in the country, so much lightness and joy. You feel you're actually doing something. Up from the country, my son and the two Raevsky students came to see me and made me feel quite terrible—telling me how everything was going so well, how they had bought firewood and procured grain.[8] I just wanted to go right back . . . "

(We stood up, for we both felt awkward keeping the old man further. In great agitation I took the money from my wallet and put it on the desk. . . .)

As soon as we were outside, our first words burst forth as we exclaimed: "He's a saint, he's a real saint!" We were so moved that we almost cried. There was something unimaginably sincere, something touching and saintly in the very being of this great man. You'll laugh, but long after embracing him we could still smell his beard. Of course, at first we could talk of nothing else, and the next day I felt the terrible desire to obtain a copy of his visiting card with his signature so as to have some kind of material record of our conversation. Before you could say Jack Robinson, I decided to write a letter, not to Lev Nikolaevich, however, but to his daughter Tatiana Lvovna, who looked after all his correspondence.[9] This is what it said:

"Dear Countess Tatiana Lvovna,

"Yesterday I had the honor to be received by your father. Our conversation has produced such a profound and indelible impression upon me that I would like very much to possess some kind of material souvenir. I wonder, therefore, whether you could ask Lev Nikolaevich to sign the portrait enclosed herewith. You can well understand how important this is to me.

"I remain yours very faithfully,

Serge Diaghilev, student

Someone will call for the portrait tomorrow evening."

I should note that both here and in my second letter I observed the rule of writing as curtly and as clearly as possible, avoiding all emotional words and sentences. I sent off my letter to Tatiana Lvovna the morning after the conversation. When I came home around two o'clock, I found that same envelope in which I had mailed the portrait, but with my address in Tatiana Lvovna's hand: "Serg. Pavl. Diag., Esq., Hotel Dresden, from Tolstaia," while the portrait now carried Lev Nikolaevich's caption: "To Serge Diaghilev. Lev Tolstoy, 17 January 1892...."

Such were my meeting and correspondence with Tolstoy. I don't know whether I'll ever have the chance to meet him or write to him again in my lifetime. I certainly desire this with all my heart because such moments and impressions remain in the soul forever, like specks of light. Nobody else has ever produced such an original and strange impression upon me. As soon as I saw him, I realized that through self-perfection one can attain a moral sanctity, and I realized that the prophets and saints we read about in the Holy Scriptures are not a myth, are not impossible. I learned that fighters in the search and advocacy of truth can exist even today. I know that when I reread these lines in thirty years' time, I'll find them very funny. My delight and zeal will pass, but if such zeal demands release, why hide it?

Serge Diaghilev

Excerpt from *"The Wandering Exhibition,"* Novosti i birzhevaia gazeta,
5 and 9 March 1897

What a joy it is each time to visit our Wandering Exhibition![10] You feel that the constant source of all the finest and most vital things that Russian art has produced is this fresh and young exhibition. This year it celebrates its twenty-fifth anniversary, and we should offer our most heartfelt congratulations on the importance it has assumed in the history of our art. First, the Wandering Exhibitions were a protest, and, like any protest by youthful and noble forces against trends that are not easy to vanquish, they had to work hard to make society reject the false views of the academic hegemony. Of course, the Wandering Exhibitions have also made mistakes, been guilty of tendentiousness and *peredvizhnichestvo* [lit.: art of the Wanderers]. The spirit of the Wanderers, with their narrowly national bias, their unabating narrative in art, and their constant need for an idea in painting, is the other side of the coin. The Wandering Exhibitions have taught us to "think painting," not feel it. Before confronting the concept of beauty, we were obliged to experience the cult of the idea, that is, a mode that is not purely artistic. The cult of "idea" went together with the cult of "nature," and one of the main yardsticks for artistic evaluation was the requirement that [the work of art] be close to nature, something that often led to a kind of photography. No longer were we much interested in the artist's character and temperament. The main thing was truth and the message. Certainly, one can understand these two conditions from the standpoint of evolution. Truth derived from a protest against the clumsy conventions of classicism that dominated all of Europe at the beginning of the [nineteenth] century, while the need for a message was based on the ideas of the 1860s, finding support in German painting, which has always influenced our art. The Wandering Exhibitions started up just as German sentimentalism and social ideas were in ascendance. . . .

Added to this was yet another requirement—that art be a mirror of what's going on—and this is when something very unusual happened. Painting turned into illustration, into a newspaper chronicle of everyday life. . . . In any case, the Wandering Exhibitions were the only Russian art society that made tolerance a primary condition and where fresh talent, regardless of orientation or style, could find refuge. If the Wanderers possessed their unfailing bias for so long, it is not because they excluded everything else but simply because such was the vogue of the time and nothing else was available. Yet now, year by year, each Wandering Exhibition is distancing itself from that initial bias and becoming more diverse, a situation that can be ascribed to two conditions: a common shift in the demands [of society] and the appearance of a new Moscow school that is investing our painting with a completely new impetus. Hence, it is from this group and from this exhibition that we should expect a new trend that will win us our place in European art. Europe firmly believes in us, has waited a long time for us, but we still lack strength; we need to believe in ourselves more and—above all—move forward. But this is exactly what could let us down: we might gain in strength and self-confidence and then become bogged down, something that is typical of our character. A Western artist never gives up trying, never abandons the search, whereas we love to take time out and admire what we've been doing. This is our misfortune, for we can boast very few artists who have matured and grown strong and are still looking ahead.

Letter from Serge Diaghilev to Princess Maria Tenisheva, 4 February 1897, St. Petersburg

Dear, kind Maria Klavdievna,

I have been in such haste recently that I had to postpone writing my letter to you for a while, although I really needed to write to you and perhaps should have done so long ago. The main point is that my exhibition has been the subject of many changes.[11] I have brought in more paintings than I intended, both in quantity and, in some cases, in size. When I realized this, I recognized that your house, which you had offered so graciously, could in no way accommodate me and my artistic family. That's when I had the idea of using the hall in the Baron Stieglitz Museum; it has not been used [as an exhibition space] before, but it has all the essentials for a big show. Contrary to my expectations, the matter was easy to arrange, and, consequently, I had to reject the idea of organizing my exhibition in your lovely home. In recent times you have given such attention to my projects, such interest, that I would like to thank you once again, Princess, for your support. Had it not been for your support, I would never have begun to organize such a complex thing as an exhibition.

I must confess that I am satisfied with the results of my trip and feel that the exhibition will be interesting. Shura [Benois] has put aside three pieces for you, which I think you'll like, and he wanted to discuss a few other pieces with you. I shall be sure to send you a catalogue and to tick off the most interesting works.

A lot is being said about your exhibition—a lot of good things, of course, although people are afraid to write about it, first, because a critical article (rather than a short notice) on such a wide-ranging collection requires a certain amount of knowledge, and, second, because it's a terrifying thing to have to judge you.[12] You have done, and are doing, too much for [us] to assail the shortcomings of your collection, while no one is willing to offer you indiscriminate praise, for that would be interpreted as partiality. I don't have the time to write anything sensible. I'd start off with you and then go on to the Russian watercolor exhibition, which makes me seasick.[13] I cannot hide the fact that I don't like most of the Russian part of your collection. Anyway, my slogan is Westernism and, consequently, I am not impartial. I would just love to throttle Messrs. Karazin et al. with my own hands.[14] If you were to supplement your rich collection with some foreign pearls, it would be one of the foremost in the whole of Europe.

Please give my respectful greeting to the Prince.[15] I remain yours very faithfully,
Serge Diaghilev

Excerpt from a letter from Serge Diaghilev to Alexandre Benois, April 1897, St. Petersburg

My dear Shura,

How could you imagine that I had become your enemy after your wonderful, sincere letter?[16] Not everyone can write such letters, and not everyone has the ability to sense their subtlety.

Nonetheless (and in spite of the "nouvelism" that runs through me),[17] I am intolerably fond of friendship, frankness, sincerity, family life, in a word, of the most bourgeois simplicity devoid of outer complexity. . . . The gist of your letter is that you don't like my packaging—from the way I dress to the insincere tone that I adopt in speaking and writing about you in the press. Incidentally, all your sermonizing about your attitudes toward your well-wishers and enemies, while somewhat cynical, is infinitely true and engaging in its sincerity. . . .

Naturally, I am not going to exaggerate my eccentricities, but I consider them too trivial and unworthy to change my physiognomy. I shall be as I was and that's that. If need be, I'll go around in rags. As for the impression that I make on those around me, well, that's a rather more complex question, and I ask you to trust my every word inasmuch as I am offering you the same sincerity. All my life, from age sixteen onward, I have done everything in defiance of everyone else. At first my family, so near and dear, was up in arms, causing me many complicated and dramatic moments (once an almost tragic moment); then came war with a myriad distant relatives who couldn't stand me. I was censored for my every move; I was sworn at. And then came my acquaintance with you, which also began with countless mockeries and with your "nonrecognition" of me.

Remember how long you thought of me as an *inner hussar*? Then society began to attack my vacuous outward appearance, my bombast, and my foppishness. Now things have gotten so bad that everyone regards me as a scoundrel, a debauchee, a salesman— in brief, hell knows what. I know all this intimately, but I still retain my brilliant front as I go into the Assembly of Nobles. You'll say that this is mere bravado. No. Two feelings combine here. First, a purely human feeling of hostility toward the world of ill-wishers that in no small measure is mingled with my scorn of them; and second, a deep belief that this phase will pass if my life is crowned with success. Heavens above, it is success and only success that saves us and supersedes everything else. My family now dotes on me; my relatives are almost praising me, and, assuming a serious visage, society has already begun to go on about "this really decent man, *très bien habillé*, just like a foreigner"— and these are the same people who scoffed at my chic elegance. If I am successful as the champion of certain ideas or attract a following and, of course, success, then I shall be better than anyone else around. *Tout est là, mon ami* [That's all there is to it, my friend]. But the moment I fail—all the old wounds will open and no one will let me forget it.

I possess a certain boldness of spirit and the habit of spitting people in the eye. That's not always easy, but it's usually useful. Let me pause here. There is a small, very small group of people before whom my boldness wanes and whose judgment I await with bowed head. They are Dima, you, occasionally Valechka, and, in certain matters of everyday life, Sasha Ratkov.[18] Before you all I become a man deprived of will and freedom of action.

I even think that everything I do, I do precisely for you or, rather, because of you: as you judge, so will it be. Consequently, for me you are a second "I."[19] As for you personally, well, previously my sentiment toward you was one of injured self-esteem for, truly, back then you did much to demonstrate that you had no liking for me. But after your marriage, you took an extraordinary turn for the better, and all your seriousness and simplicity date *de là*. Of course, sometimes, you, too, adopt poses—maybe more often than I do—and beneath them conceal attitudes that are less than flattering to those around you, but, strange to say, your outer appearance has never really shocked me. I was truly indifferent. Many things about you have often seemed trivial, and I feel that this is your greatest defect: for all your breadth of views, your sophisticated nature, and your life "beyond the necessities," there still remains within you a kind of human paltriness and trivial servility that is quite alien. This is the greatest hindrance to clarity—to *sérénité*.

As for you the artist, well, that's more complex for me to analyze, and I cannot separate you from me. One moment I am excessively stern, the next sweetly partial. I know this of myself and, therefore, keep to the mean—criticizing your technique, which, certainly, does not seem to be up to the level of your talent, although perhaps I understand nothing. But I really love your sense of creativity and fantasy and enjoy your every new success as if it were my own. However, the public knows this and won't believe me, saying that I'm partial and nepotistic. But it's all the same to me and, anyway, the results are zero. Basically, I'm fond of you, value you, depend upon you, and view much through your spectacles.

Excerpt from a letter from *Serge Diaghilev to Alexandre Benois*, 20 October 1897, St. Petersburg

Dear Shura,

I have absolutely no time and, consequently, just couldn't get round to answering your kind letter. You already know from Kostia that I'm full of projects, each more grandiose than the next.[20] I'm now planning this journal in which I hope to bring together all our artistic life, that is, to place genuine painting in the illustrations and to say frankly what I think in the articles.[21] I also wish to organize a series of annual exhibitions under the aegis of the journal and to link it up with the new and developing branch of industrial design in Moscow and Finland. In a word, I see the future through a magnifying glass. But for this I need help, and, of course, to whom should I turn, if not to you? In any case, I can rely on you as on myself, right? I expect at least five articles from you each year, not especially long ones, but good articles, malicious and interesting; it doesn't matter what they're about. Kostia has already helped by promising a cover and poster. Incidentally, Kostia—what a great talent he has! He's so interesting and fills me with unending joy. He says that I get carried away in praising him. But, my friends, does it really matter if one gets carried away? You won't believe what progress he's made. The pieces he painted this summer are charming. I expect the same from you. The Finns are remarkable.[22] Such refinement, such subtlety. Two or three of the young Finns are simply superb. Beware of competing with them, but do try to eclipse them. I await your missives with impatience.

The Princess is in St. Petersburg.[23] *We're good friends*. She'll stay in St. Petersburg the whole winter until March. She definitely wishes to engage you for a fortnight or so and

Léon Bakst, cover design for Mir iskusstva, 1902

wants you to convey her new acquisitions from Paris. She's full of energy and, apparently, money. She'd like to purchase something at the Scandinavian exhibition and has asked me to make suggestions. Of course, I'm not going to palm off trash on her.

I'm expecting Zorn, Thaulow, and Edelfelt any day.[24] Can you imagine, Zorn and Thaulow will be staying with me! The Princess has commissioned a portrait from Zorn. While we were in Finland, I kept on about Kostia to the Princess, and I'm going to take all his pictures round to her and make her buy something. What do you think about Vrubel?[25] In any case, write as soon as you can, and tell me what you think about all of this. Remind Kostia that I am expecting his poster any day now. I still don't know what the title of the journal will be. Is it true that Anna Karlovna is not well?[26]

I kiss you,

Seriozha Diaghilev

What about Ober? Can we get something by him for the exhibition? Not too big?[27]

"The Arts and Crafts" (An Interview Concerning the Goal of the Journal Mir iskusstva), Peterburgskaia Gazeta, 25 May 1898

Russian art has now reached a moment of transition.[28] It is a moment in which history places all emergent directions, when the principles of the old generation clash with new and developing needs. Hence the protest of youthful forces that we observe in the Paris Champs de Mars salon, the Munich Secession, the London New Gallery, and so on.

The Wanderers sprang up twenty-five years ago;[29] they shouldered the burden, but have now given in. They have grown old.

In the meantime, however, our art has not diminished. There is a group of young artists scattered throughout different cities who, if gathered together, could demonstrate that Russian art is fresh, original, and capable of bringing much that is new to the history of art.

Our debuts in the West have failed, and in Europe we are seen as something decrepit, slumbering upon necrotic traditions.

That is why we must explain these young forces, let our artists speak for themselves through the new journal, and render a substantial service that, through the crafts, will be for the common good.

Alexander Golovin, cover design for Mir iskusstva, 1899

Letter from Serge Diaghilev to Vladimir von Meck, 27 July 1900, St. Petersburg

Dear Vladimir Vladimirovich,

After receiving the subsidy, Mir iskusstva is now in a position to exist without the assistance and contributions by those private individuals who are sympathetic to the enterprise.[30] When *Mir iskusstva* was in need, your attitude was one of such sincerity and you manifested such concern for its collaborators that I have decided to propose the following: I feel that there is a vast lacuna in the field of Russian book publishing—a total absence of truly artistic editions pertaining to our artists. In France and Germany you can procure cheap and de luxe editions on Böcklin, Menzel, Puvis, Liebermann, Degas, and others at whatever price you like, whereas here in Russia, apart from Bulgakov's foul editions on Semiradsky, Aivazovsky, and Fedotov, there are no good collections on either good modern artists or the Russian masters.[31] My dream would be to undertake a series of such publications, both cheap and de luxe. First off, spurred by the memory of the death of my friend, the artist Levitan, I would really like to give this still underrated, great Russian master his due.[32] A very interesting collection of photographs of his works could be put together and a fine, de luxe edition made. In this case, I do have in mind a de luxe edition—because first, I consider Levitan worthy of such an honor, and second, landscapes lose their effect in mediocre reproduction, and only decent heliogravures can produce the right impression. Obviously, this should not be a large edition, but the main thing is for libraries and art lovers to possess this work in its entirety. You can cook a good dinner for just ten people, and the same with books, but one also has to be a gourmet.

So this is why, once again, I turn to you for help. If you were to give the two thousand [rubles] that you gave *Mir iskusstva* [to publish] such an edition, then we could produce a superb Levitan volume in time for the posthumous exhibition that I hope to organize in December in St. Petersburg. Such a publication would be a mark of respect for a talent of which there is such a dearth in Russia. He was truly one of "us," and "we" should care about him. Your contribution does not have to be regarded as a subsidy, because most of it would be returned to you through sales and maybe even refunded or used for other publications. In this way it would be great to resurrect Levitsky, Borovikovsky, Venetsianov, but more on this later.[33]

As in my exhibitions, so in these publications, I see an important expansion of *Mir iskusstva* activities, and you well know how essential every new accomplishment is to our common good now. I await your reply with impatience and shake your hand.

Ser. Diaghilev

Excerpt from "*The Ballets of Delibes*," Mir iskusstva, September–October 1902

I hadn't been in the Maryinsky Theater for eighteen months, but recently, after an extended sojourn abroad, I went to see the presentation of Delibes's *Coppélia* there. . . .[34]

Coppélia is the most enchanting of all ballets. It is a pearl, and there is really nothing like it in the whole of our ballet literature. But my goodness! What efforts had to be made to render this ballet so colorless, to depersonalize it so mercilessly that ill-starred evening. I just cannot remain silent. . . .

Delibes has left us barely three ballets, of which *Coppélia* has become part of our basic repertory—and it is presented as a stopgap, with decors in rags, dirty costumes, and third-rate dancers. Through their collective efforts the administration managed to turn Delibes's second ballet, *Sylvia*, into a flop last year with a production that was even worse—more casual and more economical—than the productions of Offenbach's *Tales of Hoffmann* or Ivanov's *Zabava Pitiatia*.[35]

I have just mentioned "economy," which seems to have become the motto of the present administration. A laudatory intention—to cut some of the vast, unproductive expenses for which the Imperial Theaters have long been famous. But as is always the case, the new administration got so carried away with this tempting operation that what merited regal pomp and awesome circumstance also fell victim to this fervent "economy." So that's why *Sylvia* was a flop and went quite unnoticed. . . .

But let us return to *Coppélia*. At last there resounded the majestic chords of the overture of Delibes's immortal work—and we sat through an entire evening of dancing up and down, arm waving, and a twisting and turning of third-rate dancers in threadbare costumes with a tiny, totally unremarkable dancer in the lead role. The many coryphées in our huge ballet company fulfill their obligations decently, but the administration felt that for *Coppélia* there was no need to trouble the real ballerinas and that any old dancer, even Madame Trefilova, would suffice to interpret the pranks of Delibes's doll as long as she was fairly pretty and could dance.[36] So there we were the whole evening watching this nice-looking doll do her tedious pranks, run around the stage, and occasionally even dance something, against dead and faded backdrops and to the flaccid strumming of an indifferent orchestra. Here we saw the eternal [Marie] Petipa storming around so clumsily,[37] the corps de ballet idly going through its tedious *pas*, and the lanky Coppélius who scared no one, impressed no one, and interested no one. I cannot remember such an exhausting tedium in our ballet, and this is the more vexing because the future promises only other disappointments, perhaps even more offensive than what I am describing now.

В. А. ТРЕФИЛОВА.   W. TREFILOWA.

Nicolas and Sergei Legat, caricature of Vera Trefilova

Dear Anton Pavlovich,

I am sending you the latest number of *Mir iskusstva*. You might be interested in Filosofov's article on *The Seagull*, and I'd be glad if you'd read it.[38] I do regret not seeing you again in Moscow. At the exhibition we were interrupted at just the most interesting moment: "Is a serious religious movement possible in Russia right now?"[39] Indeed, this is, in other words, a question of whether our contemporary culture is to be or not to be. I do hope to see you on another occasion and to take up our conversation where we left off. As a matter of fact, today saw the publication of the first number of *Novyi put* [New Path].[40] A tentative beginning but very talented. Quite extraordinary the impression one gains from a literature that is bound up with tendentious philosophy. They [the editors] have come over from literature and have shaken off its ashes quite deliberately, but at the same time I fear that they will be unable to escape religious and philosophical dilettantism. You regard Merezhkovsky as a hothouse plant. I am very fond of him but am earnestly afraid when he transplants himself from one soil to another. Anyway, in my view I think that their worst mistake is that they should be remaking not art but society: if art is abstract and, so to say, "devoid of principles," then it is not the fault of art. As long as society is deprived of a religious consciousness, then the latter cannot manifest itself in art, so to shake off the dust of aestheticism is absurd. They are scared stiff of literature as if it were a "sin" and of aestheticism as if it were the "devil." For them it's just too seductive. I fear for their "tendentious mysticism." Can it generate a true art? Forgive my chatter. Do please write the "Levitan" that you promised. We're waiting impatiently. Do you expect to go to Moscow again?

I shake your hand. Yours sincerely,

Serg. Diaghilev

Excerpt from "Contemporary Art," Mir iskusstva, March 1903

In the West the applied art movement has secured brilliant victories.[41] But for those cultured if careless tourists, who, in pursuing the contemporary movement, have gulped down Darmstadt, Turin, Vienna, and other "sacred groves" abounding in innu-

Dmitry Filosofov (center), Dmitry Merezhkovsky, and the poet Zinaida Gippius drinking tea, early 1900s. Around this time Gippius, who was married to Merezhkovsky but also had relationships with women, became obsessed with Filosofov, whom she managed to seduce, exploiting their shared religious interests. Filosofov, however, seems to have been infatuated with Merezhkovsky, who did not reciprocate (he was apparently asexual). Moreover, until about 1902, Filosofov was still involved with Diaghilev, who was enraged by his lover's defection. By 1905 Filosofov had moved in with Merezhkovsky and Gippius.

Léon Bakst, portrait of Zinaida Gippius, 1905. Gippius, who felt herself to be a male both spiritually and intellectually, donned eighteenth-century attire for this portrait.

merable imitators of Olbricht, Van de Velde, Eckman, and the like, the movement has become tedious indeed.

The new style has quite saturated Europe. It has become as cosmopolitan as a car of the Nord Express galloping across Germany, Belgium, and France in a single day.

I do not know whether it is the change in track gauge or the general sluggishness of our trains that has kept us from entering this international convention, this "contemporary style." But the fact is that in Russia most of our endeavors to create an applied art have always led to results quite contrary to what was intended in the West, and instead of the gregarious principle, so diffuse in the industrial art of the West, we encounter the individual, albeit fortuitous efforts of Vasnetsov, Vrubel, Polenova, and Maliutin.[42] They charm us with their unexpected projects, which often generate, however, a certain vulgarity and, from a technical standpoint, imperfection. . . .

The initiators of the new enterprise on Bolshaia Morskaia Street wished to move off the beaten path and, above all, to enter into a direct relationship with the consumer. In this way, they hoped to create something considered, permanent, and practical, independent of the artist's caprices. . . .

As for the artistic projects themselves, we take immediate note of a significant fact, one that has major consequences: all the workers who built this curious little palace are talented artists, but not one of them is a builder or architect, not even a mediocre one. In this we're very different from the West! In the West you have Olbricht, Hoffmann, and Mackintosh, experienced and studious architects who have ended up making artistic compositions. But here we have Benois, Bakst, and Korovin, very refined and extremely talented artists, who concern themselves with the architectural nature of their artistic projects.

So take note of this extraordinary feature: the main characteristic of the new enterprise is that the hand of the architect is absent. This is not a building by Olbricht or a work in the style of the Viennese Secession, where artists are given assignments under the main guidance and supervision of Julius Hoffmann or some other talented, leading architect. . . .

Let us take a stroll through the new palace of these gifted artists and take a closer look at the details of their work.

If we analyze Benois's charming dining room, it seems to consist of an entire series of the watercolors that he created under the influence of the apartments at Mon Plaisir or Oranienbaum. . . . Hence, two immediate consequences: a kind of prefabricated quality in the ensemble of the room and a certain theatricality of impression. Next to the elegant window and exquisite column we see the straight chessboard design of the Dutch tiles on the fireplace; next to the corners of the mirrors, with their charming inventiveness, seeming to derive from the effect of the transparent architecture of the halls of Peterhof, we see the green doors of a modern English cottage; next to the magnificent,

World of Art exhibition, 1901. Diaghilev paid great attention to the display of works of art and frequently solicited help from Bakst and Benois in mounting exhibitions.

resplendent candelabrum, so regal in its sumptuousness, we have the plain, white side-boards vaguely reminiscent of [Charles Rennie] Mackintosh. In its individual parts all this is beautiful, the concept of a true artist, but absent is the magic hand that could "architecturalize" these painterly designs or transform these watercolors in their expensive antique frames into a dining room where one might drink a glass of fine wine or eat a piece of rare steak with relish. But let us pass into the next room.

Once again, in the fragrant boudoir designed by Bakst we experience the same sensation: executed in wood, the room is essentially one of Bakst's subtle vignettes. With its delicate composition and excellent design, this playful salon is nothing less than a work of graphic art. It is, so to speak, a charming design, a decor for a marionette theater in which a tiny princess dwells; we know how this enchantress dances, how she powders herself, how she plays the coquette, but how she lives—we have no idea. Missing, once again, is the architectural practitioner who could transform this little princess into a contemporary lady of fashion, and her bower into a boudoir for a real-life rendezvous in today's world.

I would say that, architecturally and practically, Korovin's highly distinctive and very pleasant tearoom fulfills its function. Here Korovin has revealed all the charm of his decorative and pictorial talent. But again, in Golovin's theatrical chamber we leave life behind and have no idea how to behave in this Baba-Yaga kingdom in our dark suits and starched collars. Instead of picking up an interesting book and losing ourselves reading in this room, we have the constant impression that a band is about to strike up and extremely poetic and enchanting melodies will pour forth, compelling the terrifying eagle owls to blink and the heavy flowers to intertwine and fuse yet more intensely above our heads.

Need we mention that Prince Shcherbatov's "turquoise" furniture, again, extremely refined and noble in proportion, von Meck's picturesque dresses, and Vrubel's figurines depicting Neptune, Sadko, and Kupava enhance the general impression of a fairy tale?

Even the Somov exhibition and Lalique's fantastic jewelry serve to extend the same picture, the same impression; and here, too, as everywhere else, we miss the pragmatic expert, the architect who could transform this fabulous castle into a real house and this theatrical stage into everyday life.

I now return to what I began with. I would say that for all the great importance of the new enterprise and for all its many merits, it has not yet succeeded in avoiding the rut of patronage that . . . continues to guide the entire history of our applied arts. Of course, we do not have to turn into a society of wagons-lits, but I do think that for Contemporary Art to achieve the goals that it has set, it must come closer to life and apprehend the real demands of life. Only then will Contemporary Art become an enterprise instead of a fantasy.

Excerpt from a review of The Twilight of the Gods, Mir iskusstva, March 1903

(1) Concerning the Performers

The Twilight of the Gods was put on at the end of the season, for us, a typical phenomenon: the theaters have nothing going the whole winter long because everyone is busy preparing the novelty that will be produced two weeks before the end of the season.[43] But the novelty is missing in the spring season and only appears the following autumn, in September, with understudies and an old mise-en-scène and for season ticket holders only. Such was the case with Siegfried and The Demon, and that's how it will be with The Twilight of the Gods, presented (some kind of joke?) for three performances only, despite the fact that [Felia] Litvinne was free and in no hurry to leave St. Petersburg.[44]

The production of the above-mentioned Wagner opera has been the only event that has interested the management this whole winter. So we should be especially rigorous in our approach.

I should say straight off that my general impression after the first performances is indubitably positive or, at least, out of the ordinary.

I am extremely fond of Litvinne's singing: its sound is perfect for Wagner. As an Erscheinung [in appearance], certain German Brünnhildes are closer to the image of the aerial and fantastic Valkyrie, but not one of them has succeeded in showing us how Wagner should be "sung" or how to come to grips with the very rich vocal material encountered throughout the scores of The Ring and Tristan. That is why Litvinne is so special. . . .

(2) Concerning the Production

At this juncture we should try to answer two questions: Is our production better than foreign ones, and is it really the model production of which we have dreamed so long and ought to find satisfying?

As for the first question, we should certainly give a positive answer. Our Twilight was arranged unlike any Western staging. In layout, composition, and color our designers tried to steer as far away as possible from the new German-French model that has now become a must for any production of Wagner's operas, especially in their homeland.

On the one hand, the sacred traditions preserved at Bayreuth and, on the other, the same old absurd routine that dominates stage design in the West have created that stagnant atmosphere from which neither the designers nor the painters of the Bayreuth Festspielhaus can break loose.

In this respect, the St. Petersburg opera company has taken an initiative that deserves our praise and gratitude. To produce Wagner differently from the way Cosima understands it (and by now she has confused the behests of her brilliant husband and teacher with her own fantasies) and to put on *The Ring* without recourse to the special "Wagner production" factories that have sprung up in Germany is a not insignificant project and one worthy of respect. But unfortunately, in Russia everything is done by halves, so instead of developing the concept and taking it to its desired conclusion, our theater management possesses a special gift for depersonalizing and spoiling everything and screwing it up.

In this instance two artists worked on the production of *The Twilight of the Gods*— Benois and Korovin. The very names of both artists would indicate that we have the right to expect a really special splendor in the work under discussion. Benois is a poetic landscapist, a true man of the theater who worships Wagner but is an enemy of Wagnerian "traditions," and, finally, an individual of profound erudition. Korovin is a great virtuoso, an experienced designer, and a charming colorist. It would be hard to imagine a better union. But to my total bewilderment, on more than one occasion it has fallen to my lot to wonder at the unexpected results of Benois's work and to stand in disagreement with much of what Korovin is doing. . . .

Letter from Serge Diaghilev to Princess Maria Tenisheva, 21 April 1904, St. Petersburg

Dear Princess,

You have quite forgotten us. You didn't send us the photographs you promised of your new works and buildings. How's the church? Can it be photographed now?[45] We would like very much to publish all your new things in Mir iskusstva. I went by your exhibition at the Society for the Encouragement of the Arts, and I must say that its only defect is that it just doesn't jell with the surroundings.[46] I mean that against the background of all the homespun studies and sketches saturated by the stagnant spirit of our institutional workshops that are on sale there, your showcase introduced something rural, distant, and unsullied by the mangy ways of our "true art."

May I come and visit you in the spring, to take a look at your new projects and

Pavel Shcherbov, Milking the Cow, *a caricature of Diaghilev and Princess Tenisheva, early 1900s*

get away from my own? Life is terribly tiring, but you, too, know and understand that well.

Right now I'm awfully busy with a new and grandiose enterprise. Decorated with all manner of imperial and supreme patronage, next January I am organizing a huge exhibition of Russian portraits from the time of the emergence of the aristocratic portrait under Peter the Great to the present day.[47] In this way I hope to present the entire history of Russian art and society. I assume that we'll put together as many as 2,000 portraits. Just imagine the surprises we'll have, the reevaluations; entire epochs may come to light, while others may lose their false significance. There's so much to do. So with your permission, I'll come down alone or with Filosofov just to take time out.

Are you coming our way?

Greetings to Princess Ekaterina Konstantinovna.[48]

I shake your hand.

Yours, Serge Diaghilev

P.S. May I trouble you with a request? To make your contribution of 2,000 rubles? I have a large expenditure to make on 2 May, and for that I am counting on your help, if it will not be too much of a burden.

My apologies for troubling you.

S. D.

РУССКАЯ
ЖИВОПИСЬ ВЪ ХVIII ВѢКѢ.
ТОМЪ ПЕРВЫЙ.
Д.Г. ЛЕВИЦКIЙ.
1735 * 1822
СОСТАВИЛЪ С.П. ДЯГИЛЕВЪ.

Title page and four portraits by Dmitry Levitsky from Diaghilev's study of the painter, the first volume in an unrealized series on eighteenth-century Russian painting, an area—particularly portraiture—in which Diaghilev had great interest

N. S. Borshchova

E. N. Nelidova

Denis Diderot

Princess E. N. Khovanskaya and Mlle. E. N. Khrushcheva

"At the Hour of Reckoning," April 1905

The honor that you have bestowed upon me by today's festivity is as joyous as it was unexpected.[49] Yesterday, when I learned about the imminent meeting, I felt very disturbed and quite unprepared to accept this moving expression of appreciation for something that we have all done, suffered through, and fought for. Every festivity is a symbol, and the convention is to extend every celebration of merits, great and small, from the individual to the idea that he represents. However, I would like to speak about the veracity of our convictions and the validity of our endeavors. We are accustomed to thinking we are right; and only the strength of the conviction that "it's us or nobody" could sustain us in this unequal struggle for all too obvious truths. I would venture to regard the meaning of this evening in a rather different light. There can be no doubt that any festivity is a reckoning and that every reckoning is an end.

Of course, I am far from thinking that this festivity is in any way an end to those aspirations with which we have lived hitherto, but I think that many of you will agree that in these days the question of reckoning and end comes to mind ever more frequently. And it was this question that I encountered continually during the last phase of my work. Do you not feel that the long gallery of portraits of people great and small with which I tried to populate the splendid rooms of the Tauride Palace is but a grand and convincing reckoning of a brilliant but, alas, dead period of our history? Steeped in an aesthetic worldview, I stand moved before the theatrical splendor of the favoritism of the eighteenth century, just as I do before the fabulous prestige of sultans of '18. Only elderly nannies remember those fables, while, with a touch of elusive sarcasm, the fertile Dawe makes us realize that we can no longer believe in the romantic heroism of terrifying helmets and unvanquishable gestures.[50]

I have earned the right to say this loudly and decisively, for with the last whiff of the summer breezes, I ended my long travels across the boundlessness of Russia. And it was precisely after these avid wanderings that I became especially convinced that the time of reckoning had come. I observed this not only in the brilliant images of our forefathers who are so obviously remote but also in their descendants, eking out the rest of their days. They show that the end of a way of life is imminent. Remote estates boarded up, palaces terrifying in their dead splendor are strangely inhabited by the nice, mediocre people of today, unable to endure the gravity of past regalia. Here it is not people who are dying but a way of life. And that is when I became quite convinced that we are living in a terrible moment of crisis: we are destined to die so that a new culture can be resurrected, a culture that will take from us the relics of our weary wisdom. This is what history tells us, and this is what aesthetics confirms. And now, plunged into the depths of artistic images and thereby invulnerable to reproaches of extreme artistic radicalism, I can say boldly and with conviction that whosoever is certain that we are witnessing a great historical moment of reckoning and ending in the name of a new, unknown culture is not mistaken—a culture that has arisen through us, but will sweep us aside. And hence, with neither fear nor doubt, I raise my glass to the ruined walls of the beautiful palaces, as I do to the new behests of the new aesthetics. And all that I, an incorrigible sensualist, can wish for is that the impending struggle not abuse the aesthetics of life and that death be as beautiful and as radiant as the Resurrection!

Letter from Serge Diaghilev to Alexandre Benois, 16 October 1905, St. Petersburg

Dear Shura,

Don't be indignant at my silence.[51] It's impossible to describe what's going on here. Everything's locked up, in total gloom, no pharmacies, streetcars, newspapers, telephones, or telegraphs—and machine guns any minute!

Yesterday evening I was walking along Nevsky, part of an innumerable, black mass of the most variegated people. Total blackness. Just the shaft of electric light from the huge naval searchlight atop the Admiralty Building illuminating the length of Nevsky. The sidewalks were black, while the middle of the street was a dazzling white. People like shadows, houses like cardboard decor.

I don't want to think or speak about anything. You can understand that.

I managed to take down the exhibition without any real scandals, thank heavens. Actually, I'm not entirely certain that the paintings on consignment will return to their owners! I dream of getting down to my *Dictionary of Russian Portraits,* but right now I'm just waiting for events to unfold.[52] Tedious and dull. I've no idea where they'll take us.

Dima wants to go abroad and "Herzenize" as part of the Merezhkovsky suite.[53] Just how essential or opportune that is—well, I let each judge as he wishes. In any case, at the moment there are two escape routes: either go out on the square and subject yourself to every madness of the moment (naturally, of the most reasonable kind) or wait in your study, cut off from life. I cannot take the former because I like squares only in operas or in some small Italian town, but a study needs a "studious" individual, and that's just not me. Hence a negative consequence—there's nothing to do, just wait around and waste time. It has a certain elemental beauty, but when will this wild bacchanalia pass? Like any hurricane, it is causing many ugly disasters. That's the question everyone's asking and that we're all living with.

Until its moment of resolution I envy you and would give countless riches to get out of here. So, don't grumble at me. I believe that our time will come, too. I kiss you.

Yours,

Seriozha Diaghilev

Pl. 1 *Léon Bakst, portrait of Diaghilev with his Nanny, 1904–1906*

Pl. 2 Léon Bakst, portrait of Alexandre Benois, 1898

Pl. 3 *Léon Bakst, portrait of Dmitry Filosofov,* 1897

Pl. 4 Léon Bakst, self-portrait, 1906

Pl. 5 Léon Bakst, portrait of Walter Nouvel, 1895

Pl. 7 *Alexandre Benois, set design for the Garden or Dream scene in Le Pavillon d'Armide,* 1909

Pl. 6 *Konstantin Somov, self-portrait,* 1898

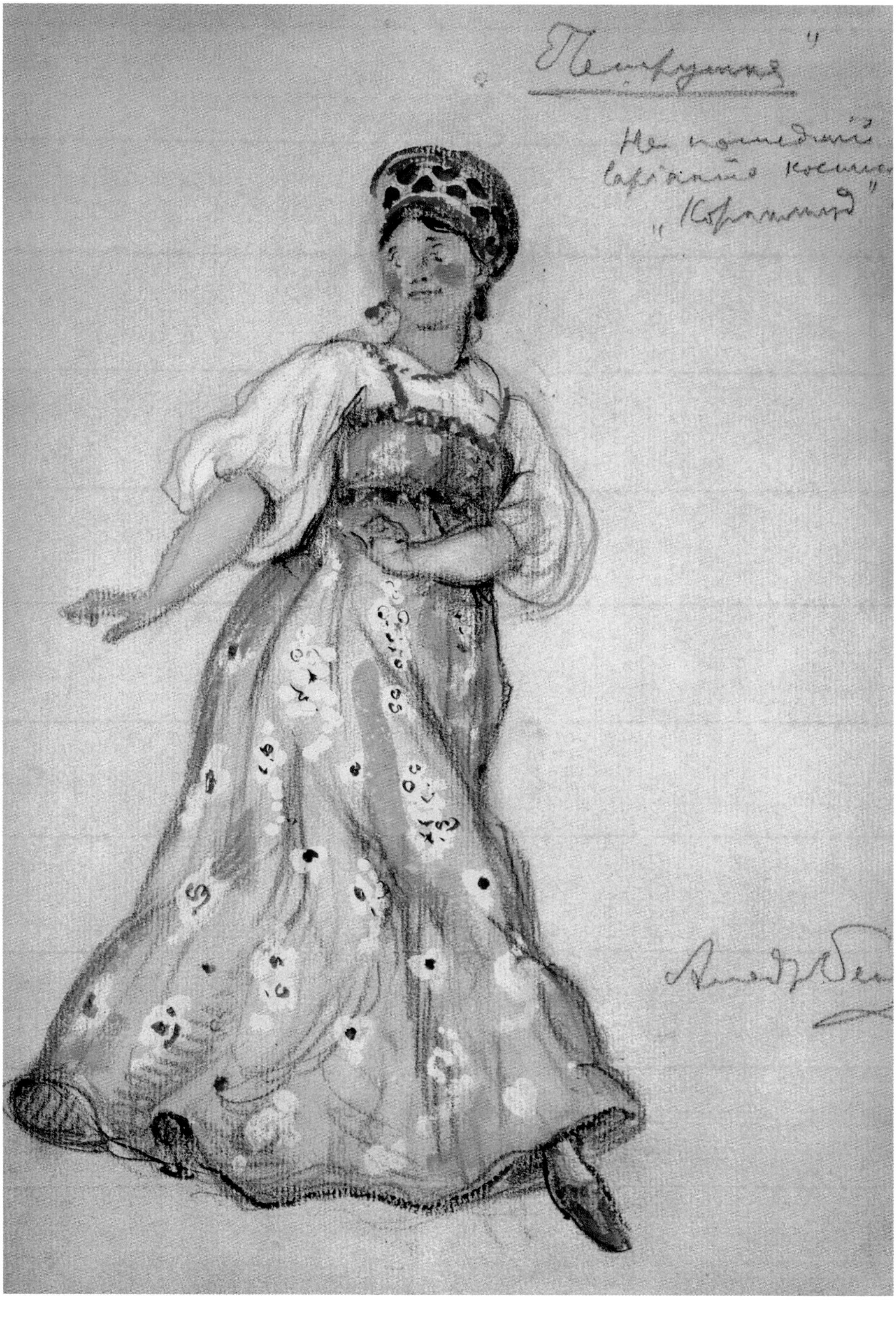
„Петрушка"
Не последний вариант костюма „Кормилицы"

Pl. 9 *Léon Bakst, set design for* Schéhérazade, 1910

Pl. 8 *Alexandre Benois, costume design for a Wet Nurse in* Petrouchka, *1911. Inscribed "Not the last variant of the costume for the Wet Nurse."*

Pl. 10 Léon Bakst, costume design for the Bacchantes in *Narcisse*, 1911

Pl. 11 *Léon Bakst, costume design for Iskender in La Péri, 1911*

Pl. 12 *Léon Bakst, costume design for a Negro Dancer in* Le Dieu Bleu, *1922, after 1912 original*

Pl. 13 *Léon Bakst, costume design for Potiphar's Wife in* Legend of Joseph, *1914*

Pl. 14 Natalia Goncharova, *set design for* Les Noces, *first version, ca. 1915*

Pl. 15 Natalia Goncharova, *set design for* Le Coq d'Or, 1914

Pl. 16 Mikhail Larionov, *curtain design for* Midnight Sun, *1915*

four Diaghilev's "Complicated Questions"

Edited and with an introduction by Joan Acocella

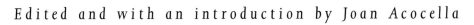

In the first two issues of his journal *Mir iskusstva* (World of art), Diaghilev published a four-part manifesto under the general title "Complicated Questions." According to Alexandre Benois, these four essays—"Our Supposed Decline," "The Eternal Conflict," "The Search for Beauty," and "Principles of Art Criticism"—reflected the views of the entire Mir iskusstva group. In particular, Dmitry Filosofov, Diaghilev's cousin and close friend (also, at this point, his lover), is said to have helped write them (pl. 3).[1] But the essays are signed by Diaghilev. We must take them as an expression of his views on art and his goals for *Mir iskusstva*, of which he was, at age twenty-six, the founder and editor-in-chief.

The basic purpose of the manifesto was to wean the educated Russian public away from the realism that had long dominated Russian art and to introduce them to the more subjective and lyrical styles—nabi, neo-idealist, aesthetic, secession, art nouveau—that had recently arisen in Western Europe and which, for the sake of discussion, I shall group together under the term *symbolism*. The conflict between realism and these anti-

Cover for Mir iskusstva, 1899

realist movements was the major issue in Western art in the second half of the nineteenth century. In Russia, however, the situation was different. In the 1860s, with the rise of the Wanderers in painting, the nationalist movement in music, and the utilitarian school in criticism, realism captured the front ranks of Russian art. Art was expected to be Russian in subject matter, accurate in depiction, liberal in politics, and socially useful, that is, understandable to

and supportive of the "common man." In the hands of such artists as Tolstoy and Mussorgsky, great works were produced under this banner, but by the 1890s realism's inherent weaknesses—tendentiousness, sentimentality, indifference to formal values—were more evident than any remaining strengths. "Taste was deplorably low and narrow," writes D. S. Mirsky in his *History of Russian Literature*. "There was among the intelligentsia no active feeling for form, no artistic culture."[2] Yet the realists still controlled classrooms and selection committees, and because of Russia's intellectual isolation, fostered by the Slavophile realists, there was little knowledge of the alternative, antirealist styles flourishing in Europe. In the West the argument between realism and symbolism had been going on for thirty years; in Russia it had not yet begun. Diaghilev's purpose in "Complicated Questions" was to initiate it, by introducing his readership to the principles of European symbolism and making the case for them.

His argument comes down to two basic points. The first is that art must be free. "The great strength of art," he writes in "The Eternal Conflict," "lies precisely in the fact that it is an end in itself, that it serves only itself, and above all that it is free." Contrary to the realist program, Diaghilev asserted, artists need not embrace any social or political purpose, need not adopt any given style or subject matter. They did not have to seem "sincere" (a value dear to the realists); they did not have be nationalist. In Diaghilev's now-famous words, "The only possible nationalism is the unconscious nationalism of the blood." An artist either had it or didn't, but any attempt to fake it led only to crudeness.

Diaghilev's second point is that, contrary to the realists' demand for truth-to-life objectivity, the power of art lies in its subjectivity. As he says in "Principles of Art Criticism," the value of any artwork lies in the extent to which it reveals the artist's personality and in the degree of sympathy between that personality and the beholder's. In this enthronement of individuality, as in his insistence on the freedom of art, Diaghilev was no doubt influenced by Nietzsche, whom he quotes on these matters. We hear another echo of Nietzsche, and of the European decadents, in Diaghilev's attack on those who would place moral strictures on art. His generation, he says, finds beauty "both in good and in evil."

This last point is made rather hastily, however. Although Diaghilev's two main arguments are adopted directly from European symbolist aesthetics, we find him elsewhere in the manifesto placing a certain distance between himself and the symbolist program.

The most striking example is his discussion of the subject matter of art in "The Search for Beauty." After describing the realist position, that art must address nature or "real life," and the symbolist position, that the subject of art is the inner life, he tries to station himself midway between the two. Or rather, in dealing with the symbolists, he uses the old

Léon Bakst, World of Art symbol designed for the 1898–1899 volume of Mir iskusstva

Léon Bakst, nude figure, Mir iskusstva, 1901. Bakst's illustration expresses Diaghilev's opposition to realism.

rhetorical tactic of pushing them to the radical fringe and then claiming the judicious middle ground for himself. Such maneuvering is clearly due in part to an anxiety over being called decadent—a label that had already been applied to the Mir iskusstva group, and would continue to be, by such realist critics as Vladimir Stasov. Diaghilev's entire first essay, "Our Supposed Decline," is devoted to refuting this charge, which he knew would not help him in wooing the pious Russian arts public. (It should be added that the initial funding for Mir iskusstva came from two arts patrons, Savva Mamontov and the Princess Maria Klavdievna Tenisheva, who had close ties to the realist movement.) But conciliation was probably not Diaghilev's only motive. He and his friends were Russian too, and they were still young. At this point, the lower depths of symbolism, with its weird brew of mysticism, sensuality, and satanism, no doubt frightened them as much as it titillated them. More than outrage, what they wanted was lyricism. As Janet Kennedy points out in her book on Mir iskusstva, the group showed a decided partiality for "paintings of landscape, sunlit meadows, animals grazing, and similar subjects."[3] Such paintings out-number the works of Aubrey Beardsley, Charles Conder, Félicien Rops, and other decadents in the magazine's reproductions, though the latter group is well represented.

Because of the urgency of its purpose, "Complicated Questions" is not as relaxed or debonair as other critical writings that Diaghilev published in the 1890s. In it we see a young man facing a formidable enemy. If his arguments are occasionally prolix and overwrought; if he appears to cite in his defense every book he has ever read or heard of; if he sometimes bangs on the table, sometimes bursts into song, this is to be expected. Nor will anyone familiar with the story of his youth be surprised by the boldness, the strength of feeling, and the willingness to lead that he shows here. Not just in these moral qualities but also in the intellectual and philosophical characteristics of the manifesto—the broad culture, the eagerness for growth and change, the defense of Westernizing, the interest in subjectivity, the ability to synthesize, to pull many things together into one thing, and (if it is true that his friends contributed to the manifesto) the talent for collaboration—in all of these, we can read Diaghilev's future.

It has been said of the manifesto that it is not a notable contribution to the philosophy of art. "An alloy of elements from the aesthetic of Kant and Schopenhauer, complicated by Nietzschean individualism," the Russian art historian V. N. Petrov called it, according to Kennedy. Such criticisms are sound, and beside the point. No one ever claimed that Diaghilev was a major aesthetician. In the Russia of 1898 what was needed was not so much a new theory of art as an argument that there might be more than one theory—an argument for breadth. This is what Diaghilev provided in "Complicated Questions." The magazine and the art exhibitions produced by the Mir iskusstva group exemplified that breadth, and in the process they changed Russian culture. "In 1890," writes Mirsky, "the sole function of art in Russia was to 'express ideas'; in 1915, Russian society was one of the most cultivated and experienced in Europe."[4] In his list of the people who effected that change, the first name is Diaghilev's.

To my knowledge, "Complicated Questions" has never been reprinted in any language. In *Sergei Diaghilev and Russian Art*, the two-volume collection of writings by and about Diaghilev edited by Ilya Zilbershtein and Vladimir Samkov and published in Moscow in 1982, "Complicated Questions" was omitted on the grounds, as the editors argued, that it was actually written by Filosofov. The manifesto's attack on realism, which in 1982 was still enthroned as official art in Russia, seems a more likely explanation.

For reasons of space only the first and fourth essays can be included here. In the second essay, "The Eternal Conflict," Diaghilev addresses the debate over the purpose of art: the art-for-art's-sake position versus the utilitarian view espoused by the realists. He scathingly criticizes the latter—he calls Nicholas Chernyshevsky, the founder of Russian utilitarian criticism, a "barbarian who stretched out unclean hands toward art, seeking to destroy it"—and he implicitly sides with art for art's sake: "The artist must love beauty alone and commune with it alone." In the third essay, "The Search for Beauty," he takes up the question of subject matter: the realist view that art must portray reality versus the symbolist/"decadent" view that art's province is the inner life, the dream world. He finds both prescriptions inadequate, for they would restrict the free play of the artistic personality, which, as he grandiloquently concludes, is "the primary cause of the whole creative world, the sole link between all the branches of art, the lord of it all, the only creative force."

A Note on the Translation: In quoting, Diaghilev sometimes used secondary rather than primary sources. Most of his quotations of Ruskin, for example, come from Robert de la Sizeranne's *Ruskin et la religion de la beauté* (Paris, 1897). In other words, he gave his reader a Russian translation of a French translation of the original. Furthermore, like many people of his time, he thought nothing of making silent cuts and other small changes in quoted materials. In many cases, the sources were traceable, but it seemed inadvisable here to replace his wording with the original—or, in the case of languages other than English, a translation directly from the original—for the goal was fidelity to *Diaghilev's* text. Therefore his translations have been translated. The one exception is discussed in note 14.

Our Supposed Decline

He who follows others will never pass them.—Michelangelo

"Ideas fly around in the air, but always according to laws; ideas live and spread by laws too difficult for us to grasp; ideas are contagious, and did you know that in the general pattern of life an idea hitherto accessible only to a highly educated and sophisticated mind can suddenly be passed on to a rough creature who never concerns himself with anything, and instantly infect his soul with its influence?" These are the words of Dostoevsky, and I have decided to use them to start my essay, as it seems to me that there is no better way of explaining the indefinable but also undeniable unity I feel with my

epoch, with a generation that has not yet expressed itself—a unity that gives me the right to state everything of which I have gradually become aware, sometimes to my pain and sometimes to my joy.

Yes, the air is saturated with ideas, as with a precious perfume that fills the hearts of all who wish to experience it and, through it, to unite themselves with other hearts in the highest spiritual communion.

My task is not an easy one. I must state the essence of my artistic convictions—that is, I must enter upon a sphere which from ancient times has consisted of insoluble dilemmas and complicated questions. To reject is not difficult, and we, with our habitual and beloved skepticism, can do so with a fine sophistication. But how is it possible to proclaim in what way the unsifted and chaotic inheritance we have received from our forebears should be sorted out, when a single assessment—or, one should say, reassessment—of these innumerable inherited treasures would take our generation their whole lives? And how can we take on trust the arguments of our predecessors and the convictions of our fathers, we who seek only what is personal to us and believe only in what is our own? This is one of our main characteristics, although anyone wishing to understand us should give up the idea that we have a narcissistic love of ourselves. True, we love more intensely and more broadly than anyone before us, seeing everything in terms of ourselves: it is in this sense, and only in this sense, that we love ourselves. If one of us were to remark carelessly that we love ourselves as we love God, he would be expressing only our everlasting desire to translate everything into our own terms and to find only in ourselves the divine authority to solve terrifying riddles. What may seem to be the artistic anarchy of the new generation, with its flouting of cherished authorities and its building of castles in the sand—this whole wrong attitude toward an epoch that is not yet understood—stems precisely from an endless repetition of the assessments of past generations, judgments that, though predictable, still take the multitude by surprise. And despite the fact that the whole recorded history of ideas affirms over and over that gods were overthrown, new ones set up, these too overthrown with comic regularity right up to the present day—nevertheless, our every step is conditioned by a passionate struggle, full of wild and senseless accusations.

And now we have appeared with our new demands, simply confirming the general correctness of the course of historical development. It is true that we have departed somewhat from well-known, well-studied forms; we took a few timid, innocent steps away from the main, well-trodden road, and, my God, how wrongly we were understood, how ignominiously branded. Classicism, romanticism, and the noisy realism that romanticism provoked—these perpetually alternating categories of the past hundred years summoned us, in our fresh bloom, to cast ourselves in a mold adorned with one of these labels. And what was most surprising, and taken as a symptom of our degeneracy, was that we were not sullied by the paints mixed and laid out for us, and showed no desire to be. We remained skeptical observers, by equal measures accepting and rejecting all that had gone before us.

But how could one allow this pale and ineffective generation, vulgarly called the fin de siècle, cunningly to rise to a point where it might coolly synthesize all these "small deeds,"[5] seeing itself as the sole interpreter of the truth and fate of the world's art? This was beyond the endurance of our critics. They could not admit that this deformed, fallen generation, these decadents, had learned to see everything clearly, had been inquisitively reading the whole of the long book of successive mistakes, and had decided to reassess everything, to laugh openly at the uncritical judgments of the past but at the same time to respect their own elect—indeed, to bow down before them, without any preconceived conditions and a priori requirements.

We have been called children of the decline, and we bear the senseless and humiliating label of "decadents" coldly and humbly. Decline follows bloom, weakness comes after strength, and faithlessness after faith; that is our sorry condition. We constitute yet another pathetic epoch when art, having reached the apogee of its maturity, gives off "the final, slanting rays of the setting sun of civilization."[6] This is the eternal law of evolution, the law by which a flower is doomed to bloom and die, dropping tender, frail petals. This is what happened in Greek tragedy at the time of Euripides. It happened to the school of Bologna, which understood development only in a superficial way;[7] it happened to French drama at the time of Voltaire; and so it is with us, involuntary witnesses of and participants in the new decline.

But I would like to know: Where was that flowering, that apogee of our art from which we are determined to sink into the abyss of disintegration? Let us turn back a few pages and see what those who boldly proclaim our demise have passed down to us. They left us the eternal struggle between their worn-out personal interests. They left us a century consisting entirely of conflicting tendencies of equal value, where school fought against school, generation against generation, and where the strength and significance of contending impulses were defined not by epochs but by years. They created "fathers and sons."[8] They invented this; it is their creation, the eternal conflict between the two closest generations. They broke up helplessly into factions and fought each other bitterly, in a real war, each defending its own importance and identity. When, then, was the heyday of this whole epoch, the period in which, convinced of their mutual worth and of the unity of shared ideas and tasks, they calmly created masterpieces? Where is that renaissance of which we are the decline? Would you like to recall a moment from the old, already forgotten history? Remember, for instance, romanticism, one of the great epochs, and the appearance of Delacroix—whom they now praise for his *Barque of Dante*, one of those things which not only they but we too gladly take pride in, as a wonderful expression of the human spirit. And how did they respond to it? Already in 1824 the classicists saw whom they had to deal with, and not only did old Gros call the picture "le massacre de la peinture" but the critics spoke of barbarism and prophesied the ruin of French painting if it followed this path. "All contemporary schools," said Delécluze, "exist and flourish only by adherence to the principles of Greek art. Even if it is admitted that Delacroix has achieved a certain success with color in his works, all the same this picture belongs to a lower level of painting, and no superiority of color can overcome ugliness of form."[9] And this was said when Balzac, still of course unrecognized, was quietly creating his *Human Comedy*, a work of genius owing to the strength of truth and realism. It is funny to think that it was only after the posthumous exhibition of his work in 1865 that Delacroix became what he has remained for us ever since—in 1865, that is, when Zola wrote bitterly, "I hate weak fools who shout contemptuously that our art and our literature are dying an inevitable death. These are the most empty minds—people buried in the past page scornfully through works that are alive and vibrant with our times and declare them to be worthless and narrow." And later, addressing a friend of his, he says: "Surely history will not always be like this? Surely it will not always be necessary to say what others say or be silent? We said that the slightest new truth could not be revealed without stirring up anger and hissing. And now, in my turn, I have been hissed and condemned."[10] Finally, remember that precisely at that time Baudelaire wrote sarcastically, "Decadent literature!" (*Décadence* had come in already.) "Empty words that we often hear issuing with a demonstrative yawn from the lips of those distant, enigmatic sphinxes who guard the holy doors of classical aesthetics."[11]

What confusion, what a mixture of interpretations, tendencies, and ideas in one period, on the same day—the struggle for classicism and the victory of romanticism, the defeat of the realist and the attack on the "decadent." What a convenient time for quiet creativity! All of this was swarming about, going back and forth, without anything being eliminated, without any one element being transformed into another, as in a proper evolutionary process, but all of it existing independently and having deep, ancient roots.

This heterogeneous history of the artistic life of the century had its main source in the fearfully shaky aesthetic foundations of the epoch, which never for a moment remained stable, nor did they develop logically or freely. Artistic questions were tangled up in the overall knot of social turmoil, with the result that a talent as independent as Pushkin's had to suffer, in the course of thirty years, three quite different evaluations: the materialist denunciation of Pisarev, the Slavophile praise of Dostoevsky, and the subjectively rapturous judgment of Merezhkovsky.[12] A few incidents from English artistic life in the last half century offer a curious portrait of this whole tangle.

In 1850, when the English Pre-Raphaelite paintings were just beginning to be shown, there occurred what usually happens when anything new and important arises, as witness the work of Glinka, Wagner, and Berlioz—there was a scandal. Everybody was outraged over the insolence of these young artists who dared to have their own aesthetic views and were working to propagate them. The famous Dickens was infuriated and struck like lightning in an article: "Approaching Millais's *Holy Family*, you have to drive out of your mind any religious concept, every lofty thought, every connection with tender, dramatic, sorrowful, noble, holy, dear, or beautiful ideas, and prepare to drop down into the abyss of all that is awful, shameful, repulsive, and disgraceful." This thunderous communication drew a sharp protest from one of the greatest aesthetes of our time, John Ruskin, who replied in two bold letters, roundly condemning the famous novelist and, with all the beauty of youthful conviction, rising to defend the weak in this unequal struggle.[13] And how funny it is for us, after the passage of a very few years, to reencounter this romantic young man, now old and famous, doing battle once more over the same unresolved artistic question. But there is no end to the tricks of fate, and this front-rank fighter, who has now heedlessly gained a position among the famous, has given up his former, brave role to one who has dared to violate his fixed doctrine. Here again we see the terrible law in operation: the period of nonacceptance, the period of struggle, is the period of true creativity. But from the moment of triumph, all that remains is an honored place in history.

And so the roles were reversed, and in 1878 Ruskin unwittingly took the place of Dickens and declared war on Whistler, one of the greatest artists of our time. Ruskin felt the approach of a dangerous enemy and attempted quickly, with his authority, to discredit him. On the occasion of the exhibition of Whistler's *Falling Rocket*, Ruskin fell upon the artist. "For Mr. Whistler's own sake, no less than for the protection of the purchaser, Sir Coutts Lindsay ought not to have admitted works into the gallery in which the ill-educated conceit of the artist so nearly approached the aspect of wilful imposture. I have seen, and heard, much of Cockney impudence before now; but never expected to hear a coxcomb ask two hundred guineas for flinging a pot of paint in the public's face."[14] This forceful statement led to a totally unexpected result: one of the most interesting legal cases of our time, in which the public saw the apostolic figure of Ruskin in the person of the defendant, the nervous, irritated figure of Whistler as the plaintiff, and the puritanical Burne-Jones as an expert witness. The whole tragicomedy lasted two days, the question being whether Whistler's picture could actually be considered an empty joke. The painting was brought into court for experts to examine; incidentally, Burne-Jones declared that the price put on it was too high, especially in view of the amount of conscientious work that was done for far smaller sums. The case ended with Ruskin's having to pay a farthing in damages, whereupon grateful England opened a public subscription to cover the sum, together with the legal costs, which came to four hundred pounds. The grateful country did not understand that this fight marked the end of Ruskin's career, and a very commonplace end, unworthy of his forceful personality. But here at least there was a battle over principles, and it is difficult to blame a man for falling into the same error against which he had once so energetically risen. This is the fate even of great men, but, unfortunately, everlasting mutual misunderstanding is due not only to matters of principle but also to the fact that the protagonists often see in each other only the extremes, without which nothing new can come forward. The fatal mistake of wounded pride is the eternal obstacle to the development of every innovation in society. Of course, children have their childish desire to do everything except what their fathers did, and smugly defy whatever limits have been set. But how can we explain the shortsightedness of fathers who swallow the bait of their children's fervor? How can they not understand that every age is filled to overflowing with unnecessary, senseless ballast, all sorts of extremes, which interest people of the time only for a moment and are then discarded and forgotten forever, like the husk after the kernel has been extracted. Does anyone now remember the innumerable artistic excesses of the reign of Louis XV, or does it make any difference to our enjoyment of Shakespeare that around him there was a pléiade of writers like Marlowe, Ford, Massinger, and others whose names we do not even know? Is it not as ridiculous and unreasonable to draw conclusions about our age on the basis of the paintings of van Gogh and La Rochfoucauld or the writings of Mallarmé and Louÿs?[15] These examples are comical, and prove nothing. Epochs must be judged on the elements that seriously represent them and not on a random enlistment of famous names.

And so, weakened by all this strife, artistic movements broke up into separate, independent impulses, with the result that no one can discern in the present century a gradual development, beginning at the start of the century, reaching greatness, and dying in our generation.

Let me repeat my question: What should we consider our heyday? Which of these different epochs constitutes a decline? Where is our Sophocles, our Leonardo, our Racine, who would contemptuously see in us merely a feeble distortion of the art he created and smile in farewell at our poor, moribund generation? Are we the decadents of the pompous classicism of the 1820s, the decade that revered David's *Coronation*?[16] But this is a joke, for we are worshipers of Baudelaire and Böcklin. We cannot endure the pathetic leavings of the false imitators of pseudoclassicism. We hate precisely that which ought to be called decadent classicism, and which, of course, is not called that by all those Poynters, Tademas, Bouguereaus, Cabanels, Lefebvres, and Semiradskys.[17] No, we are not worthy of the honor either of destroying or of renovating "the grandiose colonnades of those marble masses." Perhaps, then, we are the decadent romantics, we who carried Zola around on our shoulders, who put a laurel wreath on Tolstoy, and who are in love with Bastien; we who bow before the gigantic sincerity of Balzac and reject the theatrical verbiage of Victor Hugo? Well, perhaps we are the sad remnants of realism? No, do not forget that it was you who reproached us for our cult of the Pre-Raphaelites and our ardent worship of Puvis de Chavannes.[18]

How is it that such a simple riddle, simple enough for a child, is not understood? All these groups and tendencies developed by themselves and achieved a complete evolutionary cycle. They all reached their apogee, gave us David, Victor Hugo, Flaubert, and many others, and forever completed the circle of their existence. Finally we arrived, with our new demands, and, believe me, if we were in the least like our predecessors, even though decadent, they would have forgiven us rapturously and clasped us in a fatherly embrace. But what they cannot forgive is that we are not a continuation of them and that they themselves are the decadents of their renaissance, weeping over their decline and longing to rebuild their ruined structures on a foundation of dead and decaying ideas. Who in fact are they—our enemies, our teachers? They can be divided into categories according to three periods of the past. The first group continues in blissful numbness, like Chinese dolls, bowing before the worn-out splendor of pseudoclassical monuments and admiring through lorgnettes the works of the Tademas and Bakaloviches, as glossy as parquet.[19] These are the decadents of classicism, the most decrepit and therefore the most incorrigible of our enemies. The second group is the sighing sentimentalists, who swoon over Mendelssohn lieder, who consider Dumas and Eugène Sue serious reading, and whose taste in painting has not progressed beyond the innumerable Madonnas produced by the prolific German factories. These are the decadents of romanticism—terrible foes, because their name is legion. Finally, there is the third group, a recent group that fancies it has amazed the world with its bold frankness, dragging rags and peasant shoes onto the canvas, even though this had already been done immeasurably better and more vividly fifty years earlier by the great Balzac and Millet. This group talks too much and repeats the tail ends of what was said long ago and better. These are the decadents of realism, boring enemies still boasting of the courage in their flabby muscles and of the freshness of their moldy truths. These are the people who threaten us! And so, what unbelievable absurdity it is to speak of our decadence. There is no decline, nor can there be, *because there is nothing for us to decline from*, because in order for anyone to dare speak of decadence, a great edifice should have been created earlier to give us something to fall from and shatter our-

Alexandre Benois,
"L'Echange des
Favorites," Mir
iskusstva, 1902

selves on the stones beneath. What temple of human genius do we destroy? Show it to us, take us to this temple, since we longingly search for it, so that then, unable to hold on, we shall fall from it without fear, understanding our past greatness.

Principles of Art Criticism

The highest expression of personality, irrespective of the form it takes, is beauty created by man. The artist is the all-embracing source of the innumerable artistic moments that we have experienced. Why, then, should we seek an explanation apart from him? It is surely a matter of indifference to us where he draws the inspiration for his work or in what outer form his thought takes shape. If he is wedded to nature, then let him enslave her fearlessly, wresting from her all that will help him express himself. Why should we not accept a passion for nature? We fully sympathize, yet the essential thing for us here is not nature but the personality dominated by that passion. Insofar as we find this personality in a loving relationship with nature, we accept the work. And the man who worships nature must surely understand us best of all, for if all the beauty of the world is a manifestation of divine will, then surely it is concentrated most intensely in the nature of man, the highest emblem of the divine spirit.

Should not the same be said of those who seek beauty far from the world and concentrate on it just as exclusively? We cannot agree with them. We cannot concede that happiness consists of intoxication, that it can be "bought at any drug store, and carried around in one's coat pocket."

One must seek manifestations of beauty but not the condition of such manifestations. That is why we cannot accept formulas for seeking beauty if on principle they are distant from reality, just as we do not agree that a work of art is a piece of nature observed through temperament.[20] *Beauty in art is temperament expressed in images*, and therefore it is of no concern to us where those images are taken from, as a work of art is not important in itself except as an expression of the personality of its creator. The history of art is not the history of works of art but the history of the manifestation of human genius in art forms. In opposition to this, it could be argued that instances of the highest manifestation of human creativity occurred precisely during those epochs in which inchoate mobs, about which we know little, most suppressed the power of individual personality. In man's three greatest epochs of creative activity, the epochs that produced the art of Egypt, Greece, and the Middle Ages, individual personality appears to have been submerged and to have hidden itself behind the inspired trembling of the mob, in the shadow of great works of art. But do we really know whether it was by chance or design that these stern times erased the names of artists from the monuments they created as the greatest treasures in the world? Do we understand why it is not given to us to know on whom we should bestow the laurels? And what if this oblivion is not accidental? What if these simple masons, who raised Gothic cathedrals in the infinite ecstasy of their worship of God, considered it a great sin, an act of vainglory, to wish to proclaim their identity, which had become totally absorbed in the greatness of the common task? Is it not a higher manifestation of human existence, greater than all others, when a human creator forgets himself in the divine creator?

Furthermore, in an epoch so intensely consumed by unity of outlook and purpose, an epoch when both faith and the meaning of life seemed clear and uncomplicated, and united the whole mass of people in one service to one God, then of course there was not, nor could there be, a differentiation of human personality such as we, with our tormenting eclecticism, have now achieved. It is not important for us, in such epochs, to distinguish different physical entities; all equally reflect the common idea; the epoch itself appears to us as a complete unity, apart from its constituent elements. For us what is essential is the expression of the human spirit, whatever form it may take, whether in a collective or singular personality. And finally, even in such epochs, some individual world-

Right and opposite:

Aubrey Beardsley, illus-

trations for "Principles of

Art Criticism," Mir

iskusstva, 1899

views and forces overcame the burden of their age and reached us, thereby allowing us to admire Phidias, suffer with Sophocles, and smile with Horace.

It is only in the development of the artistic personality, independent of any objective conditions, that I see a progressive movement in the whole of art history, and from this perspective all epochs have equal importance and worth. That is why I could never agree that the Renaissance, for instance, is greater than the eighteenth century in its expression of personality; both of them, like all ages and all forms, seem to me equally capable of its manifestation. Everything is commensurate at least in the degree of expression of the human spirit, and that is why I can compare Giotto with Watteau, but not the Gothic period with the Rococo. One of the chief merits of our time and our generation is that we have precisely this capacity to sense personality under a number of guises and in all ages. We have not only accepted Wagner, we love him passionately, but that does not prevent us from eternally admiring Don Juan and adoring Orpheus.[21] And how shortsighted it is to see in this an absence of logic and hence a sign of decay, when it shows the breadth of our understanding and our good fortune. Of course we cannot follow the prescriptions of Mr. Nordau's lowbrow little book, which gives "Village Honor" as an example of powerful music and the novels of Oné as powerful literature.[22] We can merely congratulate him on his judgment and then and there close the book. But the fact that we do not accept Mr. Nordau's ideas in no way narrows our scope, since our refusal is due not to an inability to pick up pearls of this sort but to a conscious aversion to them; for apart from the insignificance of the personality manifested, we find here an absence of what constitutes the second and final of our demands in evaluating a work of art—*accord between us and the artist*. In addition to the contemplation of a manifestation of personality, full appreciation and understanding of a work of art consist not in obliteration of the individual "I" in a realm of higher perception, nor in any alteration of my being, but, on the contrary, in a discovery of myself in the personality of the artist, in accord and solidarity with the creator; if we can take delight in what is unexpected and new when we encounter it in works of art, then—precisely because of that ability—we must unite with it, for it already exists within us but has only revealed itself because of the divine clairvoyance of the fortunate artist.

"This has always been the form of influence exerted by the thinker, the spiritual hero," says Carlyle. "All men were not far from saying what he said; they all wanted to say it. An idea may come to anyone as if in a tormenting, spellbound sleep, rushing toward him, answering him: yes, this is how it is."

Of course, accord between the viewer and the artist is a purely subjective condition, but with people who are completely in agreement it can take on a certain objectivity. For we must not forget that ideas are always flying around in the air, and although the level of agreement between generations changes, each generation thinks in its own way and has its own values, and in this sense it is united. The generation that preceded ours was more fortunate than we because it was more united. It is harder for us, as we have no ready-made standards or principles. Although questions re-

Léon Bakst, "Stars," Mir iskusstva, 1901

garding the level of development of the artist's personality and the accord between that personality and our own will forever be changing, nevertheless the essence of criticism lies in these two points, and in them alone. The task of criticism seems to me to have very little to do with the pedantic classification of things according to exact but absolutely changeable criteria. Of course it is extremely important to clarify what influenced Rembrandt's style and what Racine contributed to the history of French tragedy. From the scientific point of view it is extraordinarily interesting to make a microscopic study of the emergence of lyric poetry from religious prophecy, but is this the main purpose of criticism? Surely it is not necessary to don thick professorial spectacles and lock oneself up in a scholar's study in order to judge the subtle grace and harmonious beauty of art, clear as a stream. There is a delicate dust on art, as on a butterfly's wing, and it vanishes when exposed to all these methods and systems. Surely the essence of criticism was better understood when the greatest works of art were being created in the blessed period of the Renaissance, when criticism had yet to become a separate discipline and Donatello's statues and Leonardo's pictures were appearing. At that time anyone, even someone unknown, who had the ability and was inspired by the greatness of a new work of art, wrote a sonnet to it, extolling the artist in a burst of exalted feeling dictated by his imagination. He brought his sonnet and laid it at the foot of the work he praised, and artists were glad

and proud of the quantity and beauty of the sonnets praising them. "On the next day," writes Benvenuto Cellini in his memoirs, "I uncovered Perseus for exhibition to the public. There was a crowd jostling at the entrance to the loggia, which I had draped artistically, and in those few hours when the statue was uncovered for examination, more than twenty sonnets in its praise were affixed to it. Then I again covered up the statue so that it should not be seen by strangers. Not a day passed without learned professors and students of the Pisa school leaving numerous Latin and Greek poems at the loggia. I was truly proud of the praise I received from the painter Jacopo da Pontormo and from Bronzino, his famous pupil."[23]

Surely we see here the whole principle of criticism; surely there can be no better, more beautiful, or more artistic appreciation of a work of art? It seems to me that the praises of art should be sung, that every new manifestation of talent should be triumphantly acclaimed, and hymns can be sung only when there is boundless joy and ineffable human rapture. I do not in the least deny the usefulness and importance of so-called scholarly criticism, but I must point out that a scholarly attitude toward art, the desire to make criticism a science, will never solve the problem of how to measure artistic worth.

Just as the astronomer, observing the movement of the planets, does not concern himself with the significance of the mysterious beauty of the stars, so the artist, in evaluating his impressions, would never dare perform a vivisection on art according to methods stolen from the natural sciences. And if, in the words of Taine, criticism neither condemns nor forgives, but looks with sympathy on all forms of art, then what is its purpose other than to pile up books on the dusty shelves of centuries, nationalities, and races? Brunetière can show us the whole development of the French novel with mathematical accuracy, but in doing so can he actually prove that a novel is really a work of art?[24] "It is interesting," he says, "to compare the platypus with the kangaroo; then, for exactly the same reasons—derived from a desire to know and therefore to compare—it is interesting, even essential, to compare the plays of Shakespeare with the tragedies of Racine." This is true, but what does it have to do with art criticism?

We can plot the evolution of pornographic literature quite scientifically, starting with *Les Liaisons dangereuses* and ending with Louÿs's *Aphrodite*, but by doing this we shall not endow it with any significance in the history of art, nor will we in any way touch on its artistic meaning. And this is not because criticism has failed to establish more or less stable criteria but because, with the passing of the years, whatever criteria might be established will turn into dry, worn-out formulas and lose even the unfading charm of subjective judgment, which reveals not only the work of the artist but also the soul of the critic. If subjective criticism makes the diagnosis, then objective criticism, totally indifferent to the facts of the case, notes the illness in the index of scientific statistics.

Thus for any beholder the value and significance of a work of art consist in the clarity with which it expresses the artist's personality and in the accord between the artist's personality and the beholder's. Understandably, one often finds only one of the necessary elements in a work of art: the artist's personality, though agreeable to the beholder, may not achieve its highest expression, or, vice versa, an unsympathetic personality may express itself in a magnificent form. Both variations can be permitted, as an expression of even one side of the embodiment of beauty. It is only the products of anti-art, such as the above-mentioned novels of Oné and "Village Honor," that we must expel from the sphere of aesthetics with a clear conscience.

This general position explains the whole of our attitude toward art. Spontaneously emerging from it, for instance, is our passion for "modernization," that is, for taking exactly the same approach to the present as to the past. Those who reproach us for a blind fascination with what is new and for a rejection of history do not understand us at all. I have said, and I repeat, that we were brought up on Giotto, Shakespeare, and Bach, and these are the first and greatest gods of our artistic pantheon, but it is true that we are not afraid to set Puvis de Chavannes, Dostoevsky, and Wagner beside them. And this conjunction is based quite logically on our fundamental premise. Rejecting any idea of authority, we approached all these artists independently and with our own demands. We looked at history from our present standpoint, according to our personal worldview, and we bowed only before what we valued. We plunged into past ages, applying to Shakespeare the same yardstick—development and accord of personality—by which we had measured Wagner and Böcklin the day before. We respected art too much to accept any of it on faith, fearing that it might not stand up to an agnostic judgment. We loved art too much to regard it solely from the point of view of authority or history. In the whole of our attitude toward art we demanded, first of all, independence and freedom, and if we allowed ourselves the freedom of judging, we gave the artist complete freedom in his work. We rejected any suggestion that art might not be independent, and we placed man himself, as the only free being, at the point of origin. All existing limitations had to be removed. Nature, imagination, truth, content, form, style, nationalism—all had to be examined through the prism of personality.

Nationalism is another painful problem in contemporary art, particularly Russian art. Many see it as our salvation and try to keep it artificially alive within us. But what can be more destructive for an artist than the desire to become an expression of nationalism? The only possible nationalism is the unconscious nationalism of the blood. This is a rare and most precious inheritance. The sensibility must in itself be truly of the people and involuntarily, even against its own will, perpetually reflect the brilliance of deep-rooted nationality. One has to carry nationality within one—be its lineal descendant, so to speak—with the pure, ancient blood of the nation in one's veins. Then there is a value in it, and that value is immeasurable. But nationalism on principle is a pretense and an insult to the nation. All the crudeness of our art to some extent springs from these false attempts; one cannot seize and interpret the essence of the Russian spirit at will. But these seekers come forth and, with their superficiality, lay hold of things they consider typical —things that are actually discreditable to our character as a nation. This is a fatal mistake. We shall not have any real art until a grand, shapely harmony, a regal simplicity, and a delicate beauty of color can be seen in Russian national art. Just look at our real pride, the ancient art of Novgorod and Rostov. What could be more noble and harmonious? Think of our great men—Glinka and Tchaikovsky. In their work, all is elegance and delicacy, and how gigantic is their depiction of Russia and everything purely Russian. Of course our art inevitably contains a stern element derived from the Tatars, and when this surfaces in an artist like Surikov or Borodin—who cannot feel any other way, because this was the spirit in which he was nourished—then the outcome of his sincerity and openhearted frankness is beauty. But these other, false fellows, the Stenka Razins of our art, are not truly Russian and are our scourge.[25]

Here we must answer another question. Should we preserve this Russian spirit, and how should we protect it? There are many who say that we have no need for the West—that its sweet, seductive fruits intrude too much into our lives, destroying precisely that precious, tender Russian quality. This is not true; it is profoundly untrue. You can understand yourself only when you see what others are like. One must immerse oneself in all aspects of human culture, even if only to reject them later. The true Russian nature is too pliant to be broken under the influence of the West. Let us look again at some examples. Think of the art of Pushkin, Turgenev, Tolstoy, and Tchaikovsky, and you will realize that it was only their detailed knowledge of Europe and love for it that helped them describe our peasant huts, our legendary heroes, and the inexpressible melancholy of our songs. To put any restriction on oneself or to take one's inspiration from a strident nationalism is as sad an error as, for instance, to make insistent demands on nature or on truth. We can demand a wholehearted sincerity and truthfulness in the artist's relationship to his work, but this does not mean that we should seek for sincerity and truth as essential conditions in the product. An artist's nature is such a complicated and fragile apparatus that we dare not ask it to shine with a light that seems sincere to our crude and imperfect gaze. *Art and life are indivisible* and reflect each other. If the sincerity of an

Ivan Bilibin, small Russian church, Mir iskusstva, 1901

artist consists of what we, in our harsh judgment, would call mannerisms, then let him express himself in the mannerism that is natural to him, without fearing the mockery or impotent fury of the blind crowd. The history of the world is full of the names of people who struggled bravely against the accepted views of their time. The names of those who walked peaceably in their time have, however, been wisely erased from the annals of the past as unworthy of mankind's gratitude. May higher powers guard the artist from seeking a preconceived truth that is contrary to his own nature and life, for this is a relative truth, one that he will not find, and the illusion of it will destroy his delicate talent. Of course we are not recommending falsehood, but at the same time we are not the slaves of truth.

> The deceit that elevates us is dearer to me
> Than a host of lowly truths.[26]

Above all, we are a generation that thirsts for beauty. And we find it everywhere, both in good and evil. We have no formulas to blind us with their bright light or cause us to mark time. What can we do when Ruskin, the mighty aesthete of our age, concludes his views on aesthetics by saying, "The best part of every work of art is always inexplic-

Ivan Bilibin, church in northern Russia, Mir iskusstva, 1899

able. *This is good be-cause it is good*, and elegant, growing like the grass upon the earth and falling like dew from heaven." We should not seek for a general definition of beauty, acceptable to everyone, for that would

be sacrilege. We should all of us carry beauty within us so that later we can join together in a general hymn to its everlasting might. "I go away alone," said Nietzsche, in the words of the superman Zarathustra, "and you should go alone too. This is what I want. Go far from me, and save yourselves from me, and, moreover, be ashamed of me, for maybe I have deceived you. You say you believe in Zarathustra, but what is the use of believing? You did not seek yourselves, and therefore you found me. This is what all believers do, and that is why your faith is in vain. Now I order you to lose me and find yourselves, and when you have all denied me, only then will I come again unto you."[27]

We must be free as gods in order to become worthy of tasting this fruit of the tree of life. We must seek in beauty a great justification for our humanity, and in personality the highest manifestation of beauty. Here, as at the beginning, I summon up the image of a great thinker and say, "There is no more arduous or perpetual task than that of the man who, having been set free, immediately seeks out someone before whom he can bow down." But we want to be free, because it is in this torment of freedom that the laurel wreath of all-embracing art is to be found, even though we know that there is nothing more burdensome than to "agree to endure freedom."[28]

—Translated by Olive Stevens

II Tradition and Innovation

What contradictions Diaghilev harbored! Noble-born, he was a barin of the old school, a

master of men who held on to the traditions and prerogatives of Old Russia. Yet he was also a

man of the twentieth century, a liberal and cultural progressive, an aesthete who embraced the

clean-edged poetry of modernism. In a time of international artistic experiment, Diaghilev

made ballet a crossroads of the contemporary, a haven for the new, and a laboratory for

experiment. He brought Le Sacre du Printemps into the world, as well as Les Noces

and Prodigal Son. But he also produced The Sleeping Beauty, that pinnacle of

nineteenth-century classicism. He was a revolutionary with the habits—and top hat—of

an oligarch.

five

Isadora Duncan and Prewar Russian Dancemakers

Elizabeth Souritz

I n December 1904 Serge Diaghilev attended a supper at the St. Petersburg home of Anna Pavlova. Although the party was given by one of the most celebrated ballerinas of the day, the guest of honor was Isadora Duncan, the barefoot American dancer who had just made a triumphant debut in the Russian capital; the supper party actually followed her second program of dances. "I sat between the painters [Léon] Bakst and [Alexandre] Benois," Duncan wrote in *My Life*, "and met, for the first time, Serge Diaghileff, with whom I engaged in ardent discussion on the art of the dance as I conceived it, as against the Ballet." On Michel Fokine, the future choreographer of a score of Ballets Russes works, including such prewar classics as *Les Sylphides*, *Firebird*, and *Petrouchka*, she is curiously silent. In all likelihood he was present. With Pavlova, a frequent partner, he had crowded into the Hall of Nobles the night Duncan made her debut. Other performances found him there in the company of Diaghilev. Many years later the impresario would write: "I attended [Duncan's] earliest performances with Fokine. Fokine was mad about her, and [her] influence on him was the initial basis of his entire creation."[1]

Pan & EKAO

Russia had begun to hear about Duncan at the time of her earliest European tours. Often she was described as walking through the streets in a Grecian tunic and sandals in the hope that French and German ladies would adopt them. But already in 1903, sensitive critics like Sergei Rafalovich were predicting that "she would revive [the] decrepit art" of ballet.[2] Indeed, the first serious discussion of Duncan in Russia came from poets, painters, and thinkers who viewed dance within a broad cultural and artistic framework.

By and large, poets were the first to respond to Duncan's art. The earliest Russian article to describe Duncan in performance was by the poet Maximilian Voloshin, who saw her dance at the Trocadéro in 1904. Here, he wrote, was a young girl "dancing in the night. . . . Stars were born from every movement, . . . gold and crimson circles swam in the air, . . . and thousands of palm branches started to move. Her fingers . . . were like the . . . pistils of white lilies, or the fingers of Bernini's statue 'Daphne,' bursting with laurel branches. Her dance is that of a flower waltzing in the arms of the wind, . . . a rose petal taking flight from the music."[3]

Between 1905 and 1908, other poets wrote about her: Sergei Soloviev, Andrei Bely, Fedor Sologub, even Alexander Blok. Blok's wife, Lubov, who became a ballet historian in the late 1920s and 1930s, wrote that the dancer Serpantini in Blok's poem "Nesnakomka" (The unknown woman) was inspired by Duncan. Her dancing fascinated the Bloks, and they attended many of her performances, sometimes in the company of Bely. In 1905 Duncan was often mentioned in Blok's correspondence with Bely and Soloviev.[4]

Duncan also attracted the attention of thinkers like Vasily Rosanov and Akim Volynsky, and critics like André Levinson, Valerian Svetlov, Yury Belyaev, Sergei Volkonsky, and Alexandre Benois. In most cases, their articles were published in art journals—*Vesy* (The scales), *Zolotoe runo* (The golden fleece), *Apollon* (Apollo), and *Studiia* (The studio). Far more than a dance novelty, Duncan was viewed as an artist embodying a new mentality and an aesthetic of broad significance. Her appearance was an event of general interest, important to art and culture as a whole, not just dance.

At this time revolutionary changes were taking place throughout Russian life. In literature, painting, music, and theater, old ideas were rejected, and new ones advanced. What Duncan proclaimed was closely attuned to the new thinking, and among intellectuals, her call to defy convention and follow the promptings of instinct and the dictates of nature met with ready and sympathetic understanding. In a society where theatrical dancing was taken seriously as an art, Duncan's ideas appealed to all who opposed obsolete traditions and old ways. The free movement of a body liberated from constraint offered the possibility of forming a new generation of emancipated individuals.

Duncan was not the only one who considered ancient Greece a model to imitate; in 1904, on the eve of her first Russian tour, the philosopher Viacheslav Ivanov published *The Hellenic Religion of the Dying God* and *Nietzsche and Dionysus*, works that enjoined the modern theater to return to ancient forms. Valery Bryusov had advanced the same idea even earlier in an essay published in Diaghilev's journal *Mir iskusstva* (World of art).[5] Indeed, the ancient world was an ever present theme in the illustrations reproduced in many of the era's art magazines, including *Vesy* and *Zolotoe runo*, as well as the subject of numerous paintings and poems.

Léon Bakst was among the first of the *Mir iskusstva* artists to discover ancient Greece. His enthusiasm for Greek art may well have been prompted by Rosanov, although he had little use for the philosopher's ideas. Rather, what appealed to Bakst were the external manifestations of Greek art and myth: the ruined temples, the statues, the nymphs and satyrs that appear repeatedly in his early drawings. The ancient world also figured in his earliest commissions for the Alexandrinsky Theater, Euripides' *Hippolytus* (1901) and Sophocles' *Oedipus at Colonus* (1904). In his first work for the ballet stage, Bakst designed costumes for Diaghilev's ill-fated *Sylvia*, which also had a Greek subject; in certain respects they anticipated ideas associated with Duncan. Indeed, in a long article published at the time of her first Russian concerts, Benois described Bakst's designs for the costumes of the ballerinas in *Sylvia* as being "virtually identical to the costumes worn by Duncan."[6]

Among Duncan's greatest admirers was Konstantin Stanislavsky, a founder of the

Elizabeth Duncan

Moscow Art Theater. He attended all her Moscow performances, including the first, where, as he later recalled, he found himself surrounded by the most celebrated artists, sculptors, and writers of the day, all applauding. In his diary he wrote of being "charmed by her pure art and her taste," and in his letters to her (all written in French) he was even more effusive. In one, dated early January 1908, shortly after the two had met, he wrote: "It was you who was the first to tell me in a few simple and convincing phrases the important and basic things about Art that I wanted to create. This awoke energy in me at that moment when I intended to give up my artistic career altogether." Another, written 29 January, after Duncan had left Moscow, bemoans: "You have shattered my principles. Since your departure I am seeking in my art for those things you had created in yours. This is beauty, as simple as nature itself."[7] But even before he came to know Duncan personally, Stanislavsky had revealed his admiration for her art in 1907 by engaging one of her Russian followers to teach in his studio.

But Duncan's greatest influence, not surprisingly, was among dancers and choreographers. Eli Ivanovna Kniepper was the daughter of a German bakery owner in Moscow who first saw Duncan perform in 1905; so great was her enthusiasm for the dancer that she took to wearing Grecian dress in public. The next year Kniepper went to Germany to study at the school directed by Duncan's sister Elizabeth. Returning to Russia, she began a successful career as a performer, followed by an equally distinguished career as a teacher and choreographer at the Moscow Art Theater. As Alisa (Alice) Koonen, a celebrated actress with Alexander Tairov's Kamerny Theater, recalled, Kniepper owed many of her ideas to Duncan:

Anna and Theresa Duncan. This photograph was used on the cover of the 1911 prospectus for the Elizabeth Duncan School in Darmstadt, Germany.

> Highly cultivated and a wonderful teacher, she knew how to make her classes interesting and absorbing. All the exercises that we worked on— from the simplest to the most complicated—were always organic and natural; . . . we jumped across ropes and chopped imaginary firewood; we even played leapfrog. Eli Ivanovna thought that this developed dexterity and strengthened the muscles. In all this, at the same time, there was the plasticity and beauty of line of Isadora Duncan's art.[8]

In 1907 Kniepper staged the dances for the Moscow Art Theater's production of Leonid Andreyev's *The Life of Man*. As the critic Lubov Gurevich described in her review, the choreography recalled the effects of symbolist drama: "Swaying from side to side to the sound of the violin, innumerable old women in black crept in unnoticed and filled the stage. Their arms, looking white in the darkness, were outstretched, dancing some strange tragic dance: here, symbolist theater joined the art of spontaneous dance, with its poetry of rhythmic movements arising from the spirit of the music."[9]

In 1910 Kniepper (who by then had adopted the name of her second husband, Rabenek) opened a school in Moscow and formed a company. Its performances received wide coverage in art journals, especially after the 1911 tour that included dates at the London Hippodrome (where the troupe was billed as the Moscow Aesthetic Dancers) and in Germany (where the program was called "The Dance Idylls of Ellen Tels": Tels was a shortened version of the choreographer's maiden name, Bartels). Kniepper-Rabenek set many of her dances in ancient Greece. Not all were pastoral idylls, however. In her *Scythian Dance*, to music by Gluck, a favorite composer of Duncan's, "girls in red tunics and gold headbands" formed "two enemy armies, both savage, angry, and ruthless," wrote critic Nikolai Kurov in 1911. "They change places, . . . strike each other as if with long spears, pretend to fight with swords, and cover themselves with shields. Some fall down; others celebrate victory."[10] In these *plastique études*, as they were called (*plastique* was the standard Russian term for "free dance" or dance emphasizing "pure" movement), pantomime played an important part. Alexei Sidorov, whose book on the free dance—the only such study in Russian—was published in 1922 at the height of the movement, commented on this aspect of Kniepper-Rabenek's work, linking it to a larger phenomenon: "It was the intrinsic dramatic content of her dancing that caused one to remember it. Everything was well thought-out, suggesting literature rather than music. . . . In our opinion her choreography led the spectator from dance to the theater stage. The main trend in post-Duncan dance is its progress in the direction of pantomime and ballet."[11]

A rapprochement with drama was indeed the direction in which the free dance developed in Russia. This was especially the case in Moscow, where, from its beginnings a century earlier, ballet had favored narrative forms and dramatic content over pure dance. Typical of the progression referred to by Sidorov was the "dance play" *Chrysis*, presented in 1912 by Natalia Miliukova and a group of plastique dancers that included two of Kniepper-Rabenek's students, Tatiana Savinskaia and Vera Voskresenskaia, both former actresses with the Moscow Art Theater. A play in three acts and twelve scenes inspired by Pierre Louÿs's *Chansons de Bilitis* and *Aphrodite*, *Chrysis* combined dance and pantomime. The piece depicted the evolution of sensual love, from Chrysis's awakening to the pleasures of the flesh as a young girl to her despair as an aging woman at the loss of her physical allure. In between she is loved and betrayed: she wanders through Greece, reaches the isle of Lesbos, mingles with bacchantes, and becomes a hetaera at the temple of Aphrodite. All the dancers were barefoot, and the choreography throughout was in Duncan style: there were no ballet steps and much of the action was mimed.

During the 1910s other groups of free or plastique dancers emerged. Most began as Duncan exponents but gradually enriched their expressive means through the assimilation of other styles. Of some importance was the St. Petersburg–based group Heptachor, so-called because it consisted of seven women. Originally an amateur ensemble, it was founded in 1907 under the inspiration of Duncan's second tour. The members studied Greek literature, history, and art and danced for their own pleasure; it was only in 1914 that they began to perform professionally. Ludmila Alexeeva, who worked with Kniepper-Rabenek from 1910 to 1912, was another Duncan-inspired dancer who opened a studio in

THE FIERY DANCERS: THE LATEST RUSSIAN INVASION.
THE NEW ÆSTHETIC RUSSIAN DANCERS AT THE LONDON HIPPODROME.

Moscow, although it was only in the postrevolutionary period (when, among other activities, she staged performances for workers under the aegis of Proletcult) that she came into her own as a choreographer. Yet another was Inna Chernetskaia, who had studied not only with Elizabeth Duncan but also with Emile Jaques-Dalcroze and Clothilde and Alexander Sakharoff; returning to Russia in 1913, she opened a studio in

Moscow two years later. Still others who took inspiration from Duncan, although their work moved in other directions, were Vera Maya, Francesca Beata, and Nikolai Posniakov, all of whom had flourishing studios in the postrevolutionary period.[12]

But it was not only in the realm of free dance that Duncan's ideas took root in Russia. Ballet, too, succumbed to her influence in the transitional period that began with the new century. In 1904 Marius Petipa was relieved of his long stewardship of St. Petersburg's Imperial Ballet. And in Moscow a new choreographer had appeared, an artist who even before Duncan made her Russian debut had shown himself eager to shake the cobwebs out of ballet and give it new life. This was Alexander Gorsky, whose production of Don Quixote in 1900 marked the dawn of a new era at the Bolshoi.

The production was a first on many counts. It had sets and costume designs by Konstantin Korovin and Alexander Golovin, easel painters who now made their debut on the Imperial stage. Instead of the usual tutus decorated with pompoms, the women wore genuine Spanish costumes, which imparted both authenticity and a sense of unhampered movement to the dancing. Equally innovative was Gorsky's staging, especially in the crowd scenes, where he individualized the characters and required the dancers to act. The production owed its most startling innovations to the influence of Stanislavsky's newly founded Moscow Art Theater. But it also pitted Moscow against Petersburg—Russia's "old" capital, with its crooked streets, gleaming onion domes, and eclectic art nouveau buildings, against the country's "new" capital, all harmonious vistas, elegant palaces, majestic columns, and the stately flowing Neva.

Members of the Vera Maia studio, Moscow, 1925

Gorsky came from Petersburg, but he yearned for freedom of expression, more natural forms of behavior, and greater respect for the individual. Hence his revolt against the carefully arranged lines, identical postures, and compositional regularities of the aca-

demic ballet style. When defining the innovative aspects of his choreography, Gorsky stressed its "lack of symmetry" and the "continuous movement of its groupings." "When something is performed on the right," he told the critic Fedor Troziner in 1902, "and something different on the left, and something different still at the back of the stage, everything . . . becomes interesting to the spectator: there is variety in the performance, and the action becomes picturesque."[13]

In 1901 at the Novyi (New) Theater (a stage sometimes used by the Bolshoi), Gorsky choreographed a divertissement for the company's young dancers. The program consisted of dances to Chopin (a polonaise), Edvard Grieg (Anitra's Dance from *Peer Gynt*), Glinka ("Valse Fantaisie"), Yusef Veniavsky (a mazurka), Schubert ("Les Mousqué-taires"), and two little-known composers, Ivan De Lazari, who worked at the Bolshoi, and one Goldstein. Of special interest are the dances to Glinka and Grieg.

In *Valse Fantaisie* the women wore longish dresses à la Marie Taglioni and danced in a style reminiscent of the romantic ballet of the 1830s. A precursor to Michel Fokine's *Chopiniana*, the work testified to Gorsky's desire to free ballet from the rigidity of the late nineteenth-century "grand" style. In *Anitra's Dance*, Gorsky seems to have gone even farther.

A somewhat fanciful description of the work appears in S. Grigorov's biography of Sofia Fedorova, who interpreted the solo at its premiere. For Grigorov, the dance was "a poem of the crimson northern autumn": "Under a scarlet light, wearing a cape the color of fantastic crimson leaves, appears the Queen of the Night. She waves her myste-rious veil, and autumn secrets are born: pale air flows, and something inconsolable and irrevocable is created. . . . The autumn wind sighs; the autumn sun sheds tears; the leaves of the farewell season rustle for the last time. Magic and mystery proudly reign." In the 1920s, when Mikhail Gabovich saw the work performed, the dancer wore a Grecian tunic and gold sandals, her hair streaming down her back.[14]

Gorsky admitted to being influenced by Duncan. He spoke of her in a rare 1914 interview on the day of the jubilee celebrating his twenty-five-year career in the theater. "Duncan," he said, "had an important role in the development of ballet."[15] Neither here nor elsewhere does he say when he saw her dance or what he thought of her. But we can assume that he attended her first performances in Moscow in 1905. Not only did he as-siduously follow all that was new, but the ballets choreographed after 1905 showed even greater stress on freedom of movement than he had placed in his earlier ones. His first full-length works—*Don Quixote, The Little Humpbacked Horse* (1901), *Gudule's Daughter* (1902), *The Goldfish* (1903)—had broken with tradition through changes in the libretto, new pantomime sequences, a modified use of the corps de ballet, and historically accurate dress replacing tutus. But after Duncan, he rejected such compositional forms as the traditional pas de deux, especially in his one-act ballets, while exploring plastique and oriental styles as well as the possibility of blending free dance movements with classical steps.

Like many Duncan works, Gorsky's 1907 *Etudes* was really a suite of dances united around a single theme, in this case, autumn. In the opening dance, "Les Feuilles tombées," to Anton Rubinstein's Etude no. 1, groups of "leaves" rushed from the wings, flew around the stage in groups, and fell. A romantic duet, "En orange," to music by Ernest Guiraud, followed, as did a second duet, "Pensée," to a Chopin mazurka. The moon now turned red, and like a storm in the night, Sofia Fedorova made her entrance for *Anitra's Dance*. In "La Fin," to a reprise of the Rubinstein etude, leaves whirled in the wind; then the stage was plunged in darkness. In keeping with the theme, the costumes were in autumnal shades of red and yellow.[16]

Later that year Gorsky staged a new ballet for the dancer who was to be one of his most important inspirations. Vera Karalli had been Gorsky's favorite student at the Moscow Theater School, and when she graduated in 1906 he immediately began to choreograph for her. A great beauty, she had the physical expressiveness that Gorsky valued more highly in his dancers than technical prowess. *Nur and Anitra*, to a commissioned score by Alexander Ilyinsky, was the story of an Indian princess-cum-sorceress (Anitra, danced by Karalli) who lures a handsome warrior (Nur, danced by Mikhail Mordkin) to an enchanted grotto. Based on stylized "oriental" movements, the choreography called for intricate partnering, with unconventional forms of support, much intertwining of limbs, and deep, Duncanesque backbends that ended with the ballerina falling into the arms of her danseur.

In an interview with the magazine *Teatr* (Theater) published in January 1908, Karalli spoke of *Nur and Anitra* as being created under the influence of Duncan. She expressed great admiration for the American dancer, adding that "both our ballet master, Monsieur Gorsky, and his assistant, Monsieur Mordkin, are admirers of hers as well."[17] Karalli also mentioned that at her request the celebrated Shades scene of *La Bayadère*, which the Bolshoi was then rehearsing, would be "danced à la Duncan." As it turned out, when the ballet was actually produced the changes in the scene were minor. Only in 1917, when Gorsky radically revised the ballet, would the Shades finally appear in saris.

In an unpublished memoir written shortly before her death in 1972, Karalli spoke of Duncan's influence on Gorsky's teaching: "He added to the daily class many

dance movements by Duncan. Sometimes he would fly about the room in Duncan attitudes, making us laugh. But at the same time we were very interested in her ideas. . . . Our backs, which had been taught always to be straight as . . . a poker, became more elastic and, even in classical dance, not so stiff. And in the plastic movements the body and the arms were completely free. All the strength was in the legs and in the small of the back."[18]

Gorsky choreographed numerous dances for Karalli, including many for films. Indeed, by 1914 she had become one of the most famous actresses of the Russian cinema, with credits including *Chrysanthemums, War and Peace* (in which she played Natasha), *The Dying Swan,* and *Do You Remember?* In *Chrysanthemums* she performed a Duncan-style dance that ended with her dying on a bed of flowers.[19]

Duncan-style dances also appeared in various full-length Gorsky ballets. Among these was his version of *The Little Humpbacked Horse* at the Maryinsky in 1912, a production that was sharply criticized for combining Duncan and classical movements in the pas de deux for the Ocean and the Pearl.[20] In his 1914 Moscow production of the ballet, among the most Duncanesque of his works, Gorsky replaced this pas de deux with a pas de trois and dressed the Pearls in Grecian tunics. The arms were fluid, the upper body free of restraint, and the feet placed in parallel. Reclining in one another's arms, the Pearls seemed to be exchanging loving caresses.

Gorsky employed many Duncan-style movements in ballets depicting ancient Rome and Greece. In *Eunice and Petronius* (1915), Sofia Fedorova danced a barefoot mazurka, while Karalli, when she took over the role of Eunice from Ekaterina Geltzer, discarded the latter's blocked shoes in favor of sandals. In Gorsky's 1916 ballet to Alexander Glazunov's

Fifth Symphony—the first Russian dance work to be choreographed to a symphony—barefoot maidens played with balls and long transparent scarves, while boys did exercises with hoops.

For Gorsky, and Russian intellectuals generally, Duncan was a symbol of freedom, a freedom Gorsky himself could never attain at the Bolshoi. He may have dreamed of building a new repertory, but his main job consisted of preserving the company's existing one. In staging new ballets, he had to cater not only to Geltzer, the Bolshoi's prima ballerina, but also to her partner and husband, Vasily Tikhomirov. There were struggles and, on Gorsky's part, many compromises, especially in his restagings of old ballets. In *Le Corsaire*, for instance, Geltzer wore a Greek tunic, but she also danced a variation that displayed her pirouettes. Gorsky's last version of *Giselle*, choreographed in 1922, had "free" movements in the second act but retained the traditional character dances in the first. He tried several versions of *Swan Lake*, the last and most radical in 1920 with Vladimir Nemirovich-Danchenko, a founder of the Moscow Art Theater. It has been said that this *Swan Lake* was choreographed in Duncan style,[21] but this is true only to the extent that the term implies a deviation from the laws of academic classicism, regardless of the origin of the actual movements. Indeed, by the 1920s ballet and concert dance in Russia had gone far beyond "Duncanism."

Michel Fokine also fell under the influence of Duncan, though he was less willing than Gorsky to acknowledge it. In fact, he categorically denied that her influence was the source of "all his creative work," as Diaghilev had asserted. "The

Lydia Sokolova and Nicolas Kremnev in Daphnis and Chloé, 1910s

reason for my very great enthusiasm," the choreographer explained to Arnold Haskell in 1934, "was . . . because I felt that here were so many of the elements that I was practising and preaching." In his memoirs, which he began writing in 1937, Fokine states that it was in 1904, before Duncan's first appearance in Russia, that he submitted the libretto of *Daphnis and Chloé* to the Maryinsky authorities laying out the program for his "new" ballet. His suggestions for staging the work demanded major changes in ballet practice: music, he wrote, had to express the emotional content of a work; the "dance pantomime and gestures" had to fit the style of the period; and the costuming had to be consistent with the plot. In *Daphnis* he wanted the women to wear light tunics and sandals instead of ballet shoes, or even go barefoot. Did Fokine write this, as he insists, before seeing Duncan dance? Historian Vera Krasovskaya thinks it highly unlikely. She points to certain discrepancies in Fokine's memoirs as well as to the fact that his first ballet, *Acis and Galatea*, produced in 1905, was highly conventional in approach. A more likely date for his *Daphnis and Chloé* proposal, she feels, is 1907, possibly when he was choreographing *Eunice*.[22]

And indeed, the year 1907 was an important one for Fokine. With *Eunice*, which came to the stage in February, he scored his first major success. Fokine's protestations notwithstanding, the ballet made generous use of elements associated with Duncan. As Valerian Svetlov wrote at the time: "This ballet can serve as an answer to whose who ask whether 'Duncanism' has a future and how it will develop in relation to 'real' ballet. In *Eunice* we see many features of Duncanism, both those that touch its essence and those that are its superficial signs: bare feet, tunics, plastique, port de bras, circling ensembles, ancient Greek style, etc.!"[23]

Chopiniana also premiered in 1907—it was given on the same program as *Eunice*— as did *Le Pavillon d'Armide* and *The Dying Swan*. In January 1908 Fokine presented *The Night of Terpsichore*, a "survey" of dances past, present, and future that included a "Duncan" solo for Lydia Kyasht. "Will this be a literal copy of Duncan?" Fokine was asked by the *Peterburgskaia gazeta* a few days before the premiere. "No," he answered. "The poses will be Greek, but, of course, Mademoiselle Kyasht will combine them."[24] Other numbers, such as the Assyrian-style *Dance with a Torch* performed by Tamara Karsavina and the Chopin waltz danced by Anna Pavlova in an evocation of Taglioni, were snippets from his evolving repertory: both *Egyptian Nights* and the definitive version of *Chopiniana* would be presented some six weeks later. In December 1908, in a concert program at the Conservatory, Ida Rubinstein performed his *Dance of the Seven Veils*. Then in 1909 came the first of Diaghilev's Paris seasons.

All these works recalled Duncan in some way—in their movements or groupings, in their use of music, or in their new attitude toward dance, a quality more difficult to define. Lubov Blok later wrote that Duncan "opened up a whole universe of new possibilities: one could explore new directions, elicit dance images from . . . symphonic music, inhabit one's free dancing body without feeling the constraints of real or imaginary convention. Even more important, one could be serious about dance, think of it not as an amusement or a form of theater, but as one would think of music. All these revelations inspired Fokine and shaped his creative life." After *Chopiniana*, Blok continues, everything changed: "Before, everyone danced with a vacant smile . . . even during an adagio. The unsmiling faces of our dancers today, with their air of self-absorption, are from *Chopiniana*. The tendency toward cantilena movements, the fluid 'melting' arms, the notion that costume is part of the dance—all this, too, derived from *Chopiniana*." And finally: "*Chopiniana* taught us how expressive and full of meaning dance can be: just dance, with no plot or story to tell. The ballet revealed the symphonic possibilities of classical dancing, that it can be captivating and interesting to look at, even without technical tricks or acrobatics."[25]

Chopiniana was indeed greatly influenced by Duncan. Not only did Fokine incorporate two of the pieces—the Mazurka in C Major (for Pavlova's solo) and the Prelude in A Major (for Olga Preobrajenska's)—used by Duncan at her first Petersburg concert, he also borrowed some of her gestures, as when the dancer in the Prelude raises her hand to the ear as if harking to voices in the surrounding woodlands.

Chopiniana also marked the appearance of a style that came to be associated with Pavlova. Pavlova had first danced Fokine's *The Dying Swan* on 22 December 1907, two weeks after Duncan's second visit to Petersburg, where her program included not only Gluck's

Iphigénie en Aulide but also dances to Schubert and Chopin. With its white tutu and bourrées on pointe, at first glance *The Dying Swan* appears traditional in conception, recalling Odette's solo in *Swan Lake*. In reality, however, the dance is anything but a conventional variation. Both Krasovskaya and Galina Dobrovolskaia have called *The Dying Swan* a monologue, similar to the so-called inner monologues of Anton Chekhov's plays.[26] Krasovskaya, moreover, likens its improvisational quality to the spontaneous feeling of Duncan's dances, as though Fokine had set out to prove that improvisation and music visualization were possible even within the classical idiom.

Kay Bardsley also finds Duncan elements in *The Dying Swan*. The solo, she writes,

> may possibly owe its . . . origin (certainly that portion which relates to the arms and upper torso) to the movements set forth by Isadora in the Chopin Prelude no. 20, op. 28. This dance, which continues in Duncan repertory today, is a dance of grief in which the motivation for the arm movements, as taught by Maria-Theresa Duncan, is to push away unhappy memories that keep returning and returning, so that one is overcome, and falls to the ground exhausted. Maria-Theresa's title for this prelude was "The Clouds." When Duncan performed the prelude in St. Petersburg in 1904, Nikolai Shebuev had referred to it as a "funeral dance."[27]

In an interview published in 1913, Pavlova expressed her admiration for Duncan's great talent, admitted that the dancer had opened new vistas, and spoke of her influence on Fokine beginning with *Eunice*, although she also insisted on the advantages of ballet technique over Duncan's "dilettantism." Sensitive as she was, Pavlova found much that was congenial in Duncan's way of moving. To Anna

Lydia Lopokova, 1910s. Lopokova was a pupil of Fokine's and the "baby ballerina" of the 1910 Ballets Russes season.

Duncan, one of the dancer's adopted daughters, Pavlova confessed that she had learned the fluidity of her arm movements in *The Dying Swan* from Isadora. *La Nuit*, a solo to music by Anton Rubinstein that Pavlova choreographed for herself in 1909, revealed Duncan's influence as well. In this wordless "fairy tale of the white night," declared Yury Belyaev, "Pavlova had created her own genre," which he called "dance melo-declamation."[28]

Fokine's ballets for Diaghilev also attested to the Duncan influence. This was evident not only in the costuming for his "Greek" ballets—*Narcisse* and *Daphnis and Chloé*—but also, and above all, in the freedom of movement that now appeared in his choreography, which frequently blended Duncanesque "free" movements with steps from the classical idiom.

Reviewing *Egyptian Nights* in 1908, Valerian Svetlov used strong language for the ballet that, as *Cléopâtre*, would be a triumph of Diaghilev's 1909 season. *Egyptian Nights*, he

Anna Pavlova, 1910s

Vera Fokina and Bronislava Nijinska as Bacchantes in Narcisse, 1911

wrote, was a "violation of every tradition of the good old times," "a rejection of 'turned-out' classical technique," a "violation," even, "of the ballet 'canon.'"[29] Some of the dances had "natural" Duncan movements; others, staged in profile (a device previously used by Gorsky), imitated Egyptian murals. The idiom was eclectic: at one point, the slave girls did typical Duncan skips, then entrechats-six supported by partners. Duncan's influence was also felt in the bacchanal, which presaged the ecstatic revelry of *Narcisse* and *Daphnis and Chloé*. She was a presence, too, in other Diaghilev ballets: in *The Polovtsian Dances*, where the captive maidens glided chastely across the stage, concealing their faces with gestures of girlish modesty; in *Firebird*, where the enchanted princesses danced barefoot in a moonlit garden, playing with golden apples; in *Schéhérazade*, where the languorous beauties curved their seminaked bodies into sinuous love offerings.

In *Narcisse* "free" Duncan movements appeared throughout the ballet; in *Daphnis and Chloé* they occurred in the sculptural groups and processions and in the "infinite variety of pose and gesture" as "the maidens [wound] about the altar [of Pan]." In *Les Préludes*, the Souls of Light triumphed over the Spirits of Death in an ecstatic tableau that combined Duncanesque movements with classical *pas*. Parts of the ballet, which was choreographed in 1913 for Anna Pavlova's company and quickly remounted at the Maryinsky, recalled *The Three Graces*, one of Duncan's most popular dances and a tribute to the Botticelli painting. Reviewing the St. Petersburg production, André Levinson wrote: "The hero . . . carries on a mimed dialogue of love with a pale maiden . . . [in] a delicate tunic covered with rare flowers, like a Botticelli nymph. Nine companions dressed in soft colors . . . echo their movements, dividing into three groups like the 'three graces' of the Florentine romancer; they join hands in a circle and rise on *demi-pointe* (Duncan's favorite motif) or else, coming out of the circle into a curling line, they move in single file like a display of rhythmic gymnastics."[30]

Isadora Duncan danced throughout Europe, but her influence was nowhere stronger than in Russia, above all in the decade preceding the First World War. Among her followers were the "free" or plastique dancers who emerged in the 1910s and the groups appearing in the 1920s who derived from them. Under her influence, Alexander Gorsky recast the Bolshoi at least partly in her image, assimilating her ideas into numerous ballets and the performance style of his favorite dancers. Her greatest long-term influence, however, was through Michel Fokine, whose works entered the international repertory thanks to his association with the Ballets Russes and the numerous companies that laid claim to its legacy. In Russia few of his works survived the onslaught of Stalinism. As an émigré, he was persona non grata: a cloak of silence lay over his accomplishment, even if artists like Fedor Lopukhov and Leonid Yakobson acknowledged their debt to him and kept his memory alive.

By acknowledging Fokine's influence, dancers and choreographers also acknowledged Duncan's. She had dreamed of changing the face of the world through her new dance, a utopian goal that forever eluded her. But she did change the face of dance. She did so less through her own performances or the schools she founded than by the influence she exerted over others. She opened paths to the future and people followed—paths as different as the dancemakers themselves and the dances they conjured into being.

Daphnis and Chloé, 1914. This picture, taken around the time of the ballet's London premiere, is a rare example in this period of a photograph taken from the stage.

six Firebird and the Idea of Russianness

Sally Banes

I t is often said that Diaghilev's Ballets Russes purveyed both orientalist and Russian exotica to Western Europe, and that this very exoticism was the wellspring of the company's immense and astonishing popularity in the first decade of its existence. Both Lynn Garafola and Martin Battersby have suggested that market considerations led to the abundant stream of orientalist and Russian folkloric ballets in the 1910s; Garafola, Richard Taruskin, and others track the sources of those two categories of ballets to two separate currents: Léon Bakst's travels in the Middle East and the roots of the Ballets Russes in the neonationalist Russian artistic colonies at Abramtsevo and Talashkino.[1]

But Garafola suggestively comments that " 'Russianness' defied neat categories; it was tinged with . . . orientalism. . . . Even at Abramtsevo a fine line had divided nationalist material and exotica." It seems the orientalist and "russki" ballets were not two separate strands at all. Nor, as some have argued, were the orientalist ballets a sign of Fokine's artistic exhaustion.[2] Rather, these apparently distinct strands seem to constitute an interwoven, unified project. The constant supply of these ballets was probably not simply market driven. Diaghilev's orientalist and Russian folkloric ballets were two inseparable aspects of a single search for a Russian national identity—a persistent, troubled quest that grew historically out of resistance both to the epoch of Tatar domination and to the forced Westernization of Russia by Peter the Great, and that posited Russian identity as one of mixed heritage: Eurasian.

As Garafola points out, "In an empire that spanned the Trans-Siberian railway, that included Bukhara, the Muslim holy city of Central Asia, Bakhchisarai, and Odessa, arguably the cultural 'other' was not the East, but the West." And Charles Spencer notes that the Russian Orthodox Church grew from Byzantine roots; its Christian practices—especially its artistic practices—contain distinctly Eastern, non-European elements.[3] These are important observations, but they still pose Eastern and Western as terms in a binary opposition. But Diaghilev and his set produced a third term by circulating an idea of Russia as operating in a field where it has not one, but two semantic "others." This was an ethnic self-conception of Russia as a double negation, rejecting parts of both its Eastern and Western heritages, that thereby dissolved the binary and constructed a positive, unique national identity.

Russia's vexed hybrid identity was literally incorporated on the Diaghilevian ballet stage through the creation of what might be termed an alternative bodily canon in the ballet, one that set itself in opposition to the canon of beauty in classical ballet inherited from European Renaissance values.[4] More specifically, *Firebird*, often called the first "truly Russian" ballet by Diaghilev's company, in fact belies the timeless fairy-tale narrative of the imaginary homogeneity and authenticity of Russian national identity so often ascribed to it. It does so by engaging and dramatizing the post-Petrine tensions between the European and Asian faces (and bodies) of Russianness. *Firebird*, that is, undermines the myth of "pure Russianness" by showing that Asian blood courses through the veins of the Russian body.

Valentine Gross, "Petrouchka," 1912

Léon Bakst, costume design for the Firebird, 1909. Bakst designed this costume for the Firebird pas de deux, which Tamara Karsavina danced with Vaslav Nijinsky in the 1909 divertissement Le Festin. The title notwithstanding, the dance was actually the Bluebird pas de deux from the last act of Petipa's Sleeping Beauty.

In addition to the Asiatic thread woven firmly into this most "Russian" of the Ballets Russes ballets, it should also be remembered that there was another image of the body on Diaghilev's stage that supplied an alternative to the canonical ballet body: that of the peasant. The etherealized, graceful, symmetrical, international body of the Russian nineteenth-century ballet—which had been refined and reconstituted in Russia based on ideals imported from Western Europe—was every bit as disrupted, vernacularized, and brought down to earth by the turned-in, clumsy, earthbound movements in ballets like *Petrouchka* and *Le Sacre du Printemps* as it was by the angular, entwined gestures and twisted torsos of *Schéhérazade*, *Les Orientales*, the unrealized *La Péri* (pl. 11), and *Firebird*. This rupture

Valentin Serov, portrait of
Michel Fokine, 1909

opened a dominant space on the ballet stage for representations created by means of the body that had previously been known but given inferior status, relegated to the minor genre of character dancing. In reversing the status of Western and non-Western codes of gesture and posture and in bringing previously marginalized aspects of ballet dancing to center stage, the Ballets Russes participated in a longstanding, far-reaching debate about the nature of Russian national identity. The pagan body of both the Islamic Orient and pre-Christian Russia in the above-mentioned ballets, as well as the peasant, folkloric, premodern body—epitomized by the familiar figure of the traditional folk-theater puppet Petrushka—became the site in Western European performances where the assertion of a distinctly Eurasian, non-Western Russian national identity took place, even as the stage was being set for an internationalist political cataclysm at home.

Created for the first season in which Diaghilev presented newly commissioned ballets (rather than works choreographed earlier for other venues, including the Maryinsky Theater), *Firebird* (*L'Oiseau de Feu*) was choreographed by Michel Fokine to commissioned music by Igor Stravinsky and first performed at the Théâtre National de l'Opéra in Paris on 25 June 1910, during the second Russian ballet season produced by Diaghilev. The creation of this ballet therefore signaled a new purpose: the exportation to Paris of exotic high art based on Russian folklore.

It is important to note that this was not "authentic" folklore; rather, it was "manufactured" for the Western audience. The Ballets Russes chronicler Prince Peter Lieven writes that the French audiences demanded "what they, as Frenchmen, understood to be 'du vrai Russe,'" and he complains that "the ballet was jumbled together from rags of various classical Russian fairy tales. The resulting patchwork, although colourful, was not convincing for a Russian. It was as if Alice of *Alice in Wonderland* were partnered with Falstaff in a Scotch jig." Even Stravinsky himself later recalled that when he arrived in Paris just before the ballet's premiere, his excitement about the project dampened at the first rehearsal, since "the words 'For Russian Export' seemed to have been stamped everywhere, both on the stage and on the music."[5]

The music historian Richard Taruskin aptly describes the irony of *Firebird*'s situation: "This very deliberately, in fact self-consciously 'Russian' work had no antecedent in Russian art and was expressly created for a non-Russian audience." Although he points out that the figure of the Firebird was a neonationalist cliché, "a stereotype, a *traforetto* (to use Benois's sneering word)," nevertheless Taruskin also acknowledges that "she was part of every Russian's prepackaged dreamworld," a profound emblem not only for the symbolist movement out of which Diaghilev's project partly emerged but also for artistic Russian neonationalists at least up to 1921.[6]

While members of Diaghilev's inner circle thus criticized the synthetic nature of the ballet as well as its export-commodity status, *Firebird* still stood as a signal creation of their own artistic and national identity. Indeed, the patchwork *Firebird* was a remarkably effective "invented tradition" that, in the face of political upheavals in post-1905 Russia, created a link to a historic past and set the stage for an effective "imagined community."[7]

Firebird is often said to be the earliest truly collaborative project of the Diaghilev "committee," but Fokine is usually credited as author of the libretto. The scenery and costumes were designed by Alexander Golovin, with Kostchei's court and castle imagined as a sumptuously orientalist fantasia; Bakst designed the costumes for the Firebird, Ivan

Tamara Karsavina and Adolph Bolm in Firebird, 1910s

Tsarevich, and the beautiful Tsarevna. The libretto was an amalgam of motifs and images taken from various sources: Russian fairy tales collected by Alexander Afanaseyev; symbolist elements in the writing of Fyodor Solugob and Alexei Remizov; and probably Rimsky-Korsakov's 1902 opera *Kostchei the Immortal*.[8] The narrative, as set down in the libretto, involves the standard Russian fairy-tale hero Ivan Tsarevich (Prince Ivan), who captures a magical Firebird. During their struggle, she bargains for her freedom,

Ivan Bilibin, "Ivan Tsarevich and the Firebird," 1899

which she wins in exchange for a magic feather. Ivan then spies twelve dancing princesses, captives of the evil sorcerer-king Kostchei. He falls in love with the beautiful Tsarevna (or Princess Unearthly Beauty), but his very presence summons Kostchei with his monsters and court retinue. Just when the sorcerer-king is about to turn Ivan Tsarevich to stone, the Prince uses the magical feather to call on the Firebird. She sets the entire grotesque retinue to dancing until they fall down exhausted, then instructs Ivan to find Kostchei's soul (or death), hidden in an egg. When Ivan breaks the egg, Kostchei dies. The final scene celebrates the coronation and wedding of Ivan Tsarevich and the Tsarevna.

At first glance, both the plot and the structure of this ballet seem odd for a number of reasons. The storyline lurches, rather than advancing smoothly. In accordance with Fokine's advocacy of ballet reform, the ballet is only one act long (although the act has two scenes).[9] Refusing the classical bifurcation of abstract dance and mimed sign language, it mixes classical ballet steps with expressive movements of the entire body, especially the arms and torso. But this is not achieved seamlessly, for there seems to be an uneasy mixture of styles here.

Indeed, a complete stylistic shift deliberately marks each section of the ballet: the Firebird dances classical steps with angular, narcissistic, Asiatic arm gestures; the twelve captive maidens walk and skip with Duncanesque simplicity; members of Kostchei's retinue either cavort grotesquely (that is, they violate the classical bodily canon) or perform orientalist "ethnic" dances; and in the coronation scene the members of Ivan's court file off in strict, quasi-military formation. Fokine himself notes: "In the composition of the dances I used three methods vastly different both in character and technique. The evil kingdom was built on movements at times grotesque, angular and ugly, and at times comical. . . . The princesses danced barefoot with natural, graceful, soft movements and some accent of the Russian folk dance. The dance of the Firebird I staged on toe. . . . [It] was highly technical."[10]

Finally, some critics have complained that the love interest is subsumed by the magical element—Ivan's alleged liberation of Kostchei's kingdom by means of the Firebird's feather. In fact, the love between Ivan and the Tsarevna seems rather passionless, while the central pas de deux is not only performed at the beginning, rather than the climax, of the ballet; it is danced by the wrong personages. Instead of Ivan and his love, Ivan and the Firebird form the duet. What is the relation of Ivan to the Firebird that they are paired in this way?

Before answering this question, it is necessary to note that for a ballet celebrating Russian folklore, the Asian references here are striking. As we have seen, many have commented that the "vogue for Orientalism," as Dale Harris puts it, was a Parisian fire the Ballets Russes seasons mightily fanned, especially with the company's production of *Schéhérazade*, which had its premiere in June 1910, the same season as *Firebird*. But in fact, the Asian references in *Firebird* are as important as those to a purely Russian "mysterium," and they signal far more than simply a fashionable Western European rage for exoticism and luxury.[11]

In analyzing *Firebird*, the paradox that demands attention first is the apparent miscasting of the heroine. Why is the Firebird, rather than the beautiful Tsarevna, the protagonist of this ballet, and why does the Firebird, rather than the beautiful Tsarevna, dance the ballet's crucial pas de deux? Of course, ballet history is full of pas de deux between inhuman, biologically improper love objects and human heroes. In *Swan Lake*, Prince Siegfried dances with Odile, a fatally erroneous choice of dancing partner. But his most important pas de deux is with his beloved, the human Odette (if temporarily enchanted in bird form). In ballets that end with marriages, like *The Sleeping Beauty*, the happy couple express the perfection of their romantic union in their duet. But although *Firebird* ends with a wedding, the happy couple never consummate their love in dance terms. Most puzzling is that at first glance, the pas de deux of Ivan and the Firebird seems to be about power—his struggle for domination and hers for freedom—rather than love.

In the Russian fairy tales the ballet is based on, the Firebird is a marginal, ambivalent (if not entirely negative) character. So it is noteworthy that for this ballet the "committee" made the Firebird a positive figure and a donor with enormous power, who is ultimately responsible for the defeat of the evil despot Kostchei (figured as an Asian despot) and the liberation of the kingdom. In fact, a close analysis of the ballet—the choreographic structure and the dancing—shows that she is much more powerful and central than the libretto itself suggests. For the Firebird is not simply a donor who in the manner of a conventional fairy tale serves as one of a series of helping figures. Rather, she is the author of the entire escapade. It is she who engineers Ivan's entry into Kostchei's court and the overthrow of the evil sorcerer, as well as Ivan's wedding and coronation. In other words, *Firebird* fully fleshes out the suggestion, only latent in the fairy tales, that the Firebird reigns supreme in both the earthly and the inhuman realm and that in inaugurating Ivan's adventures, she underwrites his entire narrative. Indeed, as the title of the ballet itself suggests, this is not so much a tale about a human hero's triumph but a story of cosmic political struggle: the luminous Firebird's defeat of Kostchei, a spirit of darkness.[12] It is also, crucially, the story of the unseating of an Asiatic oppressor through the agency of an Oriental woman.

When the Firebird makes her first appearance flitting across the stage, her movements are strong, direct, and quick. Her arms often push outward from her body, giving the impression of powerful wings cutting through the air. Her broad leaps imply flight, but they also symbolize freedom. Her body is often open, arms spread wide against the air, and she seems constantly in motion. Occasionally she stops in a proud pose, wrapping her arms around herself in a narcissistic preening gesture that is also strikingly Asiatic. Her musical motif is radiant, and her fluttering fingers suggest both feathers beating against the air and rays of the sun.[13] She boldly takes a golden apple from the tree, bites it, and throws it away.

Fokine later wrote that he based the Firebird's dance on jumps and made it "highly technical but without *entrechats, battements, ronds de jambes,* and, of course, without a

turnout and without any *pré-paration*. The arms would now open up like wings, now hug the torso and head, in complete contradiction of all ballet arm positions." Further, "in the ornamental arms of the bird, as in the movements of Kostchei's servants, there was an Oriental element."[14] In one of Bakst's costume designs for the Firebird, her slippers (with their curled-up toes), her jeweled armband, and her curved, at-tenuated fingers all brand her as an orientalist fantasy. Photographs of Karsavina in the role show two different costumes; in one, although she wears pointe shoes, her headdress (dripping with strings of pearls) is strikingly similar to that of Schéhérazade. This imprint of the East both marks the Firebird as an exotic "other" woman (in contrast to the beautiful, Russian Tsarevna) and identifies her with Kostchei's realm, which is also pictured as oriental (that is, Middle Eastern). But if Kostchei is a negative oriental figure, the Firebird is the positive Asian element.

Ivan captures the Firebird, and they struggle. This in itself is not necessarily new; after all, Siegfried captured Odette in much the same way in *Swan Lake*. But this is, perhaps, the first time that a pas de deux is framed as a combat between two equals, without any romantic outcome. For even though the Firebird has been caught, she has already been shown as physically powerful. Later, of course, when she returns to rescue Ivan, we learn just how powerful she is in terms of magic. She is easily capable of subduing Kostchei's entire grotesque retinue, and she repulses the evil sorcerer himself. And yet ostensibly, her magic cannot protect her from a mere mortal's grasp. This presents a conundrum, until we look more closely at the structure of the pas de deux.

Tamara Karsavina and Michel Fokine in Firebird, 1910

The duet indeed begins with a struggle. Garafola describes it thus: "Ivan Tsarevich stands behind his prey, clutching her with the arrogance of a cad; she twists, bends, turns, reaching for his hands, aspiring to the distancing clasp that will return each of them to their separate spheres."[15] But midway through the duet, the music shifts from staccato dissonance to a flowing, melismatic melody in a minor, Middle-Eastern-sounding key. The Firebird, forced into a kneeling position with her arms angled around her head, looks seductively at Ivan, then rises on pointe, turns to face him, and does a deep backbend in his embrace. She allows him to support her in a more traditional set of partnering steps. And then she strikes a series of deferential poses, ending up on the floor. Each time, she glances at him, as if to make sure the message has sunk in. The pas de deux is indeed manipulative, but after the shift, it is the Firebird who manipulates Ivan, not the other way around.

And the pas de deux reinforces the identification of the Firebird as an oriental woman. Taruskin describes the music as "shot through with languorous 'Arabian' and 'Central Asian' melismas," quoted not only from nineteenth-century Russian music in general but in particular from Rimsky-Korsakov's opera Le Coq d'Or (1909). In fact, the Russian neonationalist composer Mily Balakirev had himself begun writing an opera based on the Firebird figure in the 1860s, a Georgian song that (Taruskin suggests) may have been borrowed by Stravinsky for the Firebird pas de deux, precisely for the moment when, according to Stravinsky's annotations, the entrapped Firebird beguiles Ivan with "visions of the fantastic Orient." Throughout, the Firebird's music is related to Kostchei's; the magic of both supernatural beings is expressed by chromatic and diminished harmonies that also create an orientalist ambience.[16]

Given the Firebird's skills and powers in the rest of the ballet, the only way this pas de deux makes sense is to understand it as a benign deception. Like a master spy, the Firebird lets the simple Prince think he has mastered her, in order to send "her man Ivan" as a poison pawn into her enemy Kostchei's court. Although she strikes deferential poses, she is clearly the dominant figure, and Ivan is literally her support. But in a partnering gambit that hints of the same sadomasochistic eroticism featured in Schéhérazade, she creates the fiction that he is dominating her.[17]

For this magical forest is not Kostchei's realm alone; it is also the Firebird's. The ballet opens with her marking out her territory, establishing it, circling it, flying through it with abandon. If she stands for life and freedom, Kostchei is her enemy because he represents death, slavery, and Asiatic despotism. But in this narrative, the battle between these two forces requires human intervention, perhaps in order to lure the sorcerer outside his castle into the Firebird's realm, the forest. Or possibly human intervention is required because in the ballet's fiction it is in and through human beings (or at least, fleshily embodied creatures) that those forces are incarnated. The Firebird is an extremely powerful female figure, but she is also a designing woman who uses indirect stratagems—also culturally identified as Asiatic—to gain political control.

Ivan's meeting with the princesses and his falling in love with the beautiful Tsarevna underscore the contrast between the two kinds of female figures populating this ballet, partly through Ivan's reaction to them. The Firebird is powerful; Ivan immediately grasps her and struggles with her. The beautiful Tsarevna is demure, and Ivan keeps a civil distance from her. Indeed, the beautiful Tsarevna is first seen not as an individual but as a kind of clone, part of a group of identical female Russian folk figures whose movements are light and contained, close to the body. Their heads cant like an icon of the Virgin; their hands constantly touch their faces; they bow and strike decorative poses. (In later sections, they weep, they implore, and they pray.) Stravinsky describes them as "insipidly sweet."[18] When Ivan sees the maidens, a Russian folk-song motif emerges in the music, evoking nostalgia and comfort, a sense of "coming home," in counterpoint to the energetic dissonance and enigmatic orientalism of the Firebird's theme. Barefoot, loose-tressed, clothed in long traditional Russian dresses, and dancing simple steps that hint at Russian folk dances, the princesses appear to remind Ivan of his "pure Russian" identity. They are, in this sense, familiar and "natural," while the Firebird is strange, exotic, Asiatic, and supernatural.

Although Ivan is immediately attracted to the beautiful Tsarevna and tries to kiss her, he approaches her gently, focusing on her face rather than her waist. In true fairy-tale fashion, it takes three attempts before he succeeds in kissing her. The contrast between Ivan's view of the Firebird's sexuality and his view of the Tsarevna's is striking. The first could be termed body-sex, while the second is person-sex. He seizes the Firebird's torso intimately, while the Tsarevna merits dignity: he humbly requests her permission to make the first touch. Their love has the blessing of the community, for the other princesses ceremoniously escort Ivan and the Tsarevna toward each other, as if in a preordained ritual betrothal.[19] It is noteworthy that both the Firebird and the Tsarevna try to escape Ivan's touch, yet he allows the Tsarevna to turn away, while he brutally seizes the Firebird.

It could be argued that Ivan treats the Tsarevna with civility because she is human, while his relationship with the Firebird is in some way a nonhuman encounter, not at all concerned with love. But then, one is led to ask, why does the Firebird have to be a woman at all? Nijinsky wanted to dance the role and pointed out to Diaghilev that the Bluebird in *The Sleeping Beauty* had been danced by a man.[20] Perhaps the way to answer this question is to note the several, intertwining levels on which the relationship between Ivan and the Firebird as a female force may be interpreted.

At one level, she is, literally, an animal—a bird—while the Tsarevna is human. At a second level, the Firebird is "nonhuman" in the sense that she is non-Russian. She is the consummate "other" woman in more ways than one: oriental, sexual, seductive, both powerful and submissive, she is everything desirable that the "nice" Russian

Tsarevna cannot be. Thus the Firebird's relationship with Ivan may not be about love (as in love and marriage), but it is erotic. This relationship concerns power, and power is sexy. Moreover, the Firebird's costume emphasizes her voluptuousness, as opposed to the virginal quality indicated by the beautiful Tsarevna's long, loose gown. The

Michel Fokine with Vera Fokina as the Tsarevna in Firebird, 1910

Firebird's incessant self-touching in the form of preening is another marker of her sexual allure.

At a third, more metaphoric level, however, although the Firebird is supernatural and Asiatic, she simultaneously symbolizes nature itself, Mother Earth (and Mother Russia)—unattainable and untamable, often benevolent yet mysteriously unpredictable. There is a moment in the Infernal Dance when the princesses circle the Firebird as if to worship her, invoking the mythological associations between the Firebird, the *rusalka* (thought to be an early Slavic female deity concerned with fertility, the seasons, and the weather, and worshiped by female cults), and a female sun god.[21] A pagan cult of ancient Russia is thereby associated with an Asiatic figure.

At any level of interpretation, it is not the Firebird but the beautiful Tsarevna whom Ivan must marry, in order that the race (both Russian and human) continue. And yet the Firebird is emphatically his more significant partner—his most significant "other." The story ends happily, and we see Ivan Tsarevich together with the beautiful Tsarevna in the final scene. Yet although they have obviously become partners, this is a coronation rather than a wedding. And even though the beautiful Tsarevna is Ivan's consort, the power behind the man on the throne is clearly the Firebird, who presides over the scene. If she represents nature, then the happy ending of this story is that the natural and political domains have been correctly aligned, and thus the proper monarchy has been established, firmly rooted in a moral, spiritual, and natural order. For the tsar's dominion is considered part of the natural order. And it is the legitimation of the political order as part and parcel of the natural order that underwrites the relationship of Ivan and the Firebird throughout this ballet. Ivan is the agent of the natural order and also its client, since nature—personified by the Firebird—protects him. But crucially, the "true" Russian political/natural order retains an Asiatic fiber.

Fokine writes that it was Stravinsky who suggested ending the ballet with the coronation scene. "Stravinsky was of the opinion that it would otherwise resemble other ballets, which usually ended in weddings and dances."[22] In any case, Fokine managed to have his wedding dances, turning the Infernal Dance into an upside-down nuptial celebration in which all the monsters, warriors, and maidens of Kostchei's entourage come forward to do their "national" dances, but "out of order," because they are not given as gifts to the happy couple.

Stravinsky's notion had other repercussions besides formal innovation, however. It created a particularly resonant political message. It has been said that this is a ballet about the defeat of evil or about the liberation of an oppressed people from tyranny. According to Garafola, "Like Rimsky-Korsakov's opera *Kostchei the Immortal*, the ballet is a fairy tale of tyranny punished. . . . The whole ballet, in fact, turns on the conflict of freedom and authority, the latter embodied not only in Ivan, the future king, but in the monster Kostchei, the tyrant tumbled from his throne by a demos of enchanted princesses, *bolebochki*, Indians, and Youths armed with the Firebird's golden feather."[23]

Although Ivan is as much an autocratic figure as Kostchei, I don't see the liberation in the ballet as democratic, because defeating tyranny can still be compatible with monarchy—especially when the new monarch is backed by nature (or the personification thereof). With the aid of the Firebird, Ivan "liberates" the enchanted oriental kingdom in the most imperial Russian sense: he delivers it into colonial status in his own empire. This he accomplishes with the imprimatur of nature, in the figure of the Firebird —Mother Nature, Mother Russia, but still, paradoxically, Asiatic.

Created as a Russian neonationalist ballet, *Firebird* nevertheless presents an indissoluble mix of Russian and orientalist imagery. For the French audience, according to a contemporary critic, the tale "embodie[d] all the picturesque, strange, and invincible charm of the tales of Slav mythology."[24] It was the ultimate symbol of Russianness. Then why the orientalist theme? In the original tales, the lands to which Ivan travels are distant but not necessarily Eastern. But Kostchei's court, with its Persian-carpet decor, its women straight from the seraglio, and its warriors armed with scimitars, is clearly related to the court, taken from *The Thousand and One Nights*, of Shah Shahryar in *Schéhérazade*.

There is, I think, a deeper answer beyond the obvious point that orientalism has historically served as an attractive form of exotic entertainment for Western Europeans and has supplied dance and theater themes at least since Jean-Georges Noverre's eighteenth-century ballets *Les Fêtes Chinoises* and *Le Turc Généreux*.[25] Certainly one answer is that often the Orient itself is symbolized by femaleness. But there is another answer that has to do with more than representations of women.

As I have suggested, together the Firebird and Ivan assert a double dominion, one that seems to validate and naturalize the monarchy of the then-waning Romanov dynasty, according to the strict tsarist principles of autocracy, nationalism, and religious orthodoxy (all depicted in the final coronation scene). But crucially, Ivan's is a monarchy that has been established by both subjugating and incorporating "the Eastern horde." In this way, the ballet rewrites history, reversing the medieval Tatar conquest of Kievan Russia, the stalemate of the Crimean War, and the recent defeat by Japan in 1905.

Mlle KARSAVINA
Première danseuse dans l'OISEAU D'OR.
Photo. Bert

Tamara Karsavina as the Firebird and in Le Pavillon d'Armide. These roles illustrate some of the oppostions in the Ballets Russes: East and West, fairy tale and historical time.

The struggle for control of Central Asia was a constant theme in Russian imperial policy in the second half of the nineteenth century, and nationalist uprisings in the region were brutally suppressed by the Russian state. The tsarist government pursued a vigorous policy of "russification" of the nationalities in the empire's southern and eastern possessions right up to the 1917 revolution. (Military intervention in the Asian borderlands, of course, continued under the Soviet and post-Soviet regimes as well; note the late 1990s occupations of Afghanistan and Chechnya.) So *Firebird* not only rewrites the past but also celebrates the contemporary Russian empire of 1910, stretching eastward, north of China and the former Russian colony of Mongolia, to Vladivostok, Kamchatka, and the Bering Strait, and southward, through Kazakhstan and Turkestan, to Persia and Afghanistan. That Fokine refers to the final scene of the ballet as the transformation of Kostchei's "evil kingdom" into a Christian city underscores the strong implication that the conquered territory is Muslim. The "Russian export," not surprisingly, presents the Russian nation to Western Europe as politically powerful, especially in its suzerainty over its eastern and southern possessions.[26]

And yet, as I suggested earlier, the ballet is not simply a binary opposition between Russia and the East. For since the incursion of the Tatars in the early thirteenth century, these categories have not been easily separable. Indeed, the Firebird herself, a hybrid creature containing elements of both these realms, embodies Russia's split identity. In many ways she represents the ancient Russian-Slavic strain. She makes possible, perhaps even engineers Ivan's accession to the throne, and thus she stands for Russian supremacy. In Russian folklore she is associated with at least one pre-Christian Slavic agrarian deity. Yet she is also an exotic outsider, mistress of a distant land, literally framing herself with her Asiatic arm gestures as an oriental temptress. (In fact, the critic Vladimir Stasov had suggested in the 1860s that the Firebird of traditional Russian folklore was a borrowing from East Indian epics.)[27] Although the fairy tale is set in some distant time, the Firebird, like Russia itself at the turn of the twentieth century (seeking a national identity but torn between East and West, Moscow and St. Petersburg), is of mixed heritage. And by making her his partner, Ivan Tsarevich not only acquires new eastern territories, but also acknowledges that Russia itself is as much Asian as European.

Indeed, this turn to the East was a familiar theme among artists during the period between the Russian revolutions of 1905 and 1917. The Russian neoprimitivist painter Alexander Shevchenko wrote in 1913, "We are called barbarians, Asians. Yes, we are Asia, and are proud of this, because 'Asia is the cradle of nations,' a good half of our blood is Tatar, and we hail the East to come, the source and cradle of all culture, of all arts."[28]

It is true that Ivan Tsarevich marries the "right" woman, in that the beautiful Tsarevna is both Russian and (therefore?) human. With this gene pool, the Tsarevich can create a dynasty. But Ivan also maintains his relationship with his donor, the Firebird. Given that there is a happy ending in the form of a marriage and that both the human (Russian) and the inhuman (Asian) female not only survive but flourish, this is not so much (like earlier ballets involving an inhuman "other" woman) a cautionary tale against straying from the appropriate marriage class or from the marriage bed as it is an endorsement of a more liberal sexual arrangement. This attitude is hardly surprising since the ballet was created by a group of artists with mixed heterosexual, homosexual, and bisexual orientations and liberal views (or at least behaviors) toward extramarital sex—and it was marketed to a sophisticated Parisian audience with similarly liberal mores.

The ballet could also be seen as an advance in the representation of women as agents, for even though the Firebird still has all the old markings of an exotic "other" woman (in both senses), she is nevertheless a positive female figure of enormous power. She is Carabosse redeemed, the witch and the Lilac Fairy rolled into one. The apparent docility of the Firebird in the libretto's narrative—her effortless capture by Ivan and the immediate forfeiting of her feather—is belied by the character's deeds onstage, embodied in the dancer's powerful actions. That is, paying attention to performance as much as plot in this case creates a different narrative flow from the one suggested by the libretto.

But as I noted earlier and as Natalia Goncharova's design for the 1926 revival makes abundantly clear (pl. 30), the final scene is far more coronation than wedding. The women in Firebird are less gendered beings than political symbols. Ultimately, this ballet concerns not sexual politics or female agency but national ideology. It hints at liberal sexual alliances, as well as at a respectful acknowledgment of female power, but its deeper message is political conservatism in regard both to the West and to ideas of empire. The beautiful Tsarevna is a "true" Russian maiden, an ideal of racial purity and national superiority. But the Firebird is a more complex, multivalent sign, merging metaphoric images of Mother Russia and Mother Earth with those of the oriental "partner." She links Russia to nature and the supernatural forces that rule nature, yet at the same time she is a discreet and mighty concubine who makes possible the Russian empire. The agent of destruction of the Asiatic despot Kostchei, she nonetheless symbolizes the "barbaric" oriental element within.

seven

Fernand Léger and the Ballets Russes

An Unconsummated Collaboration

Judi Freeman

To design for the Ballets Russes was, by 1914, an aspiration shared by many avant-garde artists working in France. Although a number of visual artists became involved in a variety of stage productions, a commission from the Ballets Russes was considered a plum. Artists periodically offered their services either directly to Diaghilev or via third parties. Some even arrived with elaborate proposals for productions, many of which were developed to greater or lesser degrees but never realized.

One hitherto unknown—and ultimately unconsummated—Ballets Russes collaboration was with the artist Fernand Léger. Today Léger is best known to ballet students for his two collaborations with the Ballets Suédois, a company headquartered in Paris that presented programs at the Théâtre des Champs-Elysées from 1920 through the beginning of 1925. Much has been made of Léger's emergent interest in the stage and in non–easel painting endeavors in the early 1920s.[1] But a voluminous correspondence between Léger and his wife-to-be, Jeanne Lohy, written between

1914 and 1917 has recently come to light that sheds new light on Léger's ambitions for the stage, aspirations already nascent during the First World War, when Léger served in the French armed forces, first as a sapper and then as a stretcher-bearer at the front.[2] In conjunction with what we already knew about Léger's life and activities, this material makes it clear that the artist was making a conscious, active effort to present his work on the stage. It is in these years, at the close of the second decade of the twentieth century, that Léger's world and that of the Ballets Russes intersect.

"I am selling a prewar painting and two drawings done in Verdun to Diaghilev, the organizer of the Ballets Russes," wrote Léger in February 1917 to his longtime friend Louis Poughon. "He's a great collector and I am delighted [that my work] will become part of his collection and then, when Diaghilev is in Paris with his company, we shall be able to go and watch them in the director's loge! That is always a treat. Diaghilev, a perfect European type, likes my painting very much and would absolutely like to know me. Good work." He wrote enthusiastically of Diaghilev's purchase to another old friend, Charlotte Mare (wife of the artist André Mare, also a childhood friend), ten days later. Yet despite his confident assessment of his chances, just four days later he was writing to Lohy urging her (as he had been doing for some time) to get closer to the impresario because he felt that personal contact was essential.[3] Léger had already asked his friend Natalia Goncharova to intercede on his behalf with Diaghilev; his request to Lohy was a follow-up to Goncharova's effort. That same day, 17 February 1917, Jean Cocteau and Pablo Picasso left Paris for Rome to complete work on their ballet *Parade*.

Lohy had been the one who originally encouraged Léger to become involved with Diaghilev and his company. She floated the idea in early January 1917 during Diaghilev's brief visit to Paris to negotiate his spring season and finalize contractual arrangements for *Parade*. Léger replied sarcastically that only the rich could afford such advice.[4] But by February the idea was at the forefront of Léger's mind. The collaboration would be the logical culmination of personal and professional contacts he had been cultivating before the outbreak of war and which he had maintained, sometimes during his leaves from the front, at other times via Lohy.

That Léger was conducting such a fruitful and active artistic life while serving at the front is surprising; but although he was present during some of the bloodiest and most prolonged battles of the war (in Verdun and the Argonne region generally), much of his time was sufficiently unoccupied that he could ruminate on artistic matters. His six leaves during his more than four years of military service enabled him to resume his artistic relationships in Paris, negotiate the sale of his work, and solicit dealer representation and projects.[5]

Among these projects was an initially vague idea that he design a ballet or stage production. Lohy's suggestions in mid-winter 1917 may have focused Léger's thinking, but his growing friendship with Mikhail Larionov and his companion Goncharova had already brought Léger closer to the notion of being an artiste-décorateur-collaborateur, roles that Larionov and Goncharova themselves played in their work for Diaghilev. That Léger's involvement with the pair intensified during the period when their partnership with Diaghilev was rapidly changing makes the link all the more significant.

Following their first joint visit to Paris from April through July 1914, a trip occasioned by their work on Diaghilev's production of Le Coq d'Or, Larionov and Goncharova had returned to Russia.[6] Like Léger, Larionov was drafted to serve at the front. There he was wounded almost immediately, hospitalized for three months, and released from military service in January 1915. While he was recovering, the couple received a series of increasingly anxious telegrams from Diaghilev, then in Switzerland, requesting that they join him and a small group of company members at the Villa Bellerive, on the outskirts of Lausanne. The last sealed their decision to go: "Leave immediately. Waiting anxiously. Diaghilev, Stravinsky."[7] Departing Russia for what would be the last time in their lives, the pair arrived in Geneva in July and joined Diaghilev. The two not only planned costumes and decors but also served as jacks-of-all-trades and were called upon to supervise the work of new choreographer Léonide Massine. Larionov oversaw Massine's choreography of Liturgie, which was developed only through rehearsal stage, while Goncharova designed the ballet's decor and costumes. Subsequently, Larionov worked closely with Massine on both the choreography and the design for Soleil de nuit (Midnight sun; pl. 16). Massine later acknowledged that Larionov's participation was integral to the production, presented in December 1915:

> Larionov was again asked to supervise the choreography. He was intrigued and suggested that it should revolve around the person of the sun-god Yarila to whom the peasants pay tribute in ritual ceremonies and dances, fusing it with the legend of the snow maiden, the daughter of King Frost, who is destined to melt in the heat of the sun when she falls in love with a mortal. I also decided to incorporate into the action the character of Bobyl, the innocent or village half-wit, and to end the ballet with the traditional dance of the buffoons. . . . It was through Larionov that I first came to understand the true nature of these old ritual peasant dances.[8]

Other projects were embarked upon but never realized during this period: Larionov designed sets and costumes for *Le Bouffon* (staged as *Chout* in 1921) and Goncharova for *Les Noces* (1923). In effect, the pair replaced Diaghilev's principal prewar designers, Alexandre Benois and Léon Bakst, and because of the reduced size of the enterprise became much more closely involved with the administration of the company.

Larionov and Goncharova moved with the Ballets Russes company to Paris to present *Soleil de Nuit* at the Paris Opéra on 29 December 1915. From there, the company left for the United States while the couple remained in Paris through early July 1916, when they rejoined the company during its tour of Spain.

Léger had met and befriended Goncharova and Larionov before his departure for the front in 1914. Although they had stayed in Paris only three months the couple had been hailed by the avant-garde community. Guillaume Apollinaire wrote the preface to the catalogue of their exhibition at the Galerie Paul Guillaume (17–30 June 1914), proclaiming Goncharova the "head of the Russian Futurist school" and Larionov "the head and the creator of the Rayonnist school" while noting what an honor it was for Goncharova to be invited to design the decors for Diaghilev's *Le Coq d'Or*. Léger, meanwhile, was working intensively in Paris and delivered the second of two lectures at the Académie

Left to right: Léonide Massine, Natalia Goncharova, Mikhail Larionov, Igor Stravinsky (seated), and Léon Bakst in the garden at the Villa Bellerive, 1915

Natalia Goncharova, costume design for an *Apostle* in *Liturgie, 1915*

Wassilieff on 9 May 1914.[9] Although no documentation exists to confirm that Goncharova and Larionov attended the lecture, clearly they met and came to know Léger during this period. Marie Wassilieff, who ran the academy, was a Russian émigré whose work was deeply influenced by Russian folk art and illustration. Her academy was a mecca for Russian as well as Scandinavian artists; Goncharova and Larionov, as well as Diaghilev, were among its frequent habitués. In addition, Apollinaire squired Goncharova and Larionov around town and was particularly close to Léger in 1914.

While at the front, Léger was eager to maintain his friendship with Goncharova and Larionov. Toward the end of 1915 or perhaps in early 1916, he sent them an ink drawing, one of his many *dessins de guerre,* inscribed "To Larionov, to Goncharova, two great Russian artists, your admirer and friend, F. Léger." In January 1916 he wrote to Larionov from the Argonne, telling him that he had just received the pair's Paris address from their mutual friend Volochine (a friend of Wassilieff's) and was eager to hear what Larionov and Goncharova had been working on. Léger anticipated a leave from the military soon (in fact, one came through at the end of the month) and hoped to see them shortly. Two weeks later, he wrote to Poughon, "I would like you to meet Larionov and Mme. Goncharova, the author of decors for the Ballets Russes, a very talented and kind young artist. Jane [Léger's nickname for Lohy] is often with them and they are good friends." Léger's only leave from the front that would have overlapped with Larionov and Goncharova's stay in Paris was his two weeks in late January–February 1916. Otherwise, he relied upon Lohy to relay news to and about the pair to him during his military service. He inquired several times about Goncharova's work that March and enclosed a letter to Larionov in one of his missives to Lohy.[10]

In the ensuing months Léger's interest in Goncharova and Larionov's activities waned, replaced in his letters to Lohy with discussions about the sale of his work, wartime and financial difficulties, and interest in his work from abroad. It is during this period that Rolf de Maré, the future theater and ballet impresario, purchased his first pictures by Léger through a friend, the artist Nils von Dardel. Though de Maré at this time was not involved with the stage, he was becoming an enthusiastic buyer of works of art by members of the emerging French avant-garde, an activity that would later result in many important artists working with his company, the Ballets Suédois, in the first half of the 1920s. Léger's concern with the Dardel–de Maré purchases preoccupied him throughout April and May 1916.

By early June, Léger's mood had shifted again. He resumed his friendship with Marie Wassilieff in a series of letters. Wassilieff, who remained in Paris during the war (except for a brief trip to Russia), was a catalyst for many of the avant-garde interactions in the cafés and restaurants. Her personal situation was less fortunate, however; as a Russian citizen with an illegitimate son born in France, she was imprisoned briefly. In desperation, she contacted Léger and Lohy, who came to her aid. "Léger, who dared as a soldier to concern himself with a child who had been declared an enemy of the country," Wassilieff later recalled, "was so generous and good that, even now, I see Léger as a soldier and his wife Jeanne as an apparition of saints."[11] Wassilieff's son Pierre became Léger's godchild. Although their correspondence is now lost, references

Léonide Massine and Lydia Sokolova rehearsing the Annunciation scene in Liturgie, 1915

to Wassilieff in Léger's letters to Lohy in these months suggest that the two were in close contact.

Concurrently, Léger began to invoke Picasso's name with increased frequency. In early June he urged Lohy to see what he described as Picasso's exhibition. In fact his reference was to the contemporary art exhibition at the Salon d'Antin from 15 through 31 July, the first public showing of Picasso's little-seen *Demoiselles d'Avignon* (1906–1907), on loan from its owner, Jacques Doucet. Léger, who also participated in the Salon d'Antin that year, perceived the exhibition as Picasso's event, characteristic of the prominent media attention Picasso was receiving in these years.[12]

Is this an innocent statement, or is there a touch of sarcasm in Léger's remark? He and Picasso were peers, born just nine months apart (Léger was older). By 1907 Picasso had become an emerging star in avant-garde circles while Léger was just beginning to exhibit his work and was spending long stretches of time in his native Argentan in Normandy and in Corsica with friends. Once Léger settled more permanently in Paris, in 1908, he moved to La Ruche in Montparnasse, a building he shared with Amédéo Modigliani, Henri Laurens, Jacques Lipschitz, and Marc Chagall. By 1911 he had moved to the Left Bank, but his associations continued with these artists as well as with artists working in Puteaux (Marcel Duchamp, Jacques Villon). He had exhibited regularly in the Salon d'Automne and contributed notably to the Maison Cubiste of 1912, conceived by his childhood friend André Mare. His name had appeared in press coverage of the period along with artists like Albert Gleizes, Jean Metzinger, and Robert Delaunay. But although many critics who championed Picasso also admired Braque, Léger's advocates seemed to link him to a different wing within the Cubist cause. Léger tried to push the view that he was a pioneer of equal importance to Picasso and Braque; as Apollinaire wrote of Léger's 1914 lecture at the Académie Wassilieff: "He showed that although other kinds of painting are possible today, the only kind of realistic painting possible is the one by which he, together with Picasso and Braque, has been seeking to represent, simply but forcefully, the world as it exists today."[13]

While Léger and many of his fellow artists were away in the military, Picasso remained in Paris, where he substantially increased his visibility. One of the artists presented by the dealer Daniel-Henry Kahnweiler (Léger was another), Picasso principally showed his work at his own studio. Although he had only one exhibition during the early 1910s—at Vollard's gallery from 20 December 1910 through 11 February 1911—during the war his studio became a gathering place for artists, writers, and critics who had re-

Rehearsing the Garden of

Gethsemane scene in

Liturgie, 1915

mained in the city as well as for those home on leave. Picasso participated in a group exhibition at Germaine Bongard's in December 1915, which was followed by the June 1916 showing of *Demoiselles d'Avignon* at the Salon d'Antin, a highly anticipated event, evident in Léger's own exhortation to Lohy to see it. Thus, when Picasso embarked on his collaboration with Serge Diaghilev and the Ballets Russes in mid-1916 that resulted in *Parade*, it was a noteworthy event.

According to Boris Kochno, Diaghilev had met Picasso that spring and offered him the commission. It took some time for Picasso to decide whether to accept; a letter from Jean Cocteau to his friend Valentine Gross of late July indicates that Picasso had not yet made up his mind. But he seems finally to have agreed on 12 August 1916, an occasion documented by Cocteau in a series of revelatory photographs taken that day.[14]

Parade marked Picasso's first foray into the theater. It also signaled yet another shift in Diaghilev's involvement with artist-designers. Whereas during the war Goncharova and Larionov had largely replaced Bakst and Benois, Picasso and other visual artists subsequently and more prominently participated in ballet productions toward the end of the war and afterward. Cocteau, for instance, had approached Picasso about the production sometime during the spring of 1916; he had already devoted significant effort to the project by that time.

Léger returned to Paris for his third leave in mid-August 1916. Whether he was in Paris on 12 August is unclear. In his letters to Lohy of 8 and 10 August, he refers obliquely to Picasso; soon thereafter he returned to Paris.[15] There is no doubt that he saw his friend Wassilieff, now running a canteen for artists in Montparnasse, during his visit. Wassilieff was definitely present for the 12 August lunch at La Rotonde, photographed by Cocteau, at which Picasso apparently agreed to collaborate on *Parade*. Thanks to Wassilieff, Léger would certainly have learned of Picasso's decision soon afterward.

In general, Léger was acutely aware of events transpiring in artistic circles in Paris, especially shifts within the avant-garde. In January 1916 he had written bitterly to Poughon, "And I know that behind me, the artistic life, all my old artistic life, is resuming. They *all* avoided fighting. All of them, they knew the fingers to push [to avoid going to war] when they needed to. All of them, I am telling you. One paints, one works, one sells in Paris *more than before the war*. I am telling you this because I know it. Jane was able to sell my pictures for 1600 francs to the Swedes [Rolf de Maré, via Dardel]. These people had admirable thoughts[:] 'How is it,' they say, '[that] Léger is *still* there?' "[16] Léger, eager to maintain his profile in Paris, had encouraged the publication of a brief reference to his work in *Mercure de France*:

> The Cubist painters, almost all of whom are now at the Front, are fighting two battles—one military and one artistic. And their works have found new and enthusiastic admirers there, from the common soldier of the second-class to the highest ranks among the staff officers. . . . The decorative capacities of the artist [Léger], which have perhaps been even more stimulated by eighteen months in the Argonne, do not appear at all revolutionary to all these "stout hearts" who, free of any great obsession with yesterday, are engaged in forging for us the beauty of tomorrow.[17]

Léger wanted the public to believe that something significant was happening among the artists at the front, symptomatic of the transformation taking place in his own work.

The *Mercure de France* article was one small element in Léger's effort; his own monitoring of events in Paris was another. Amid pages and pages of letters describing life at the front, concerns about finances, and amorous feelings expressed with restraint, Léger had managed to keep abreast of current news from Paris. In a letter to Lohy from mid-March, he inquired about the artists Serge Férat and Irène Lagut; Lagut had by this time embarked on a liaison with Picasso. He expressed renewed interest a month later.[18]

Léger's return to Paris at the end of the summer of 1916 must have hardened his perception that events were to some degree passing him by. Notwithstanding his assiduous correspondence with his artist friends and his numerous drawings inspired by the terrain and the carnage he had witnessed that pushed his prewar Cubist idiom in new directions, he perceived that he was out of step with artistic trends in the city, which were subtly but significantly shifting. Picasso's increased prominence and willing visibility underscored this. Picasso was achieving the seniority sought but not realized by his colleagues. Even Braque was off at the front, out of the picture both literally and figuratively.

Léger sought avenues beyond easel painting. Early on he saw the possibilities in the movies. Accompanied by Apollinaire, Léger frequented the cinema whenever he was on a leave. The seeds of his passion for film were planted at this time; it would be more clearly articulated in the 1920s, when he wrote and lectured on the subject and collaborated on his own film, *Le Ballet Mécanique* (1924). But during the war he was already producing films in his mind: in one, he envisioned a country scene that would center on the fantasies of a Parisian woman.[19] Involvement with the theater was a natural outgrowth of such interests. Cocteau may have claimed that "in 1916 a dictatorship hung heavy over Montmartre and Montparnasse. Cubism was going through its austere phase, and to paint a stage set for the Ballets Russes [as Picasso was doing for *Parade*] was a crime," but Léger did not share that view. He was receptive to such partnerships, as many of his fellow French artists would be in the following decade. He welcomed Diaghilev's apparent receptivity to new projects and collaborators, heralded in the journal *SIC*: "We have learned with pleasure that M. Daghileff works and searches for new things."[20]

Given Léger's concern about his own artistic eclipse toward the middle and end of 1916, coupled with the public departure of Picasso and Cocteau for Rome to complete work on *Parade* in early 1917, it is not surprising that Léger, initially dismissive of Lohy's suggestion that he become more involved with Diaghilev and his company, would switch gears and begin to lobby more actively to attract Diaghilev's interest. To have received a commission would have placed him on a par with Picasso and helped to compensate for Léger's sense that Picasso and others had been far more active and successful in wartime than he had been.

Via Lohy, Léger urged Larionov, and especially Goncharova, to open a dialogue for him with Diaghilev. Repeatedly throughout the late winter and early spring of 1917, he inquired after Larionov and Goncharova, asking Lohy to forward letters to them; in addition, he requested information about Picasso's activities. Since September 1916 Goncharova and Larionov had been in Rome with Diaghilev and Massine; they returned to Paris in April 1917, just before *Parade*'s Paris premiere on 18 May. Toward the end of April, Léger was still hopeful, telling Poughon that "with Diaghilev and the Ballets Russes, I wish to be able to have perhaps a proceeding that would help us."[21] But despite whatever intercession Goncharova and Larionov might have made on Léger's behalf, he was unable to interest Diaghilev in a collaboration.

Parade debuted before Léger had a genuine opportunity to advance a relationship with the impresario. In view of this failure, Apollinaire's comments in the program notes for the Paris performances of *Parade* must have been difficult for Léger to read: "The Cubist painter Picasso and the most audacious of choreographers Léonide Massine have realized it [notions of modernity] in consummating for the first time this alliance of painting and dance, of plastic art and music, which is the clear sign of the approach of a more complete art."[22] After he returned from the front, it must have been highly upsetting for him to learn that first Sonia and Robert Delaunay, then André Derain and Picasso for the second time, and finally Matisse had been engaged by Diaghilev to design ballets for

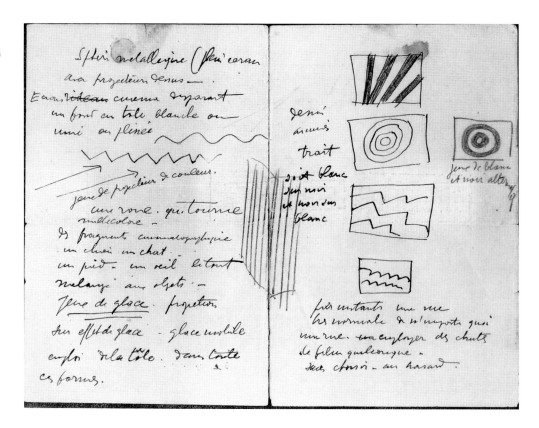

the company, all encouraged by Larionov. Though eventually his interest in working on the stage would be realized in 1922 and 1923 through his collaborations with the Ballets Suédois, his desire to be part of the Ballets Russes enterprise never entirely vanished.

In autumn 1919, following two book collaborations with his friend the poet Blaise Cendrars, and just before he and Lohy were married, Léger traveled to Scandinavia, a trip rarely mentioned in literature on the artist.[23] He visited Oslo in late October through early November as the guest of artists Thorvald Hellesen, who was having a one-man exhibition of his work at Tivoli, and Hélène Perdriat, whose work was showing at the Kunstnerforbundet. Léger had written the foreword to the catalogue for Perdriat's exhibition. Extensively interviewed and well received, Léger was fêted grandly in Norway. He then proceeded to Stockholm in early–mid-November, hosted by Ragnar Hoppe, curator (later director) of the Nationalmuseum and a habitué of artists' studios in Paris who had known Léger since 1914. During Léger's visit to Stockholm, Hoppe acquired from him a drawing and a watercolor for the museum.

En route back to Paris, Léger made a little-known stop in London. There he saw the Ballets Russes firsthand in its postwar incarnation. "We found the Ballets Russes here having a huge success," he wrote to Hoppe, "I have had a loge at my disposal and we enjoyed Derain's excellent ballet—with Massine in his loge. Saw Matisse—Jacques Blanche—all of Paris!"[24] Léger's trip, in mid- to late November, quite likely overlapped with Matisse's second visit to London; he had been there in October for two weeks, working with Vladimir Polunin on sets for the forthcoming *Le Chant du Rossignol*, and returned at Diaghilev's request to create a drop curtain for the production.[25] Léger would have seen the London debut of *Parade* (his first view of the actual production), as well as Derain's *La Boutique Fantasque* and possibly Picasso's *Le Tricorne*.

Léger's trip to London was not merely coincidental. He was concerned about the sale of his work and eager for new audiences. His repeated letters to his new dealer, Léonce Rosenberg, from late 1917 onward, are riddled with urgent references to money and demands and recommendations for pricing and selling his work. It is obvious from these letters that Léger had been talking with fellow artists about their respective situations. After Rosenberg's return from a visit to London in the summer of 1919, Léger had queried him on the situation in England. "Your hopes are our hopes," he told Rosenberg,

and proceeded to describe Derain's experience in the city during the three-month preparations for *La Boutique Fantasque*. Though not close to Derain, Léger kept abreast of work for
the stage; evidently, in Léger's view, Derain, a fellow artist also represented by Kahnweiler
before the war, was more approachable than Picasso, who had concurrently been in London working on *Le Tricorne*. According to Léger, Derain's impression was that people were
more open-minded toward contemporary avant-garde art in London than in Paris, a view
that no doubt resulted from the enthusiastic reception his ballet (and subsequently his
paintings) received in England.[26] In the same letter, Léger mentioned that he was con-
sidering sending a large canvas to London under the auspices of Osbert Sitwell; Sitwell's
close friendship with Diaghilev could not have escaped his notice. In September, at
Sitwell's urging, Léger had exhibited *La Ville* at Heal's Mansard Gallery. It is likely, therefore, that Léger's stopover in London was deliberate.

But once again, Léger failed to attract Diaghilev's attention. How frustrating this
must have been for an artist whose interest in performance had by this time developed
into a thematic element of his work. His friendship with the circus performers the

Fratellini brothers had inspired his 1918 depictions of the Cirque Médrano in at least a half-dozen canvases. Particularly fascinated by clowns and acrobats Léger began focusing on them in a group of increasingly mechanomorphic paintings. These images culminated in 1919 in the studies leading up to *La Ville*, which reads as if it were an urban stage set of interlocking geometric decors populated by a series of seemingly interchangeable anonymous figures. The serial paintings that follow in his 1919 oeuvre—*Le Pont du remorqueuer*, *Le Passage à niveau*—announced the possibilities for decors and sets to be populated by Léger's increasingly tubular figures. (My reading here is based on my assessment of how Léger shifted in the years 1918–1920 from the repetition of one type of motif to another in his work, rather than on how he disposed of these particular canvases.) His repeated oscillation from "backdrop" imagery to "figurative" pictures in these brief years—a practice not inconsistent with his prewar tendencies but intensified in the immediate postwar era—suggests that he still had his mind on doing stagework.

Several studies for a set design and costumes that clearly emanate from such urban images as *La Ville* or the subsequent *Disques dans la ville* series suggest that Léger may have gone so far as to produce preliminary sketches for a proposed ballet for the Ballets Russes. These studies place the action in a French café, with phrases from a menu scattered across the decor. The characters are elegant men and women, dressed in the latest fashion. Their attire is no doubt influenced by Sonia Delaunay's contemporary work (which

Fernand Léger, costume design for a Beetle in La Création du Monde, 1922

Léger had seen by this time, before the exhibition of her dresses at the Bal Bullier in 1923) but is specifically drawn from Léger's disk motifs of 1918–1919. Traditionally, these drawings have been dated 1922 but they have not been persuasively associated with a particular production.[27] Their close resemblance to Léger's 1918–1919 canvases supports an earlier dating.

Unquestionably, Léger's designs for the Ballet Suédois *Skating Rink* emanated from these designs. His obvious pleasure in working with the company had everything to do with his familiarity with the principals, especially Rolf de Maré. His studies for the company's *La Création du Monde*, while clearly grounded in his keen interest in tribal sculpture, was also a genuine collaboration with his old friend and student of African legend Blaise Cendrars. Léger's memory of the Ballets Russes remained close at hand; his study for the beetle in *Création* closely resembles Larionov's design for the cricket in *Histoires Naturelles*, and his design for the Messenger of the Gods in *Création* incorporates elements of Picasso's American Manager and Chinese Conjuror (pl. 20) from *Parade*.[28]

In 1914 Léger painted a large canvas and several other images devoted to the theme of the stairway, *L'Escalier*. The painting was typical of Léger's "contrastes de formes" imagery that dominated his prewar oeuvre. This was the painting Diaghilev acquired in February 1917; very soon thereafter he gave it to Massine. As Massine later confirmed to Alfred H. Barr, Jr., Léger himself changed the title to *La Sortie des Ballets Russes* (Exit the Ballets Russes; pl. 19).[29]

Mikhail Larionov, *study for a Cricket from* Histoires naturelles, 1917–1919

Is the new title revelatory? Was Léger consciously or perhaps unconsciously signaling to Massine and to himself the closure of this particular avenue among his collaborative activities? It could be argued that by 1925 the Ballets Suédois, particularly in the ballets of Cocteau, Léger, Gerald Murphy, and Francis Picabia, had become even more avant-garde in the visual arts arena than the legendary Ballets Russes. Léger's wartime ambitions had been replaced in the mid-1920s by a solid record of collaborative achievements, a considerable array of lectures and publications—notably on the subject of the intersection of painting and performance—and the significant reception of his work by collectors. Essentially, Léger's need for involvement with the Ballets Russes had metaphorically exited, closing a brief but fascinating chapter in his life.

eight Classicism and Neoclassicism

David Vaughan

Throughout the twentieth century, choreographers have argued over the question, what is ballet? On one side, Michel Fokine, Léonide Massine, and later Antony Tudor and Jerome Robbins have demanded that dance be expressive—that it imitate some action other than "mere" dancing. On the other, George Balanchine and Frederick Ashton have used stories, if at all, as pretexts for pure dance. The conflict, manifested in works presented by Serge Diaghilev's Ballets Russes, has continued into our own time, with the emergence of "dance theater" in Europe, in part, at least, in reaction to the so-called abstraction of Balanchine and Ashton. The struggle has even been found in modern dance, in the dichotomy between the mythological narratives choreographed by Martha Graham and the pure dance works of Merce Cunningham.[1]

In its first seasons, the Ballets Russes was primarily the vehicle for Michel Fokine's reform ballets, in which he replaced what he saw as the empty and artificial spectacle of the late

nineteenth-century Imperial Russian ballet with expressionist dance dramas like *Cléopâtre*, *Schéhérazade*, and *Petrouchka*. Even so, items from the classical repertory of the Imperial Theaters were in fact presented in the programs of the Ballets Russes from the beginning, if only to display the brilliant technique of the dancers from St. Petersburg and Moscow who formed the personnel of the initial seasons. Fokine himself did not entirely reject classicism: his *Pavillon d'Armide*, the opening ballet on the first Ballets Russes program in 1909, was conceived by its librettist Alexandre Benois as a ballet *à grand spectacle* in the Petipa manner and had been presented at the Maryinsky Theater in St. Petersburg in November 1907. (Benois's design for scene 2 bore a striking resemblance to Matvei A. Shishkov's design for act 3 of the original production of *The Sleeping Beauty*.)[2] (See plate 7.)

Le Festin, the third ballet on that opening night program, was a kind of prototype of the "highlights" programs presented later by the Bolshoi Ballet and other companies: it included excerpts from Petipa's *Sleeping Beauty* (the Bluebird pas de deux, temporarily renamed "The Firebird") and *Raymonda* (the Grand Pas Classique Hongrois). The Bluebird pas de deux remained in the Diaghilev repertory as a separate number, under various titles, until the complete ballet was given as *The Sleeping Princess* in 1921; in 1911 Mathilde Kchessinska danced the act 3 Wedding pas de deux (or "Aurore et le Prince," as it was styled for the occasion) in London with Nijinsky. *Le Festin* itself was, so to speak, a movable feast in which new ingredients could be inserted (such as the pas de deux from

Alexander Gorsky's version of *The Daughter of Pharaoh* that Pavlova danced with Mikhail Mordkin). The title could also be used for any ad hoc collection of divertissements, as in 1925, when it again included the Grand Pas Hongrois from *Raymonda* as well as new numbers by George Balanchine.

Les Sylphides (as Diaghilev renamed Fokine's *Chopiniana*), which opened the second program in 1909, could be considered a neoclassical ballet *avant la lettre*—it comprised a plotless suite of dances to piano pieces by Chopin, orchestrated by Alexander Glazunov, Alexander Taneyev, and Igor Stravinsky. In later seasons Diaghilev continued to present classical works: *Giselle* (which had been considered—and rejected—for the first season) in 1910, and a two-act condensation of *Swan Lake* that included divertissements from act 3 in 1911, again for Kchessinska and Nijinsky. A similar version of *Swan Lake* was presented   Les Sylphides, 1909

Tamara Karsavina and Vaslav Nijinsky in Giselle, Paris,

1910

in Monte Carlo in 1923 with Vera Trefilova and Anatole Vilzak. Fokine himself made revisions to the choreography of both *Giselle* and the 1911 *Swan Lake*, and at some point it seems that Balanchine made some to the later production: this may have been the first time that Odette's mime scene in the second act was replaced by dancing, as became standard practice in versions given by later Ballet Russe companies. In 1925 Diaghilev presented *Le Bal du Lac des Cygnes*, largely consisting of the divertissements from act 3. Meanwhile, Balanchine also rechoreographed the pas de trois of Florestan and his sisters for *Aurora's Wedding* (1922), which Diaghilev salvaged from *The Sleeping Princess*. And former company member Ninette de Valois once told me that when Balanchine and his colleagues first joined the Ballets Russes in 1924, Diaghilev instructed Alexandra Danilova to teach the women of the company variations from Petipa's *Paquita*.

Indeed, in 1921 Diaghilev reengaged Bronislava Nijinska, who had danced in the first seasons of the Ballets Russes, as a choreographer because she had staged a complete production of the Petipa-Ivanov *Swan Lake* in Kiev in 1919. Her initial assignment was to add interpolations to *The Sleeping Princess*, the production that was Diaghilev's most important statement of belief in classicism.

Throughout the successive phases of reform (Fokine), modernism (Nijinsky and Massine), and, finally, constructivism and neoclassicism (Nijinska and Balanchine), the dancers of the Diaghilev company were trained in the technique of the classical *danse d'école*, notably by Enrico Cecchetti, formerly a member of the Imperial Ballet; and Diaghilev continued to demand academically trained dancers, although his reason was originally, as André Levinson suggested, "to combat the Classic Dance successfully." Both Fokine and Massine used classical technique when it suited their purposes; Nijinsky only by negation (by abandoning the turn-out fundamental to the technique, for example), except, apparently, in *Jeux* (1913), which his sister Nijinska called "the forerunner of Neo-classical Ballet." The first of Fokine's Five Principles (of the so-called "new" ballet), enumerated in his famous letter to the London *Times* on 6 July 1914, was "to create in each case a new form corresponding to the subject."[3] (This meant that in ballets in which the goal was ethnic or historical authenticity, for example, the danse d'école was banned.) Massine, for his part, developed in his early ballets a style influenced by the neoprimitivisim of painters like Natalia Goncharova and Mikhail Larionov, by futurism, by the gestural language of theatrical innovator Vsevolod Meyerhold, and even by the cinema.

But in the years following the production of *The Sleeping Princess*, classical technique was reinstated as the dance language commonly used in new ballets presented by the Ballets Russes, and in this sense these works could be called neoclassical. I am using the terms *classical* and *neoclassical* as they are commonly used in ballet, where they have a different meaning from that of music or literature. Classical ballets like *Swan Lake* are often romantic in their subject matter; *classical* refers to the dance technique they employ. Similarly, *neoclassical* indicates a contemporary stylization of the technique, sometimes with the admixture of elements derived from jazz or social dancing, but often also a use of contemporary subject matter. It is in both these senses that Nijinsky's *Jeux* can be seen as prototypically neoclassical. It introduced a kind of

Olga Spessivtzeva as Aurora in The Sleeping Princess, *1921*

stylization—in the way the hands were held, for instance—that became common in ballets of the last decade of the Ballets Russes, and it was also the first ballet to depict contemporary sexual mores (even, by implication, homosexuality).

Certainly, Nijinska followed the example of her brother in both these senses in *Les Biches* (1924). Technically, the ballet's vocabulary consisted to a large extent of the kind of petit allegro—small jumps and beaten steps—taught by Cecchetti; the subject matter was contemporary sexual mores, as exemplified in the antics of a group of Bright Young Things in a house of assignation (pl. 28). (*The House Party*, the English title given the ballet by Diaghilev for his London seasons, was surely euphemistic.)

But already the year before, Nijinska had proposed a radically innovative use of classical technique in *Les Noces*, where she put the women on pointe, but in parallel position. When the ballerina had risen to her toes a hundred or so years earlier, the purpose was to give an illusion of ethereal lightness, to enable her to portray a creature

*Vera Savina in Le
Astuzie Femminili*

of another world. Petipa added a further dimension, greater speed in allegro movement. But in *Les Noces*, Nijinska sought the opposite effect: greater weightedness, in which the women appeared rooted in the earth. Where Nijinsky in *Le Sacre du Printemps* (1913) had used an idiom characterized by percussive flat-footed stamping, Nijinska employed stabbing pointes. Even the jumps, which occurred only rarely, seemed to have a downward thrust instead of giving the impression of flight.

In *Le Train Bleu* (1924), on the other hand, Nijinska abandoned the use of pointe in favor of a method closer to that of Massine, inventing a choreographic idiom derived from sports and newsreels. Massine's version of modernism involved experimentation with movement in which the danse d'école played only a limited part. Thus, in *The Good-Humoured Ladies* (1917) he was led "to invent broken, angular movements for the upper part of the body while the lower limbs continued to move in the usual harmonic academic style"[4]—which sounds a lot like Merce Cunningham in his most recent use of the computer program LifeForms.

Although Stravinsky's score for Massine's *Pulcinella* (1920) is generally considered to have initiated the neoclassical movement in contemporary music, Massine's choreography was hardly neoclassical: it was more in the modernistic vein of *The Good-Humoured Ladies*. (However, Massine's divertissement for the opera *Le Astuzie Femminili*, produced by Diaghilev shortly after *Pulcinella*, was a suite of dances in the Petipa manner. It entered the repertory as a separate ballet under the title *Cimarosiana* in 1924.)[5] When Massine returned to the Ballets Russes in 1925, his first assignment was to take over the choreography of *Zéphyr et Flore* (which Serge Lifar had begun and quickly abandoned). This ballet *was* neoclassical, both in the sense that it treated a classical myth in contemporary terms and that it used a stylized academic technique. During the same period Massine also choreographed the character ballets *Les Matelots* (1925) and the Soviet-style, mechanistic *Pas d'Acier* (1927), in which the dancers portrayed factory workers, as well as restaging *Mercure*

Ode, 1928

(1927), which he had originally made for Etienne de Beaumont's Soirées de Paris in 1924. *Les Matelots* was a popular success and continued to be performed after the demise of the Diaghilev company, but Massine's most important and innovative work in this period was the neoclassical *Ode* (1928).

Designed by Pavel Tchelitchev, *Ode* was a forerunner of the mixed-media works of the 1960s and 1970s, when such stage effects as light projection and even use of film became commonplace not only in experimental theater but also on the commercial stage. Although the ballet's subject matter, derived from an ode by the eighteenth-century poet Mikhail Lomonosov, was apparently impenetrable, "never before," wrote the British critic A. V. Coton, "were the senses so delightfully assaulted with unrelated and unrelatable forms of movement, music, lighting, and colour." Some of the dancers were dressed in what would now be called unitards and made geometric shapes with a length of rope; in these sequences Massine came closest to creating choreography that was not just neoclassical but even abstract. "The actual movements," noted Cyril W. Beaumont in his 1928 "annal" of the company, "were in the manner of the classical ballet whose linear beauty was here given its full value by reason of the bodies being, for all practical purposes, unclothed. But the lines had an unusually austere and chaste quality, a geometrical rather than an emotional beauty."[6]

It is often said that the last years of the Ballets Russes were a period of decadence, in which Diaghilev turned to an ever more desperate pursuit of novelty at all costs, particularly in visual design, to the detriment of choreography and music. As Serge Grigoriev, Diaghilev's faithful régisseur, saw it, Diaghilev was possessed of an "almost morbid taste for everything fashionable."[7] And in fact, when Balanchine joined the company in 1924, after defecting from Soviet Russia, he tried to satisfy Diaghilev's taste in this direction, drawing on his knowledge of the experimental choreography of the immediate postrevolutionary period (some of which he had himself created). After proving with his first ballet assignment, a new version of Stravinsky's *Le Chant du Rossignol* (1925), that he could put a dance work together, he was given the ballet-bouffe *Barabau* (1925), in which the movement seems to have been grotesque, if not vulgar.

Indeed, Balanchine, as an apprentice choreographer, was willing to turn his hand to anything. He choreographed dozens of opera ballets for the seasons at Monte Carlo, and it is easy to imagine that for these he also drew upon his knowledge of the classical repertory he had danced at the Maryinsky. His next full ballet, *La Pastorale* (1926), was certainly the product of the search for novelty, even while Diaghilev sought to repeat the success of *Les Matelots* by using the same designer (Pedro Pruna) and composer (Georges Auric). The action concerned the activities of a movie company shooting a film on location, with Lifar as a messenger boy arriving on a bicycle and falling for the star, danced by Felia Doubrovska. Tall and elegant, with a beautiful line, Doubrovska was the first typical Balanchine ballerina, and she inspired what little dancing there was in *La Pastorale*, which included a passage in which Lifar rotated her in arabesque by turning her leg, a movement that Balanchine incorporated into *Serenade* some years later. (Apparently Doubrovska's long, elegant line also inspired, or made possible, Massine's experiments with abstraction in *Ode*.)

Meanwhile, the fairy scenes in the English pantomime ballet *The Triumph of Neptune* (1926) enabled Balanchine to include a classical *ballabile*, or ensemble dance, as well as classical and demi-caractère variations for Danilova, Lydia Sokolova, and the choreographer himself. "There was a scene in a Frozen Forest with a flying ballet," wrote W. A.

Finale, Le Chant du Rossignol, 1925

Propert, "and another in Cloudland that took one back appropriately to Sylphides, with Danilova, [Lubov] Tchernicheva, Lifar, and the rest of them in their most classical mood.[8]

Having hit his stride with this ballet, Balanchine now began to eliminate extraneous elements from his work, a process that culminated in the absolute purity of *Apollon Musagète* in 1928. *La Chatte* (1927) was his first completely neoclassical work, a ballet in which all the ingredients matched: Balanchine's spare choreography, Henri Sauguet's bittersweet music, and the constructivist setting and costumes by Naum Gabo and Anton Pevsner—"all of it," as Propert remarked, "as transparent as crystal."

Alice Nikitina (who replaced Olga Spessivtzeva after the first performance) was "the most adorable cat who ever danced in a talc petticoat" (a reference to the clear plastic skirt of her tutu).[9] She even did a tap step—in pointe shoes.

But it was *Apollo*, as the ballet came to be called, that finally confirmed Balanchine as a neoclassicist. First performed a few days after the premiere of *Ode*, it brought together as the Muses the three ballerinas who were the most classical in style: Danilova (who had to turn the first night performance over to Nikitina because the latter's protector was footing the bill), Tchernicheva, and Doubrovska. Lifar danced Apollo. Balanchine's response to Stravinsky's neoclassical score is famous: "In its discipline and restraint, in its sustained oneness of tone and feeling the score was a revelation. It seemed to tell me that I could dare not to use everything, that I, too, could eliminate. . . . I began to see how I could clarify, by limiting, by reducing what seemed to be multiple possibilities to the one that is inevitable."[10]

Four more ballets remained to be presented by Diaghilev, three of them choreographed by Balanchine. *The Gods Go a-Begging* (1928) was a hastily assembled *pièce d'occasion*, an end-of-season tribute to conductor Thomas Beecham, who had arranged the Handel numbers that made up the score. In spite of the mostly hand-me-down costumes and scenery, the ballet was an unexpected hit, a work of great charm in which Balanchine relaxed his usual austerity, especially in the lyrical pas de deux.

Le Bal (pl. 31) and Prodigal Son, presented within a couple of weeks of each other during Diaghilev's final season, found the choreographer once again at his most extreme. In Le Bal, Balanchine seems to have made a conscious effort to find a choreographic equivalent of the architectural elements in Giorgio de Chirico's scenery and costumes. The result was the kind of modish deformity that is often held to be typical of late Diaghilev ballets. Still, Coton, who called Le Bal Diaghilev's "final ballet of épatisme," also found the choreography to be "mature and beautiful."[11]

With Prodigal Son, Balanchine renounced neoclassicism, not in favor or classicism or modernism, but in order to return to his early Soviet, even expressionist style—though once again Doubrovska inspired him to create some extraordinary, if totally unclassical movement. Ironically, this least typical of his ballets is the one from this period that is most often performed.

Lubov Tchernicheva (left), Léon Woizikovsky, and Felia Doubrovska in The Gods Go a-Begging, *1928*

Meanwhile, the ballet's librettos were undergoing a change as well. If Jean Cocteau aspired to be the artistic arbiter of the postwar Ballets Russes (he made a small contribution to the scenario of *Les Biches* and a larger one to that of *Le Train Bleu*), it was Boris Kochno who assumed this role in the second half of the 1920s. A poet who joined Diaghilev's entourage as his secretary while still in his teens, Kochno found his true métier as the author of pretexts for ballets. Of the works mentioned here, eight had libretti by Kochno—*Zéphyr et Flore, Les Matelots, La Pastorale, La Chatte, Ode, The Gods Go a-Begging, Le Bal,* and *Prodigal Son.* Diaghilev did not care for abstract ballets, and Kochno's specialty was the concoction of what were often the thinnest of pretexts for dancing. He collaborated with all three of Diaghilev's postwar choreographers—Massine, Nijinska, and Balanchine—both with the Ballets Russes and for later companies. The works Kochno helped create are often called neoromantic rather than neoclassical, but his ideas provided a vehicle for the neoclassicism of Balanchine's *Cotillon* (1932) and Nijinska's *Les Cent Baisers* (1935), which were made for the post-Diaghilev Ballet Russe company directed by Colonel W. de Basil. Once Balanchine moved to America the most important ballets he created were neoclassical: *Concerto Barocco* (1941), *The Four Temperaments* (1946), *Agon* (1957). But he did not abandon the neoromanticism associated with Kochno, as in *La Sonnambula* (1946), *La Valse* (1951), and the short-lived *Gaspard de la Nuit* (1975). The first and last masterpieces he created in the United States—*Serenade* (1934) and the final version of *Mozartiana* (1981)—combined elements of both neoclassicism and neoromanticism.

From the first decade of the Ballets Russes, Fokine's *Les Sylphides, Carnaval* (1910), and *Firebird* (1910), Massine's *The Good-Humoured Ladies, La Boutique Fantasque* (1919), and *Parade* (1917), and Nijinsky's *L'Après-midi d'un Faune* (1912) have a strong enough choreographic structure to warrant survival—yet few are in current repertory—whereas the second decade, when neoclassicism began to replace expressionism, produced *Les Noces, Les Biches, Apollo,* and *Prodigal Son,* all of which are frequently performed today. The Ballets Russes was among the most important artistic manifestations of the twentieth century, and what it finally proved is that modernism in ballet can only be fully cogent when it goes hand in hand with classicism.

Pl. 17 Mikhail Larionov, costume design for a Young Peasant Girl in Midnight Sun, 1915

Pl. 18 David Bomberg, *study for Russian Ballet lithographs, ca.* 1914

Pl. 19 Fernand Léger, Exit the Ballets Russes, 1914

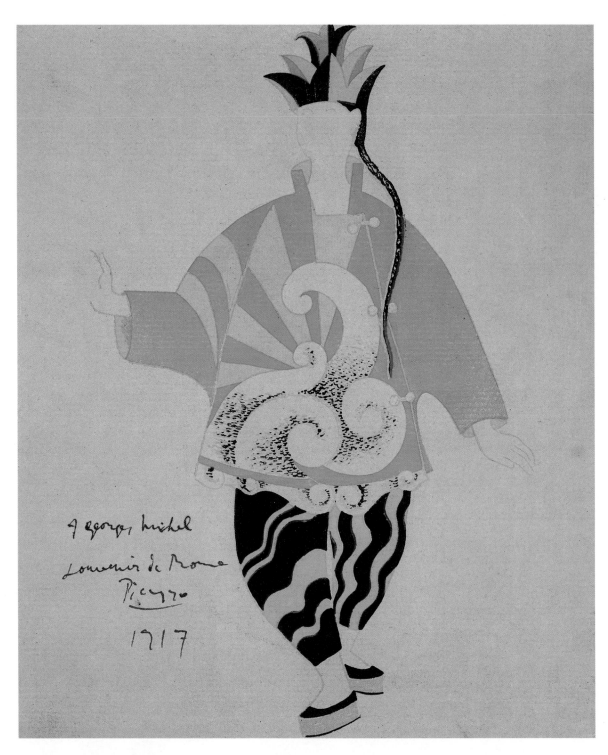

Pl. 20 Pablo Picasso, costume design for the Chinese Conjuror in Parade, 1917

Pl. 21 *Pablo Picasso, set design for Pulcinella, 1920*

Pl. 23 Mikhail Larionov, *set design for Le Renard*, 1922

Pl. 22 *Pablo Picasso*, Pulcinella with a Guitar in Front of a Curtain (Massine taking a bow), 1920

Pl. 24 Léopold Survage, set design for Mavra, 1922

Pl. 25 *Pablo Picasso, study for curtain, Le Train Bleu, 1922*

Pl. 26 *Alexander Vesnin, program cover design, Kamerny Theater's Phèdre, 1922*

Pl. 27 Natalia Goncharova, poster for the Bal Travesti, Paris, 1923

Pl. 28 Marie Laurencin, *design for the drop curtain in Les Biches*, 1924

Pl. 29 Maurice Utrillo, *set design for Barabau*, 1925

Pl. 30 Natalia Goncharova, *set design for Firebird*, 1926

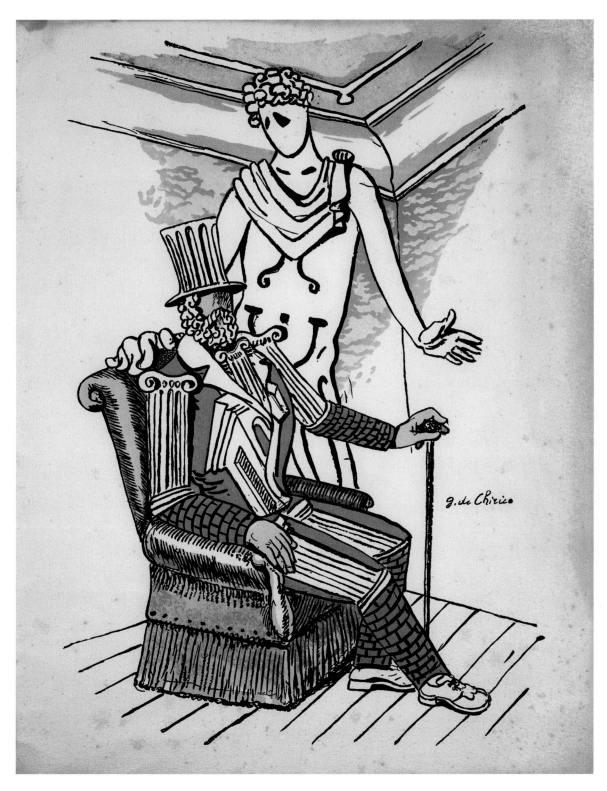

Pl. 31 Giorgio de Chirico, design for Le Bal, 1929

Pl. 32 Natalia Goncharova, curtain design for Le Coq d'Or, 1914

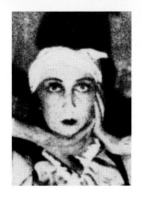

nine Bringing Les Noces to the Stage

Drue Fergison

Les Noces, arguably the most important Ballets Russes production of the 1920s, premiered at the Théâtre de la Gaîté-Lyrique, Paris, on 13 June 1923. Plagued by problems of artistic gestation, financial difficulties, even a dancers' strike, the ballet was in the works for eleven years before finally reaching the stage. Since its premiere this collaboration of some of the most important artists of the 1920s—Stravinsky, Bronislava Nijinska, Natalia Goncharova, and Diaghilev—has entered the repertory of ballet companies round the world. But how Les Noces first got to Paris is a fascinating story, and one that illustrates the way the Ballets Russes productions fused the various arts to create a whole new aesthetic.

As suggested by its title, the ballet depicts a wedding, a Russian village wedding under the old regime. The music and text are by Igor Stravinsky, who called the former a "cantata" and took the latter from several sources in Russian popular literature, most notably Pavel Kireyevsky's compilation of folk songs, which included a number of wedding songs. Although the text of Les Noces is in many ways wedded to the Russian language, Stravinsky's collaboration with the Swiss writer Charles-Ferdinand Ramuz, whom he met in 1915, resulted in an excellent French translation that is often performed.[1]

The text is characterized by fragmentation and repetition, by ritual lamentation and prayer, and by folk imagery. In his vocal writing, Stravinsky paired these textual qualities with chantlike melodies based on repetitive, interrelated, and gradually varying melodic cells, incorporating as well rhythms, shouts, exclamations, calls, and drunken sounds that mimic those of everyday speech and life.[2]

Les Noces is divided into four musically unbroken tableaux—The Braid (At the Bride's), At the Groom's, the Departure of the Bride, and the Wedding Meal—each based on an actual Russian ritual. The characters, as suggested by their generic names, are distinguished by their lack of individuality, which is musically reinforced by having the same singers perform the parts of different characters. Thus, the bride and groom become mere symbols of the socializing ritual of marriage. The work is a tribute to the power of community.

Stravinsky's own community when he was composing Les Noces was a remarkable one. Exiled in Switzerland during World War I and under constant financial strain,

Stravinsky spent much of his time visiting friends in the towns on and around Lac Léman. (Stravinsky later described these years as "the bicycle stage of my life.") Among his new acquaintances was Ernest Ansermet, the future conductor of Les Noces, whom he had met by 1914 and who introduced him in turn to Ramuz and to Aladár Rácz, the Hungarian cimbalomist who stirred Stravinsky's interest in the instrument. Ansermet may also have intro-

duced him to Vasily Ki-
balchich, the choirmaster
of the Russian church in
Geneva, who later con-
ducted the Russian cho-
rus in the first perfor-
mance of *Les Noces*.[3] All
lived close by, as did Diaghilev, who spent the
second half of 1915 at the
Villa Bellerive in Ouchy,
just outside Lausanne.

In his orchestra-
tion for *Les Noces*, Stravinsky struggled through
different versions, including arrangements that
exemplified the "mecha-
nistic" and impersonal
qualities of the wedding

ceremony itself. Over the course of composition, which began in late 1914, his conception shifted from a huge *Sacre*-like orchestra of about 150 players to a smaller group including mechanical instruments and Hungarian cimbalom to a final compromise of four
pianos and percussion (xylophone, timpani, crotales, bell, side drums, drums, tam-
bourine, bass drum, cymbals, and triangle). "I completed the first tableau," he told
Robert Craft,

> for an orchestra of the size of *Le Sacre du Printemps*, and then decided to divide
> the various instrumental elements—strings, woodwinds, brass, percus-
> sion, keyboard (cimbalom, harpsichord, piano)—into groups and to keep
> these groups separate on stage. In still another version I sought to combine
> pianolas with bands of instruments that included saxhorns and flügel-
> horns. Then one day in 1921, in Garches, where I was living as the guest
> of Gabrielle Chanel, I suddenly realized that an orchestra of four pianos
> would fulfil all my conditions. It would be at the same time perfectly ho-
> mogeneous, perfectly impersonal, and perfectly mechanical.[4]

These orchestrational shifts reflect Stravinsky's growth away from his so-called Russian works and toward neoclassicism. In fact, *Les Noces* embodies elements of both: one of Stravinsky's most purely Russian works, it also exemplifies the clean, mechanical precision of the 1920s aesthetic and its fascination with pianolas, radios, phonographs, and other new technologies. Thus, his experiments with the cimbalom and its mechanistic qualities and, more broadly, his search for the means of fusing the "folkloristic" with the "technological," the "Russian" with the "cosmopolitan." The genesis of *Les Noces* coincided with the first of many "moltings" by the composer, a process that allowed him to metamorphose, chameleonlike, from an identity that no longer served him creatively and make himself afresh as an artist.

Like Stravinsky's orchestrations, the stage and costume designs by Natalia Goncharova went through a number of versions. The earliest, which dated to late 1915 (pl. 14), emphasized the festive aspects of the subject, with "full, highly coloured, much ornamented, typical peasant costumes" that recalled her neoprimitivist designs for the 1914 production of *Le Coq d'Or* (pl. 15). In the next, she eliminated floral decorative elements, replacing them with "stripes, circles, squares and splashes." The third version, which she described as "clear cool colours with silver and lace, or rather embroideries in silver with rather high hair styles adorned with silver and seed pearls," was a lyrical vision of nature in Russia's north.[5] It was only in the fourth version that resurfacing memories of the "tragedy" of Russian village weddings prompted the monochromatic simplicity of her final designs. In articles describing this progression, Goncharova implied that she had stumbled upon each solution independently or with minimal guidance from Stravinsky, Diaghilev, or Mikhail Larionov. Pointedly, she hardly mentioned the ballet's choreographer, Bronislava Nijinska.

Nijinska, for her part, implied that it was she who deserved credit for the look of *Les*

Mikhail Larionov, portrait of Natalia Goncharova, 1918

Noces. In an account written many years later, she described being overwhelmed by the music when she first heard it in 1922. "At that moment I saw the picture of *Les Noces* and my choreographic line for this ballet." But when Diaghilev took her to see Goncharova's designs, she told him that they did not correspond to the music or to her vision of the ballet, in which all the costumes had to be "both simple and alike." Diaghilev took her off the project, explaining that he and Stravinsky had already approved the designs. Nijinska heard no more about the ballet until the spring of 1923, when Diaghilev informed her of its imminent production and his decision to go ahead with her idea. "And so," Nijinska wrote, "the costumes and sets were created as a direct and whole response to my choreography. . . . Diaghilev was particularly attentive to me in my work at this time, and *Les Noces* was the only ballet in which he allowed the choreographer to have a deciding influence over the entire production."[6]

Although most scholars agree that Nijinska probably was the final arbiter of the "look" of *Les Noces,* the truth undoubtedly lies somewhere between the two accounts. Coming to the project last, Nijinska struggled with it much less than the others. Indeed, she was the only collaborator who knew from the first what she wanted to do and who stuck with her ideas consistently.[7]

Whatever the collaborative scenario, the final result was a synesthetic success. Although in varying degrees the three artists worked independently, *Les Noces* revealed a compelling unity of musical, visual, and choreographic elements.[8] The look of the ballet, with its sculptural and architectural massings, stylized movements from the vocabulary of Russian folk dance, and uniform brown and white costumes inspired by Russian peasant dress, underscored the communal, ritualistic, austere, and mechanistic aspects of both libretto and score.

Initially, Diaghilev had hoped to produce *Les Noces* at the Paris Opéra in 1919. When this didn't happen, he planned to produce it, again at the Opéra, in 1922. We don't really know why his plans fell through each time, but the sequence of events can be pieced together from contracts, correspondence, and telegrams, and Diaghilev's so-called black books, or notebooks.

Three contracts, in various forms of draft, between Diaghilev and Opéra director Jacques Rouché indicate that Diaghilev initially intended to present *Les Noces* in October–November 1919 or May–June 1920. For unknown reasons—which could well include Stravinsky's not having finished the score—this plan fell through sometime after early July 1919. However, as indicated by the signed contract between the two dated 8 October 1921, Diaghilev agreed to produce the ballet at the Opéra during the company's May–June 1922 season. A telegram from Stravinsky to Ansermet on 18 April 1922 confirmed the plan, while also indicating that Stravinsky had worked out the final orchestration and that Diaghilev wanted Ansermet to conduct the premiere.[9]

However, between 21 and 26 April a cryptic series of telegrams and letters between Stravinsky, Diaghilev, Stravinsky's publisher Chester, and Rouché indicate that things were not going well. The implication, corroborated by other evidence, was that rehearsals for the ballet had already begun, but Nijinska was not going to be ready in time. Arrangements were made to replace *Les Noces* with Stravinsky's opera *Mavra*.[10]

So yet again the plans to produce *Les Noces* at the Opéra came to nothing. Several factors were probably at work: Nijinska was not ready; Stravinsky was not as far along with the score as he should have been; Diaghilev was experi-

Stage photograph of the
Kamerny Theater's
production of Phèdre,
1922

encing revenue difficulties, possibly involving Chester; Chester was not ready. A letter
from Chester's Otto Kling to Stravinsky on 25 April asserts that it was not Chester's fault
the ballet could not be produced but Diaghilev's (since the latter had not yet paid for the
piano and vocal scores); Kling also reminded the composer that Chester had yet to receive
the orchestral accompaniment. Numerous and complicated legal tussles over issues of
rights, royalties, contracts, performances, dates, and publishing had occupied the three
since at least 1919; some of the machinations involved Les Noces. The only thing that is clear
is that blame was passed freely around.[11]

But Diaghilev was determined to premiere Les Noces at the Opéra, and he tried
again in 1923: in his black book for the period the ballet is listed as the centerpiece of
performances that were projected as part of a Stravinsky Festival at the Palais Garnier.[12]
(When it became evident that the Ballets Russes would be forced to put on its 1923 season
elsewhere, his notes reflect this.) In addition to what we can assume was his frustration
at the continual postponement of Les Noces's premiere, therefore, was the disappointment
he must have felt when it finally took place at the Gaîté-Lyrique, a far less prestigious

venue. The existence of signed contracts must have made the collapse of his hopes that much more painful.

What sparked Diaghilev finally to mount the work in 1923, even though it meant no Opéra premiere? Although the evidence is unclear, two explanations are likely. In the first place, a contractual agreement signed in late 1922 with the Société des Bains de Mer made the Ballets Russes a six-month resident of the Monte Carlo Opera, an arrangement that helped stabilize Diaghilev's precarious finances. Second, Alexander Tairov's Kamerny Theater, which paid its first visit to Paris on 6–23 March 1923, scored an unexpected success. Performing its avant-garde *Phèdre* (pl. 26), among other pieces, at the Théâtre des Champs-Elysées, the Moscow-based troupe attracted an enthusiastic following of artists and intellectuals, including all the collaborators of *Les Noces*. According to his biographer Arnold Haskell, Diaghilev "did not miss a single performance, watching every detail eagerly and jealously."[13] Diaghilev must have felt that the time was right for *Les Noces*.

If we examine the notebooks of Diaghilev's assistant régisseur Nicolas Kremnev, in the Serge Lifar Papers at the Archives de la Ville de Lausanne, we can try to piece together exactly how the long-delayed premiere came about. These notebooks hold by far the most detailed record of day-to-day life in the Ballets Russes in the years 1922 and 1923. Written in Russian and French, the notes, covering tours as well as the months spent in Monte Carlo, offer a fresh glimpse into the inner workings of the company, including its daily schedule and Diaghilev's rehearsal and programming practices.

Aside from a trip to Paris in early March 1923 for the Kamerny premiere, Nijinska apparently spent the entire spring in Monte Carlo working with the dancers. Stravinsky and Diaghilev, by contrast, shuttled back and forth between Paris and Monte Carlo, while Goncharova seems to have remained mostly, if not entirely, in the French capital. (Among her commissions that winter was the poster for the Bal Travesti, an artists' costume ball held at the Salle Bullier on 23 February; see plate 27.) Unfortunately, the surviving documentation sheds little light either on the order in which the var-

Serge Sudeikin, portrait of Vera Sudeikina, 1920

Felia Doubrovska as the

Bride in Les Noces

ious parts of the ballet were choreographed or on how the collaborative process worked at this stage.

Although we shall probably never know if Nijinska's choreography influenced Stravinsky's final orchestration of *Les Noces* (which he completed in Monte Carlo on 5 May), we do know that rehearsals were under way by 27 March. We know, too, from Stravinsky's letter to Nijinska of that date explaining the reprise in the ballet's opening measures, that she tackled the choreography "from the top" rather than beginning with one of the later scenes. Exactly when Stravinsky arrived in Monte Carlo is unknown, although it is reasonable to assume that he accompanied Vera Sudeikina, his mistress and future wife, who arrived there on 9 April. According to Robert Craft, the role of the Bride was intended for Sudeikina, who had to withdraw because of illness. Vera Rosenstein, in 1993 the only known surviving principal from the original cast, had no memory of Sudeikina's participation in rehearsals, although she vividly recalled Felia Doubrovska, who danced the Bride at the premiere.[14]

According to Serge Lifar, another member of the original cast, the rehearsals were exhausting and difficult, and Diaghilev, a terrifying presence, attended regularly. Lifar wrote vividly of Stravinsky's banging out the rhythms on the piano, although the composer did not (as Lifar asserts) attend every rehearsal:

> Every rehearsal of Les Noces was attended by the composer, Igor Stravinsky, but not by any means as a simple spectator. . . . To begin, he would only indicate roughly what was meant, but soon he was angrily gesticulating, and then, thoroughly aroused, would take off his coat, sit down to the piano and . . . begin singing in a kind of ecstatic, but terrible voice. . . . Often he would go on in this way till he was completely exhausted. . . . [He] infused . . . new life . . . into the rehearsal, and the whole company would start dancing for all it was worth.[15]

Stravinsky's presence at the piano raises a fascinating issue. His dependence on the tactile nature of the instrument as a compositional device is well documented, but his attendance also relates to the sense of his own physicality and his preoccupation with the choreographic aspects of his ballets. It is clear that Stravinsky wished to participate in the rehearsals of his ballets and that Diaghilev encouraged him to do so. It is also clear that he was unusually gifted at conveying the rhythmic and kinesthetic elements of his music, as well as ideas about movement. Still, this is far from being responsible for the ballet's choreographic ideas, as he seemed close to implying in an interview published in L'Excelsior the morning of the premiere.[16]

Although Kremnev's records are of limited usefulness in charting the choreographic development of Les Noces, they tell us a great deal about how the company used its time — where it went, when and what pieces it rehearsed and performed. They also reveal Diaghilev's programming strategies in this period: how he saved his older, less challenging ballets for locales outside Paris while keeping his more daring works for the sophisticated, cosmopolitan audiences of the French capital. They show, for example, that he needed to retrench after the financial reverses brought on by the early London closing of The Sleeping Princess, a difficulty that may also have prompted him to rely on older works while preparing a single new splash — Les Noces — for Paris in 1923.

Jean Cocteau, "Stravinsky Playing Le Sacre du Printemps," 1913

From 27 March to 16 April, the company rehearsed full-time in Monte Carlo. As indicated in Kremnev's notes, *Les Noces* was rehearsed nearly every day, and the intensive rehearsals continued after the four-week Monte Carlo season began on 17 April. The following synthesis of the company's rehearsal and performance schedule from 17 April to 14 May indicates the primacy of *Les Noces* in the schedule.

Tues., 17 April   10–1, rehearsal (*Prince Igor*); afternoon off; evening performance (*Carnaval, Aurora's Wedding, Schéhérazade*)

Wed., 18 April   10–1, 2:30–5, and 9–11, rehearsals (*Prince Igor, Les Noces, Prince Igor* on the stage)

Thurs., 19 April   10–1 and 2:30–5, rehearsals (*Les Noces, Petrouchka, Cléopâtre*); evening performance (*Les Sylphides, Aurora's Wedding, Prince Igor*)

Fri., 20 April   10–1, 2:30–5, and 9–11, rehearsals (*Petrouchka, Les Noces, Le Sacre du Printemps*)

Sat., 21 April   10–1 and 2:30–5, rehearsals (*Petrouchka, Les Noces*); evening performance (*Carnaval, Contes Russes, Schéhérazade*)

Sun., 22 April	Morning off; matinee performance (*Papillons, Aurora's Wedding, Prince Igor*); 9–11, rehearsal (*Cléopâtre, Petrouchka*)
Mon., 23 April	10–12:30, 2:30–5, and 9–11, rehearsals (*Les Noces, Cléopâtre, Petrouchka, Le Sacre du Printemps*)
Tues., 24 April	10–12, rehearsal (*Les Noces, Cléopâtre, Petrouchka*); afternoon off; evening performance (*Les Sylphides, Petrouchka, Prince Igor*)
Wed., 25 April	10–12, 2:30–5, and 9–11, rehearsals (*L'Après-midi d'un Faune, Les Noces, Le Sacre du Printemps*)
Thurs., 26 April	10–1 and 2:30–5, rehearsals (*Les Noces, L'Après-midi d'un Faune*); evening performance (*Papillons, Aurora's Wedding, Le Spectre de la Rose, Prince Igor*)
Fri., 27 April	10–1, 2:30–5, and 9–11, rehearsals (*Les Noces, L'Après-midi d'un Faune, Les Noces*)
Sat., 28 April	10–1 and 2:30–5, rehearsals (*Cléopâtre, Les Noces*); evening performance (*Carnaval, L'Après-midi d'un Faune, Le Spectre de la Rose, Schéhérazade*)
Sun., 29 April	Morning off; matinee performance (*Petrouchka, Les Sylphides, Schéhérazade*); 9–11, rehearsal (*The Good-Humoured Ladies*)
Mon., 30 April	10–12, rehearsal (*Les Noces*); afternoon off; 9–11, rehearsal (*Les Noces*)
Tues., 1 May	10–12, rehearsal (*Les Noces*); afternoon off; evening performance (*Contes Russes, The Good-Humoured Ladies, Cléopâtre*)
Wed., 2 May	10–12, rehearsal (*Les Noces*); afternoon off; 9–11, rehearsal (*Les Noces*)
Thurs., 3 May	10–12 and 2:30–5, rehearsals (*Les Noces, Pulcinella*); evening performance (*Les Sylphides, Petrouchka, Schéhérazade*)
Fri., 4 May	10–12, 2:30–5, and 9–11, rehearsals (*Les Noces, Pulcinella, Les Noces*)
Sat., 5 May	10–12 and 2:30–5, rehearsals (*Les Noces, Le Sacre du Printemps, Les Noces*); evening performance (*The Good-Humoured Ladies, L'Après-midi d'un Faune, Le Spectre de la Rose, Cléopâtre*)
Sun., 6 May	10–12 and 2:30-[?], rehearsals (*Les Noces*); matinee performance (*Papillons, Petrouchka, Contes Russes*); evening off

Mon., 7 May	10–12, rehearsal (*Les Noces*); afternoon off; 9–11, rehearsal (*Les Noces*)
Tues., 8 May	10–12 and 2:30–5, rehearsals (*Les Noces*); evening off
Wed., 9 May	10–12, rehearsal (*Les Noces*); afternoon off; 9–11, rehearsal (*Les Noces*)
Thurs., 10 May	10–12 and 2:30–5[?], rehearsals (*Les Noces*); matinee performance (*Aurora's Wedding, The Good-Humoured Ladies, L'Après-midi d'un Faune, Prince Igor*); evening off
Fri., 11 May	Rehearsals [all day?] (*Les Noces*)
Sat., 12 May	Rehearsals [all day?] (*Les Noces*); evening performance (*Papillons, Contes Russes, Cléopâtre*)
Sun., 13 May	Morning off; matinee performance (*The Good-Humoured Ladies, L'Après-midi d'un Faune, Le Spectre de la Rose, Schéhérazade*); evening off
Mon., 14 May	10–12, rehearsal (*Les Noces*); afternoon off; 9–11, rehearsal (*Les Noces*)

The most impressive thing about this schedule is how hard the dancers worked. The daily norm was either three rehearsals or two rehearsals and a performance. A typical day might include a morning rehearsal from ten to twelve or one, possibly beginning with a class conducted by Nijinska, an afternoon rehearsal from two-thirty to five, and an evening performance at nine. On Sundays, a matinee at three might be followed by an evening rehearsal from nine to eleven. Fridays were usually devoted entirely to rehearsals. Although the dancers had an occasional morning, afternoon, or evening free, they did not have a single full day off during the entire four-week period.

The dancers who brought *Les Noces* to the stage were as dedicated as the artists who "created" it—with less tangible reward. Contracts and payroll sheets, corroborated by the recollections of Vera Rosenstein as well as by Lifar's memoirs, indicate that a typical salary for a member of the corps de ballet was 800 francs a month when the company was performing—enough to live on, so long as the dancers shared rooms at modest boarding houses. During rehearsal periods, however, only half this salary was usually paid. Moreover, the dancers had to provide their own practice clothes, including shoes, and tights for performances. And because their shoe allotment for performances was so meager (one pair for every twelve acts), they typically had to dip into their own funds to buy extra shoes.[17]

Moreover, under the terms of their contracts, the dancers were barred from sup-plementing their income by performing elsewhere. It was a hard life, sustained by the ex-ceptional prestige of the company, by Diaghilev's personal charisma and remarkable pow-ers of command, and possibly by the irregular legal situation of the company's many stateless Russians. A tribe apart, engaged in an undertaking of high importance worthy of sacrifice, the dancers gave Diaghilev the gift of their loyalty and hard work.

After the Monte Carlo season ended on 14 May, the company took a few days' break. This was followed by a brief season in Lyons. The company traveled to Paris on 1 June, performed at the Festival des Narcisses in Montreux on 2 and 3 June, then returned to Paris on 4 June to begin final preparations for the Gaîté-Lyrique season. Consisting of only eight performances, each of which included Les Noces, this began on 13 June.

Conditions did not improve with the company's arrival in Paris. If anything, they deteriorated. Exhausted by the weeks of rehearsals and performances, the dancers had dif-ficulty finding affordable rooms in the hot, crowded, and expensive city. The first night in Paris they slept in the rehearsal room on the top floor of the Gaîté-Lyrique, a "long, bleak room," as Lydia Sokolova remembered it, "with a bar[re] down one side."[18] None of this boded well for the coming season.

According to one observer, Paul Budry, the rehearsals for Les Noces—at least those with musicians that Stravinsky attended—were stormy:

> I see once again those morning rehearsals at the Gaîté Lyrique. Les Noces was mounted in an atmosphere of divorce. Stravinsky had decided to accom-pany his ballet with four solo voices and four pianos. [Georges] Auric, [Francis] Poulenc, Marcelle Meyer, among others, were at the keyboards. [Poulenc did not perform at the premiere.] In the enormous empty, dark hall, this made a shrill, macabre din, traversed with furious and contradic-tory orders, Ansermet in the middle, hardly angry, with the patience of a shepherd.
>
> At the end of the session, everyone talked like Jews and four her-culean men entered: "M'sieurs-dames!" and picked up the four pianos to take them back to Pleyel, while Stravinsky and Ansermet, hanging onto the truck, between the furniture, pursued their pianistic controversy across Paris.[19]

Since Ansermet was familiar with the score, the problems likely arose from the difficulty the musicians were having with Stravinsky's extremely challenging music.

Similarly, despite the weeks of rehearsals in Monte Carlo, the dancers were still struggling with the ballet—with its rhythmic elements and, especially, with the coordination of the music and the choreography. Finally, fed up by their recent travails, they went on strike. Ostensibly, they were demanding higher wages, but exhaustion and frustration must have contributed to their decision as well. The strike was brief. As Lifar recalled:

> About this time our company went on strike for higher wages, and though we all gathered in the Gaîeté-Lyrique, not one of us would begin rehearsing. A little later Diaghilev appeared, easy and confident as ever, and in the presence of us all listened patiently to our collective demands through the mouth of a spokesman, after which, very calmly (though one might guess at a certain nervousness by his pallor) he said:
> "Ladies and gentlemen, you demand the impossible. I take good care of you, you know that, and I do the utmost I can. I know your wages are not sufficient, and should like to be able to increase them, because I value your work; but there are limits that can't be overstepped, if one wishes to preserve our great common cause, which you should love and cherish as much as I do. Calm yourselves, ladies and gentlemen, think it all over and, I beg of you, begin working, we can't afford to miss even a day or an hour." Then, as though detecting some indication of "persuasion" in his words, he stopped short, and ending somewhat dryly, added: "Of course, you are at liberty to do as you please, so whoever feels loath to work may leave the Russian Ballet. Good-by, ladies and gentlemen."
> Whereupon the whole company became aware that it had entered into collision with the wall of Diaghilev's immutable will, impregnable to any of their futile, petty assaults, and immediately began rehearsing.[20]

Although this act of rebellion was quashed by Diaghilev's appeal to the pride and esprit de corps of the dancers—along with his threat of dismissal—it is possible that he used the *audition privée* of the music of *Les Noces*, to which, unusually, the entire company was invited, as a means of reconciling them. Held two days before the premiere at the home of the Princesse Edmond de Polignac, one of Diaghilev's earliest and most generous benefactors, the event offered the dancers a glamorous validation of their work while giving them an opportunity to assimilate what the company's chief régisseur Serge Grigoriev called the ballet's "complicated and unusual score."[21]

The audience for this semiprivate concert was elite and cosmopolitan: it included artists, aristocrats, and Romanovs, as well as several members of Diaghilev's gala patronage committee. Officially, the event was not a performance but, as Jacques Brindejont-

Offenbach noted in the society column of *Le Gaulois*, "the 150th and next-to-last rehearsal
of Stravinsky's new score," a figure that was probably somewhat exaggerated.[22] Lifar described the evening in his biography of Diaghilev:

> Stravinsky was conducting. Round Diaghilev were Nijinska, all our leading
> artists, and the whole musical world of Paris. I sat on the floor, absorbing
> the music and rhythms, and floating away, as it were, into the inner world
> of this ballet. The powerful sounds enthralled me, swept me on, thrilled me
> with their mystery, their timelessness and illimitable space, their wild Rus-
> sian upsurge. . . . Diaghilev looks at us kindly and smiles the smile of a
> great, loving, omniscient father. Princess de Polignac embraces Stravinsky,
> and loads us all with attentions. We, Diaghilev, Stravinsky, the leading ac-
> tors, the *corps de ballet*, are all overwhelmed with a happiness which brings
> us close to each other, and we know our success is assured.[23]

The warm reception in the Polignac salon set the stage for the ballet's more public
triumph.

The Théâtre de la Gaîté-Lyrique was a large Italianate theater that in its heyday had been a temple to light opera and operetta. Although the dancers disliked it (possibly because of its waning reputation), the Gaîté-Lyrique held distinct advantages over the infinitely more prestigious Opéra. As Gérard d'Houville wrote at the close of the season: "The Gaîté's stage is not too big, and nothing is lost there; all the fervor, instead of dispersing, as at the too-vast Opéra, concentrates itself and shoots forth in a flashing blaze; all the forces, all the graces, all the gestures keep all of their details and all of their importance there, contributing to the splendor of the total and magnificent effect!"[24] Nevertheless, it was a big theater, with two thousand seats, and night after night they were filled. Its one drawback was the orchestra pit, which was too small to accommodate the two double pianos needed in Les Noces. Eventually, these instruments were placed on each side of the stage.

That Diaghilev "saved" Les Noces, Le Sacre du Printemps, and Pulcinella for Paris indicates that he considered the city a venue capable of supporting both the expatriate/Russian and cosmopolitan/avant-garde sides of his repertory, as well as works like Les Noces that straddled the two. And these categories were mirrored in the social physiognomy of Diaghilev's audience, as well as in that of Les Noces itself. The production required a huge contingent of artists, both French (pianists Auric and Meyer, conductor Ansermet) and Russian (all the principal singers, Vasily Kibalchich's Russian chorus, and many of the dancers). The double pianos came from the Pleyel Company, the percussion from the Couesnon Company, and the costumes from the firm of Marie Muelle—all representative of the French patrimoine, its cultural and national heritage.

Like the audition privée, the premiere of Les Noces was a social event, a charity gala that raised more than 100,000 francs for several Russian expatriate organizations, including a student group.[25] The patronage committee was extremely cosmopolitan—more so, even, than the audience of the audition privée. It was headed by Grand Duchess Marie, one of the most illustrious members of the Russian émigré community. In the audience sat the rich, famous, talented, and titled—a glittering cross-section of that international high society that made Paris a mecca during les années folles.

We know little about the debut performance itself. The artists involved have left few comments, although Grigoriev contended that, on the whole "its success was far greater than we had expected. It even reminded us of our triumphs of 1909. All eight performances were received with equal enthusiasm. . . . Diaghilev was delighted with this ballet and its triumph; and thenceforward Nijinska was known as 'La Nijinska.'" Lifar noted that after the audition privée the dancers gained in confidence, convinced that their success was assured. On opening night, he added, "after *Les Noces* some of the audience begin hissing, but only to be drowned by the applause, which goes on increasing until it becomes a veritable ovation."[26] We also know that there was talk by reviewers—who repeatedly mentioned the audience's rapturous response—of extending the sold-out Ballets Russes season. But this did not happen. Still, it appears that once *Les Noces* finally made it to the stage, it was a success, delighting artists and audiences alike.

The critical response was generally positive as well, both to the season as a whole and to *Les Noces* in particular. Of the ballet's three collaborators, Stravinsky came in for the greatest censure, with many writers objecting to what they saw as his exploitation of novel effects for their own sake; nonetheless, nearly everyone agreed that his music was the most important and original being written at the time. Nijinska's choreography was generally praised. The groupings, architectural effects, and mimetic elements were most often singled out, although critics disagreed as to whether the choreography worked with the music. Goncharova's designs were thought to enhance the music and choreography, and the "austerity" of the "black and white" costumes was fre-

The Sketch's *view of six women dancers in* Le Sacre du Printemps, *1913*

quently noted. (Oddly, not a single reviewer accurately described the colors as brown and off-white.)

The ballet was most often compared to *Le Sacre du Printemps*, but the comparisons themselves differed substantially. Some critics believed that *Les Noces* was a logical extension of ideas first explored in *Sacre*. Although a few comments attested to the perception that *Les Noces* was anachronistic (Stravinsky's long compositional period was duly noted), this was not the general view, and, in spite of the implied similarities, *Les Noces* was essentially considered a new work. *Sacre* evoked an imagery of savagery and barbarity, which was complemented in *Noces* by references to mechanization and impersonality, showing the synthesis in the latter work between the "old" exotic primitivism and the "new" technological neoclassicism of 1923. As Emile Vuillermoz wrote in *L'Excelsior*:

> The only thing he [Stravinsky] needs, in order to create his special pathos, is a solid machine with which to forge lovely accents, a machine to hit, a machine to lash, a machine to fabricate automatic resonances. His genius resides in the organization of the rhythmic puffing of this sonorous factory, a puffing so new, so strong, so precise, which dominates you, which carries you along, which subjects you to its fantasy without a reviving break.
>
> What good does it serve to burden oneself with the fragile and nuanced timbres of a flute, an oboe, or a viola in order to drive in these repeated blows, these organic shocks whose return is so knowingly calculated and which owe nothing to the out-of-date material of old harmonic and contrapuntal writing? The metallic groan of the four skillfully illtreated pianos, the hallucinating cry of the castanets whipped at every blow, the rippling of the xylophone, and the muffled detonations of kettledrums surround the melodies and the cries of the singers with a rhythmic atmosphere which is marvelously exact and sharp.[27]

Vuillermoz went on to describe the stage as "a vast cinematographic screen," the dancers as "synthetic marionettes," the wedding as "mechanical, machine-like," and the orchestra as "the forge where one sees the great blacksmith Ansermet brandish his menacing fists in order to bend all of his workers on their anvils!" But he also mentioned the score's "savage and barbarous exaltation," which, like the terms "organic" and "hallucinating," underscored the link between the primitive and the mechanical.

Raymond Charpentier, writing in *Comoedia* on 16 June, noted how Stravinsky joined irreconcilables: "That the most illustrious representative of contemporary Russian art, a master of sounds, possesses a thousand excellent recipes and special manufacturing secrets, no one would know how to deny that now. One also accepts of him, even with eagerness, that he profits from his virtuosity in order to try to join even irreconcilables: the noise of music, the primitive and civilization, by the magic of rhythm and the sovereign intervention of science—in this case, 'the writing.' "[28] This recognition of the melding of "primitive" and "civilized" was the most significant feature of the response to Les Noces. The critics had astutely pinpointed the two elements of Les Noces that even today reveal it clearly as a product of the early 1920s.

Writing in L'Eclair, Roland Manuel described the fatalistic characters of Les Noces as "schematized, living expressions of the inexorable mechanism which rules the actions of men, even to their loves. . . . Under the surveillance of the chief engineer Ansermet, . . . the machines from the Stravinsky factory obtain, in Les Noces, an output which surpasses the most optimistic forecasts."[29] Anticipating what would come to be known as neoclassicism, he noted that the "particular romanticism of Sacre gives way to a kind of grand stripped-down classicism, which clearly valorizes an orchestral make-up whose simplicity is extremely bold."

Perhaps the most illuminating reviews were the three by the émigré dance critic André Levinson. Though strongly negative, they must be treated seriously because of their insightfulness and the author's unique perspective: he had lived in Soviet Russia. In his 16 June review in Comoedia, Levinson highlighted Goncharova's austerity, "as excessive [here] as was the voluptuousness of orgiastic color not long ago." He was less tolerant of the choreography, using descriptions like "stadium," "parade-ground," "mechanical reproduction of rhythm," "spirit possession," and "soldiers at the rifle-range." He criticized the ballet's architectural elements as static arrangements of "regimented and mechanized personnel" and called Nijinska a "pedantic and stubborn vampire," likening her style to that of Dalcroze eurhythmics, one of his bêtes noires.[30]

Two days later in the same daily, Levinson mounted a general attack on the Ballets Russes. This time he announced that Les Noces should be given only as a concert work, referred to the choreography as Marxist, and declared that Nijinska had "passed through the collectivist reveries of the Soviets and the Swiss theories of physical culture"—another reference to Dalcroze. Most significantly, he claimed that the innate Russianness of the work was diminished by its visual elements.[31]

In a review published in an unidentified émigré newspaper, Levinson returned to these themes.[32] But he also expanded on points calculated to appeal to Russian readers. Thus he wrote that the wedding ritual "represents the solemn and austere reality of the Russian heart"; in the "pulsation of the wedding games and calls one can hear the mag-

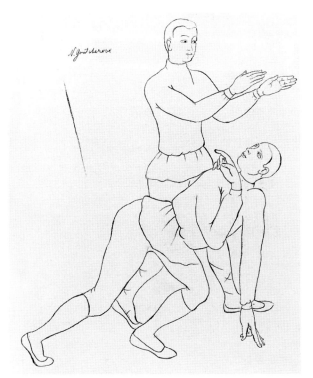

nificent breathing of our land." With respect to the music, he noted a "heightened spiritual state of being" that had been "partially overlooked by the French critics." Moving to the text of *Les Noces*, Levinson asserted that not even Mussorgsky—a master of prosody—had so effectively embodied the "natural rhythm and intonation of Russian popular speech": "Not only the Russian heart is embodied in the melos of these 'choreographical scenes,' but the genius of Russian language as well."

Levinson's French reviews had mentioned the ballet's "mechanical reproduction of rhythm" and debt to Dalcroze and "rhythmic gymnastics." But it was only in this Russian essay that he linked these phenomena to manifestations of the Soviet avant-garde—the Kamerny Theater, constructivism, the "Soviet 'mass' theater," among others. An "entire Red army division [seems] to be involved in the show as well as crowds of working-class people," he wrote at one point. At another, he claimed that the ballet's "automatized motions (the so-called 'biomechanics' of Meyerhold) make such choreography look like machinery: mechanical, utilitarian, industrial. It seems like electrification applied to ballet." At the same time, Levinson allied the ballet with overarching themes—the Russian soul, the genius of the Russian language, peasant masses, Mother Russia—characteristic of prerevolutionary opera and literature. In linking this Russian past with the Soviet present, Levinson, perhaps without realizing it, echoed both the dualism present in French criticism of *Les Noces* and tensions in the ballet itself. These tensions—between primitivism and mechanization, exoticism and neoclassicism, Russianness and cosmopolitanism, Soviet and émigré—may have placed the work squarely in 1923, but they also give it the energy that appeals to audiences today. The ability of *Les Noces* to negotiate so many different boundaries, to stand for so many different things, accounts in no small measure for its timely, as well as timeless success.

ten Diaghilev and Stravinsky

Charles M. Joseph

Diaghilev's tangled relationship with Igor Stravinsky—two larger-than-life personalities locked in a twenty-year struggle over money and power—easily has the makings of a romantic novel. Diaghilev was a jumble of unlikable personal traits. He could be utterly malicious in his treatment of friends. It took little to infuriate the quixotic impresario, and when crossed, he unhesitatingly sought vengeance against those foolhardy enough to question him. For Stravinsky, a similar description obtained. Countless pages dissect Stravinsky and Diaghilev's often antagonistic yet immensely productive association. We have become obsessed with the acrimony of their remarks, their obduracy over finances, their intransigence in quarreling over every artistic issue.

Both were bullheaded and inflexible, refusing to speak to each other for periods that

Serge Diaghilev and Igor Stravinsky, Beausoleil, 1911. The figure in the background is General Bezobrazov, a well-known St. Petersburg balletomane and sometime member of Diaghilev's circle.

sometimes extended to years. Stravinsky's correspondence, much of which remains unpublished or has been editorially sanitized, is astonishingly cruel in its criticism of Diaghilev. As was the composer's habit, he did not address his venomous remarks to Diaghilev directly but expressed them in letters to friends. The rhetoric in this correspondence steadily escalates in vituperation over the years, at first questioning Diaghilev's moral integrity, then accusing him of duplicity, and finally disparaging him as no more than a common swine. Diaghilev was no less coarse, crassly complaining that Stravinsky's interests began and ended with money. He impugned the composer's loyalty to the Ballets Russes and resented Stravinsky's readiness to deal with anyone willing to pay his price. On more than one occasion he openly chastised the composer for his preoccupation, even obsession, with money. Stravinsky, in response, would order Diaghilev to compensate him immediately for services rendered, otherwise he would refuse to complete a composition already in progress. Diaghilev, in turn, would balk, imploring the composer to be reasonable and at least somewhat flexible. And so the wrangling continued for years.[1]

All through those years, however, Stravinsky continued to move freely in Diaghilev's world. He worked closely with many members of the Ballets Russes, forming friendships, influencing trends, manipulating agendas, and sometimes competing with Diaghilev himself for the upper hand in dealing with dancers, artists, designers, choreographers, and even other composers. With remarkable swiftness, the self-assured, "imperial" Stravinsky, as Nijinsky characterized him, became a formidable presence in Diaghilev's oligarchy, as well as a constant irritant.

To appreciate the full complexity of the Diaghilev-Stravinsky relationship, one must turn to unpublished letters, Stravinsky's compositional sketches and drafts (particularly those—and there are many—exhibiting a sensitivity to choreographic concerns), and, perhaps most unexpectedly, the numerous cans of invaluable footage trimmed from several television documentaries about Stravinsky. Dating from the 1950s through the 1980s, these films include interviews with a number of Diaghilev familiars, including George Balanchine, Tamara Geva, Boris Kochno, Serge Lifar, Igor Markevitch, Alicia Markova, and Marie Rambert. Particularly important is Tony Palmer's documentary *Aspects of Stravinsky*. Made for London Weekend Television in 1982, it is undoubtedly the most extensive film record of the composer's life.

Palmer's biopic, first shown at the 1982 San Diego International Stravinsky Symposium marking the centenary of the composer's birth, attempted to cover the whole of Stravinsky's life. Palmer interviewed many Ballets Russes veterans (in a number of cases this was their last interview on film), although owing to time constraints, a good 90 percent of their remarks were cut.[2] With these collective sources (along with the composer's own archives) now available for consultation at the Paul Sacher Stiftung in Basel, we are able to test purported truths, verify or reject long-held assumptions, and even broaden the discussion of this amazingly fertile period in twentieth-century music and dance. From these combined materials, a sharper portrait of Stravinsky's interactions with the Ballets Russes emerges. The particulars of that portrait begin with Diaghilev's "discovery" of Stravinsky at the dawn of the Ballets Russes. The early years of their relationship are worth briefly retracing.

The Ballets Russes was the catapult for Igor Stravinsky's sudden and phenomenal success. It was Diaghilev, of course, who sprang the switch, launching the young composer, as he launched so many others. Certainly, without Diaghilev's intercession, Stravinsky's meteoric rise to international celebrity might never have occurred. Some contend that *Firebird* (1910), though not particularly innovative in its musical vision, signaled

*Igor Stravinsky, 1912.
This is the last known
photograph of the
composer before he left
Russia.*

Stravinsky's ability to match Michel Fokine and Diaghilev as a purveyor of "orientalism" through his successful collaboration in the retelling of this familiar story. Others note that *Petrouchka* (1911), although historically inseparable from Nijinsky's haunting portrayal, represents the true turning point in Stravinsky's compositional progression—a genuine musical leap extricating the ambitious composer from nationalistic strictures that others were unwilling or unable to abandon. Finally, who could argue with Pierre Boulez's anointing of *Le Sacre du Printemps* (1913) as the genuine "birth certificate" of modernism, a work so familiar from virtually every aesthetic perspective that its status appears self-evident? Although some music scholars have methodically searched for seeds of greatness in Stravinsky's pre-Diaghilev works, the truth is that Rimsky-Korsakov's young student was hardly headed toward an auspicious career, let alone one that would ultimately redefine the boundaries of music. With *Petrouchka* and *Sacre*, Diaghilev and Stravinsky compelled the youthful century to rethink its preconceptions not only about music but also about how music and ballet were partnered.

It was in 1909, on the eve of his first Paris ballet season, that Diaghilev heard Stravinsky's *Scherzo fantastique* and came away impressed by his potential usefulness. Appreciating Stravinsky's flair for instrumental color, Diaghilev invited the composer to re-orchestrate the opening and closing Chopin waltzes of *Chopiniana*, the ballet by Michel Fokine that Diaghilev would present during the coming Paris season as *Les Sylphides*. Although young and unknown, Stravinsky was by no means naive: he instantly understood the opportunities to be seized from collaborating with Diaghilev on his exciting new venture. Shortly after completing this compositional audition, the twenty-eight-year-old composer was invited by Diaghilev to write the music for what would become his most familiar score: *Firebird*. Stravinsky was not Diaghilev's first choice, nor, when Anatoly Liadov failed to deliver the score, even his second. In fact, as Richard Taruskin has convincingly demonstrated, he was closer to a last resort.[3]

Firebird was Stravinsky's rite of passage as a ballet composer. He worked closely with Fokine, the ballet's choreographer (although his contribution to the scenario was minimal), a fact that in later life annoyed him extremely. Stravinsky's autobiography attests to the closeness of the collaboration: "Fokine created the choreography of *L'Oiseau de feu* section by section," he wrote, "as the music was handed to him. I attended every rehearsal." Fokine's memoirs offer further corroboration: "I have staged many ballets since *The Firebird,* but never again, either with Stravinsky or any other composer, did I work so closely as on this occasion. . . . I did not wait for the composer to give me the finished music. Stravinsky visited me with his first sketches and basic ideas, he played them for me, I demonstrated the scenes to him. At my request, he broke up his national themes into short phrases corresponding to the separate moments of a scene, separate gestures and poses."[4]

Stravinsky's compositional sketches at the Pierpont Morgan Library confirm these memories.[5] There is an abundance of specific annotations regarding tempi, how long notes should be stretched, which passages to stress, accents, the dynamics of loudness and softness, and similar performance details. They are particularly evident in the piano score that Stravinsky probably used in rehearsal (even piano fingerings are inserted, demonstrating that Stravinsky worked out his own performance of the piano reduction carefully —something he regularly did in all the piano scores for his ballets).

It is also clear that the composer dutifully followed Fokine's directions throughout their collaboration. Numerous musical passages—some quite extended—are crossed out, rewritten, or transferred to other sections of the ballet. From a purely musical viewpoint, these changes reflect Fokine's choreographic conception, for compositionally they functioned well as they were originally written. In other words, if Fokine needed more or less time to embellish the scenario, Stravinsky accommodated him, deleting or expanding a few measures. Especially revealing is their collaboration on the sparkling Infernal Dance of Kostchei, where music is cut, rewritten, and reinserted at a number of different points. The struggle to find the right pacing is evident, although in the end Stravinsky was disappointed with Fokine's staging. He was also unhappy with certain ineffectual passages written at Fokine's request—filler that undercut the power of the music. In an unpublished letter to his older son Theodore written in 1945, Stravinsky reiterated his reservations about the original production: Fokine, he says, forced him to write "too much music expressly for useless pantomime."

All too quickly, Stravinsky turned against his first choreographic tutor. Even as *Petrouchka*, their second collaboration, unfolded, the relationship between the two deteriorated. As early as 1912, in a letter to his mother, Stravinsky described Fokine as evil and greedy, a once-progressive artist who now had nothing new to say. Over the course of his life, Stravinsky's opinion did not change. He complained of Fokine's offensive manner, suggesting that of all his collaborators Fokine was by far the most unpleasant and boorish. Years after the choreographer's death, Stravinsky still bristled at the memory of Fokine casually dismissing the *Firebird*'s score as nothing more than a necessary accompaniment to his much more important and memorable choreography. And with outlandish but, alas, typical revisionism, Stravinsky added that it was at his behest that Diaghilev had assigned the ballet to Fokine in the first place, implying that he, Stravinsky, was already, at that early juncture, part of Diaghilev's inner circle.

Stravinsky's relationship with Nijinsky was even more complex and typically duplicitous. Indeed, as the Russian dance historian Vera Krasovskaya told Palmer, Stravinsky initially wanted Fokine to "stage" *Sacre*, although when Diaghilev gave the assignment to Nijinsky, the composer was "delighted." This would tend to support Stravinsky's claim, as reported by Stravinsky's assistant Robert Craft in a recent essay, that "Fokine had to some extent blocked out the remainder of the ballet before Nijinsky superseded him in June 1912."[6] Moreover, there is little question that Stravinsky, privately at least, admired Nijinsky's abilities as a choreographer, although his later remarks suggest that he was unhappy with certain aspects of the ballet's staging. Whatever his true feelings at the time of their partnership, the composer expressed genuine concern for the troubled dancer's welfare. One finds numerous poignant unpublished telegrams at the Sacher Stiftung in which Stravinsky arranges diversions with Nijinsky, accompanies him to the zoo, and expresses concern for his welfare. In contrast, Nijinsky's daughter Kyra told Palmer (in another ex-

Nijinsky, as
photographed by Igor
Stravinsky, Monte Carlo,
1911

cised segment) that her father believed that Stravinsky blamed him for ruining the ballet, almost certainly a response to the composer's later and often caustic criticism of the dancer's ideas. That Stravinsky was more pleased with Léonide Massine's revival in 1920 is a matter of public record, and his private papers do indeed confirm that his respect for Massine, both in restaging *Sacre* and in their other collaborations, was genuine. Moreover, documents in the Sacher Stiftung dispel the long-promulgated fiction that after Massine's production the composer lost interest in restaging the ballet. Not only did Stravinsky discuss the possibility with Balanchine, but he also weighed a proposal from Jerome Robbins in 1960 to stage the work at Copenhagen's Royal Theater, an offer Stravinsky reluctantly declined because the orchestra pit was too small.[7]

Retracing the evolution of *Sacre* has occupied musicologists as well as dance historians. In reconstructing the collaboration of composer and choreographer, Craft's essay "The Stravinsky-Nijinsky Choreography" (an appendix to the 1969 facsimile reproduction of Stravinsky's sketches for *Sacre*) is as revealing as the musical sketches for *Firebird*.[8] Stravinsky's notes are both copious and exacting. In the four-hand rehearsal score for *Sacre*, for example, the composer provides, in astonishing detail, precise directions for the dancers. He specifies where certain movements are to begin, how groups are to be divided, the direction they should move, how a dancer should "twirl" at a certain point in the action. In another spot he scribbles on the score what the dancers should be doing for a certain number of measures and how those measures should be counted. He directs Nijinsky to take charge and keep count for the ensemble. Clearly, the composer expected the dancers to maintain the recurring beats steadily as the hitherto unheard-of rhythms unfolded in the complicated score (recalling the scene, as described by Stravinsky and others, of Nijinsky in the wings pounding out the rhythms). Yet elsewhere in the score Stravinsky admonishes the dancers not even to attempt to count the beats. There are hundreds of such instructions, demonstrating that Stravinsky had a far greater say in the stage action of *Sacre* than of *Firebird*.

After Nijinsky's death, Stravinsky's memories tended to focus less on their collaboration than on Nijinsky's personal troubles—a topic that interested the general public and was thus, as Stravinsky quickly perceived, marketable. In preparing a draft for one of his so-called conversation books, Stravinsky spoke in some detail about Nijinsky and his family, specifically about their mental and physical problems. He went so far as to quote Diaghilev's contention that the entire Nijinsky family was syphilitic. Unpublished documents in the Sacher Stiftung reveal that when Nijinsky's widow, Romola, read the proofs, she protested through her attorney that such remarks were false, and she threatened litigation unless revisions were made. In his reply a few weeks later, Stravinsky argued that the overall content of his remarks was now "far more friendly and fair"—"a retribution for my remarks about [Nijinsky] in my *Autobiography*."

By the time Stravinksy came to write *Apollon Musagète* (later *Apollo*) in the late 1920s, he had become an even more formidable presence in the ballet world, and not only did he stop deferring to choreographers, he took on Diaghilev himself. A major point of contention between the two was Diaghilev's highhanded decision to ax the whole of the variation Balanchine had choreographed for Terpsichore, a role created for Balanchine's muse Alexandra Danilova. (Unlike Stravinsky, however, Balanchine did not have sufficient clout to argue when Diaghilev put in Alice Nikitina instead.) Tamara Geva, Balanchine's wife during his early years with the Ballets Russes, recalled the episode in an excised segment from her interview with Palmer:

> One of the variations in *Apollo* was not to Diaghilev's taste. He thought it was too long, too repetitious. . . . He told George that the variation was no good, and that he didn't like the music. George said, "It is your dancer that isn't good." (It was [Alice] Nikitina.) George wouldn't change the variation, so Diaghilev took it out. One day, in Covent Garden, just before the performance of *Apollo*, Diaghilev rushed in looking for George . . . in such a state of fear that George said he was trembling. . . . "Put the variation in quickly. . . . Stravinsky is in the audience." So George had to grab the lady who was dancing Terpsichore and quickly rehearse her just before she went on stage. That shows you . . . the relationship between Diaghilev and Balanchine, and who was the boss.

It also said something about Diaghilev's relationship with the composer. For Stravinsky there was no more explosive issue than cuts. It led to his estrangement in the late 1930s from his old friend Ernest Ansermet (after the conductor suggested pruning certain passages from *Jeu de Cartes*) and was a precipitating factor in his final break with Diaghilev. For Diaghilev, cuts were one of the most effective ways of controlling composers. As the composer Nicolas Nabokov remarked: "Few things seemed to give Diaghilev more pleasure than to make cuts in a new score; it was kind of a delightful ritual with him." To this rite he brought considerable knowledge and a surgeon's scalpel. He unhesitatingly marked passages of Stravinsky's scores for excision. This matter of "cuts" had long been

a sticking point in Diaghilev and Stravinsky's relationship. As early as 1916 Diaghilev ordered Stravinsky to eliminate several sections of *Le Rossignol*, feeling that the stage action would improve as a consequence. He was not shy in identifying the exact measures to delete in a particular passage. Nor was he reluctant to dictate, with *ex cathedra* authority, that a certain section needed to be revised or that music must be added to improve the dramatic action on stage. And anticipating the composer's likely reaction, the shrewdly perceptive Diaghilev could peremptorily add: "And there is no reason for anyone to go off into a temper about this! I am a man of the theater and not, thank God, a composer." Nor did Diaghilev's attitude change over the years, even though Stravinsky's masterful compositional skills (leaving aside his well-established reputation) needed no editorial help. Stravinsky's continuing complaints about Diaghilev's unthinkable interventions often boiled over in letters to Ansermet and others.[9]

In another television interview that ended up on the cutting-room floor, Serge Lifar, who created the ballet's title role, claimed that Diaghilev found Stravinsky's music for *Apollo* "just tolerable," an opinion that is probably closer to the truth than generally acknowledged. Although Diaghilev lauded *Apollo* in public, privately he resented Stravinsky's acceptance of Elizabeth Sprague Coolidge's commission. The ballet premiered at the Library of Congress with choreography by Adolph Bolm six weeks before it was first presented in Paris with Balanchine's. Yet even though Coolidge funded Stravinsky's writing of the work, the composer intended *Apollo* from the start for the Ballets Russes. While the work was being composed, Diaghilev, Lifar, Kochno, and Balanchine were contributing to its progress. In a segment deleted from the Palmer documentary, Soulima Stravinsky, the composer's younger son, recalled many conferences around the Stravinsky kitchen table in Nice during early 1928 to discuss the evolution of the ballet (even as Bolm, an ocean away, was left in the dark until almost the last moment). "I remember when Father was composing *Apollo*, he played for Diaghilev as he was composing what he had already achieved and asked me to help him play [since] he couldn't grasp all the notes of the score."

The rough sketches for *Apollo*, now in Basel, strongly suggest that Stravinsky initially planned an additional variation either for one of the three muses who ultimately appeared in the scenario or possibly for a fourth muse. Indeed, several pages of compositional sketches survive for what appears to be a variation that never materialized. The music simply disappeared. This is highly unusual, for Stravinsky seldom left any music unused. Ever frugal, he was far more likely to rework his sketches, incorporating virtually every scrap of music into other sections of a work. Such transformations appear repeatedly in the sketches not only for *Apollo* but also for *Jeu de Cartes, Orpheus,* and *Agon.* Even if at first he did not know where the music would work best, he almost always made room for whatever he had composed. Why then in *Apollo* did he completely abandon this "lost" variation, whose compositional notations appear rather late in the sketches themselves? Could it be that Diaghilev's need to control the length and content of the ballet for the Paris premiere in some way influenced Stravinsky's original compositional plan? For although Stravinsky was

Alexandra Danilova, late 1920s

unwilling to have others tamper with his music once it was completed, he was amenable to discussing the overall shape of a work before or during its composition.

Diaghilev's way of exercising authority—"without appeal and without discussion," in Lifar's words—also perturbed Stravinsky. Ten years Diaghilev's junior and himself notoriously abrasive, how did he function within Diaghilev's tightly controlled kingdom? Was he capable of the kind of compromise—let alone outright submission—that Diaghilev expected of company members and associates? Conversely, how did the overbearing Diaghilev, well aware of his role in plucking Stravinsky from obscurity, deal with an equally supercilious composer who became increasingly demanding and querulous as his fame grew? As Lifar and others affirm, Diaghilev and Stravinsky were constantly testing one another, vying with each other for control. Stravinsky's typical approach to confrontation was to walk away, dismissing whatever conflicts existed as unworthy of his time while privately fuming over how unjustly he had been treated.

Although much of his antipathy toward Diaghilev arose from the conviction that he had been persistently cheated of his rightful royalties, even more vexatious was Stravinsky's feeling that Diaghilev treated him shabbily, without the deference a composer of his reputation deserved. And as Lifar suggests in another excised film clip, Stravinsky was especially sensitive to being viewed by Diaghilev as yet another of his "serfs." Stravinsky was easily offended and would toss off criticism with an indifference (as his archives demonstrate) that was completely feigned. He frequently grumbled bitterly that Diaghilev's statements about him should be viewed as suspicious and untrustworthy. He dismissed Diaghilev as an unimportant figure in his life, one whose friendship he neither needed nor relied upon in making his mark. His rage, and surely his hurt, sometimes surfaced more menacingly, as when he threatened personal reprisal by declining further collaborations in the face of what the composer estimated to be Diaghilev's waning fortunes. The need to retaliate was clearly part of each man's character.

But though Diaghilev may have considered Stravinsky merely one of many capable composers pressed into service for the Ballets Russes, others closely identified Stravinsky with the company and its aesthetic. After Diaghilev's death in 1929, many of Stravinsky's friends assured him that the very existence of the Ballets Russes had been entirely dependent upon the composer's contributions. Indeed, some have wondered whether Diaghilev's always financially precarious enterprise could have continued over its two decades without the blockbuster ballet scores that Stravinsky provided, upon which the company, musically at least, built its international reputation. Whether such an assessment is inflated is less important than the fact that Stravinsky himself believed it. Surely this is why he often secretly negotiated commissions independent of the Ballets Russes, going so far as to ask his friends to conceal from the "ringmaster," as he referred to Diaghilev, his efforts to secure work elsewhere, especially in America. Even after patching up his differences with Diaghilev in 1920, Stravinsky continued to seek commissions whenever he could. In fact, the composer's final rupture with Diaghilev came about when Ida Rubinstein offered him a new ballet, *Le Baiser de la Fée* (1928), and Stravinsky accepted with alacrity.

Stravinsky was not the only one to find Diaghilev's artistic acumen a point of contention; Balanchine had differences with his mentor as well. In fact, Balanchine and Stravinsky bonded, at least in part, because neither of them ever completely trusted Diaghilev and each resented Diaghilev's unwillingness to acknowledge his gifts. Pierre Suvchinsky, one of Stravinsky's closest friends, contended that Diaghilev never really recognized Stravinsky's genius, although he did wonder whether Diaghilev simply refused to concede it out of obstinacy. As for Balanchine, the young and confident choreographer (in many ways as defiant and cocksure as Stravinsky) was not about to stand by passively while Diaghilev labeled his work "stupid." According to Geva, Diaghilev and the choreographer clashed from the start. One conflict centered on Balanchine's superior musicianship. "Diaghilev considered himself a great musician," she told Palmer, "and then he met George who [was] a better musician. That took a bit of wind out of Diaghilev's sails. Diaghilev always mixed his emotionalism, his personal life, with the person he promoted. . . . George . . . was not emotionally connected to Diaghilev." Not only did Balanchine question Diaghilev's understanding of music, just as Stravinsky had, but both recognized that Diaghilev's decisions were often sexually colored. As Balanchine confided to Robert Craft fifty years after *Apollo*'s premiere: "Nobody will believe me of course, but Diaghilev did not know anything about dancing. His real interest in ballet was sexual. He could not bear the sight of Danilova and would say to me, 'Her tits make me want to vomit.' Once when I was standing next to him at a rehearsal for *Apollo*, he said 'How beautiful.' I agreed, thinking that he was referring to the music, but he quickly corrected me: 'No, no. I mean Lifar's ass; it is like a rose.'"[10]

The clashes between Stravinsky and Diaghilev were as often the result of their similarities, however, as of their differences. Like Diaghilev, Stravinsky expected fealty

from those around him. Stravinsky was particularly jealous of composers who caught Diaghilev's eye and suspicious of music that he knew was equal to his own. Diaghilev's 1929 production of *Prodigal Son*, with a wonderful score by Prokofiev (whose relationship with Stravinsky was less than friendly, given their competitive natures and opposing politics), was difficult for Stravinsky to swallow—especially because a decade earlier Diaghilev had relied on Stravinsky to "fix" one of Prokofiev's early ballet scores. Stravinsky continued to see himself as an indispensable component of the Ballets Russes, all the while professing that he didn't need the company (even, in the early 1920s, casting aspersions on the legitimacy of ballet as an art form). Yet one need only examine the Ballets Russes souvenir programs over the years to see how prominently Stravinsky was touted as the marquee composer. As his numerous portraits in company programs attest, Stravinsky, far more than any other composer, was given top billing, despite Diaghilev's unwillingness to concede his importance. And although the composer loudly declared his indifference to productions that did not include him, he kept close watch on them, even after he and Diaghilev had severed relations completely. "Don't speak of [Diaghilev]," Stravinsky told pianist Arthur Rubinstein. "He is only out to '*épater son public.*' He produces ballets by Auric and Poulenc and God knows who else."[11]

Tamara Geva in Zéphyr et Flore, 1925. She is holding one of Oliver Messel's masks.

The bitterness of those final years was exacerbated by Diaghilev's sponsorship of a promising young protégé. Igor Markevitch, born in 1912 in Kiev, had quickly joined the ranks of Nadia Boulanger's "super-children," as Léonie Rosenstiel calls them in her biography of the famous pedagogue. As with her other prodigies, Boulanger actively pushed Markevitch's career, and before he was out of his teens his music was being played everywhere, even in the salon of the Princesse Edmond de Polignac—for Stravinsky an inner sanctum, where several of his own works had been introduced.

At the same time, the seventeen-year-old wunderkind became Diaghilev's close companion during these, the final months of his life. Like Boulanger, Diaghilev actively promoted Markevitch's first compositions, including his Sinfonietta (written in 1928, the same year as *Apollo*) and, especially, his Piano Concerto. Inevitably, the two Igors were compared. Writes Rosenstiel: "A new shining star, Igor Markevitch, had joined Stravinsky in Nadia's Russian émigré pantheon. She fervently believed in Markevitch's not inconsiderable talent, but she was also much impressed by his aristocratic origins."[12] The old Igor was being replaced by "the little Igor"—a message that was not lost on Stravinsky. Diaghilev praised Markevitch's talent as the "indubitable birth of a new generation of composers." Stravinsky was by now embittered by Diaghilev's every action, and the fact that his own son, Soulima, was also studying with Boulanger can only have added to his anger.

Against the advice of less partial observers, Diaghilev even introduced Markevitch's still studentish music to London during the company's final season there. As régisseur Serge Grigoriev observed: "I feel sure that Diaghilev half realized at least that it was too soon as yet for Markevitch to make his debut. But Diaghilev was impatient by nature and he could not endure any delay before showing the world his latest find; moreover, to perform at Covent Garden with the Diaghilev Ballet was an opportunity for Markevitch which might not recur."[13]

With undisguised bitterness, Diaghilev's former lover Lifar recalled Diaghilev's infatuation with Markevitch. "It was because of

Christian Bérard, portrait of Igor Markevitch, 1929

this encounter that Diaghilev died at fifty-seven," he asserted to Palmer. Ignoring his physician's advice and his own deteriorating health (he was suffering from diabetes), Diaghilev went off to Salzburg, Baden-Baden, and Munich, introducing the young composer to operas by Mozart, Strauss, and Wagner—everything from *Don Giovanni* to *Tristan*. He doted on him, while Markevitch eagerly imbibed Diaghilev's aristocratic tastes and wide-ranging knowledge. How different this was from Diaghilev's efforts to "educate" Balanchine in Italy five years earlier—attempts Balanchine brashly resisted. Lifar told Palmer that toward the end of his life Diaghilev spoke of his three musical "children": "First was Stravinsky, second was Prokofiev, and third was to be Nabokov, but he failed, so [Diaghilev] took on Markevitch."

His London debut notwithstanding, the French journals and newspapers of the late 1920s sang Markevitch's praises, proclaiming (much to Stravinsky's annoyance) that Markevitch was the most extraordinary talent since Stravinsky. *Le Monde musical*'s coronation of Markevitch as "the new Igor" was surely the coup de grâce. Little is known about Markevitch's first attempt for the stage, a virtually forgotten ballet completed in 1928 to a libretto by Kochno entitled *L'Habit du Roi*. His second ballet, *Rébus*, was composed in 1931, and in fact Stravinsky attended a concert performance of it on 15 December at the Salle Gaveau. The older composer's opinion of the young musician was, perhaps predictably, less than laudatory, and he was quick to take exception to those who saw remarkable promise in Markevitch's blossoming career. Certainly he was not about to concede Markevitch anything other than a modicum of talent and nothing close to the wunderkind title being applied more and more to the new Igor. But one wonders what choice Stravinsky had other than to offer a cool opinion, especially given Diaghilev's flamboyant—and to Stravinsky's way of thinking, unfounded—sponsorship of the young composer. Stravinsky's opinion aside, Markevitch's third ballet, *L'Envoi d'Icare*, written in 1933, represented a new level of maturity. Even though Lifar pronounced the ballet "anti-danceable" and "reminiscent of Stravinsky with all the defects that suggests," it brought the young composer his greatest acclaim. Henri Prunières, one of the period's most influential critics, wrote that its premiere marked a date comparable in music history to the premiere of *Sacre*, yet another incendiary comparison that must have infuriated Stravinsky, all the more so because his own music was rapidly falling out of favor with Parisian audiences.

Markevitch's own view of the matter was expressed in an extensive interview with Palmer (not one frame of which appears in the final film).[14] There Markevitch (who after Diaghilev's death married Nijinsky's daughter Kyra) reported that Diaghilev had reacted "with great bitterness" when Stravinsky accepted Ida Rubinstein's commission for *Le Baiser de la Fée*. He also spoke of Stravinsky's wariness of other composers: "I believe that Stravinsky was very jealous when Diaghilev became keen on other people's music." Markevitch was not unaware of the growing animosity between Stravinsky and Diaghilev, and of his own role in their eventual rupture. As he described the situation to Palmer, "Diaghilev was very interested in me as a young composer, and I believe that Stravinsky was quite annoyed about this and only found fault with me." Markevitch balked at discussing the final years of the Ballets Russes. He preferred to stress his friendship with Stravinsky, noting that after Diaghilev's death the two "became good friends . . . and always kept up correspondence." Initially, this was far from true, although as Markevitch's career moved away from composition and toward conducting, the relationship improved. By the 1950s,

Stravinsky's friends reported that Markevitch had matured considerably, even conducting the composer's own demanding works with remarkable skill, perception, and sensitivity. And Markevitch went on to compile many important recordings that would place him among the more respected conductors of his day.

Alicia Markova was another Diaghilev "discovery" of the 1920s, but her arrival did not cause friction between Diaghilev and Stravinsky. On the contrary, she seems to have appealed to another, less frequently shown, side of the composer, one that was important for his work with the Ballets Russes. Only fourteen years old when she joined the company, she was soon cast by Balanchine in the 1925 revival of *Le Chant du Rossignol*, his first ballet for Diaghilev and the start of his association with Stravinsky. Markova had vivid memories of the composer that she shared with Palmer, although, again, the entire interview was cut from the documentary:

> My first meeting with the great man was when I was fourteen in Monte Carlo. . . . I was in a flood of tears because Balanchine was choreographing for me, and suddenly I was thrown into Stravinsky, and I really panicked; it was something I felt

I was never going to be able to cope with. . . . Diaghilev walked in to the rehearsal after dinner that evening and he found me in tears. He said "what's the matter," and I said I'm very sorry, I know I've lost the chance of a lifetime, [but] I'm never going to be able to dance this. And he inquired why. And so Stravinsky took me by the hand . . . over to the piano, and he said now come with me, little one, as he always used to call me, and he sat down and . . . started to demonstrate a little bit. . . . The most important thing he said [was] "Now you have to learn everything by ear," and from that moment on, if you can imagine, at fourteen, I learned all the Stravinsky scores by ear, the instrumentation, everything. . . . He would . . . drop in often . . . in Monte Carlo for the . . . rehearsals for *Rossignol*. We [didn't] have a pianist, it was all on pianola. We had to use a pianola. . . . [Later], when we revived . . . other Stravinsky ballets, . . . we had a wonderful pianist . . . Rika Fox, who we called "Foxy." . . . She could always deal [with the music], and Stravinsky used to work with her a lot. . . . Often if she was playing, he'd get up and go over and add the other two hands, making it four hands.

How kind and patient Stravinsky appears in Markova's affectionate recollection, so different from the brusque composer of other memoirs. And how sincere appears his concern for the dancers entrusted with the physical realization—or "externalization," as he liked to call it—of his music. Stravinsky's natural attraction for dance was steeped in his attraction to physical movement of any kind. He himself was always in motion. As Craft told Palmer, "He knew ballet [and] . . . could demonstrate dance steps to the end of his life." In 1918 he nearly danced the role of the devil in the premiere of *L'Histoire du Soldat*. He was willing—in fact, eager—to demonstrate gestures and movements to the dancers in his ballets. Indeed, nothing enraged him more than being credited merely as the composer of a ballet. Fokine, Benois, Nijinsky, and of course Diaghilev himself were all accused by the composer of denying his contribution to the choreography of his works, a mistake that Balanchine knew better than to repeat. Stravinsky was unable to refrain from coaching dancers, not only youngsters but also seasoned professionals: he acted in rehearsals as if he were the choreographer. Even as late as 1947, when Stravinsky and Balanchine were collaborating in New York on an early Ballet Society production, the composer could not refrain from demonstrating to the dancers, with great animation, his clearly envisioned ideas. He never hesitated to take complete charge. Leo Smit (who served sometimes as Balanchine's rehearsal pianist) and others vividly remember Stravinsky refashioning choreography on the spot, regardless of what Balanchine had initially planned.

And it was not only Balanchine who was instructed. From *Firebird* on, the impatient Stravinsky would often push the rehearsal pianist aside to demonstrate for the dancers the tempo and "feel" of the music. Pierre Monteux, who conducted the premiere of *Sacre*, remembers the first time Stravinsky rehearsed the ballet: "With only Diaghilev and myself as an audience, Stravinsky sat down to play a piano reduction of the entire score. . . . The very walls resounded as Stravinsky pounded away, occasionally stamping his feet and jumping up and down to accentuate the force of the music. Before he got very far I was convinced he was raving mad."[15] In her own interview with Palmer, Marie Rambert, Nijinsky's assistant while he was choreographing the ballet, recalled the composer's restlessness during rehearsals and the way he would sit down at the piano, playing with the frenetic motions of a "mad man," to demonstrate what he wanted. He was especially insistent about the tempo (extremely fast in *Sacre*, according to Rambert) and about which beats he wanted the dancers to stress.

Although Markova implies that the pianola was an alternative born of necessity since a "live" rehearsal pianist was too expensive, Stravinsky may well have preferred the preprogrammed instrument. Having very clear—even inflexible—ideas about tempo, he tended to regard any rehearsal pianist other than himself as risky. In fact, the pianola was used to rehearse a number of Stravinsky ballets, including *Les Noces*. According to Lifar, when Stravinsky was not around, "he had a barrel-organ sent down from Paris and on its rolls was inscribed the music of the ballet. We then had the extraordinary spectacle of an accompanist transformed into a mechanic and turning the handle!"[16]

The pianola had begun attracting the attention of serious musicians in the first decade of the twentieth century. We know that as early as 1912 the Grieg Piano Concerto was "pedaled" in a live performance with the London Symphony Orchestra. That same year, as confirmed by a telegram on 18 December from Diaghilev to Stravinsky, the Ballets Russes was regularly making use of pianola arrangements for rehearsals of *Sacre*. Indeed, as the composer's archives reveal, Diaghilev himself asked Stravinsky to "record" the ballet (meaning to perforate the rolls of paper that the player piano would then "read") to help Nijinsky deal with the ballet's rhythmic complexities. The dating confirms Diaghilev's interest in the pianola (although probably for financial rather than artistic reasons) long before Stravinsky began exploring its possibilities. The composer's first set of piano rolls was made in 1914 (a transcription of a set of early piano etudes). The advantages of having an instrument reliably reproduce a regularly calibrated tempo for dancers to follow in rehearsal were obvious. But the disadvantages were also evident, since

Stravinsky working at

the Pleyela, 1922

Stravinsky would often change his mind about tempi in performance. As Geva once remarked, when Stravinsky conducted *Firebird*, "everything was suddenly three times as fast. To keep up with Stravinsky's tempo, everybody was tripping and falling over each other."[17] In addition, not all conductors chose to follow Stravinsky's tempo, a complaint that prompted the composer to devote huge amounts of time to recording his music, including all his Diaghilev ballets, on roll.

Stravinsky's passion for the instrument spilled over into the Ballets Russes in critical ways, even beyond rehearsals. Prompted by Diaghilev, he considered incorporating it into several compositions, most notably *Les Noces*, where the composer once envisioned the use of four pianolas as part of the orchestral sound. In 1922–1923, when this possibility was considered (and rejected), Stravinsky "perforated" *Sacre, Pulcinella, Petrouchka,* and *Le Chant du Rossignol*. Later came several pianola versions of *Firebird* as well. Stravinsky repeatedly insisted that his purpose in "reconstituting" already composed works, as he put it, was to ensure that performers strictly complied with his intentions. What could be more clear than the dictum enunciated in his *Autobiography*:

> In order to prevent the distortion of my compositions by future interpreters, I had always been anxious to find a means of imposing some restriction on the notorious liberty, especially widespread today, which prevents the public from obtaining a correct idea of the author's intentions. . . . The means enabled me to determine for the future the relationships of the movements (tempi) and the nuances in accordance with my wishes. It is true that this guaranteed nothing, and . . . I have had ample opportunity of seeing how ineffective it has proved in practice. But these transcriptions nevertheless enabled me to create a lasting document which should be of service to those executants who would rather know and follow my intentions than stray into irresponsible interpretations of my musical text.[18]

Although in fact liberties in tempo were still possible (Ansermet reported to Stravinsky that undesirable rubati would sometimes creep in to the pianola performances), Stravinsky forbade the slightest nuance. The pianolist should set the tempo at a regular, unvarying speed, made possible by a hand lever. As Rex Lawson (the most knowledgeable scholar of the subject) comments, "For his Pleyela rolls, Stravinsky indicated his preferred speeds by setting down the length of paper (actually the number of perforations) that he wanted for each beat in various sections of the music."[19] Although the pianola would seem to preclude synchronization with live performers, this, in fact,

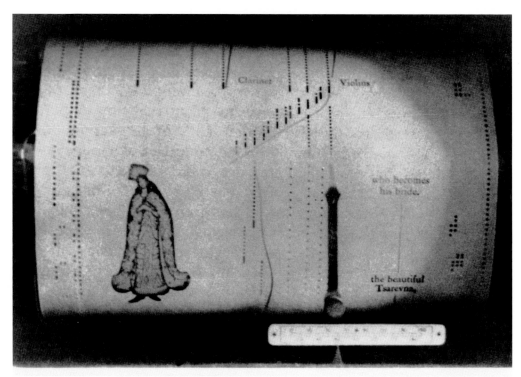

A Duo-Art Pianola Roll of Firebird, with one of Vladimir Polunin's "pictorial decorations." Polunin and his wife, Elizabeth, worked as scene painters for the Ballets Russes in the late 1910s and 1920s. The written text was by the British musicologist Edwin Evans, who was Stravinsky's close friend and a strong supporter of the Ballets Russes.

was Stravinsky's goal. As Markova's comments reveal, the composer welcomed the use of the pianola with "live performers" since at heart he distrusted choreographers, particularly with Diaghilev looking over their shoulders ready to impose his own wishes.

In an excised clip from the 1965 documentary on *Apollo* filmed in Hamburg, Balanchine and Stravinsky were caught off guard while the film was rolling.[20] They chatter about tempo and Diaghilev's attitude toward the ballet, reminiscing that he thought it moved too slowly and needed more stage action and quicker tempi. And in a whole can of film that was never released, Stravinsky rehearses the Hamburg musicians, recording the audiotape that would later be used by Balanchine for a production of *Apollo* by the Hamburg Ballet. But later in the film, when Balanchine hears the tape, he confides to a group of New York City Ballet dancers that Stravinsky's conception of the work had changed over the years and that the tempi in 1928 had been much, much slower. In another deleted segment, Balanchine says that he will have to make some choreographic adjustments to accommodate the new tempi.

Tempi were not the only changes that exercised the composer. He was afraid that "inappropriate" ideas might be introduced by the choreographer. When Stravinsky could not personally monitor rehearsals, he became deeply apprehensive about the fate of his work. In his *Autobiography*, he recounts the circumstances surrounding the first production of *Le Baiser de la Fée*:

> I was unable to follow the work of Bronislava Nijinska, who was compos-
> ing the choreography in Paris bit by bit as I sent the parts from Echarvines
> as completed. Owing to this, it was not until just before the first perfor-
> mance that I saw her work, and by that time all the principal scenes had
> been fixed. I found some of the scenes successful . . . but there was . . . a
> good deal of which I could not approve, and which, had I been present at
> the moment of their composition, I should have tried to get altered. But it
> was now too late for any interference on my part.[21]

An unpublished letter in the Basel archives indicates that in October 1928, Stravinsky reluctantly sent the piano score of *Baiser* to G. G. Païchadze, his representative, instructing him to withhold it from Nijinska as well as from Ida Rubinstein: "For even though the arrangement is well done, it is necessary for people such as they are, who are not particularly initiated, that . . . I play the music for them myself. . . . Nijinska will howl, but don't you pay any attention to it."[22] Three days later, in an unpublished letter, Païchadze was informed: "I see that Ida will not make it if I do not allow the production before my arrival. . . . Therefore she may give the music of the end to the pianist and de-mand from her the strict observation of the metronomic markings. I didn't want to show the music without being there because I am never sure of the choreographer's tempos."[23]

During his interview with Markova, Palmer asked about Vera Sudeikina, Stravin-sky's mistress at the time and his future wife. Sudeikina's contribution to *Le Chant du Rossi-gnol* is often underestimated. Markova explained that after rehearsing the ballet in Monte Carlo, she went to Paris to have her costume designed by Matisse. About two weeks be-fore the premiere, she was taken to Sudeikina's apartment for a fitting. She remembers Diaghilev, Matisse, Stravinsky, and Kochno being there in addition to Sudeikina, all con-ferring about her costume. She was to wear "all over white silk tights." "Then they de-cided I would just have these large diamond rhinestone bracelets on my ankles, and one on the arm, the other on the wrist and a little diamond necklace." Matisse, who wanted no hair showing, designed "a white chiffon bonnet also studded with rhinestones." To soften the effect, Sudeikina suggested a white osprey, which Kochno objected to because of the expense, but which Stravinsky and Matisse offered to buy. Markova concludes, "It was Madame Stravinsky, Vera, who did my costume, and then of course [at] the opening performance, Stravinsky conducted for me himself." In fact Markova always remained close to the couple, and even after Diaghilev's death the composer thought of her for roles in his ballets.

Diaghilev had introduced Sudeikina to the long-married Stravinsky in 1921. Their love affair quickly blossomed, with Kochno often acting as a go-between. Sudeikina appeared in Diaghilev's 1921 production of *The Sleeping Princess*, for which Stravinsky, as he later wrote, had reorchestrated several passages that unfortunately had been trimmed from the original Tchaikovsky score by order of the Imperial Theatre in St. Petersburg. Sudeikina often worked for the Ballets Russes, making costumes for Stravinsky works like *Le Chant du Rossignol* and *Firebird*, as well as for *Les Biches* and *Prodigal Son* (when Diaghilev found fault with Georges Rouault's designs).[24]

Sudeikina was also fond of Kochno and introduced the young poet to Diaghilev. (Kochno and Diaghilev briefly became lovers.) Palmer's interview with Kochno, only one snippet of which was retained, indicates that the latter's relationship with Stravinsky was much closer than previously recognized. In 1921, around the time he met Sudeikina, Stra-

Alicia Markova as the Nightingale in Le Chant du Rossignol, London, 1925

vinsky asked Kochno to write the libretto for an opera on a Spanish theme. It was to portray, in Kochno's words, "life in contemporary Spain, with bullfights, castanets, guitars, flamenco." The scenery was to be done by Picasso (who had designed two of Diaghilev's Spanish ballets, *Le Tricorne* and *Cuadro Flamenco*), and the title was to be *The Barber of Seville*. But like Diaghilev's 1910 proposal that Stravinsky write a ballet based on Poe's "The Masque of the Red Death," nothing came of this. In 1922 Kochno proved his skill as a librettist in Stravinsky's opera *Mavra*, which was based on a Pushkin text and anticipated the many libretti Kochno would write for Diaghilev as the decade progressed.

Astonishingly, given his well-known secrecy about works in progress, Stravinsky apparently opened his sketchbooks to Kochno. The musical sketches for *Oedipus Rex* (now at Basel) indicate that Kochno contributed some sections of the text, a Cocteau-Stravinsky collaboration. Stravinsky also shared his sketches for *Apollo* with Kochno, whose calligraphic flourishes on the manuscript pages in Basel are unmistakable. That Stravinsky would permit anyone to make a mark on his manuscript is almost unthinkable, suggesting the unusual trust and friendship that existed between the two.

In the end, however, it is Stravinsky's relationship with Diaghilev that remains at issue. And Palmer's interviews, along with the other documents now surfacing, begin to fill in the memory holes—or, at least, urge us to rethink those memories, upon which we have modeled our understanding of this most important pairing of iconoclasts. There is no question that once the fictions and aggrandizements are swept away, along with the the public and private derogations, an abiding affection remained between them. The tragedy is that at the end they stopped speaking to each other. In his *Autobiography,* Stravinsky claims that the last time he saw Diaghilev was "on the platform of the Gare du Nord, where we were both taking the train for London." But even here, Stravinsky prevaricates: he cannot admit that he and Diaghilev passed each other on the train and did not speak. Yet if Stravinsky was quick to attack Diaghilev for his despicable actions, misjudgments, and "poor artistic taste," he also defended the "Russian *barin,*" as he called Diaghilev, against all other assailants. "Diaghilev's death was hard on my father," Soulima Stravinsky told Palmer. "It was as if it was a brother or more, even more." Stravinsky's feelings about Diaghilev were equivocal and complex. Gratitude, indebtedness, admiration, anger, guilt, hostility—they ran the gamut.

Soulima remembers, too, that Diaghilev's glittering world of stars, pomp, and spectacle never ceased to fascinate his father. Stravinsky was a man of the theater, and perhaps more than music history cares to admit, the Ballets Russes was deeply and spiritu-

Stravinsky taking flowers

to Diaghilev's grave on

the island of San Michele

in Venice, 1932

ally his home. In spite of his later impugning of the entire enterprise, the Diaghilev era was a time of extraordinary growth for the composer. In a 1958 diary entry, Christopher Isherwood describes a dinner conversation in which "Igor said that Diaghilev surrounded himself with people who were inventive. 'And inventions,' Igor added, 'are the only things worth stealing.'"[25] As Arthur Rubinstein recalled, when Diaghilev died, many composers, especially Stravinsky, felt orphaned. The composer visited Diaghilev's grave often. Little more need be added than the simple unpublished telegraph Vera sent her husband in 1958 while he was in Switzerland and she in Italy: "Went with flowers to cemetery. Venice cold. Love, Vera." Thirteen years later Stravinsky was buried in Venice, only a few yards from Diaghilev. It was a bittersweet reunion in death, a reconciliation that speaks to us still through the legacy of their bold and imaginative creations.

III Influence and Afterlife

Not even Diaghilev, prescient though he sometimes seemed, could have predicted the long

reach of his ideas or the influence of his company on generations to come. Men and women

who had never known him sought to emulate his example, adapting the art he had fostered

and the kind of artists he had nurtured to the circumstances of another time and place.

They imitated his style and his willfulness, even if only a few had his breadth of vision, his

strength of character, or his will to recast ballet in the image of *Apollo*. Still, they carried

on his name and his ideas, latter-day apostles spreading his cult of beauty, love, and art.

eleven *Adolph Bolm in America*

Suzanne Carbonneau

Serge Diaghilev despised America and loathed Americans. Twelve years after he last set foot on American soil he could still rant to Tamara Geva that "America is a barbaric country. They know nothing about art! It is all Indians, and bankers, and gangsters in checked suits. They are cave people!" Although his company made two American tours in 1916–1917, Diaghilev had acquiesced to Metropolitan Opera Board Chair Otto Kahn's powers of persuasion to cross the Atlantic only because the war in Europe had made business impossible and because he had conceived of the idea that gold-grubbing American philistines could finance his European artistic experimentation. In his autobiography, Edward Bernays, the brilliant young publicist who handled Diaghilev's American tours, asserted that American suspicion of ballet and, in particular, the hostility to male dancers was matched by Diaghilev's prodigious contempt for his American hosts and audience. Still, Bernays was able to conclude that the tours made all America aware of ballet—that they were, in fact, "a turning point in the appreciation of the arts in the United States."[1]

Although the tours represented the end of official Ballets Russes activities in America, they had lasting consequences on American dance via the dancers and choreographers who left the Diaghilev company to pursue careers in the United States. On the whole, these dancers were content to re-create in America a combination of what they had learned from the Russian Imperial Ballet and from the Diaghilev repertory during the Fokine period. They were aware that the American public, relatively unsophisticated in its tastes, was uninterested in artistic experimentation. The mirth, anger, and derision aroused among the general public by the New York Armory Show of 1913 was proof enough that the average American was not ready for the kind of avant-garde experimentation being pursued by Diaghilev after 1914. Indeed, the dancers themselves tended toward aesthetic moderation and rarely expressed a desire to extend that outlook. The bargain these dancers made with America was driven by fiscal rather than artistic concerns.

There was, however, one notable exception to this conservatism, in the person of Diaghilev dancer and choreographer Adolph Bolm. Bolm was fascinated by America and saw in its youth, naïveté, and mass culture the very stuff of ballets of the future. Unlike Diaghilev, who viewed America's lack of refinement as creating an unreceptive environment in which to instill art, Bolm believed that the country would be a potent medium in which to cultivate artistic change. Precisely because it was unencumbered by centuries-old cultural traditions of which it would have to divest itself in order to accept the "new," this audience was, for all intents and purposes, a tabula rasa on which to inscribe a forward-looking art. In fact, Bolm was able to realize Diaghilev's aesthetic in America and then to extend it in a repertory that unmistakably parallels the modernist experimentation being pursued by Diaghilev in Europe.[2] In this seemingly inhospitable climate, Bolm managed to create ballets that harmonized Diaghilev's avant-garde concerns with Bolm's own fascination with American culture. Almost ballet for ballet, Bolm's American works find an analogy in the style, subject matter, music, and decor of the Ballets Russes repertory.

Like Diaghilev, Bolm was an artistic polymath and ambitious entrepreneur, eager to spread the gospel of modernism. His intellectual and artistic interests extended to painting, sculpture, architecture, literature, and music. Born in St. Petersburg in 1884, he graduated from the Imperial Ballet School in 1903 with first honors in dance, music, painting, and academic studies, and upon his graduation made a grand tour of Western European museums and theaters. Returning to the Maryinsky, he became allied with the Fokinitsy faction of the troupe, supporters of the early experiments and ideas of Fokine. De-

termined to break out of the confines of the Imperial Ballet, Bolm organized a small company in 1908, with Anna Pavlova as his partner, and they made a triumphant tour of
Helsinki, Stockholm, Copenhagen, Prague, and finally Berlin, where they returned the following season. Bolm was entertaining offers from French impresarios when a stream of

telegrams from Diaghilev began to arrive, asking him to forgo any Parisian appearances until Diaghilev's own first ballet season, in which he would be featured. Acceding to Diaghilev's request, Bolm filled in the time at the Empire Theatre in London, where he partnered Lydia Kyasht, becoming the first of the great Russian males to be seen in Western Europe.[3]

Bolm joined Diaghilev as the principal character dancer for the first Paris season in 1909. His performance as the Chief Warrior in *The Polovtsian Dances* from *Prince Igor* created a sensation, causing the audience, in a frenzied response to his ferocious masculinity, to tear off the orchestra rail of the Théâtre du Châtelet. Fokine asserted that it was Bolm who achieved perhaps the greatest success of the first season and emerged as its star.[4] Bolm skipped Diaghilev's second season to appear again with Kyasht in London, where he choreographed, staged ballets, and directed the small company. When Diaghilev established the Ballets Russes as a permanent organization in 1911, however, Bolm took the bold step of permanently resigning from the Maryinsky to join the company. He went on to become indelibly associated with character roles in the Fokine repertory, including Pierrot in *Carnaval*, the Moor in *Petrouchka*, and King Dodon in *Le Coq d'Or*.

Bolm's choreographic and directorial aspirations could have been no secret. In addition to choreographing for his own touring groups and his London engagements, he had staged the St. Petersburg production of Leonid Andreyev's *Life of Man* in the style of

Goya.[5] But Diaghilev allowed Bolm only limited choreographic assignments, all associated with opera. These included the dances for Mussorgsky's *Khovanshchina* (1913), which he choreographed in the style of Russian miniatures, and the Russalka dances for Rimsky-Korsakov's *May Night* (1914). He also served as ballet master during Fokine's absences from the company.

It is interesting to speculate how different Bolm's career might have been if his presence in the company had not been so completely overshadowed by Nijinsky's. Although Bolm is usually regarded as second only to Nijinsky among Diaghilev's male contingent, Diaghilev's personal and professional attention was so completely fixed on his favorite that the position of also-ran carried very little weight.[6] Bolm's great success during the first season notwithstanding, Diaghilev was not terribly interested in him, so completely was he absorbed in Nijinsky's image, style, and personality. Diaghilev's determination to push Nijinsky as a choreographer—and his subsequent interest in Léonide Massine—left little opportunity for Bolm to fulfill his creative aspirations. Within the first few seasons, it must have become quite clear to Bolm that his managerial, choreographic, and performing ambitions would not be realized in Diaghilev's company.

Still, it was Bolm to whom Diaghilev turned when arranging his first American tour. Prevailed upon to serve as ballet master, Bolm trained what was virtually a new company and re-created a repertory of twenty ballets with the help of régisseur Serge Grigoriev. He kept up these responsibilities throughout the grueling tour, in addition to his performing duties, which encompassed some of Nijinsky's roles in addition to his own. When the company made its second American tour, under Nijinsky's direction, Bolm had not wanted to participate; he did so only because Otto Kahn threatened to cancel the contract unless he took an active role. During the company's stay in Spain between tours, Bolm again trained the dancers and rehearsed the repertory, while also choreographing a new version of *Sadko* when no one could remember the Fokine original. (Fokine had been absent from the company since 1914.) The *New York Times* called Bolm "the 'brains' of the Russian ballet in its American seasons." Dance writer Merle Armitage, who had directed public and press relations for the American tours, wrote that "the fact that America saw the Diaghileff ballet with its character unimpaired is largely due to the prodigious efforts of Bolm."[7] In the shambles of the second tour under Nijinsky's feeble and erratic management, however, a stage accident left Bolm with fractured vertebrae, causing him to spend time in a body cast.

By that time Bolm had made his own contacts in the American artistic community, and as he recovered from his back injury he decided to leave Diaghilev and settle permanently in the United States. He wanted, he wrote, to form a company to perform "American ballets," that is, "flashing new ballets bright with the tones of life, cymbolic [sic] of moods of wistfulness and wonder." Adolph Bolm's Ballet Intime was modeled on Diaghilev's enterprise, although, as the name implies, it was fashioned on a scale suitable for concert halls rather than opera houses, comprising only twelve dancers and fourteen musicians. In his publicity, Bolm emphasized the Diaghilev standard by calling his own group a "Petite Ballet Russe."[8] After a tour of summer resorts, the company performed in Washington and New York in August 1917. As artistic associates during his first season, Bolm took on an international cast including Roshanara, an Englishwoman specializing in Indian dances who had performed with the Loie Fuller, Pavlova, and Diaghilev companies; Ratan Devi, another India-struck Englishwoman, who played the tamboura and sang Indian melodies; the Japanese choreographer Michio Ito; and Ito's Danish wife and partner, Tulle Lindahl, as well as Russian, English, and American dancers. For Bolm,

Bolm (center) with the Ballet Intime outside the Belasco Theatre, Washington, D.C., August 1917

"American ballet" encompassed the notion of international dances representative of a nation of immigrants.

The Ballet Intime repertory included reworkings of Fokine's *Carnaval* and *The Polovtsian Dances*, as well as an Assyrian dance performed to a commissioned score by Alexander Maloof, the prototype for a series of international character studies that would become a repertory staple. But in addition to offering this international repertory, Bolm began his transformation into an American choreographer by looking toward American sources for his work. His *Danse Macabre* was loosely based on Edgar Allan Poe's "The Masque of the Red Death." Set to a Saint-Saëns score, it was a pantomimic ballet in the Fokine style, with Bolm and Rita Zalmani as the young lovers trying to outdance Marshall Hall as a leering, violin-playing Death.

For the next decade, when he was not engaged in other pursuits, Bolm toured his Ballet Intime throughout the country on the concert circuit. The repertory was similar in scope to that of the Ballets Russes, with an extensive collection of character studies, abstractions, music visualizations, and pantomimic dramas. In commenting on a performance at Carnegie Hall in February 1920, *Musical America* proclaimed Bolm Diaghilev's rightful heir: "The Russian Ballet has left in its wake a myriad of imitators and followers. But Mr. Bolm is of the manner born, and outstrips them all by his very heritage. In his own dancing he has made strides beyond even his brilliant work with the Diaghileff forces, and as a creator, these choreographic pastels, all of which he planned and staged, reveal the subtle attention to detail which makes his conception of dancing seem a focussing point for all other arts."[9] In July 1920 Bolm took the Ballet Intime to London, where it was received with great enthusiasm in the vast space of the London Coliseum, just a week after Diaghilev's substantially larger company had been applauded in the same theater.

Bolm's first American commission, for a Broadway musical, unexpectedly offered him the resources to mount a ballet along the lines of a Diaghilev production. "Falling Leaves" was created as a divertissement for the Victor Herbert—Jerome Kern musical Miss 1917, which opened at the Century Theater in New York in November. Bolm's libretto cast the ballet in Diaghilev's "Greek" mode and required a huge cast of dryads, satyrs, and dancing leaves. Bolm himself portrayed Boré, the Spirit of the Wind, and Flora Revalles, the opera singer who had mimed the Ida Rubinstein roles on Diaghilev's American tours, appeared as the Golden Birch, a nymph imprisoned in a tree.

This project was followed shortly by an offer from Otto Kahn to stage Le Coq d'Or at the Met in March 1918. Bolm knew Fokine's 1914 version of the choreography, which the Diaghilev company had performed in Paris and London before Rimsky-Korsakov's widow withdrew permission for the staging. In fact, Bolm had taken on the role of King Dodon when its cre-

Bolm in a Javanese dance, 1920s

ator, Alexis Bulgakov, left the company. In America, Bolm produced his own version of the ballet, crediting it in the program as "after the original production by Michel Fokine." The Met found itself with a genuine "modern" hit on its hands, and *Le Coq d'Or* remained in the repertory for several years, with Bolm returning to perform Dodon. Bolm became indelibly associated with the role in the minds of Americans, and he continued to restage the ballet for American opera and ballet companies throughout his life. In collaboration with Stravinsky, Bolm also staged *Petrouchka* at the Met on the occasion of the composer's first visit to the United States in 1919, and he restaged it there in 1925.

Bolm's success at the Met had persuaded the managers of the Chicago Grand Opera Company to invite him to choreograph there in 1919. This was his first association with artistic groups in Chicago, the American city that would provide Bolm with the most supportive atmosphere in which to pursue his artistic vision. He was commissioned to choreograph *The Birthday of the Infanta*, a fifty-minute ballet-pantomime based on the Oscar Wilde story, with music by Chicago composer-industrialist-arts patron John Alden Carpenter. The scenery and costumes were commissioned from Robert Edmond Jones, the noted American designer who had created the Ballets Russes production of Nijinsky's *Till Eulenspiegel*. The Spanish character of the ballet would have appealed to Bolm, who had toured through Spain with Diaghilev in 1916, absorbing the Iberian atmosphere and studying flamenco with José Otero. He had been the male star of the company then, and the Spanish experience remained one of his most cherished memories. It would resurface in his ballets over the next decade, as it also appeared in the Ballets Russes' *Las Meninas* (1916), *Le Tricorne* (1919), and *Cuadro Flamenco* (1921). Set at the Spanish court at the time of Velázquez, *The Birthday of the Infanta* told the story of Grotesque Pedro (Bolm), a misshapen hunchback whose hopeless love for the beautiful Infanta (Ruth Page) causes him to die of grief. The ballet scored a striking success, and it was repeated in New York in February 1920. Bolm described the collaboration with Jones and

*Bolm as Pedro the
Hunchback in* The
Birthday of the
Infanta, *1919*

Carpenter as "most perfect," and in consequence, he treasured the work as his first "American ballet."[10]

Back in New York, Bolm quickly made a place for himself in the intellectual life of the city. His studio and adjoining apartment on East Fifty-Ninth Street was a gathering place for an artistic intelligentsia that included composers Serge Prokofiev, Carlos Salzedo, and John Alden Carpenter, flutist Georges Barrère, set designers Robert Edmond Jones and Nicholas Roerich, Michio Ito, Roshanara, and Fedor Chaliapin.[11] The discussions often centered on the creation of a "native" American art. The salon felt that this could be

achieved only by concentrating on American thematic material and exploiting the vigor, humor, and brashness of contemporary American culture. Bolm was determined to realize this theory in practice and cast about for a project with which to make a radical cultural statement.

There could have been no subject more indigenously American than the Sunday supplement, and in 1922 Bolm again joined forces with Carpenter to create the "jazz-pantomime" *Krazy Kat,* based on the George Herriman comic strip that ran in the Hearst papers. Bolm could see that the adventures of Krazy Kat, with his immigrant accent and imprecise gender, constituted an American folktale, just as the Ballets Russes' *Firebird, Petrouchka, Le Coq d'Or,* and *Snegurochka* were Russian. He wrote that he wished to express in a ballet "some of the real spirit of America, some of the native idealism of its busy life." The comics, which reached twenty million Americans each day, seemed to

Bolm the ideal expression of that "phase of living peculiarly and wholly American." And of all the comics, none seemed to him so fine as *Krazy Kat*. "Here is whimsy that we seldom find in purposefully fantastic writing," Bolm wrote. "If you seek subtlety there are fine meanings in Krazy Kat's amazing gestures. If you are blunt, there is hearty laughter in his incessant brick dodging."[12]

Herriman cooperated enthusiastically with the project: he not only designed the sets, costumes, and makeup and served backstage as makeup artist, he also wrote the scenario, which was "a distillation of a hundred strips."[13] Herriman created a constantly shifting background for his comic strip by having the scenery unfold as a panorama on a roller mechanism. The costumes were full-body suits and masks that were simply blowups of drawings from the strip. With the ballet's live action it looked like an animated cartoon, and the comic strip came to life.

The ballet was given its first performances on 20-21 January 1922 at Town Hall in New York with Bolm as Krazy Kat, Ulysses Graham as Officer Pup, Ledru Stiffler as Bill Postem, Olin Howard as Joe Stork, and Bella Kelmans as Ignatz Mouse. The action involves Krazy's transformation into a dancer. A disguised Ignatz Mouse offers Krazy a bouquet of catnip, which makes him delirious. At the climax of the dance, Ignatz beans Krazy with a brick, and Krazy is left unconscious at the final curtain.[14] Employing the slapstick humor of the comic strip, Bolm staged *Krazy Kat* as a broad caricature. The ballet's opening was a parody of Nijinsky's *L'Après-midi d'un Faune*, designated in the score as "The Afternoon Nap of a Faun." Herriman's libretto not only allowed for pantomimic action but called specifically for dancing. The sight of a poster for a Grand Ball sends Krazy into a reverie, as he clumsily tries to waltz. When Krazy dons a tutu, he performs parodies of virtuosic movement as "a regular ballet dancer," and after an exaggerated application of makeup, launches into a long Spanish dance, another reference to Diaghilev's repertory.

The Katnip Blues section—what Herriman described as a "Class A Fit"—was a wild frenzy of jazz dancing performed to Carpenter's "Tempo di Fox-Trot." The cultural critic Gilbert Seldes described the scene as based on an actual 1919 comic strip depicting "hundreds of Krazy Kats in a wild abandoned revel in the Katnip field—a rout, a bacchanale, a satyr-dance, an erotic festival, with our own Krazy playing the viola in a corner, and Ignatz, who has been drinking, going to sign the pledge."[15] When the inevitable brick is hurled at Krazy, knocking him out, the ballet returns to its beginning with Krazy "asleep" under a tree, suggesting that the action is a ritual to be played out ad infinitum.

Krazy Kat has often been referred to as the first American "jazz ballet." The popular milieu links the work to the Ballets Russes' ballet *Parade,* in which librettist Jean Cocteau's fascination with jazz and music hall led to the appropriation of elements of popular culture. This embrace of popular culture had its grounding in Diaghilev's preoccupation with futurist artists whose aesthetic comprehended such popular entertainments as the variety theater. In *Krazy Kat,* too, Carpenter and Bolm found art in what was generally considered crass or vulgar. The ballet was part of a growing movement within the Amer-

ican intelligentsia to incorporate into their art what had formerly been considered low-brow. Seldes was directly inspired by Bolm's ballet to declare himself a cultural populist and to begin work on *The Seven Lively Arts,* his revolutionary work on American culture, which had far-ranging and lasting import.[16]

Their work together on *Krazy Kat* deepened the admiration of Bolm and Carpenter for each other and sealed their lifelong friendship. It also led Bolm to move to Chicago, where he was offered the post of ballet master of the Chicago Civic Opera in 1922. The historian John Dizikes has called Chicago's opera, constructed from the remains of Oscar Hammerstein's Manhattan Opera Company, "the most interesting in America in the 1920s." But although the Opera's singing and relatively adventuresome programming were strong, its ballet, under the directorship of sometime Pavlova dancers Andreas Pavley and Serge Oukrainsky, had become moribund. After Bolm became director, he spent two seasons with the company (1922-1924) that were, in the words of Ann Barzel, "the greatest artistic splurge opera ballet has ever known."[17]

Bolm came to Chicago at a fortuitous time in the city's cultural life. Its symphony was flourishing under Frederick Stock; it was the center of jazz and African-American performance; and Sherwood Anderson and Ben Hecht were creating what came to be known as the Chicago School of writing. Bolm wrote of Chicago that it "is truly symbolic of creative restless America, of the America I like best. New York has become a city of the world, a little jaded, a little ashamed of honest emotion. Chicago shouts and whistles and hammers constantly at new buildings. It tears up streets and builds new ones overnight. It is dirty and dangerous and daring. But it is immensely alive."[18] Indeed, the city was open to experimentation and fresh voices, and Bolm confronted Chicago with ballets that would have discomfited if not outraged the stodgy patrons of the Met.

Bolm's opera productions included *La Juive, Boris Godunov, Cléopâtre, Lakmé, Aïda, Samson and Delilah, L'Africaine,* and Rimsky-Korsakov's *Snegurochka*. Rimsky was, of course, a favorite of Diaghilev's, who staged a number of his operas, and *Snegurochka* had been presented by Savva Mamontov, whose own operatic enterprise was a model for Diaghilev's. Staged as a Russian carnival, *Snegurochka* was proclaimed the "striking success" of the 1922 season. It was Bolm's first collaboration with Nicolas Remisoff, the Chauve-Souris designer who became Bolm's most important artistic associate. (The Chauve-Souris began in Moscow as an artists' cabaret; after the 1917 revolution it relocated in the West and began touring major theater centers.) The dancers were Americans whom Bolm was training at his own school, along with two Maryinsky graduates, Anna Ludmilla and Konstantin Kobeleff, as featured performers. In describing Bolm's tenure as ballet master, Edward C. Moore wrote that "never be-

fore . . . had the Chicago Opera been given such fine, sincere, superb art in its ballet department."[19] Although Bolm raised the level of dancing and choreography at the opera, he also spent two years struggling with managerial "inertia" and finally left for a new challenge.

This was Chicago Allied Arts, a venture designed to bring together an orchestra dedicated to modern music with a forward-looking choreographer in a thrice-yearly series of performances. Bolm's friend John Alden Carpenter was a driving force behind its formation in 1924. The very name of the organization proclaimed its mission. In Allied Arts, Bolm had finally found the organizational structure and backing that would allow him to create ballets that were a contemporary version of the Wagnerian Gesamtkunstwerk, a guiding principle of Diaghilev's early Mir iskusstva (World of art) group. The music contingent was headed by Eric DeLamarter, an assistant conductor of the Chicago Symphony, who had a passion for contemporary music. Bolm was invited to serve as artistic director and choreographer. Programs were to consist of a mixture of new ballets and music for small orchestra. It was also an integral part of the group's purpose to commission decor from designers of the first rank. To a greater extent than Diaghilev's choreographers, Bolm was not simply a collaborator who supplied the steps for a work but an auteur who oversaw its general direction—choosing the music, selecting the designer, and deciding upon the concept and style.

Like Diaghilev, Bolm had a keen interest in modern music, and Allied Arts was planned around the creation of ballets to adventuresome new works. In concentrating on chamber pieces by contemporary composers, Allied Arts was filling a niche left unoccupied by the Chicago symphony or opera. With Diaghilev as their example, avant-garde composers had begun embracing ballet as a means of gaining a sympathetic hearing for their work, and Bolm's organization sought a similar rapprochement. As the only musical organization in Chicago playing contemporary music, Allied Arts became "the most important musical organization in this town," according to critic Alfred V. Frankenstein.[20] Like Diaghilev, Bolm was a trained musician whose ability to read scores and communicate with composers on technical matters made him a true collaborator. Bolm's father and brother had been professional musicians in the Russian theater; in his autobiographical writings, Bolm refers to his habit of attending their rehearsals both to soak up the atmosphere and to hear new music. Over the course of its existence, Allied Arts introduced works to Chicago by many Diaghilev composers—Manuel de Falla, Darius Milhaud, Francis Poulenc, Serge Prokofiev, Erik Satie, Igor Stravinsky—and other contemporaries, including John Dowland Batock, Arthur Bliss, Felix Borowski, John Alden Carpenter, Alfredo Casella, Henry Eichheim, Manuel Font, André Grétry, Jeanne Herscher-Clement, Arthur Honegger, Paul Juon, Clarence Loomis, Gian Francesco Malipiero, Antonio Pedrotti, Arnold Schoenberg, Jean Sibelius, Charles Sanford Skilton, Leo Sowerby, Karol Szymanowski, Alexandre Tansman, and Ralph Vaughan Williams.

Allied Arts' original plan called for a rotating roster of designers (the prospectus listed Léon Bakst, Robert Edmond Jones, and Nicolas Roerich, as well as Norman Bel-Geddes), but the Russian artist Nicolas Remisoff quickly became, to all intents and purposes, head of the organization's design "wing," occupying an advisory position similar to the one Mikhail Larionov and Natalia Goncharova had held with Diaghilev during the war years. Following his training at the Imperial Academy of the Arts in St. Petersburg, Remisoff had become known as the caricaturist Re-Mi of the weekly *Novy Satirikon*.[21] Nikita Balieff, founder and confrère of the Chauve-Souris, had based skits on his cartoons in the mid-teens, and when the two met up again in Paris after the 1917 revolution, they began to work together. Remisoff came to the United States with the Chauve-Souris in 1922 and became instantly famous for his murals on the walls and ceiling of the Century Roof Theater. After the first Allied Arts season, Remisoff moved to Chicago, where he also taught stage design at the Goodman Theatre's drama school.

The designs on which Remisoff built his reputation were in the colorful Russian peasant style associated with Larionov and Goncharova. His work for *Snegurochka*, his first collaboration with Bolm, recalled the Ballets Russes' neoprimitivist folk ballets—*Le Coq d'Or* (1914), *Soleil de Nuit* (1915), *Kikimora* (1916), *Contes Russes* (1917), *Chout* (1921)—which were all designed by either Larionov or Goncharova. Bolm and Remisoff shared an artistic vision, pushing each other toward nontraditional approaches to thematic content. The critic Edward Moore described Remisoff as having "a flair for gorgeous colorings and outlines that stray from the normal and at the same time indicate lightness and motion." Over the course of his Allied Arts work, Remisoff tried out an astonishing variety of styles, including experiments with light that put forward the idea of a fluid concept of decor. The first thing a patron saw upon entering an Allied Arts venue was Remisoff's "hypnotizing" front curtain, depicting the invasion of the Chicago skyline by the Allied Arts dancers. There Remisoff set commedia dell'arte characters "amid skyscrapers with a Pisan disregard for verticality, reaching for bulbous red clouds in a warty blue sky."[22]

The Allied Arts ballets and musical programs were aimed unabashedly at the Chicago intelligentsia, and conditions unique to Chicago were key to the group's ability to flourish there. Unlike New York's society audience, Chicago's theatergoers were relatively progressive, and Allied Arts supporters included prominent, forward-looking Chicagoans with names like Goodman, Rockefeller, Peabody, Rosenwald, and McCormick, who could add generosity to their enthusiasm. In founding the company, its directors described their patrons' contributions as a "semi-civic subsidy" designed to make ballet an art form independent of the opera, which was seen as restricting its development.

The inaugural program of Allied Arts was a gala occasion (an anomaly in the history of the organization), focusing on a guest artist rather than repertory. The organizers had guaranteed a full house for the performances on 27 and 30 November 1924 at the Eighth Street Theatre by securing the Chicago debut of Tamara Karsavina, who was making her first (and only) U.S. tour. This opening program spoke to the earliest phase of the Ballets Russes, when Fokine and the Mir iskusstva aesthetic were dominant. It featured the ballet-pantomime *Foyer de la Danse*, in which the Degas painting came to life to music by

Nicolas Remisoff's design for the front drop curtain for Chicago Allied Arts, mid-1920s

Emmanuel Chabrier. Staged in the style of *Petrouchka*, the work was a "realistic" depiction of a bustling historical scene, with the main characters emerging from the busy crowd. With the same passion for authentic detail seen in Alexandre Benois's designs for *Petrouchka*, Remisoff's decor re-created the Degas setting of a ballet rehearsal at the Paris Opéra in 1870. In addition, Karsavina danced works from her own repertory and Bolm performed solos that seemed to inhabit Diaghilev's successive imaginative worlds. "Satyr and Nymph," for instance, invoked both Fokine's *Narcisse* and, with music by Debussy, Nijinsky's *L'Après-midi d'un Faune*; there were two Spanish divertissements from the Ballet Intime repertory set to music of Albéniz and Laparra; an excerpt from *Snegurochka*; a trio to Mozart called *Elopement*; and *Précieux Ridicules*, a duet set to the music of Bolm's friend and future Diaghilev collaborator Serge Prokofiev.

It was the second program of the season, given on 1 and 4 January 1925, that proclaimed Allied Arts a progressive organization. Bolm's *El Amor Brujo* (Love, the Magician) was set to a Falla score that had been unsuccessfully staged as a ballet in Madrid in 1915. It was an extended narrative in the style of the Ballets Russes' *Le Tricorne* (set to another Falla score). Bolm used the original scenario by Martínez Sierra, and he engaged María Montero, a flamenco dancer from Seville who had also studied with Otero, to dance the role of Candelas to his own Carmelo. The scenery and costumes were the work of the artist and actor Rollo Peters.

The other major work on the program, which became one of the great successes of Allied Arts, was *The Rivals*, an ancient Chinese legend set to a score commissioned from the American composer Henry Eichheim, who also conducted. It moved beyond the exotic hokum of Fokine, reaching toward the authentic expression of Asian culture. Bolm certainly knew (and was probably influenced by) Stravinsky's opera *Le Rossignol*, which was produced by Diaghilev in 1914, and must also have known about its 1920 successor, *Le Chant du Rossignol*, a one-act ballet designed by Matisse and staged by Massine. (A new version by Balanchine was restaged in June 1925, shortly after Bolm's ballet.) But none of the Ballets Russes' productions made even a pretense of authenticity. Bolm's staging of *The Rivals*, on the other hand, scrupulously adhered to the conventions of Chinese theater, with scene changes effected by "property men" sporting pigtails and a scenario inspired by a seventh-century Chinese poem. Its fidelity to Chinese traditions caught the imagination of the audience, and it was pronounced "undoubtedly one of the most fantastic and weird things done around Chicago in a long time." Eichheim had just returned from his third visit to Asia, and he based his themes on Chinese ceremonial music, employing Chinese percussion instruments from his own collection. The costumes were likewise authentic. Remisoff's decor was universally admired. The movements for the main characters, danced by Bolm, Page, and Mark Turbyfill, were "suggestive of Chinese art and the figures seen on Chinese ware."[23] The program also included *Bal Masqué*, with music by Liszt, and Offenbach's *Little Circus*, a gloss on an indoor Russian circus, whose bareback riders, ponies, and clowns point once again toward the milieu of *Parade*. The program closed with a nod toward Bolm's first Ballets Russes triumph in the Tartar Dance from *Prince Igor*, "rearranged" by Bolm after Fokine.

By its second season, Allied Arts was taking no aesthetic prisoners. It started off on 8-11 November 1925 with a ballet indicating the futurity of its vision—Bolm's "amusing and unbeautiful" *Mandragora (The Magic Remedy)*. Possibly the move to fresh quarters had given the directors courage. The new Goodman Theatre, attached to the Art Institute of Chicago, was intended as a "laboratory of the arts," and at least one critic thought the Goodman would encourage openness in its patrons by providing "the backing of authoritative surroundings . . . that in itself will develop our willingness to give it a hearing." For, he explained, "part of our objection to futurism and cubism in painting is not that we can't understand them but that we don't want to understand them." In any case, as another critic declared, *Mandragora* established Bolm's "right to the surname of our idol Diaghileff."[24]

Superficially, *Mandragora* was a nod to Fokine's *Carnaval*, using two of the same characters, Harlequin and Columbine, who had appeared in that ballet. Its true reference point, however, was the Ballets Russes' more recent exploration of Latin period material and avant-garde form in such ballets as *Pulcinella* (1920), which featured commedia costumes designed by Picasso. For Bolm's commedia characters were "not of the moonlit gardens of Normandy, but shipwrecked on a perfectly impossible African coast where a barbaric king . . . reigns." The score by the Polish composer Karol Szymanowski had been intended as a divertissement within Molière's burlesque *Le Bourgeois Gentilhomme*, but it was reconceived by Bolm, who gave the story an African locale and subject. All that remained of Molière were Remisoff's designs, conceived in the style of Louis XIV, which coincided with the Ballets Russes' interest in French academicism. In Bolm's libretto, Columbine (Page) was shipwrecked off the Nubian coast and kidnapped by King Gagabamba (R. Aleneil). With the help of a doctor (Turbyfill) and his huge syringe of mandrake that changes the skin pigmentation of the African queen (Margaret Meaney) from black to white, Columbine is rescued by Harlequin (Bolm). Clearly, the ballet owed as much to traditions of minstrelsy and Drury Lane pantomime as it did to Molière. The production also prefigured Diaghilev's interest in British "panto," which would make itself known in such ballets as *Jack-in-the-Box* (1926) and *The Triumph of Neptune* (1926). Viewers were stunned by the outlandish setting, the irony and facetiousness of the tale, and the unfamiliarity of the music. Frankenstein declared that "there is real blood in the scene, blood that spurts perfectly in accord with the woozy tale unfolded by the dancers."[25]

The modernism of this statement was consolidated by the premiere of *Bal des Marionettes* on the same program, a ballet that was described in every review as deliberately "grotesque." It was set to a suite of seven dances from "La Piège de Méduse" by Erik Satie, the recently deceased composer who had been so influential in establishing Diaghilev's modernist credentials. Comparisons with the Ballets Russes' *La Boutique Fantasque* (1919) are inescapable, but Bolm's puppets inhabited another world entirely. The dancers portrayed puppets who seemed to dangle, slack-limbed, from invisible strings, performing rubber-legged versions of the quadrille, valse, matelot, mazurka, grotesque, and polka. The nightmarish effect was like "nothing ever seen on land or sea, but [was] conjured up from mince-pie dreams." Frankenstein could only describe it in relation to a work by a master of the grotesque: "If you want to know what it was like," he wrote, "get a copy of Poe and read 'King Pest.' The same stuffed rag dolls, the same unholy, somehow diseased and decaying figures of men."[26] Yet in spite of the difficulties it may have presented to traditional notions of ballet, *Bal des Marionettes* met with such an enthusiastic response at its premiere that it was encored. The repertory was repeated at the next program series on 27 and 29 December, with the addition of divertissements to Johann Strauss and Schubert, along with *Perpetuum Mobile*, to a score by F. Ries.

That same season, patrons were pushed even further by the third bill (3–6 January 1926), which featured the Chicago premiere of Arnold Schoenberg's *Pierrot Lunaire*, designed by Remisoff. It was only the second time the score had been performed in the United States and the first time anywhere it had been staged with scenery and costumes. As if to make amends for this extreme work, the next piece on the program was *Reverie*, a Chopin ballet that echoed Fokine's *Les Sylphides*. The evening concluded with *A Night in Arabia*, set to authentic Middle Eastern songs arranged by the Armenian composer Anis Fuleihan. As a desert maiden and her sheik, Marcia Preble and Mark Turbyfill disported themselves in Remisoff's desert designs, while the ballet suggested a serious gloss on the exotic Rudolph Valentino movies. (Diaghilev's own interest in Middle Eastern exotica went as far back as *Cléopâtre*, but his ballets were more fantastic, less realistic and "modern" than *A Night in Arabia*.) Fragments from *Petrouchka* were also offered.

The repertory of this season challenged its audience, with the result that many society patrons—although they had gone along with a great deal more than their New York counterparts—were separated from the hard-core intelligentsia. One Chicago critic dubbed Schoenberg "the Antichrist," while the *Chicago Post* questioned whether Allied Arts was not too "arty." A "lorgnetted dowager," noted the *Post*, was overheard describing *Bal des Marionettes* as "an insult to the human intelligence." Patrons complained that Bolm's ballets were "no longer classic" and had "departed from the formula of the ballet. They are lost amid barbaric settings, Paris green palms, scalloped seas, nose rings, thatched huts and black-faced Africans. . . . And as for the marionettes, they are caricatures, nightmares, bacilli come to life." Some audience members missed the tights and tutus—they even felt nostalgic affection for the Greek ballets of Fokine and Nijinsky. Thomas Fisher, the Allied Arts' secretary (and husband of Ruth Page), defended the program, saying, "What we are doing is just striking the modern note."[27]

Even in the face of such controversy, Bolm did not abandon the "modern note" in planning the next Allied Arts season. Giving no quarter to discomfited audiences, Bolm created ballets that pushed at the bounds of American taste and understanding, that even—in one instance—challenged the authority of ballet as a narrative vehicle. The 1926–1927 season opened with *La Farce du Pont Neuf*. Wholly Parisian in tone, this work shared the sensibility of the Ballets Russes' ballets of the period, with its French classical setting and modernist style. Bolm commissioned a female composer, Jeanne Herscher-Clement, who also wrote the scenario and traveled to Chicago for the ballet's premiere. Herscher-Clement had studied at the Paris Conser-

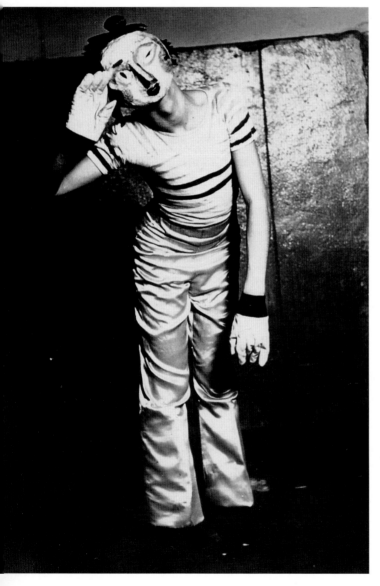

Bal des Marionettes, 1925

vatory with Gabriel Fauré (whose *Pavane Pour une Infante Défunte* was used by Diaghilev for *Las Meninas*). Her score, written in the style of Les Six, was said to "sparkle with bizarrerie." The ballet was set in the seventeenth century, when the Parisian bridge was a center of social, commercial, and theatrical life: it was where Molière first saw the commedia dell'arte. The slender plot featured commedia characters in love with a dancer. Here Bolm was evoking the same world as the Ballets Russes' Molière ballet *Les Fâcheux* (1924). The decor and costumes were by another young Parisian, Georges Valmier, whose work was being seen for the first time in the United States. The backdrop showed the Pont Neuf as dominated by the statue of King Henry IV, painted in naive style. Samuel Putnam felt that Valmier's was in the best tradition of contemporary design. "There is in it," he wrote, "a certain intrepid quality of balance, a certain memory of the Cubistic straight line . . . while the 'pointillist' sky in the background adds a touch of humor."[28]

On the same program was *Visual Mysticism*, one of the most extraordinary works of Bolm's career. This ballet marked a startling step for Bolm, who had worked within the tradition of dance drama and character studies. It was a move into pure abstraction, the same vein being mined by Nijinska in *Les Noces* (1923) and other works, and one to which Balanchine also shortly applied himself. As Lynn Garafola has pointed out, Diaghilev in his later years began jettisoning narrative, though the pretext of a plot was usually maintained. In *Visual Mysticism*, however, Bolm gave up dramatic intentions entirely. The program note announced: "This dance may be called pure plastic, just as music is frequently called pure music. In presenting Skriabin's intimate dream, it is necessary to achieve a complete fusion of movement and light and an intense and complex emotional sensitiveness."[29] Its three sections, "Longing" (Page), "Searching" (Bolm), and "Harmony" (Bolm and Page), corresponded to Scriabin's three piano compositions "Désir," "Enigme," and "Caresse Dansée," composed in 1908 and 1911 during his mystical post-*Prometheus* period. Remisoff's designs were also abstract: the costumes were vaguely Elysian short tunics, and the decor consisted of lighting effects.

Many critics referred to the experimental nature of the ballet. *Musical America* wrote that "it is not in ballet form, as the ballet is generally understood." Another critic recognized it as "a new attempt to interpret music by light and movement." Putnam saw it as supremely "daring," and thought it "one of those experiments in the doubtful no man's land of the arts which are always so fascinating, however perilous they may be." With *Visual Mysticism*, Bolm was seen as transferring allegiance from the au courant to the avant-garde. Writing in *The Drama*, Putnam noted that Bolm "[was] particularly sensitive to world currents and rather weirdly circulated with those same currents. . . . He is himself one of the generating batteries, as is shown in such an experiment as his 'Visual Mysticism.'" Hazel Moore was so overwhelmed by its novelty that she could only write of it impressionistically: "Angles, soft and sudden lights and plastic emotions, fluid body lines, earthly but unearthly." The ballet was also seen as profoundly sensuous.[30] When he later toured the work with the Adolph Bolm Ballet, Bolm renamed it *Plastic Poem*, as if to emphasize its abstraction and to obliterate any remaining programmatic references.

The same program featured the premiere of the ballet-comédie *Parnassus on Montmartre*, a "consummately frivolous" interpretation of Satie's *Mercure*, which had first been mounted in 1924 by Comte Etienne de Beaumont's Soirées de Paris and revived by Diaghilev in 1927.[31] Bolm transformed Satie's cast of gods and goddesses into Parisian art students at a masquerade, again evoking the world of the demimonde. Also on the program were Asian dances by Vera Mirova and a divertissement set to music by Anatol Liadov.

Allied Arts' final presentation was a holiday program given 26-31 December and 2 January. Bolm once again worked with uncanny synchronization with Diaghilev in choreographing *A Christmas Carol*. Based on the Charles Dickens story, *A Christmas Carol* was conceived by Bolm and Remisoff "in the spirit of George Cruikshank" and set to commissioned music by Ralph Vaughan Williams, with whom Bolm had worked closely in London that summer. It was a cousin to the Ballets Russes' *Triumph of Neptune*, which was produced that same month in London with choreography by Balanchine. *Neptune* was also inspired by Cruikshank's engravings and featured music by another British composer, Lord Berners. Bolm's choreography was based on the traditional English dances he had observed in 1920 at the Sussex gathering of the National Dancing Association under the direction of Cecil Sharpe. Remisoff continued to experiment with the idea of using lighting as decor, employing a scrim and dissolves between scenes. In response, Karleton Hackett rhapsodized, "Wonderful are the affinities between paints and lights, and Mr. Remisoff has caught their secret."[32]

Also on the program was Bolm's last major work for Allied Arts, *The Tragedy of the Cello*, which later appeared on Bolm's short list of works he considered his most successful. In this case, Bolm declared himself "fascinated by the esprit and humor of the subject and its plastical possibilities." Set to the *Sextuor* of Alexandre Tansman, a young Polish composer living in Paris, the ballet was another Parisian ballet-bouffe. Laden with irony, it was a bow to the antisentimentality of the French smart set wooed by Diaghilev. Alexandre Arnoux's scenario depicted a duel over love between the violin and the cello and its consequences for the instruments of the orchestra, who stand in for human foibles. Remisoff's "unequivocally modish designs" were among his most widely admired. Bolm's choreography, which was deliberately punctilious, was acclaimed, although many critics complained about the dissonance and distortion of the music. Olin Downes thought the score was "one more testimonial to the devastating influence of the genius of Igor Stravinsky in [the] Europe of today."[33] The program also included divertissements set to Schumann, Schubert, Mussorgsky, and Gluck, and Ruth Page's populist *The Flapper and the Quarterback*, to a score by Clarence Loomis.

Even before the company's third season began, patrons of Allied Arts had challenged Chicago—noted for its world-class symphony and opera—to make ballet a permanent civic institution. The cry was picked up by columnists and editorialists, who wrote that as the only company in the United States following Diaghilev's lead in presenting the best in new music, dance, and design, Allied Arts was indispensable to Chicago's claim to national status in the arts. And although the arts were combined under the Allied Arts rubric, ballet was its reason for being and constituted its most powerful brief for modernism. One critic wrote that "the music and the scenery are allies, but Mr. Bolm's ballet furnishes the shock troops."[34] Many writers saw this as Allied Arts' breakthrough year.

In December 1926 the Allied Arts patrons met to plan an expansion of the organization. They decided that the subsidy should be doubled so that five performances could be given the following year, and they discussed establishing the organization on the Maryinsky model with a school, theater, and company under its aegis. It was announced that the third program of the 1926–1927 season, scheduled for 6–13 March, would include three new ballets: *Maestro Pedro's Puppet Show* to a Falla score; *Karaguez (Turkish Ballet)*, with music by Marcel Mihalovici and a neoprimitivist decor based on ancient Turkish shadow theater by Larionov; and *La Guiablesse*, after a Martinique legend, with music by the African-American composer William Grant Still.[35]

Suddenly, however, on 4 March the season scheduled to begin in two days was canceled. In fact, the directors announced that all Allied Arts performances would be suspended for a year while plans to establish the company on a permanent footing were implemented. Instead, this was to prove the effective end of the organization. The ballets created for the final season were never performed. (It seems that the pleas to Chicagoans to adopt Allied Arts as a civic institution had been a signal from the patrons that they were preparing to withdraw their subsidies.) Bolm picked up the Chicago personnel and repertory, and, as the Adolph Bolm Ballet, closed the fourth season of the League of Composers series devoted to modern music at the Jolson Theatre in New York on 27 March 1927. It was a lavish social occasion, produced by a committee headed by Countess Mercati, Mrs. Charles Guggenheim, and Mrs. Otto Kahn, with debutantes serving as ushers. It was a triumph, and ironically, New York newspapers chastised local arts organizations because the city was being outclassed in ballet by an organization from upstart Chicago.

Although the demise of Allied Arts came as a crushing blow, Bolm must have been heartened by an exceedingly prestigious commission that followed soon after and acknowledged his stature as the foremost American choreographer working in the classical idiom. In 1928 he was invited to set the first season of ballet for the Library of Congress Festival of Chamber Music, sponsored by Elizabeth Sprague Coolidge. Coolidge had commissioned a score from Stravinsky for a small orchestra and a few dancers. In line with his reputation for exactitude, Stravinsky had requested specific details about the production, including the size of the stage and the orchestra pit. The library had warned that the stage would not hold more than five people.[36] Bolm's *Apollo Musagètes* [sic], the world premiere of the score, with sets and costumes by Remisoff, was performed at the library's chamber music auditorium on 27 April 1928, six weeks before the Balanchine version was presented by Diaghilev.

The commission found Bolm once again keeping exactly abreast of developments in Paris. Beginning with *The Sleeping Princess* (1921), Diaghilev had displayed his fascination with French classicism and the academy. In his choreography for *Apollo*, Bolm found himself immersed in the same world. Staged as a *ballet d'action*, Bolm's work was designed as an homage to the beginnings of classical ballet as set down by the Académie Royale. Remisoff's setting, consisting of a ruined temple and a huge outcropping of stone, was inspired by Piranesi's eighteenth-century engravings of ancient Roman scenes. As Apollo, Bolm was costumed in a plumed helmet and light armor in the style of the mythological ballets, "doubly resplendent because of the fact that he is both Greek and French, that his *cuirasse* is that of a Grecian god, his *perruque* that of the Roi Soleil." Ruth Page as Terpsichore, Berenice Holmes as Polyhymnia, and Elise Reiman as Calliope also suggested "in their arm-bands and their golden fillets, Mount Parnassus, in their pale bodices and their drooping tulle skirts, the Académie Nationale." The action of the ballet followed Stravinsky's libretto, although the prologue depicting the birth of Apollo was not staged; in its place were rituals conducted by the Muses around a burning brazier. The Apotheosis depicted Bolm rising on the stone mountain as the Muses watched from below.[37]

The tiny stage was only about 28 by 20 feet, and there were no wings. The only entrance and exit came via a door in the center of a concrete wall. Bolm wrote of the difficulties in creating "an effect of grandeur" in such a restricted space and credited the "ingenuity" of Remisoff, which he dubbed "supreme," in addressing this problem. The score and the subject seem to have evoked in Bolm a response similar to Balanchine's in its eschewal of novelty and effect and its concentration on the *danse d'école*. Bolm's choreography was described by critics as severely classical and academic "in precise pattern formalized." In his capacity as the newly created dance critic for the *New York Times*, John Martin made the journey to Washington to see the program. Martin recognized the magnitude of the occasion in his declaration that "for the first time in history a major ballet work had its world premiere in America."[38] Martin found Stravinsky's score a formidable challenge, and he expressed doubts that any choreographer "had ever been faced with a ballet score of equal length and offering any more difficulties."

In his remarks Martin could have been addressing the style and mood of Balanchine's choreography as well. His reaction to Bolm's academicism was that it "directs itself to the intellect. It is dry and unemotional in quality, but—at least in the hands of Mr. Bolm—it is far from dull. . . . Under his direction it comes forth as a gentle and subtle

Nicolas Remisoff, set design for Apollon Musagète, 1928

burlesque, witty and sparkling to the observing eye." Martin felt that Bolm's work offered tremendous challenges to Americans but rejoiced that "it has been proved possible to produce intelligent, adult ballet performances in America."

The program also included three other premieres. *Arlecchinata*, to a score by the eighteenth-century composer Jean-Joseph Casanea de Mondeville, was another masked Harlequin and Columbine fantasy. (Somehow, Remisoff fit his decor of a model Italian village onstage with the dancers.) Ravel's *Pavane Pour une Infante Défunte* was done in Velázquez style, reminiscent of *Las Meninas*. Ravel himself had been present for rehearsals and told Bolm that in watching his choreography "I begin to like my music."[39] In *Alte Wein*, Bolm tied together into a sparkling narrative several Beethoven dances found in the Library of Congress collection.

The parallels between Bolm's American career and Diaghilev's in Europe continued even to the dissolution of their experimental enterprises. Diaghilev's sudden death in the year after the premieres of the American and European *Apollos* resulted in the disbanding of his company. It was just at this time that Bolm was forced by the demise of Allied Arts and the onset of the Depression to abandon his own company. Bolm was forced to reinvent himself in a new role as an American choreographer, moving farther west to try his hand in Hollywood. Convinced that the growing importance of films would make California the artistic center of the country, he transferred his home and his activities there.[40] Bolm was disappointed in his belief that the movies would transform ballet into a form with mass appeal, however, and the remainder of his life represents his heartbreaking effort to regain the ground he had once held in leading Americans into the aesthetic unknown with his bracing experiments.

Eschewing offers from the post-Diaghilev "Ballet Russe" companies touring America (which he viewed as artistically bankrupt), Bolm continued to struggle toward his lifelong goal of establishing a permanent American ballet, becoming by turns a resident choreographer at the Hollywood Bowl, "founding director" of the San Francisco Ballet, and the first choreographer to sign with Ballet Theatre. In all these companies, he continued to create repertory on the Diaghilev model, combining restagings of Fokine ballets and operas with ballets inspired by dances from the postwar Diaghilev repertory. Yet he never ceased experimenting and never abandoned his singular vision.

Ballet is woman," George Balanchine liked to say. His first star in the West, however, was a young man named Serge Lifar. Lifar, who directed the Paris Opéra ballet from 1929 to 1945 (when he was dismissed for collaboration with the Nazis) and again from 1947 to 1958, was the last of Serge Diaghilev's leading men, one of the golden boys who made the Ballets Russes famous. Like his predecessors, Lifar was uniquely a product of that company; plucked from oblivion, he was groomed by Diaghilev for stardom and launched on a path that asserted not only his preeminence within the company as an individual but also the preeminent role within its repertory of a new kind of hero.

This hero, who made his first appearance with Vaslav Nijinsky, differed markedly from the princes of the nineteenth-century Russian repertory that formed the early dancers and choreographers of the Ballets Russes. No longer merely a consort to the ballerina or the

exponent of a chivalric ideal of masculinity, he was a protagonist in his own right, projecting an image of sexual hetero-doxy that left a deep imprint not only on the ballets of the Diaghilev period but also on their audiences. From the androgynes of *Le Spectre de la Rose* (1911) and *L'Après-midi d'un Faune* (1912) to the deco gods of *La Chatte* (1927), *Apollon Musagète* (1928), and *Prodigal Son* (1929), Diaghilev's heroes traced a spectrum of male roles that transcended conventions of gender while presenting the male body in a way that was frankly erotic. Ballet after ballet celebrated its physique, dramatized its athletic prowess, and paraded its sexual availability. Among the many excellent *danseurs* who passed through the ranks of the Ballets Russes, the "ballerino" alone haunted Diaghilev's imagination.

As a type, the ballerino had no historical precedent, so Diaghilev, with typical invention, manufactured him from the material at hand. Nijinsky was the first; Léonide Massine, Anton Dolin, Lifar, and a few lesser lights followed. For Diaghilev, they were sometime lovers, would-be sons, and muses. He made them star dancers and fashioned them into star choreographers; he shared his life with them, and his purse, and the passion, intelligence, and taste he brought to every branch of art. At a time when the memory of Oscar Wilde kept most homosexuals in the closet, Diaghilev made the Ballets Russes a venue where the public medium of ballet and the private theater of his imagination at least partly overlapped—a kingdom of "beautiful boys." Generous at times to a fault, cunning, quixotic, willful, and perspicacious, he used this peculiar collection of attributes to alter the course of ballet. Before Diaghilev, individual dancers may have been homosexual and homosexual individuals may have been present in the ballet audience. But the terrain itself remained ideologically and socially heterosexual. With Diaghilev, however, ballet in Western Europe no less than in America became a privileged arena for homosexuals as performers, choreographers, and spectators. It was a feat unparalleled in the other arts, and for gay men (to use a modern term) it was a revolution. The captain of ballet modernism was a homosexual hero who did as much for the cause of gay freedom as its more celebrated advocates.

For women, however, the consequences of this revolution were mixed. If with Bronislava Nijinska the Ballets Russes launched a major female choreographer on an international career, the company did little else to accommodate female talent, even as performers. Indeed, with the partial exception of Tamara Karsavina, the female star of the company's pre–World War I years, the ballerina went into eclipse. She did so not only as an individual but also as a category and an idea. Reversing the trend of nearly a century of ballet history, the ballerina became a subordinate or an appendage of the new Diaghilev hero, an absence in the poetics of ballet modernism at large.

Although the nineteenth-century ballerina had largely been a creature of men, she had also been a power in her own right. She dominated the stage, just as her roles dominated the ballet repertory, and she stood, in contrast to her male consorts, at the apex of the performing hierarchy, the star audiences paid to see. For choreographers, she was both a medium and an instrument; they gave her steps to dance and imagined characters for her to act, but it was only to the degree that she invested these with charm, eroticism, and the mystique of her own personality that they acquired larger meaning.

Woman, of course, was the great obsession of romantic and postromantic ballet. She came in many guises and in many national variants. But it was in her virginal, ethereal guise, ostensibly beyond class or race, that she left her deepest mark on choreography; in the "white acts" of ballets like *Giselle, La Bayadère, The Sleeping Beauty,* and *Swan Lake,* the purity of her young womanhood was identified with an Eden of transcendent form. Even if it sprang from the mind of the prince (and of the ballet masters who imagined it), this kingdom of the ideal belonged to the ballerina, as did the larger domain of subjectivity—poetry, loss, grief, beauty, desire, eroticism. Indeed, in its nineteenth-century

Vaslav Nijinsky as Harlequin in Carnaval, 1910

form, ballet was uniquely an expression of the feminine as embodied in the ideology and physical presence of the ballerina.

Diaghilev's revolution dethroned the ballerina from this seemingly impregnable position within the dance universe. In his company her role was sharply curtailed, her repertory limited, her image radically transformed. At the same time, her eroticism and physical bravura were appropriated as attributes of the new male hero. If *Swan Lake* and *La Bayadère* were meditations on the mystique of femininity embodied in the ballerina, works like *Schéhérazade* (1910), *L'Après-midi d'un Faune*, and *La Chatte* (1927) celebrated the mystery of the male androgyne or the prowess of the homosexual athlete as represented by one or another of Diaghilev's golden boys.

This shift away from inherited conventions of ballet sexuality was not immediately apparent in 1909, when the Ballets Russes first appeared in Paris. Handpicked by choreographer Michel Fokine and chosen to a large extent from the "reform" wing of St. Petersburg's Maryinsky Theater, the dancers continued to be divided according to traditional categories of *emploi*. The chief division was between "classical" and "character" dancers, that is, between dancers who excelled in the academic idiom of the *danse d'école* and those who excelled in the folk-derived idioms of character work. Although this division principally rested on technical ability, it also embraced matters of style and decorum. For the classical dancer this implied attractive physical proportions and a deportment that called for nobility and restraint; for the character dancer, it meant a freer use of the body coupled with a more overt projection of sexuality. Whether upper class or populist, the paradigm in each case was heterosexual.

Four of the five ballets presented in 1909 adhered to this traditional paradigm. *The Polovtsian Dances* celebrated the muscular masculinity of a tribe of pre-Christian warriors and the serpentine

Serge Lifar as the Young Man in La Chatte, 1927

Vaslav Nijinsky as the Golden Slave in Schéhérazade, 1910

femininity of their captive maidens; *Les Sylphides*, a poetic reverie, evoked the virginal play of ballet's traditional sisterhood. In *Le Pavillon d'Armide* the ballerina came to life in the dream of the protagonist, while in *Le Festin* classical and character dancers joined forces in a potpourri of preexisting dances.

Only in *Cléopâtre*, based on Fokine's earlier *Egyptian Nights*, was there a perceptible shift in the paradigm, and this, significantly, occurred when the work was being revised for Paris. The inspiration for the ballet was Alexander Pushkin's tale "Egyptian Nights," which gave birth to the first of the nineteenth century's "killer-Cleopatras" (in Lucy Hughes-Hallet's phrase)—a lascivious queen who has her lovers put to death once she has slept with them.[1] In the ballet her victim is Amoûn, a youth who abandons the girl who loves him for a night of pleasure with the queen. In the St. Petersburg version of the work, Cleopatra was a minor seductress; her rival, Ta-hor, a passionate innocent. For Paris, Diaghilev enhanced the role of the femme fatale (now performed by Ida Rubinstein) while playing up the ballet's decadent elements, thus transforming the Egyptian queen into an idol of perverse and deadly sexuality. He had her carried onstage in a sarcophagus, wrapped in veils that slaves peeled away one by one, disclosing, as Alexandre Benois wrote, "a divine body omnipotent in its beauty."[2] At her side, crouched like a panther ready to spring, was Nijinsky, her favorite slave, half-man, half-beast, blazing with an erotic fire stoked by her beauty and cold, majestic disdain. By contrast to the thrill of this voluptuous sadism, the romance of Amoûn and Ta-hor seemed tame and irrelevant. In later ballets that explored the same ground, the romantic pretext was discarded.

Cléopâtre proved so popular that it became the matrix of numerous Diaghilev

Olga Preobrajenska, early 1900s

works, all of which exploited the French appetite for exoticism and several of which also milked the theme of voluptuous sadism. In *Thamar* (1912), for instance, the legendary Georgian queen of the title plunged a dagger into the heart of her captive lover. In *Legend of Joseph* (1914), Potiphar's Wife (a role originally intended for Rubinstein) towered over Joseph (a role originally intended for Nijinsky), a youthful shepherd caught in the web of a Venetian courtesan. And in Diaghilev's version of *La Tragédie de Salomé* (1913), the period's most famous nymphet, now tricked out in kiss curls, tattoos, and a huge glittering headdress, danced for an all-male cast of "Negroes" and executioners, as well as the severed head of John the Baptist. It was *Schéhérazade*, however, that laid out the theme most clearly and emblematically. Here Rubinstein's "proud, cunning and unrestrained passion" as Zobéide and Nijinsky's "half-cat, half-snake, fiendishly agile, feminine and yet wholly terrifying" impersonation of her favorite Negro slave reiterated the sexual dynamics of *Cléopâtre*.[3] His death, which followed on the heels of a frenzied orgy, was a thrilling reminder of the wages of sexual sin at the hands of a grasping woman. As personified in Diaghilev's killer-Cleopatras, female sexuality and female power were a deadly combination.

Not all the women of the company found such roles congenial. Anna Pavlova, who danced Ta-hor in 1909, left the Ballets Russes at the end of the first season, miffed, among other things, at the last-minute substitution of *Les Sylphides* and *Le Festin* for *Giselle*, one of her greatest roles, at a Paris Opéra gala. That Nijinsky had received the lion's share of the season's publicity did not help matters, nor was she tempted to change her mind by the promise of the title role in *Firebird*, scheduled for production the following year. Ida Rubinstein was the next to go. Most Diaghilev apologists, echoing Prince Peter Lieven, explain that she departed because she wanted to perform dance roles as opposed to mime ones, and "Diaghileff, who knew perfectly well that she was no good as a dancer, gave her a decisive rebuff, at which she took offence."[4] Given that in the nine years following her break with Diaghilev she devoted herself to acting rather than dancing, it seems likely that she was, rather, "bored," as Lieven claims she told Diaghilev, with "caresses, embraces, and stabbing herself." In any event, like Pavlova, she went her own way. Other women principals came and went as well—Vera Karalli, Yekaterina Geltzer, Olga Preobrajenska, Mathilde Kchessinska, Elena Poliakova. Like Pavlova, all were identified with the classical repertory and its major ballerina roles.

Only Tamara Karsavina, who occupied a rung apart in the company, remained loyal to Diaghilev, although she never succumbed to his entreaties to quit the Maryinsky.

And for all the affection she bore him, by 1913 she had become sufficiently restive to demand a work of her own. He rewarded her with *La Tragédie de Salomé*, a work that was familiar to the French public from the versions produced by Loie Fuller (in 1907) and Natalia Trouhanova (in 1911) —yet was sufficiently minor that it would not detract from the season's other premieres: Nijinsky's *Jeux* and his monumental *Le Sacre du Printemps*. Unsurprisingly, the fillip endured for no more than a season.

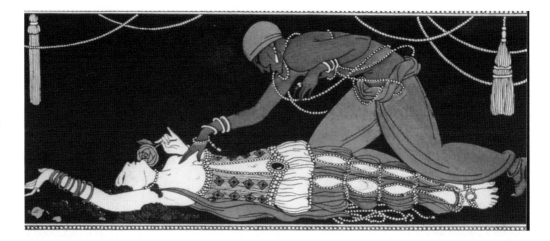

Diaghilev's dethronement of the ballerina was reflected not only in the diminished importance and overt misogyny of many female roles but also in the progressive devaluation of pointe work. This, more than any other aspect of female technique, defined the ballerina; it was her exclusive province and an analogue of the idealism traditionally embodied in her roles. In the interest of historical authenticity, Fokine typically eschewed the use of pointe except in works identified with the Western past: *Les Sylphides*, which evoked romantic-era ballets like *Giselle* and *La Sylphide*; *Le Spectre de la Rose*, set in the Biedermeyer period; *Carnaval* (1910), which introduced the commedia dell'arte theme within the context of a nineteenth-century masked ball. In exotic ballets or ballets set in antiquity—which together constituted a majority of his works for Diaghilev—pointe work was either proscribed or sharply curtailed.

In *Petrouchka* (1911), however, a different sort of authenticity was at stake. Here Fokine's choreography for the Ballerina exploited the technique of pointe for parody, both of the tricks of female virtuoso style and of the ballerina manners that typically accompanied it. Fokine had no quarrel with femininity; what he loathed was its expression as artifice. Even as he disavowed pointe, Fokine used arms and a newly pliant, uncorseted torso to create a more "natural" female body, one that moved freely and expansively, arching, stretching, twisting, bending, in a way that enhanced its plasticity and three-dimensionality. Although not exclusive to women, this unfettered body, with its curves and softened contours, was the basis of the "femininity" he prized in his women dancers. Even if Fokine never abandoned academic technique as a system of training, in much of his choreography, especially for women, he sought to neutralize its presence.

Vaslav Nijinsky and

Tamara Karsavina in

Le Spectre de la

Rose, 1911

In Nijinsky's three works for Diaghilev—*Faune, Jeux,* and *Sacre*—the conventions of the female dance all but disappeared. Only in *Jeux,* where the ballet's two women danced on high three-quarter pointe, were they present, albeit treated with the utmost minimalism. Although Fokine had opposed bravura effects in principle, he occasionally made use of bravura steps. Nijinsky eliminated these entirely. He virtually abandoned the duet and with it the system of supports by which the danseur had traditionally presented his partner: the men and women in his ballets almost never touched. At the same time, he hardened the contours of Fokine's "natural" female body. In *Faune* this body, both individually and collectively, was little more than an interplay of angles across a two-dimensional plane, indistinguishable in shape from that of the hero, although softened, to a degree, by flowing Grecian tunics. In *Sacre,* too, men and women shared a common stance and gestural vocabulary, although at certain times, such as in the ring dance that opens the second tableau (the score's only extended lyrical passage and the only dance sequence performed exclusively by women), these common gestures took on a "feminine" quality that mitigated against their normative unisexuality.

In *Sacre* as in *Faune* and *Jeux,* Nijinsky grounded the choreography in a movement

Ludmila Schollar (left),
Vaslav Nijinsky, and
Tamara Karsavina in
Jeux, 1913

idiom worked out on his own body and then passed on to his dancers. In modern dance, this is standard practice; in ballet, by contrast, a highly elaborated technique, independent of the choreographer, interposes itself between the maker and the executant of a dance. Most early modern dance choreographers were women, and initially at least, so, too, were most of their dancers. The female body was thus the model and the matrix of an enterprise that was in some measure reciprocal. In Nijinsky's case, however, both the generative body and the model body were male, and whether from ignorance or inexperience or a combination of the two, he insisted on imposing them on his dancers autocratically. Obviously, in *Sacre* he imposed them on men as well as women. But in both *Faune* and *Jeux*, his most experimental works, he was not only the "star" but also the only male presence onstage. If the female body had dominated the ideology of nineteenth-century ballet to the extent of eclipsing and, in some cases, even banishing men from the stage, in Nijinsky's ballets the male body not only claimed the stage but haunted the female bodies that shared it.

For all that Nijinsky's choreography elided traditional differences between male and female dance idioms, his ballets retained a thematic link with other Diaghilev works. Both *Faune* and *Jeux* reiterated the theme of male sexual innocence and female sexual knowledge found in *Petrouchka*. In *Faune* the Chief Nymph (a role Nijinsky initially wanted Ida Rubinstein to play, in part because of her height) dropped her veils one by one, a striptease that recalled Rubinstein's unveiling in *Cléopâtre*. In *Jeux* the two women engaged the young man in erotic games as provocative and potentially dangerous as those of *Schéhérazade*. To be sure, none of these temptresses was a classic Cleopatra. In *Jeux* they wore designer tennis dresses; in *Faune*, Grecian tunics of a sort favored by at least some of the ladies in Diaghilev's audience. Like the costumes, the settings—a garden in *Jeux*, a woodland clearing in *Faune*—were also shorn of exotica, as was the music, supplied in both cases by Claude Debussy rather than by the Russian neonationalist composers of *Cléopâtre* and *Schéhérazade*. In muting the overall tonality of his ballets, Nijinsky domesticated their erotics; instead of killer Cleopatras, his women were everyday seductresses of the international elite. Diaghilev's exotic ballets typically ended in an orgy of sex. In Nijinsky's works, by contrast, the hero avoided sexual entanglement, eschewing physical contact with women, as though the female body itself filled him with loathing.

Although Nijinsky left the Ballets Russes in 1913, Diaghilev sought again and again to emulate the pattern of his career. In Léonide Massine, a talented Bolshoi dancer, he found a youth worthy of his passion for mentorship, an instrument capable of realiz-

Léon Bakst, portrait of Léonide Massine, 1914

ing his ambitions. Diaghilev discovered Massine in the turbulent months following Nijinsky's marriage and immediately cast him in *Legend of Joseph* in the role originally intended for Nijinsky. Although Massine had completed his studies at the Bolshoi theater school, he was far from being the technical wunderkind Nijinsky had been. He lacked finish, which teachers hired by Diaghilev eventually supplied, as well as the ideal physical proportions and distinguished presence of a *danseur noble*. Given the nature of the Ballets Russes repertory, this hardly mattered. With his eye for talent, Diaghilev discerned in Massine not only the charisma of a future star but also the raw material of a future choreographer. In the months that followed the outbreak of World War I, Diaghilev took his protégé to museums, introduced him to the futurists, arranged lessons with the great Italian pedagogue Enrico Cecchetti, and watched over his maiden choreographic essays with the modernist painter Mikhail Larionov. Massine was willing, able, and malleable. It was only a matter of time before he fulfilled the high hopes Diaghilev had placed in him.

From 1914, when he joined the Ballets Russes, until 1921, when he left, Massine was the company's preeminent star, the pivot on which the repertory turned. He was the Chinese conjuror of *Parade* (1917), the Miller in *Le Tricorne* (1919), and a leading player in *The Good-Humoured Ladies* (1917), *La Boutique Fantasque* (1919), and *Pulcinella* (1920), all ballets he choreographed. He took over Nijinsky's roles in *Petrouchka*, *Cléopâtre*, *Schéhérazade*, and *L'Après-midi d'un Faune*, thus stressing the continuity of pattern between his career and that of his predecessor. And in 1920 he choreographed a new version of Nijinsky's greatest work, *Le Sacre du Printemps*.

For all his star quality, Massine was not a classical dancer in the strict sense of the term. A superb actor (for a time he had contemplated a career on the dramatic stage), he had a strong affinity for character styles of movement, especially the Spanish dance idioms that he exploited so successfully in *Le Tricorne*. He loved the "eccentric" dance forms associated with jazz and incorporated them into his ballets, along with elements from the circus, commedia dell'arte, cinema, and other vernaculars of twentieth-century folklore. Such idioms sat well on his body and formed the basis of his personal style as a performer and his early style as a choreographer. Both left a deep imprint on the company's dancers.

Léonide Massine as Leonardo in The Good-Humoured Ladies

With Massine the Ballets Russes ceased to be a classical company; it became instead a demi-caractère one. The transformation itself had started before the war; indeed, it dated to the company's earliest years. But it was Massine who completed the process. Although Diaghilev never abandoned classical technique as the physical basis of the company's training, with Massine, the danse d'école became irrelevant to the company's experiments in choreography. What was studied in class had little organic relation with what was danced onstage, even if elements of the technique coded the work as ballet. The divorce between studio and stage was all but complete.

Although rarely called upon to make full use of her powers as a classicist, Tamara Karsavina had remained Diaghilev's official ballerina up to the war. With the reorganization of the company that coincided with Massine's early essays in choreography during World War I, the title (now that Karsavina had returned to Russia) fell into abeyance. Like Nijinsky, Massine dominated the Ballets Russes as a performer; his choreography, by contrast, offered a number of women in the company (most notably Lydia Lopokova and Lydia Sokolova) roles that were meaty and challenging. But these roles and the technical idioms associated with them were rooted in the idiosyncracies of Massine's own style. Their sterling qualities as performers notwithstanding, Massine's women were formed on the demi-caractère model of his own body. Their classical potential remained largely untapped.

It was Bronislava Nijinska who put the women of the Ballets Russes back on pointe. Indeed, Les Noces, which she choreographed in 1923, was the first ballet created for the Diaghilev company in which the entire female ensemble donned ballerina footwear.[5] Yet Nijinska stressed the percussive rather than the aerial qualities of pointe, an approach that broke with nineteenth-century conventions. Moreover, in choosing to employ the technique in a work inspired by Russian folklore and staged to modern music (the score was by Igor Stravinsky), she also broke with Fokine's historicism. If technically the pointe-work of Les Noces was uncomplicated, its very use was a milestone, asserting not only its centrality to the female dance but also its adaptability as a means of expression. The following year, in Les Biches, a ballet with a contemporary setting, Nijinska again put all the women on pointe; now they were flappers with the prancing strut of mannequins. This time she also reintroduced the ballerina (albeit in the sexually ambiguous and somewhat ironic role of the Garçonne) and the classical pas de deux (which was not only distilled in form but also, to a degree, treated ironically). With these two works began the "re-classicizing" of avant-garde ballet.

For all this, a tension remained between this reclassicizing impulse and the need to showcase one or another of the company's "ballerinos." Thus, in *Le Train Bleu* (1924), choreographed by Nijinska six months after *Les Biches* and intended as a vehicle for Anton Dolin, the gymnastics (at which he excelled) were treated as bravura turns while the classical elements of the duets, along with their romantic entanglements, became occasions for parody. This tension was discernible in Balanchine's works for the company as well. The choreographer whose ballerinas would later be celebrated for the bravura and refinement of their pointe work was remarkably sparing in his use of the technique in the Diaghilev period. Indeed, unlike *Les Noces* and *Les Biches*, almost all Balanchine's ballets employed pointe selectively. But they employed it significantly: more than any other technical element, pointe identified the domain of the hero's female counterpart. This role, although it had a ballerina component, was ancillary rather than primary to the larger character of a work, whose theme remained embodied in the hero. Indeed, whether as the Movie Star in *La Pastorale* (1926), the Cat in *La Chatte* (1927), Terpsichore in *Apollon Musagète* (1928), or the Siren in *Prodigal Son* (1929), the female, however striking her choreography, was essentially a foil to the hero, presenting and complementing him, and showing off his attributes.

In the case of Serge Lifar, who was the star of all these ballets, these attributes included a pronounced athleticism and the striking good looks of a "beautiful boy." The athleticism was partly a compensation for his late start and patchy early training as a dancer. The good looks, on the other hand, were at least partly thanks to Diaghilev, who had arranged for his teeth to be fixed and his nose straightened. Ballet after ballet celebrated the young god and his slim, muscled body, selectively bared and occasionally even stripped à la *Cléopâtre* (as in the Prologue of *Apollon Musagète* or the penultimate tableau of *Prodigal Son*) to heighten the sensation of its beauty. In *La Chatte* he was borne onstage in a triumphal car formed by six youths—the apotheosis of a deco god. The *danseuse*, when she appeared at all, was no more than an accoutrement.

Indeed, even apart from *Les Biches, Le Train Bleu*, and *La Pastorale*, all of which had contemporary settings, many ballets of the 1920s, including those with mythological or period themes, alluded to contemporary fashion. In Massine's *Zéphire et Flore* (1925), for instance, the Muses wore adaptations of flapper styles, including "chic little pork-pie hats and earrings, quite in keeping with the only Olympus they had ever known—one nearer Deauville than Thessaly."[6] In Nijinska's *Romeo and Juliet* (1926), the dancers in the rehearsal scenes wore practice clothes, and in the "redressed" version of *Apollon Musagète*, the Muses

Serge Lifar and the male
ensemble of La Chatte,
1927

wore tunics by Gabrielle Chanel, the couturière responsible for *Le Train Bleu*, draped with scarves from Charveau.

In all these ballets, the accent was on youth and the celebration of the body beautiful. For men this entailed revealing the body; for women clothing it in the styles of fashionable consumption. If in his latest incarnation Diaghilev's hero was a boy with the physical endowments of a god, his new woman, by contrast, was a girl who looked like a mannequin. Slim, boyish, and decorative, she was a symbol of modern life as this was defined by deco luxury. Like the Bright Young Things (as flappers were known in England) who thronged Diaghilev's audience, she paraded her worth by what she wore on her back: she embodied a consumerist ideal rather than a physical one.

Chanel once said that Diaghilev did not know how to dress women. More to the point, he did not care to undress them; he kept their bodies hidden, except for the occasional revelation of skin that came with a tutu. What had been daring in the nineteenth century (and even the stuff of pornography), however, was now positively Victorian. At a time when short skirts routinely displayed the leg and tight-fitting bathingsuits showed off the torso, when Paris chorus girls and specialty dancers performed their acts in G-strings, Diaghilev's women, for the most part, were as sexy as matrons. If their gilt-edged style enhanced the value of the hero, it never detracted from his desirability.

In spite of his overwhelming commitment to new work, Diaghilev did not wholly eschew the traditional repertory. In 1910 he presented *Giselle*; in 1911 the first of several versions of *Swan Lake*; and in 1921 *The Sleeping Beauty* (or as he renamed it, *The Sleeping Princess*). To mount these productions, however, he faced a problem: he needed the ballerinas his company had jettisoned. His solution (except in the case of *Giselle*, which Karsavina danced) was to import them. Like Pavlova, one of his 1911 Swan Queens, most of these imports made brief appearances in the "regular" repertory: Mathilde Kchessinska, the Maryinsky's *prima ballerina assoluta* and another of the 1911 Swan Queens, in *Carnaval*; Vera Trefilova, one of his Auroras, in *Le Spectre de la Rose* and *Aurora's Wedding*. None of them stayed with the company. Even Olga Spessivtzeva, the most celebrated of his Auroras and a dancer he assiduously courted, found greener pastures elsewhere, both at the former Maryinsky Theater (to which she returned in 1922) and at the Paris Opéra, where in 1924 she danced the title role in its first revival of *Giselle* since the 1860s. Compared to such plum roles, Diaghilev's offerings were scraps: the female lead in *La Chatte*, the Swan Queen in one or another of his truncated versions of *Swan Lake*, whose periodic dismemberments he seemed to relish. Nor did it take much discernment on Spessivtzeva's part to realize that partnering Lifar, with whom she was typically paired, was a mixed blessing. For all his wooing of Spessivtzeva, Diaghilev treated her as cynically and highhandedly as he had her predecessors.

Although Diaghilev pounced on choreographic talent no matter what its sexual packaging, only his favorites reaped the full rewards of his mentorship. Indeed, without him, it is unlikely that Nijinsky or Massine, to say nothing of Lifar (whose first ballet, a remake of *Le Renard*, was produced by Diaghilev in 1929), would ever have become choreographers at all. His generosity was boundless: he gave them all the accumulated wisdom of his years and all the fruits of his broad experience, in addition to a knowledge of the arts, an appreciation of aesthetics, and an introduction to everyone who was anyone in the circles of High Bohemia. Money was no object: he paid for months of experiments in the studio and hundreds of rehearsal hours with dancers, for music by the greatest composers and sets by the finest artists. No Pygmalion ever served his Galatea as devotedly as Diaghilev served his lover-choreographers.

Obviously, women and heterosexual men were at a disadvantage. They might work for him, but they would never be his intimates; and although he might guide them, he would never fashion the company in their image or make them the instruments of his imagination. The progression from lover to star dancer to choreographer was a pattern that repeated itself again and again, and not only in the Ballets Russes. Both Rolf de Maré's Ballets Suédois and Comte Etienne de Beaumont's Soirées de Paris were conceived as vehicles for favorites (Jean Borlin and Massine, respectively), who not only starred in virtually every work of these companies but also supplied all the ballets for their repertories. Like the Ballets Russes, these companies were modernist in orientation and private rather than public in ownership. Compared to institutions like the Paris Opéra, tradition sat lightly on them; as one-man shows, they were also unhampered by bureaucracy. In this, they more closely resembled modern dance companies than the traditional ballet troupes of the opera house.

In the traditional companies, custom mitigated against women as choreographers or, more correctly, as ballet masters, for it was only in the twentieth century and in companies formed on the Diaghilev model that the ballet master's choreographic function was detached from his functions as a producer, teacher, and administrator. Where women did make inroads as choreographers was in venues that lacked the prestige of a major opera house. In music halls and other stages that catered to a popular audience or lyric theaters of secondary category (at least from a dance point of view), one finds all but forgotten choreographers like Katti Lanner and Madame Mariquita. Theoretically, the avant-garde companies should have welcomed women; as enterprises enunciating a male homosexual ideology, they did not. Yet within these companies were any number of women who harbored choreographic ambitions. The most notable (apart from Nijinska, who found favor with Diaghilev partly because of her brother's claim on his affections) were Ninette de Valois and Marie Rambert, both of whom eventually formed their own companies; Carina Ari, a principal with the Ballets Suédois who created a number of works for the Opéra-Comique; and dancers like Karsavina and Lopokova, who choreographed at least some of the numbers they performed on the music hall stage. Indeed, in the post-Diaghilev years a genuine flowering of women ballet choreographers occurred, a phenomenon encouraged by the marginal status of the companies with which they were typically associated as well as by the fact that these groups, although partly inspired by the Ballets Russes, broke with its cult of the ballerino.

If that cult had proved a serious barrier to the promotion of women as choreographers, its public expression, as evinced in the aesthetic practices of the company and its broader iconography, linked the larger enterprise of ballet modernism with homosexuality. Although Diaghilev made no secret of his proclivities, they were not general knowledge beyond the elite circles in which he traveled. But the image of the ballerino, as depicted in company programs and in numerous books, photographs, and drawings of the period, made the connection with homosexuality explicit, even if the word itself was never uttered. In Nijinsky's case, the body was progressively feminized. Released from the decorum of conventional masculinity, it openly displayed its erotic attributes—a pliant, supple middle, soft, embracing arms, eyes lengthened and darkened with liner. In the drawings of Robert Montenegro, Paul Iribe, and George Barbier especially, the pose is often languid, its curves dramatized by serpentine scarves and by gestures that circle inward on the body, as if announcing its availability: here was a houri waiting to be taken.[7] The eroticism was heightened by designer Léon Bakst's exotic packaging and by costume elements that often crossed gender lines—harem trousers in *Schéhérazade*, a peplum skirt in *Le Dieu Bleu* (1912), tunics in *Narcisse* (1911) and *Daphnis and Chloé* (1912), body stockings in *Carnaval*, *L'Après-midi d'un Faune*, and *Le Spectre de la Rose*. Such packaging revealed the con-

George Barbier's rendering of Vaslav Nijinsky in L'Après-midi d'un Faune, 1913

tours of the male body to an unprecedented degree, as well as expanses of flesh in the midriff and lower reaches of the neckline. At the same time, by identifying such revelations with the exotic, antique, or imaginary, Diaghilev neutralized the "danger" of their effeminacy. In contrast to Fokine, whose choreography for the company's women celebrated a "natural" body unfettered by corsets and free of ballerina artifice, Diaghilev made the very stratagems of femininity integral to the identity of his new hero.

For all his erotic charisma, Nijinsky was never conventionally attractive. Massine, on the other hand, was beautiful: dark, slender, with enormous Mediterranean eyes and the grave expression of an innocent. His beauty haunted Diaghilev, as it haunts the portraits of Massine that he commissioned from Bakst, Matisse, Natalia Goncharova, Mikhail Larionov, and other artists associated with the company as designers. Most of these portraits—like the works that a later group of artists made of Anton Dolin and Serge Lifar—found their way into company programs, making public the sitter's unique position within the Diaghilev enterprise.

Women, of course, did not vanish from company programs. But the space allotted to them was minimal, and almost always they were depicted in roles from the repertory. For the most part, too, the images reproduced were photographs, as opposed to the line drawings and paintings that associated the representation of the favorite with the prestige of the unique artwork and, more generally, with the modernism of Diaghilev's newest designers. Only in the numerous drawings made by Picasso in the late 1910s and early 1920s when he designed several company productions did women receive a share of the glamour. But what women! What avoirdupois! If the men in his drawings have the ideal proportions and nonchalant eroti-

Pablo Picasso, Dancers, 1919–1920

Felia Doubrovska in

Ode, 1928

cism of the youths of classical sculpture, his women—the charm of their ballerina manners notwithstanding—are as fresh and fleshy as milkmaids.

Ironically, as Picasso added pounds to Diaghilev's women, they themselves were getting thinner. "She is too fat for us," Diaghilev remarked about Lydia Lopokova in 1924.[8] And, indeed, compared to Alice Nikitina, the reed-thin newcomer whom he was then promoting as his latest female find, Lopokova did seem positively robust. By the mid-1920s the lean silhouette was high fashion, and it was only natural that Diaghilev's women, like generations of women dancers before them, would personify in some measure the elite beauty ideal of their age. In its newest incarnation, this ideal had a definite masculine component: it demanded a body as hipless and flat-chested as a boy's. Ida Rubinstein may have been slim, but her body had revealed the usual female equipment (at least until Gabriele d'Annunzio, anxious that she acquire a "man's figure" for her role as the travesty hero in his play *The Martyrdom of Saint Sebastian*, put her on the diet that made her, according to some accounts, the thinnest woman on the French stage).[9]

If before the war Diaghilev had feminized the male body, now he set about making the female body masculine. Thus in 1922, when he revived *L'Après-midi d'un Faune*, he cast Nijinska in the role originally created by her brother. The experiment was not a success. However much she strapped in her breasts, she needed more than a body stocking to camouflage her sex, even if she resembled Nijinsky in physical type and musculature. Only in Massine's *Ode* (1928), and specifically in the role created by Felia Doubrovska, was the unencumbered female body allowed to be itself. Clad in tights and a leotard (the only time, apart from Nijinska's appearance in *Faune*, that Diaghilev permitted a woman of the company to wear such revealing garb), Doubrovska displayed the harmonious line and long, lean silhouette of the prototypical Balanchine ballerina—along with small but unmistakable breasts.

Unlike Nijinsky, in whom the feminine was at least partly associated with sexual passivity, Diaghilev's heroes of the 1920s wore their sexual plumage like peacocks. Beginning in 1923, when Anton Dolin briefly joined the company, and continuing throughout the years of Lifar's preeminence, the body was not only bared but its erogenous zones were explicitly sexualized. In a remarkable series of photographs dating to the mid-1920s Man Ray recorded the various elements of Lifar's erotic uniform—trunks (to show off the legs), belts (to dramatize the waist), laces, garters, and boots (to draw attention to the calves and knees), tunics or tunic-style tops (to reveal a midriff, a shoulder, and sometimes even a nipple). Nearly always the legs were bare. Although the display might be regarded as "feminine," the body itself—hard, muscular, athletic—was that of a sexually active, "virile" male. Indeed, in the later years of the Ballets Russes, Diaghilev discarded the trappings of fin-de-siècle androgyny that had made the effeminacy of Nijinsky acceptable. With Lifar, he revealed the homosexual as an openly gay man. No wonder the theaters where the company now performed had become a privileged gathering place for what *Vogue*'s Herbert Farjeon described, with obvious disapproval, as "velvet-voiced youth."[10]

By almost any yardstick, women in the Ballets Russes counted for less than men. In a sense they were triply disadvantaged, for with the exception of Nijinska, their role behind the scenes did not make up for the loss of their traditional preeminence as performers or for their irrelevance to the ideology and practice of modernist ballet generally. That this occurred at a time when women were establishing a dominant presence in other

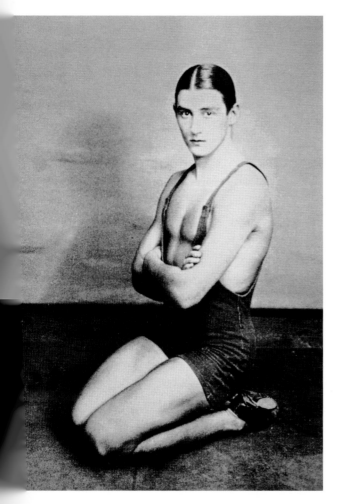

forms of concert dance only emphasizes the antifemale bias implicit in Diaghilev's homosexual radicalism. The 1930s partly redressed this imbalance: the growing trend of neoclassicism demanded women of high technical accomplishment to fill both traditional and newly minted ballerina roles, while a number of fledgling companies were either headed by women or associated with them as choreographers.

Nevertheless, the ballerino remained a force to be reckoned with. At the Paris Opéra, where Serge Lifar directed the ballet troupe for nearly thirty years, numerous works continued to foreground the hero (a role that Lifar typically reserved for himself), even to the point of eliminating women entirely (as in his 1935 revision of *Faune*). And in companies like the Joffrey Ballet, which in the 1970s and 1980s did so much to keep the Diaghilev repertory alive, or Maurice Béjart's Ballet of the 20th Century, which in the 1960s and 1970s reinterpreted works from that repertory from an openly gay perspective, the development of ballerinas has been ancillary to the celebration of male talent.

If ballet in its female-centered variety is about more than women, so, in its male-centered variety, it is about more than men. Liberation, in Diaghilev's book, was for men only, even when this entailed, as it often did, appropriating attributes associated with femininity. In the long run, the cult of "masculinity" offered no more than a temporary antidote to the "problem" of nineteenth-century ballet, which burdened women no less than men with the legacy of the feminine mystique and a system grounded in patriarchy. Nor did Balanchine's cult of "femininity," with its selective privileging of women as muses and of men as Pygmalions. Today, as in Diaghilev's time, full and equal citizenship in the ballet polity remains an elusive dream.

thirteen **In British Eyes**

Compiled by Lynn Garafola

In England, as elsewhere, the Ballets Russes inspired visual artists of every kind—painters, sculptors, photographers, graphic artists, caricaturists, illustrators. Although overshadowed by their French and Russian counterparts, British artists nevertheless left a rich and varied record of the company's seasons, works, and personalities. Many of the images that follow were published in the illustrated press, in magazines like *Punch, Vogue, The Tatler,* and *The Sketch.* Some, however, appeared in books, art portfolios, or literary or specialist journals, while a few, mainly drawings, were not intended for publication. Whatever the source, they testify as a group to the company's broad appeal, its compelling interest for many different audiences. At the same time, they tell us something about the company's public image and identity, the associations that attached themselves to it—exoticism, aestheticism, fashion, modernity, cosmopolitanism, homosexuality—and how those associations changed over time, adapted themselves to the local terrain, and were finally naturalized. Unsurprisingly, given that so many of the images are caricatures, the English sense of humor is on display, as well as the very English passion for pets and sports. What follows is a small sampling, at once humorous and serious, of the Ballets Russes in British eyes.

FIREMEN ANSWERING A CALL.

POLICEMAN ON POINT DUTY

RAILWAY PORTER INDICATING THAT THE LUGGAGE IS IN THE BRAKE VAN

STREET SCAVENGERS STREET SCAVENGING

TICKET COLLECTOR PUNCHING TICKET

DUSTMAN RETIRING EXPRESSING GRATITUDE FOR HONORARIUM.

POLICEMAN EFFECTING ARREST OF BACCHANAL

IT HAS BEEN REMARKED THAT HITHERTO IN THIS COUNTRY THE MASCULINE DANCER HAS ALWAYS LOOKED MORE OR LESS FOOLISH, AND GENERALLY TAKEN REFUGE IN FRANKLY ECCENTRIC CREATIONS. NIJINSKY, MORDKIN AND OTHERS HAVE SHOWN US THAT A MALE CAN BE MANLY THOUGH GRACEFUL. THIS DISCOVERY MAY HAVE FAR-REACHING RESULTS, AS DEPICTED ABOVE.

Thomas Maybank, caricature, Punch, 1911. "It has been remarked that hitherto in this country the masculine dancer has always looked more or less foolish and generally taken refuge in frankly eccentric creations. Nijinsky, Mordkin and others have shown us that a male can be manly though graceful. This discovery may have far-reaching results, as depicted above."

STARTLING RESULTS OF EXOTIC INFLUENCE ON THE PERSIAN NATIVE.

I.—In the Russian sphere of influence.

E.T. Reed, "Startling Results of Exotic Influence on the Persian Native: In the Russian Sphere of Influence," Punch, 1912.

In November 1911 Russian troops invaded northern Persia, provoking a crisis in Anglo-Russian relations. Although Russian dancers were still newcomers to London, their impact was such that ballet immediately became an activity associated with Russians.

"LE SPECTRE DU VERT": DANCED BY THE MIKST FOURSOMZ BALLET.

Ernest H. Shepard, "'Le Spectre du Vert': Danced by the Mikst Foursomz Ballet," The Sketch, 1913. Better known today as the illustrator of Winnie the Pooh, Shepard was a popular caricaturist whose work appeared in The Sketch and Punch.

INFLUENCE OF THE RUSSIAN BALLET ON BATHING DESIGNS.

Ernest H. Shepard, "Influence of the Russian Ballet on Bathing Designs (Salomé and The Faun)," Punch, 1913. Here, Shepherd pokes fun at Karsavina's tattoos in La Tragédie de Salomé and Nijinsky's mottled bodystocking in L'Après-midi d'un Faune.

Anne Estelle Rice, "Schéhérazade," Rhythm, 1911. An American painter living in Paris who was sometimes called "Queen of the Fauves," Rice contributed a number of Ballets Russes drawings to John Middleton Murry's literary quarterly Rhythm.

Duncan Grant, Nijinsky in the ballet Narcisse. Like other members of Bloomsbury, including *Virginia Woolf,*

Clive and *Vanessa Bell,* and *Lytton Strachey,* Grant took a lively interest in the *Ballets Russes* and

frequently attended performances.

David Bomberg, "Methodic discord startles . . ." This lithograph comes from Bomberg's *1919* album *Russian Ballet*.

BABA YAGA

I. de B. Lockyer, Baba Yaga, from Edith Sitwell, Children's Tales (From the Russian Ballet), 1920. Sitwell's

book was a retelling of Contes Russes, one of the most popular ballets in Diaghilev's postwar repertory.

July, 1919.

The Dancing Times

6D.
NET.

THE CAN CAN IN "LA BOUTIQUE FANTASQUE."

Ethelbert White, "The Can Can in La Boutique Fantasque," The Dancing Times, 1919, frontispiece. This caricature shows choreographer Léonide Massine in his celebrated role as the Can-Can Dancer.

John Nash, "Poodles!" Current Opinion, 1919. "John Nash, who thus caricatured the Russian dancers for the London Land and Water, confessed that 'La Boutique Fantasque' was really too beautiful to make fun of." After the Can-Can, the most popular number in the ballet was the pair of Dancing Poodles.

Edmond Dulac, "The Good Fairy Bakst Leads Prince Charming Diaghileff to the Shrine of the Sleeping Princess," The Sketch, 1921. In November 1921 Diaghilev produced The Sleeping Princess at London's Alhambra Theatre. The set and costume designs were by Bakst.

Vanessa Bell, cartoon of Lydia Lopokova taking a curtain call, with a smitten John Maynard Keynes bringing her flowers. Lopokova, a great favorite of the British public, married the celebrated economist in 1925.

SOME "CELEBS"—AS SEEN BY NERMAN

The names, from left to right, are: Anna Pavlova, Diaghileff, Bakst, and Stravinsky

Nerman, "Priscilla in Paris: Some 'Celebs'—*As Seen by Nerman*," The Tatler, 1922

Max Beerbohm, "Lord Berners Making More Sweetness Than Violence," 1923. *A diplomat and sometime intimate of Diaghilev's circle, Berners composed the score for the Ballets Russes's* 1926 Romeo and Juliet.

Husband (to listening-in Wife). "WHAT'S THE MATTER, DEAR? IS IT BAD NEWS OR STRAVINSKY?"

H. M. Brock, "Husband (to listening-in Wife). 'What's the matter, dear? Is it bad news or Stravinsky?'" Punch, 1926. Stravinsky's Les Noces, with choreography by Bronislava Nijinska, premiered in London to almost uniformly negative reviews a month before this cartoon appeared.

Anthony Betts, "Alice Nikitina and Serge Lifar in the Andantino from Les Biches," Vogue, *1928. Often called The House Party, Les Biches was a favorite with London's Bright Young Things and the most popular of the company's mid-decade creations.*

Félix de Gray, "A de Gray Decoration on a Russian Ballet Theme: Sauguet's The Cat," The Sketch, 1929. The

title role of the ballet, usually known by its French name La Chatte, was danced in England by Alice Nikitina.

The set by Naum Gabo and Anton Pevsner was a gleaming, transparent construction of plastic. A mica

cone completed the ballerina's tutu.

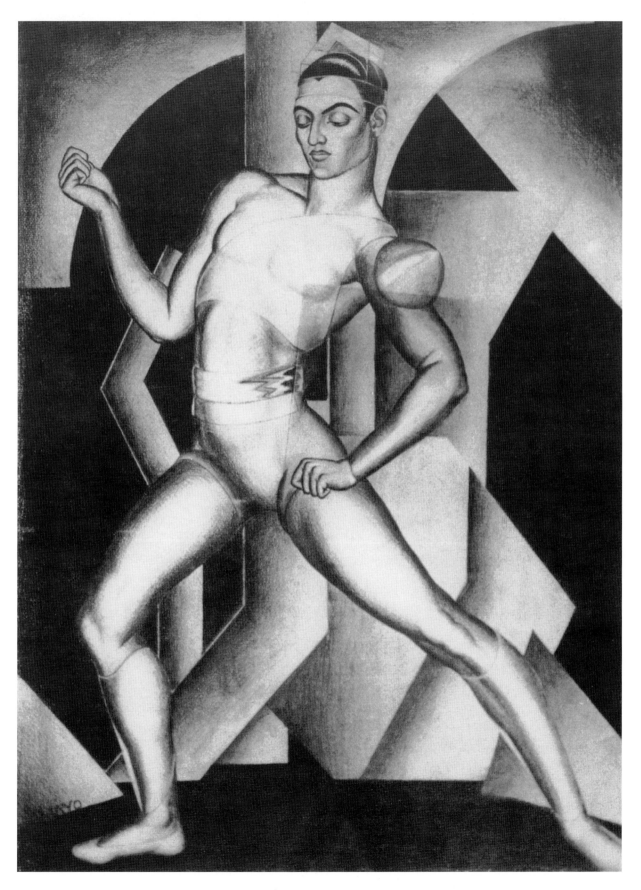

Eileen Mayo, "Portrait of Serge Lifar in La Chatte," 1928

Mrs. Maynard Keynes sits
in a box at the ballet and
watches Nikitina, Dou-
brovska, Tchernicheva and
Lifar dancing in Stra-
vinsky's ballet, " Apollo
Musagetes "

Cecil Beaton, "Mrs. Maynard Keynes sits in a box at the ballet and watches Nikitina, Doubrovska, Tchernicheva and Lifar

dancing in Stravinsky's ballet Apollo Musagetes," Vogue, 1928

MADAME ALEXANDRA DANILOVA

In "Pastorale," in which the beautiful lady—far more beautiful than this picture would suggest—dances delightfully. Her pas de deux in "Apollo" with Lifar was the best thing in that not very entrancing ballet

Nerman, caricature of *Alexandra Danilova* in La Pastorale, The Tatler, *1929*

Laura Knight, "*A Dancer Resting: An English Pupil in the School of Maestro Enrico Cecchetti,*" early 1920s. Diaghilev's in-house ballet master for nearly a decade, Cecchetti opened a London studio in 1919 that quickly became a mecca for British dancers and a gateway to the Ballets Russes.

fourteen **In His Image**

Diaghilev and Lincoln Kirstein

Nancy Reynolds

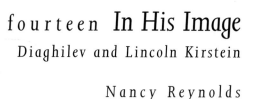

Lincoln Kirstein, American "aristocrat of life and culture," wrote often of "apostolic succession"; indeed, he made the phrase his own. Above all else, in his view, the patient and inevitable rules of such a process gave the world George Balanchine, the inheritor of a grammar of movement and a set of aesthetic beliefs practiced and honed across the centuries. Through devotion, assimilation of what had been learned before, and open-mindedness, Balanchine became an initiate of what Kirstein called a "secret society" or "higher order," an inner circle accessible only to the servants of art.[1]

By those standards of passion and service, which he combined with vision, voracious intellectual activity, and sheer audacity in his chosen sphere as impresario, patron, and catalyst in the arts, Kirstein can be recognized as Diaghilev's heir in spirit and deed—a successor-initiate himself.

Kirstein (through Balanchine) and Diaghilev (through the Ballets Russes) brought to the West new visions of ballet as a spectacular art: Diaghilev to the cultured but aestheti-

Pavel Tchelitchev,
portrait of Lincoln
Kirstein, 1937

cally exhausted soil of Western Europe, which had a long tradition and appetite for entertainments born at court; Kirstein to America, a virgin land in art and dance, where ballet had yet to sink permanent roots. A Harvard graduate, Kirstein received a classical Eurocentric education and, through his father, was an Anglophile. Still, he chose America, where three centuries of ingrained Puritanism, with its strictures against the celebration of the body and its dead hand on the development of dance, had other social consequences: Diaghilev wore his lovers on his arm and put them center stage (as did Balanchine), with incalculable import for his art. Kirstein married—as he was advised to do in order to be taken seriously—and it was not until his final book of memoirs (published when the author was eighty-seven) that he revealed his homosexual preference.[2]

Kirstein had personal wealth (although never enough to support a ballet company on his own), whereas Diaghilev had little more than the legacy he had received—and spent—as a young man. Diaghilev lived in hotel rooms and after 1917 was a citizen of no country; Kirstein owned an elegant town house in New York City that he filled with beautiful art. What they had in common was the ability to attract and cultivate many of the greatest artists of the century in movement, art, and music and to marshal an unsurpassed array of financial backers, movers and shakers, and society patrons to enable a ballet company to flourish.[3]

In this they were aided by boundless self-confidence. Toward the end of his life, Kirstein remarked, "I never had any doubt about my own opinions. They may have been wrong, but by the time I was 22 or 23 . . . I think I knew . . . as much as I know now about the relative standards." At about the same age, Diaghilev wrote home to his stepmother: "I think I have just found my true vocation—being a Maecenas. I have all that is necessary save the money"—as if such a lack were but a minor impediment.[4]

Like so many others, Kirstein viewed Diaghilev's role in the Ballets Russes as "indispensable." In the chaotic European ballet scene of the post-Diaghilev years, when several troupes vied unsuccessfully to pick up the pieces of the former company, he also called for a "Diaghilev to knock heads together[—]*the true function of the impresario*." To Diaghilev's "I work the lights," Kirstein could have replied, "I was always around. . . . I took care of the public aspects, the political aspects, the official aspects [while Balanchine made art]."[5]

Although Kirstein never met Diaghilev, there is abundant evidence in his writings that Diaghilev's example was the one he wished to emulate. In a letter written to the critic Allen Tate in 1933, he confessed, "I am merely trying to jockey myself into a position where eventually I can act as I like in relation to the employment . . . of the artists of merit in this country. And while I should never attempt to assume the career of a Diaghilev, nevertheless the parallel is useful." Nearly forty years later, in *Movement and Metaphor*, a brilliant, complexly layered work that sums up Kirstein's feelings about dance as history, artistic expression, and politics, he mentions Diaghilev far more than any other figure from the time of Louis XIV on and concludes: "Of all non-dancers in the history of ballet, Diaghilev is the greatest; he birthed an era more important to us than the *ballet de cour* (1570–1680), *ballet d'action* (1740–80), or *ballet romantique* (1830–70). . . . Diaghilev was a courtier, a gifted musical amateur, a catalyst of genius. His moral energy in bringing his ballet into being and maintaining it in spite of loss of base was heroic. He spans history. He marked the end of one epoch and named another; what he managed remains our model."[6]

As a student abroad in 1929, Kirstein stumbled on Diaghilev's funeral by accident, but it was hardly his first encounter with the great man. Kirstein caught Cocteau's "red and gold disease"—addiction to the theater—at an early age; indeed, he became infected on seeing *The Merry Widow* as a boy of five. "The malady, obsession, advanced state of unease, indeed disease, was compounded of passion for the preposterous, the tease of perfection which was an impersonation of grandeur, or in exalted cases, the superhuman and heroic," he wrote some sixty years later in his typically baroque style. His first "contact" with Diaghilev, albeit at several removes, occurred just a few years later, when his mother decided against taking him to a performance of the Ballets Russes in Boston in 1916. (For years he thought he'd missed Nijinsky, although it is likely that Alexander Gavrilov had danced unannounced in his place.) By the time he saw Pavlova as a teenager, the disease was entrenched: "Whatever it was that lurked as an imaginative need, 'ballet' stuck in my elementary judgment as a luminous magnet. This basic bias soon accumulated conviction, sharp preferences rapidly becoming what counted as 'my taste.' Reputations and fame glowed as a nimbus around the bodies of God-given performers, flaring or withering as I managed to gain first-hand impressions from their galvanic performances."[7]

In the 1920s he began making yearly visits to Europe (often mingling with the Bloomsbury set) and in 1924 saw his first Diaghilev season. He singled out Léonide Massine's *Les Matelots* as "an early statement" of post–World War I modernism. "It satisfied me," he wrote, "more as a declaration of policy than as an independent triumph of dancing, but strengthened my faith in the crusading principles of Diaghilev's policy. . . . *The past* was abandoned, rhetoric was left behind, and a new and electric sensibility was available and exploited. To be a first witness of such dynamism rarely happens in a lifetime."[8] In 1926 Kirstein saw his first Stravinsky ballet, *Firebird*, in which Balanchine appeared in the role of Kostchei, and he continued to follow the company until its collapse in 1929.

Kirstein's earliest major piece of writing on dance was "The Diaghilev Period," published in 1930. The product of impressive research and an early vehicle for his interpretive abilities, the essay gave voice to ideas on ballet as an art form that Kirstein would continue to develop. It began:

An American tourist was hunting the back alleys of Venice, one hot morning in the middle of last August, for a church in which Dominico Theotocopulos must have worshipped. . . . Not until three days later, reading the *London Times*, did he learn that he had unwittingly attended, in San Giorgio dei Greci, the obsequies of a great Russian. . . . Sergei Diaghilev, more than any other sin-

Lucian Freud, portrait of George
Balanchine, 1950

Lincoln Kirstein, 1933. The photographer, George Platt Lynes, studied in Paris with Man Ray and in 1933 opened his own studio in New York, where this portrait was taken. Two years later, he was invited by Kirstein and Balanchine to document the repertory and principal dancers of their fledgling American Ballet, a collaboration that continued until the photographer's death in 1955.

gle person, was responsible for the growth and maintenance of a tradition in contemporary painting, music, and dancing. . . . His previous training in law, in esthetics, in music, his inherent gifts of taste, his consciousness of the chic, his appreciation of social snobbery and his passion for the beauty of surprise and of youth—these in a combination of brilliant energies and practical qualifications made him the isolated genius that he was. . . . [He was] a personality of the utmost distinction, combining in his fantastic character elements of practical facility, capacity for action, and an exuberant invention which made the ballet possible.[9]

Kirstein could almost have been describing his adult self.

Of Balanchine, Diaghilev's last choreographer, the neophyte critic wrote: "In *The Cat* and *Apollo*, [he] was leading out of mere ingenuity into a revivified, purer, classicism. . . . Always in the last analysis the classical dance is the most satisfactory; its cold multiplication of a thousand embroideries . . . divested of the personal, if more romantic charm of pantomime . . . never becomes cloying."[10] Even before meeting him, Kirstein felt an instinctive affinity for Balanchine's work; at the same time, his secondary career as an impassioned historian, critic, and apologist of dance was born.

Kirstein's diaries of 1933, published forty years later in a putative reconstruction, recount the events of the fateful summer in Europe during which his choice of profession crystallized and the course of ballet in America was forever altered. At this time of attempted self-definition, Kirstein was involved in a tumultuous relationship with Romola Nijinsky, ghostwriting a good part of her book about her husband and gaining entrée into Russian émigré circles. He hoped to become a painter and harbored vague notions about establishing an "American ballet." Among his confidants that summer were the composer Virgil Thomson—who filled him in on ballet styles in Europe and told him that "the main progressive line from Diaghilev is with Balanchine rather than Massine"—and, most important, Monroe Wheeler. Wheeler, Kirstein wrote, "gave me everything I most wanted and needed, and tested my own aims. What did I actually want? What could I actually do? How much money did I actually have or could I raise[?] . . . Everything cried out for Diaghilev. . . . Could not tell whether he was suggesting I try for this." (As Kirstein later acknowledged, he was.) From Janet Flanner (Genêt of the *New Yorker*) he learned that "ballet activity is greater this year than at any time since Diaghilev's death, but there is no restraining or controlling influence; the dancers (choreographers?) are all too social and uppity; Diaghilev would have permitted none of this nonsense"; from Wheeler, that Boris Kochno, Balanchine's artistic director at the time, "is not powerful enough to last as an impresario."[11]

Finally, there was the meeting with Balanchine in London on 11 July 1933:

He said one must not revive anything, ever; dancing, a breath, a memory; dancers are butterflies; . . . the idiom of one decade has little to do with the next; must be cleansed repeatedly, like laundry. Conventions and limits of Petipa, intolerable today. Whole academic dance must be restudied from its base. . . . He would like to come to America with twenty girls and five men, in a repertory of classical ballet in his own extended academic "modern" style. . . . Balanchine seemed intense, concentrated, disinterested; not desperate exactly, but without any hope.[12]

After one more meeting, during which Balanchine confessed that America had always been his dream, Kirstein wrote a sixteen-page letter to his friend Everett A. "Chick" Austin, Jr., the director of the Wadsworth Atheneum in Hartford, Connecticut. "This will be the most important letter I will ever write you," Kirstein began. "We have a real chance to have an American ballet within 3 yrs. time. When I say ballet, I mean a trained company of young dancers—not Russians—but Americans. . . . We have the future in our hands. For Christ's sweet sake let us honor it."[13]

The medium for this visionary project was to be Balanchine, who, financed by Austin and other friends, duly arrived in the New World on 17 October 1933. By mid-1934 the School of American Ballet had been established, and its students had performed Balanchine's first American ballet, *Serenade*, on an outdoor platform in White Plains, New York. Within a year, Balanchine's American Ballet had become the resident dance troupe of the Metropolitan Opera. In 1946 Ballet Society was founded, and two years later, the New York City Ballet. It was a remarkably direct journey, even if the going was sometimes bumpy. Still, as Kirstein told an interviewer in 1983, "I never doubted the fact that sooner or later, it [the New York City Ballet] would happen."[14]

Diaghilev's collaborative ideal was one that clearly fired Kirstein's imagination and had done so at least since his first visit to Bayreuth and encounter with Gesamtkunstwerk in 1924. As his alter-ego in *Flesh Is Heir* explains, Diaghilev had taken "all the best painters and musicians and dancers. The very best and put them all together and it makes the most perfect thing an artist can do." Kirstein observed this approach at work during the summers he had spent watching the Ballets Russes; he encountered it again in the Blum-Balanchine and de Basil Ballet Russe companies, and in Les Ballets 1933, in which all six of the ballets presented were new. All were choreographed by Balanchine, and most had especially commissioned scores and decors.[15]

Within months of Balanchine's arrival in the United States, Kirstein had put the collaborative idea into practice. The American Ballet, their first, short-lived company, presented several works from the Les Ballets 1933 repertory — *Dreams, Errante,* and *Mozartiana* — as well as a new atmospheric piece called *Transcendence*, which had a libretto by Kirstein on the nature of virtuosity.[16] Gluck's *Orpheus and Eurydice*, staged in 1936 by Balanchine for the Metropolitan Opera, had an extraordinary gauze-and-wire decor and striking lighting effects by Pavel Tchelitchev. Considered one of the most magical works ever designed, it was also highly controversial: with the singers in the pit and the action mimed by dancers, it drew the ire of music critics and opera fans. After only two performances, the production was withdrawn.

Kirstein was able to realize his ideas more fully with Ballet Caravan. Founded in 1936, this chamber-sized summer touring company had a repertory consisting entirely of new works, most with decor and scores commissioned from American artists and many on American subjects. With Balanchine only peripherally involved, Kirstein's principal choreographers were William Dollar, Lew Christensen, and Eugene Loring. The composers and designers included Elliott Carter, Virgil Thomson, Paul Bowles, Robert McBride, Paul Cadmus, Aaron Copland, and Jared French, while the subject matter ranged from Pocahontas to a day in the life of a gas station attendant. Kirstein, who was full of ideas for ballets, contributed seven scenarios, including the perennially successful *Billy the Kid*, the only work produced by the company that significantly outlasted it. In its efforts to employ native talent, to treat everyday subjects unassumingly, to strip away empty

William Dollar with Holly Howard and Annabelle Lyon in Errante, 1935

Lew Christensen in the title role of Apollo, 1937. Christensen was Balanchine's first American Apollo.

glamour, and to appear in large and small towns all over the country, Ballet Caravan was a forerunner of the regional ballet movement.

Never more than a part-time enterprise, Ballet Caravan lasted from 1936 until 1940. World War II surely hastened its death, but there were other problems: the Americana formula was too rigidly followed, often at the expense of theatrical flair, and the low budget and inexperience of the dancers gave an amateurish flavor to the enterprise. As Kirstein wrote, his two-piano arrangements could not compete with ballet orchestras, nor could his earnest young performers erase memories of the likes of Alexandra Danilova, Tamara Toumanova, and Léonide Massine, who could be seen in one-night stands all over America with the various Ballet Russe companies.[17] He had learned something about dance as a spectacular art—that it had, in some measure, to provide the "luminous magnet" that had originally attracted him.

Kirstein's most ambitious attempt to re-create the Diaghilevian synthesis of the arts—and go beyond it—was contained in his plan for Ballet Society, which made its debut in 1946. As he wrote (anonymously) in the prospectus: "Each [new work] will have the planned collaboration of independent easel painters and progressive choreographers and musicians, employing the full use of avant-garde ideas, methods and materials. . . . Emphasis will be on expert musical and dance direction to insure an essential elegance and freshness, rather than on famous stars or the residual prestige of the standard ballet repertory." Unlike Diaghilev, however, who tended to use only one choreographer at a time, Kirstein, while giving Balanchine free rein, sponsored the efforts of several others: John Taras (*The Minotaur*), Todd Bolender (*Zodiac*), William Dollar (*Highland Fling*), Merce Cunningham (*The Seasons*), Lew Christensen (*Blackface*), and Fred Danieli (*Punch and the Child*). John Cage, Elliott Carter, Vittorio Rieti, and Igor Stravinsky were among the commissioned composers; Isamu Noguchi, Estebán Francés, and Horace Armistead among the designers. In its two-year existence, Ballet Society produced sixteen new ballets, including Balanchine's seminal *Four Temperaments*, *Symphony in C*, and *Orpheus*, and plans were laid for an elaborate two-act Balanchine work—unrealized—on the theme of Beauty and the Beast, with music by Alexei Haieff and decor by Francés. Operas by Gian-Carlo Menotti and dances in idioms other than ballet were also presented. The critics, who had to purchase their own tickets, were generally enthusiastic.

But Kirstein wanted more. He envisioned a select audience that, in addition to "participating" in the creation of new works, would receive monographs, a yearbook ("based on the model of the annuals of the Imperial Russian Theatres"), recorded scores of the ballets, silk-screen prints of stage designs, and invitations to films, poetry readings, exhibitions, and dance demonstrations. In short, Kirstein wanted to offer a complete environment for experiencing dance in all its intellectual, aesthetic, and sensual aspects. Not even Diaghilev had contemplated an enterprise on so vast a scale, nor, even in the best of times, could he afford to ignore the commercial aspect of his ventures as Kirstein, by restricting tickets to Ballet Society members, hoped to do.

But he could not bring it off. The company performed only four programs yearly on unsuitable stages. Dissolution seemed inevitable when, on the strength of *Orpheus,* Ballet Society's most prestigious collaborative effort (involving Balanchine, Noguchi, and Stravinsky), the group was invited by Morton Baum, chairman of City Center's executive committee, to become a resident constituent of the theater; as the New York City Ballet, it gave its first performance on 11 October 1948. After a fifteen-year struggle, Kirstein and Balanchine had achieved a measure

Lew Christensen as Mac in Filling Station, *1938*

of permanence for their vision.

In the following decade Balanchine produced some of his most felicitous creations: *Firebird*, *La Valse*, *Swan Lake* (Act 2), *Scotch Symphony*, *Western Symphony*, *Allegro Brillante*, *Pas de Dix*, *Agon*, *Episodes*, *Tschaikovsky Pas de Deux*, *Liebeslieder Walzer*, *A Midsummer Night's Dream*, and *Tarantella*. These ballets, along with such earlier masterpieces as *Concerto Barocco*, *Apollo*,

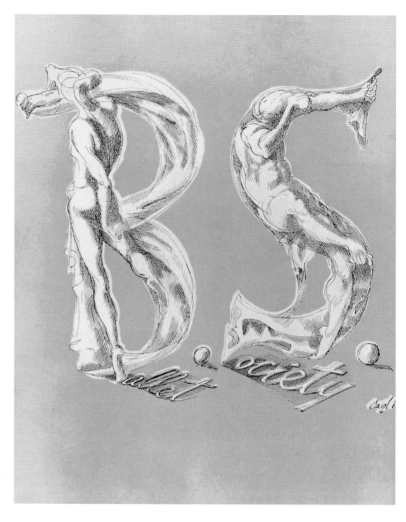

Ballet Society prospectus with cover design by Corrado Cagli, 1947. Cagli, an Italian painter, designed The Triumph of Bacchus and Ariadne *(1947).*

Prodigal Son, and *Serenade*, established him as the preeminent choreographer of his day (as well as the most prolific), one whose philosophy regarding both theatrical values and dance technique was very much his own. The 1954 *Nutcracker*, a rare mounting of an older work, may be seen as Balanchine and Kirstein's counterpart to Diaghilev's *Sleeping Princess*: a bouquet to the past and box-office security for the present and future. So successful was it as a money maker that it inspired some two hundred imitations throughout the country, starting a new tradition. True to the Kirstein ideal, there were also distinguished and experimental works by Antony Tudor, Frederick Ashton, Martha Graham, and John Cranko, a season of Japanese gagaku, and an entire repertory of original, provocative works by Jerome Robbins, including *The Cage*, *Afternoon of a Faun*, *Age of Anxiety*, *The Concert*, *The Pied Piper*, and *Fanfare*. In addition to these preeminent figures, there were ballets by Ruthanna Boris, Lew Christensen, Todd Bolender, Francisco Monción, William Dollar,

Birgit Cullberg, and John Butler, most of them new, some with new music and interesting decor, almost all with scenarios, themes, or plots.

But with time, Balanchine's vision became the dominant one. Works by outside choreographers of independent reputation were ignored; the occasional new ballet by a Balanchine follower (usually a company member) lasted only a season or two. Commissioned scores became rarer and eventually nonexistent, and decor was downplayed or dispensed with entirely; house designers, not independent artists, dressed the stage. A signal event in this evolutionary process was *Agon* (1957), quite apart from its significance as a work of genius. The last active collaboration between Balanchine and Stravinsky, performed in practice clothes on a bare stage to a twelve-tone score, *Agon* was, unexpectedly, a popular as well as a critical success, meaning that Balanchine's most radical work to date—his most stripped, reductive, and musically uncompromising—had found favor with the general public, not just the cognoscenti. Balanchine had proved he could do it all.[18]

By the 1960s, any pretense of the company's being anything but his personal laboratory had been abandoned, and it must have been apparent that the Diaghilev idea was dead for the New York City Ballet. Somewhere along the way Kirstein had made the decision to suppress his own creative vision in the interests of serving that of Balanchine. Regarding the issues involved in this choice or the precise nature of his relationship with Balanchine, the normally voluble Kirstein provided only the most circumspect observations: "We never had a contract;

Joan Junyer, costume design for a Cretan Worker in The Minotaur, *1947*

Maria Tallchief and Nicholas Magallanes in Orpheus, 1947

we never had any kind of legal connection. We never had any disagreements because we never talked about anything. . . . People don't realize the specific way in which George ran the company. . . . There was nothing except what he wished." As if in a footnote, he added, "Generally speaking, he knew what he wanted, but for specifics [in decor and costumes] he needed suggestions, so I could give them to him." The offstage Balanchine who appears in the recollections of his close friend Nathan Milstein, his biographer Bernard Taper, and any number of companions—colorful, passionate, fun-loving, mystical, and deeply religious—is all but absent from Kirstein's writings. Clearly, the two were colleagues, not friends. Kirstein described Balanchine at work as "unassertive, slim, no longer boyish, and, with his grave, alert mannerliness, the more daunting in his authority, instinctive and absolute"—a brilliant miniature portrait, born of closeness without intimacy.[19]

In 1962 the New York City Ballet toured the Soviet Union (Balanchine's first return visit since emigrating); in 1963 it was stabilized by an unprecedented grant of two million dollars (over a ten-year period) from the Ford Foundation;[20] in 1964 after an acrimonious struggle led by Kirstein and Morton Baum against John D. Rockefeller III and the board of Lincoln Center, it became the resident company of the New York State Theater (for which Kirstein had selected the architect); and in 1965 its first subscription drive was undertaken. Clearly, institutional status was at hand. This must have pleased Kirstein, a great believer in order, tradition, and continuity, as his numerous writings on dance (and other subjects) clearly and repeatedly demonstrate.

But his most creative years with the company were over. Not only was Balanchine in complete artistic command but also, as Kirstein himself confessed in the early

1980s, "When the thing became an institution, I lost interest in it. . . . The kind of thing that we did, the strength of it was based on improvisation. When it got to be as big as it is now, there are so many factors that limit the improvisation."[21]

When Diaghilev died at fifty-seven, his company collapsed. At the same age, Kirstein oversaw the inaugural season of the New York City Ballet at the New York State Theater, a circumstance that he more than anyone else had engineered and an event that

Tanaquil LeClercq and
Francisco Monción in
La Valse, 1951

heralded a new era of permanence for the company and a new phase in his own career. Driven by a sense of service inherited from his father and honed by his years at Balanchine's side, he continued on as fundraiser, troubleshooter, socialite tamer, and general advocate, supervising the creation of boards of directors for the company and the School of American Ballet and the move of the school to expansive new quarters. He did not formally withdraw from the directorship of either body until 1989, well after Balanchine's death, when at the age of eighty-two he quietly retired.

The irony surrounding Kirstein's accomplishment is that he succeeded to Diaghilev's mantle by abandoning the quest to do so. He gave up much of the creative leadership of the New York City Ballet in order that—unlike the Ballets Russes—the company might survive. But perhaps, despite his years of impassioned rhetoric in favor of the Diaghilev model, this had been in the cards all along. Recalling his second meeting with Balanchine in 1933, in which the choreographer had talked about his problems with Edward James and de Basil, Kirstein wrote: "When he spoke, I began to have a large and

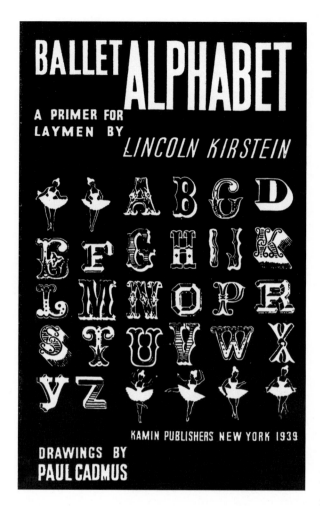

growing sympathy for Balanchine himself, not as an historic figure but as an individual, who, like others, depended on factors beyond his own extraordinary capacities, and whom perhaps I might have a real role in supporting. Perhaps it was this personal consideration, up until now quite lacking, that seemed to indicate my ultimate direction."[22]

Kirstein never had a "sole" profession. Had he never met Balanchine, he would have made a name for himself as a cultural critic and historian. After an early apprenticeship as a reviewer of dance and art, he became an outspoken advocate for various overlooked artists. Over the years he rescued or enhanced the reputations of William Rimmer, Elie Nadelman, Gaston Lachaise, and Pavel Tchelitchev and was one of the earliest to argue persuasively for photography as an art form. But he saved his choicest language for the defense of classical ballet, particularly classical ballet in America. During the 1930s his chief targets were modern dance and the expatriate "Russian" troupes that were beginning to tour the country (in the process building new audiences for the ballet, a circumstance Kirstein ignored). His invective on the subject appeared in purest form in his *Blast at Ballet: A Corrective for the American Audience* (1937), in which he attacked not only the "so-called Russian ballet" but also the managers, patrons, critics, and public that supported it, themes reiterated in *Ballet Alphabet: A Primer for Laymen*, published two years later. As his hopes and dreams began to be realized, the tone of his writings grew milder, although at the age of nearly eighty, he could still contribute "The Curse of Isadora" as a lead article to the Sunday *New York Times*.[23]

Kirstein also left a major legacy as a dance historian. While still in his twenties

Paul Cadmus, cover design for Lincoln Kirstein, Ballet Alphabet: A Primer for Laymen, 1939

he published *Dance: A Short History of Classic Theatrical Dancing* (1935), the first work in English devoted to the subject. A densely written tour de force, the book covers topics ranging from ritual dances of ancient Egypt to the Renaissance, from Dauberval to Diaghilev; some of the material, such as that on nineteenth-century dance in America, was largely virgin territory. Another work of wide-ranging scholarship and erudition was *Movement and Metaphor: Four Centuries of Ballet* (1970), in which the author examined fifty seminal ballets through the ages in their cultural, political, and technical contexts. As if to dignify the status of his notoriously elusive subject matter and its frequent lightweight treatment in print, he wrote, "The classical dance is a language, and ballets are its constructs, comparable to others formed in other idioms. The battle picture, still life, landscape; the comedy of manners, heroic tragedy; the novel of society or psychological observation create worlds based on tradition, observation, and craft. The universe projected by ballet in its brief temporal duration draws on analogous sources and is capable of maintaining similar metaphors." Reflecting his (then) forty-year association with Balanchine, he also wrote, "If there is a hero, it is choreography."[24] Like *Dance, Movement and Metaphor* is profusely illustrated with remarkable and often little-known images, many from the field of visual arts, attesting

Vaslav Nijinsky in the title role of Till Eulenspiegel, *1916. This was one of the images reproduced in* Nijinsky Dancing.

to Kirstein's broad interests, knowledge, and continuing love affair with objects in museums.

One of Kirstein's most striking contributions to dance literature was his early recognition of Nijinsky's importance as a choreographer. While other writers were still mesmerized by Nijinsky's sensational and tragic life or waxing idolatrous over his legendary performances, Kirstein was analyzing the radical underpinnings of his choreography. At the time of Diaghilev's death, Nijinsky's work was considered a failure, and, with the exception of L'Après-midi d'un Faune, none of his ballets had survived their first season. Nevertheless, in 1935 Kirstein wrote, "Great as he was in the province of the performing dancer, Nijinsky was far greater as a practicing choreographer, in which function he either demonstrated or implied theories as profound as have ever been articulated about the classical theatrical dance." He later elaborated his notion that Nijinsky's ballets "paralleled Freud's chart of man's developing psyche: in *Faune*, adolescent self-discovery and gratification; in *Jeux*, homosexual discovery of another self or selves; in *Le Sacre du Printemps*, fertility and the renewal of the race." Finally, in his handsome monograph *Nijinsky Dancing*, Kirstein wrote boldly: "Launched by sounds without precedent into a style with no history, [Nijinsky] forced himself to find a range of movement, an idiom without a model, which might serve as metaphor for an epoch before remembrance. . . . He put beauty as defined by his epoch mercilessly to the question. . . . Instinctively, or however, Nijinsky . . . for his generation murdered beauty."[25]

In 1940, with some five thousand of his own books, photographs, designs, playbills, manuscripts, and other documents as the centerpiece, Kirstein established the Dance Archives at the Museum of Modern Art, under the curatorship of Paul Magriel — the first such resource in the United States. In conjunction with the opening of the New York State Theater at Lincoln Center in 1964, this material (by now considerably augmented) was transferred to the Dance Collection of the New York Public Library, where Kirstein established a conservation laboratory in 1970. His donations to the Dance Collection continued over the years, and he deeded to this major repository his papers and his copyrights.

In 1942, with the vast material in the Dance Archives as a nucleus for research, Kirstein, Magriel, and Baird Hastings founded the periodical *Dance Index*, an unprecedented undertaking in the then barely defined world of American dance scholarship. Unlike Diaghilev's lavishly produced *Mir iskusstva*, it was modest in format and design. But it was equally adventurous in content. In existence until 1949, *Dance Index* provided a forum for the investigations of George Chaffee (on romantic iconography), Marian Hannah Winter (on preromantic ballet), Lillian Moore (on various subjects, many of them American), and Yuri Slonimsky (on Petipa and Perrot), among others. There were monographs on Duncan, Graham, Balanchine, Nijinsky, and several visual artists, photographers, and critics, in addition to the acclaimed issue "Stravinsky and the Theater," where Balanchine's most famous formulation of his dance philosophy appeared for the first time: "*Apollon* I look back on as the turning point in my life. [The score] seemed to tell me that I could dare not to use everything. . . . I could clarify . . . by reducing what seemed to be multiple possibilities to that one that is inevitable."[26]

The strength of character that permitted Kirstein to give up artistic domination to Balanchine also produced a constancy that predicated his devotion until the end. His

Vaslav Nijinsky at the piano with Maurice Ravel, ca. 1911–1913. This was another image reproduced in Nijinsky Dancing.

public reputation as someone who
was irascible and unpredictable,
bore grudges, and cut off friends
without explanation notwithstanding, on the big issues there was
nothing fickle about Kirstein and
his vision. Moreover, the fruits of
his mercurial intellect tended to
obscure his behind-the-scenes ac-
complishments as a conciliator and
facilitator, of which the fight for
control of the New York State The-
ater is only one example. Although he was "very happy to have been brought up amid the
relics and the legacy of the nineteenth century in England," he is the closest thing to a Renaissance man of culture that twentieth-century America has produced. "There can be no
second Diaghilev," Kirstein wrote in 1937.[27] A second Kirstein is equally impossible.

Ivan Bilibin, *cover for the Boris Godunov souvenir program, 1908*

appendix: Operas and Ballets Produced by Serge Diaghilev

Compiled by Lynn Garafola

Operas

Boris Godunov

Music Drama in Three Acts and Seven Tableaux

Music: Modest Mussorgsky, revised and orchestrated by Nikolai Rimsky-Korsakov

Libretto: Modest Mussorgsky, after Alexander Pushkin

Conductor: Felix Blumenfeld

Chorus master: Ulrich Avranek

Stage direction: Alexander Sanin

Scenery: Alexander Golovin, Alexandre Benois, Konstantin Yuon

Costumes: Ivan Bilibin, Dmitry Stelletsky, Alexander Golovin, Alexandre Benois, Boris Anisfeld, Eugene Lanceray, Stepan Yaremich, Konstantin Yuon

Premiere: 19 May 1908, Théâtre National de l'Opéra, Paris

Principal singers: Fedor Chaliapin (Boris), Klavdia Tugarinova (Tsarevich Fedor), Dagmara Renine (Xenia), Elizaveta Petrenko (Nurse), Dmitry Smirnov (False Dmitry), Ivan Alchevsky (Prince Shuisky), Vladimir Kastorsky (Pimen), Natalia Ermolenko (Marina), Vasily Sharonov (Varlaam), Mikhail Kravchenko (Missail), Mitrofan Chuprynnikov (Idiot)

Note: The opera was first produced in its original form in 1874 in St. Petersburg and in Rimsky-Korsakov's revised version in 1896.

Prince Igor (Act II)

Polovtsian Scenes and Dances

Music: Alexander Borodin, completed and partly orchestrated by Nikolai Rimsky-Korsakov and Alexander Glazunov

Libretto: Alexander Borodin, after a scenario by Vladimir Stasov

Conductor: Emile Cooper

Chorus master: Ulrich Avranek

Stage directions: Alexander Sanin

Scenery and costumes: Nicholas Roerich

Scene painting: Boris Anisfeld

Choreography: Michel Fokine

Premiere: 18*/ 19 May 1909, Théâtre du Châtelet, Paris

Principal singers: Elizaveta Petrenko (Konchakovna), Vasily Sharonov (Prince Igor), Dmitry Smirnov

*When a *répétition générale* preceded the official premiere, the earlier date is given followed by an asterisk.

(Vladimir), Kapitan Zaporojetz (Khan Konchak), Michel d'Arial (Ovlur)

Principal dancers: Adolph Bolm (A Polovtsian Warrior), Sophia Fedorova (A Young Polovtsian Girl), Elena Smirnova (An Oriental Slave Woman), Alexis Kosloff, Nicolas Kremnev, Leonid Leontiev, Laurent Novikov, Alexander Orlov, Georgy Rosai (Young Polovtsian Boys)

Note: This opera was first produced in 1890 in St. Petersburg.

Ivan the Terrible (The Maid of Pskov)

Opera in Three Acts and Five Tableaux

Music: Nikolai Rimsky-Korsakov

Libretto: Nikolai Rimsky-Korsakov, after Lev Mey

Conductor: Nicolas Tcherepnin

Chorus master: Ulrich Avranek

Stage direction: Alexander Sanin

Scenery: Alexander Golovin, Nicholas Roerich

Costumes: Dmitry Stelletsky

Scene painting: (?) Vnukov (Scene 1), Boris Anisfeld (Scenes 2, 4, 5), Nikolai Charbé (Scene 3)

Premiere: 24*/26 May 1909, Théâtre du Châtelet, Paris

Principal singers: Fedor Chaliapin (Ivan the Terrible), Lydia Lipkowska (Princess Olga Tokmakov), Elizaveta Petrenko (Nurse), Vladimir Kastorsky (Prince Georgy Tokmakov), Vasily Sharonov (Prince Viazemsky), Vasily Damaev (Mikhail Tucha), Alexander Davydov (Boyar Matuta)

Note: The third and final version of this opera was first produced in 1895 in St. Petersburg.

Ruslan and Ludmila (Act I)

Fairy Opera in Five Acts

Music: Mikhail Glinka

Libretto: Konstantin Bakhturin, Valerian Shirkov, and others, after Pushkin

Conductor: Emile Cooper

Chorus master: Ulrich Avranek

Stage direction: Alexander Sanin

Scenery and costumes: Konstantin Korovin

Premiere: 2*/4 June 1909, Théâtre du Châtelet, Paris

Principal singers: Lydia Lipkowska (Ludmila), Evgenia Zbruyeva (Ratmir), Dmitry Smirnov (Bayan), Vasily Sharonov (Svetosar), Vladimir Kastorsky (Ruslan), Kapitan Zaporojetz (Farlaf)

Note: This opera was first produced in 1842 in St. Petersburg.

Judith (Orgy and Finale)

Music: Alexander Serov

Libretto: A. Maykov and others, after the biblical book of Judith

Conductor: Emile Cooper

Chorus master: Ulrich Avranek

Stage direction: Alexander Sanin

Scenery: Valentin Serov, Léon Bakst

Costumes: Léon Bakst

Premiere: 7 June 1909, Théâtre du Châtelet, Paris

Principal singers: Fedor Chaliapin (Holofernes), Felia Litvinne (Judith), Dmitry Smirnov (Vagao), Evgenia Zbruyeva (Avre), Kapitan Zaporojetz (Asphanèse)

Note: This opera was first produced in 1863 in St. Petersburg.

Boris Godunov

Music Drama in Three Acts and Seven Tableaux

Music: Modest Mussorgsky, revised and orchestrated by Nikolai Rimsky-Korsakov

Libretto: Modest Mussorgsky, after Alexander Pushkin

Conductor: Emile Cooper

Chorus master: D. Pokhitonov

Stage direction: Alexander Sanin

Scenery: Konstantin Yuon (executed by G. Golov), Ivan Bilibin

Costumes and Accessories: Ivan Bilibin

Premiere: 22 May 1913, Théâtre des Champs-Elysées, Paris

Principal singers: Fedor Chaliapin (Boris), (?) Davydova (Tsarevich Fedor), Marie Brian (Xenia), Elizaveta Petrenko (Nurse), Vasily Damaev (False Dmitry), Nikolai Andreyev (Prince Shuisky), Pavel Andreyev (Pimen), Elena Nikolaeva (Marina), Alexander Belianin (Varlaam), Nikolai Bolshakov (Missail), (?) Alexandrovich (Idiot)

Note: The opera was first produced in its original form in 1874 in St. Petersburg and in Rimsky-Korsakov's revised version in 1896. The first performance in London of the Diaghilev production was on 24 June 1913 at the Theatre Royal, Drury Lane. The chorus was from the Imperial Opera, St. Petersburg.

Khovanshchina

Music Drama in Three Acts and Four Tableaux

Music: Modest Mussorgsky, completed and orchestrated by Nikolai Rimsky-Korsakov, with additional passages orchestrated by Maurice Ravel and Igor Stravinsky

Libretto: Modest Mussorgsky, Vladimir Stasov

Conductor: Emile Cooper

Stage direction: Alexander Sanin

Scenery, costumes, and accessories: Fedor Fedorovsky

Choreography: Adolph Bolm (Scene 3, Persian Dance)

Premiere: 5 June 1913, Théâtre des Champs-Elysées, Paris

Principal singers: Fedor Chaliapin (Dositheus), Elizaveta Petrenko (Marfa), Kapitan Zaporojetz (Prince Ivan Khovansky), Vasily Damaev (Prince André Khovansky), Marie Brian (Emma), Elena Nikolaeva (Susanna), Pavel Andreyev (Shaklovitz), Nikolai Andreyev (Scribe), Alexander Belianin (Varsonofiev)

Dancers: Serafima Astafieva, Lubov Tchernicheva, Henriette Maikerska, Sophie Pflanz, Kasimira

Kopycinska, (?) Konietska, (?) Dombrovska, Olga Khokhlova, Doris Faithful, (?) Chidlovska, Alexandra Wassilewska, (?) Jezierska, Ludmila Guliuk, Hilda Munnings, Anne Bromney (Broomhead)

Note: This opera was first produced in 1886 in St. Petersburg. The first performance in London of the Diaghilev production was on 1 July 1913 at the Theatre Royal, Drury Lane. According to the London program, "the orchestration of the scene of the reading of the ukases, the hymn to Prince Ivan Khovansky, the duet between young Khovansky and Emma in the first act, Maria's song, and the song of Kouska and Chorus, in the second act, [were] by Maurice Ravel from the original manuscript of Moussorgsky now in the Imperial Library of St. Petersburg."

Ivan the Terrible (The Maid of Pskov)
Opera in Three Acts and Five Scenes
Music: Nikolai Rimsky-Korsakov
Libretto: Nikolai Rimsky-Korsakov, after Lev Mey
Conductor: Emile Cooper
Chorus master: D. Pokhitonov
Stage direction: Alexander Sanin
Scenery: Alexander Golovin (Scenes 1, 2), Nicholas Roerich (Scenes 3, 4, 5)
Scene painting: (?) Vnukov (Scene 1), Boris Anisfeld (Scenes 2, 4, 5), G. Golov (Scene 3)
Costumes: Alexander Golovin
Premiere: 8 July 1913, Theatre Royal, Drury Lane, London
Principal singers: Fedor Chaliapin (Ivan the Terrible), Marie Brian (Princess Olga Tokmakov), Elena Nikolaeva (Stiosha Matuta), Elizaveta Petrenko (Nurse), Pavel Andreyev (Prince Georgy Tokmakov), Kapitan Zaporojetz (Prince Viazemsky), Vasily Damaev (Mikhail Tucha), Nikolai Andreyev (Boyar Nikita Matuta), Kapitan Zaporojetz (Messenger)
Note: The third and final version of this opera was first produced in 1895 in St. Petersburg.

Le Coq d'Or (*also called* The Golden Cockerel *and* The Golden Cock)
Opera in Three Scenes
Music: Nikolai Rimsky-Korsakov
Libretto: Vladimir Belsky, after Alexander Pushkin, revised by Alexandre Benois
Conductor: Pierre Monteux
Chorus master: Nicolas Palitzine
Stage direction and choreography: Michel Fokine
Scenery and costumes: Natalia Goncharova
Premiere: 24 May 1914, Théâtre National de l'Opéra, Paris
Principal singers: Aurelia Dobrovolska (Queen of Shemakhan), Vasily Petrov (King Dodon), Ivan Alchevsky (Astrologer), Alexander Belianin (General Polkan), Elizaveta Petrenko (Amelfa), Elena Nikolaeva (Golden Cockerel)
Principal dancers: Tamara Karsavina (Queen of Shemakhan), Alexis Bulgakov (King Dodon), Adolph Bolm (Astrologer), Louis Kowalski (General Polkan), (?) Jezierska (Amelfa), Serge Grigoriev (Guidone), Max Frohman (Afrone)

Note: This opera was first produced in 1909 in Moscow. The first performance in London of the Diaghilev production was on 12 June 1914 at the Theatre Royal, Drury Lane.

Le Rossignol (*also called* The Nightingale)
A Musical Fairy Tale in Three Acts
Music: Igor Stravinsky
Libretto: Igor Stravinsky and Stepan Mitusov, after the tale by Hans Christian Andersen
Conductor: Pierre Monteux
Chorus master: Nicolas Palitzine
Stage direction: Alexandre Benois, Alexander Sanin
Scenery and costumes: Alexandre Benois
Scene painting: Nikolai Charbé
Choreography: Boris Romanov
Premiere: 26 May 1914, Théâtre National de l'Opéra, Paris
Principal singers: Aurelia Dobrovolska (The Nightingale), Elizaveta Petrenko (Death), Marie Brian (The Cook), Pavel Andreyev (The Emperor of China), Alexander Varfolomeev (Fisherman), Nicolas Gulaev (The High Priest), Alexander Belianin (The High Chamberlain), Elisabeth Mamsina, Vasily Sharonov, Fedor Ernst (Ambassadors of the Emperor of China)
Principal dancers: Ekaterina Fokina (Dancer), Max Frohman (Dancer with the Nightingale), Boris Romanov, Nicolas Semenov, Michel Fedorov, Louis Kowalski (Warriors), Nicolas Kremnev, Nikolai Ivanovsky, Nicolas Zverev, Alexander Gavrilov, Anatole Bourman (Young Men)
Note: The chorus was from the Bolshoi Opera. The first London performance was on 18 June 1914 at the Theatre Royal, Drury Lane.

Prince Igor
Opera in a Prologue and Four Acts
Music: Alexander Borodin, completed and partly orchestrated by Nikolai Rimsky-Korsakov and Alexander Glazunov
Libretto: Alexander Borodin, after a scenario by Vladimir Stasov
Conductor: Lev Steinberg
Stage direction: Alexander Sanin
Scenery, costumes, and accessories: Nicholas Roerich
Scene painting: Orest Allegri (Prologue, Acts 1, 2, 4), Nikolai Charbé (Act 3)
Choreography: Michel Fokine
Premiere: 8 June 1914, Theatre Royal, Drury Lane, London
Principal singers: Elizaveta Petrenko (Konchakovna), Pavel Andreyev (Prince Igor), Fedor Chaliapin (Vladimir/Khan Konchak), Alexander Varfolomeev (Ovlur), Maria Kuznetsova (Princess Yaroslavna)
Principal dancers: Adolph Bolm (Polovtsian Chief); Lubov Tchernicheva, Sophie Pflanz, (?) Boniecka, Kasimira Kopycinska, Olga Kokhlova (Slaves); Vera Fokina, Alexandra Wassilewska, Margarita Frohman, Henriette Maikerska, Hilda Munnings (Polovtsian Girls); Nicolas Semenov, Michel

Fedorov, Boris Romanov, Max Frohman (Polovtsian Warriors); Alexander Goudin, Nicolas Kremnev, Alexander Gavrilov, Anatole Bourman, Nicolas Zverev (Young Polovtsian Boys)
Note: This opera was first produced in 1890 in St. Petersburg.

Nuit de Mai (May Night)
Fantastic-Comic Opera in Three Acts
Music: Nikolai Rimsky-Korsakov
Libretto: Nikolai Rimsky-Korsakov, after Nikolai Gogol
Conductor: Lev Steinberg
Scenery and costumes: Fedor Fedorovsky
Stage direction: Alexander Sanin
Choreography: Adolph Bolm (Dances of Youths and Maidens in Act 1; dances of Water Nymphs in Act 3)
Premiere: 26 June 1914, Theatre Royal, Drury Lane, London
Principal singers: Alexander Belianin (Mayor), Elisabeth Mamsina (Sister-in-law to the Mayor), Elizaveta Petrenko (Hanna), Pavel Andreyev (Clerk), Fedor Ernst (Distiller), Vasily Sharonov (Kalennik), Marie Brian (Pannochka), Dmitry Smirnov (Levko)
Principal dancers: Nicolas Kremnev, Alexander Goudin, Anatole Bourman, Alexander Vorontzov, Alexander Gavrilov (Youths); Luba (or Nadia) Baranowicz, (?) Konietska, Hilda Munnings, Doris Faithful, Henriette Klementovicz, Olga Khokhlova (Water Nymphs)
Note: This opera was first produced in 1880 in St. Petersburg.

Mavra
Comic Opera in One Act
Music: Igor Stravinsky
Libretto: Boris Kochno, after Alexander Pushkin's story "The Little House in Kolomna"
Conductor: Gregor Fitelberg
Stage direction: Bronislava Nijinska
Scenery and costumes: Léopold Survage
Premiere: 3 June 1922, Théâtre National de l'Opéra, Paris
Principal singers: Oda Slobodskaya (Parasha), Hélène Sadoven (The Neighbor), Zoia Rosovska (The Mother), Stephan Belina-Skupevsky (The Hussar)

La Colombe
Comic Opera in Two Scenes
Music: Charles Gounod, with new recitatives by Francis Poulenc
Libretto: Jules Barbier and Michel Carré, after Jean de La Fontaine
Conductor: Edouard Flament
Stage direction: Constantin Landau
Scenery and costumes: Juan Gris

Scene painting: Vladimir and Elizabeth Polunin
Premiere: 1 January 1924, Théâtre de Monte-Carlo
Principal singers: Maria Barrientos (Countess Sylvie), Jeanne Montfort (Mazette), Théodore Ritch (Lord Horace), Daniel Vigneau (Master Jean)
Note: This opera was first produced in 1860 in Baden-Baden.

Le Médecin malgré lui
Comic Opera in Three Acts with Ballet
Music: Charles Gounod, with new recitatives by Erik Satie
Libretto: Jules Barbier and Michel Carré, after Molière
Conductor: Edouard Flament
Scenery, costumes, and stage direction: Alexandre Benois
Choreography: Bronislava Nijinska
Premiere: 5 January 1924, Théâtre de Monte-Carlo
Principal singers: Inès Ferraris (Lucinda), Romanitza (Martine), Jeanne Montfort (Jacqueline), Daniel Vigneau (Sganarelle), Théodore Ritch (Léandre), Jacques Arnna (Géronte), Albert Garcia (Valère), (?) Fouquet (Lucas)
Principal dancers: Anton Dolin, Lubov Tchernicheva
Note: This opera was first produced in 1858 in Paris.

Philémon et Baucis
Comic Opera in Two Acts
Music: Charles Gounod
Libretto: Jules Barbier and Michel Carré
Conductor: Edouard Flament
Chorus master: Amédée de Sabata
Scenery, costumes, and stage direction: Alexandre Benois
Scene painting: Vladimir and Elizabeth Polunin
Premiere: 10 January 1924, Théâtre de Monte-Carlo
Principal singers: Maria Barrientos (Baucis), Alesio De Paolis (Philémon), Nazzareno De Angelis (Jupiter), Bruno Carmassi (Vulcan)
Note: This opera was first produced in 1860 in Paris.

Une Education manquée
Comedy in One Act
Music: Emmanuel Chabrier, with new recitatives by Darius Milhaud
Libretto: Eugène Leterrier, Albert Vanloo
Conductor: Edouard Flament
Stage direction: Alexandre Benois
Scenery and costumes: Juan Gris

Premiere: 17 January 1924, Théâtre de Monte-Carlo
Principal singers: Inès Ferraris (Helen of the Cherry Orchard), Daniel Vigneau (Master Pansanias), Théodore Ritch (Gontran de Boismassif)
Note: This opera was first produced in 1879 in Paris.

Oedipus Rex

Opera-Oratorio in Two Acts
Music: Igor Stravinsky
Libretto: Jean Cocteau, after Sophocles, in a Latin translation by Jean Daniélou
Conductor: Igor Stravinsky
Premiere: 30 May 1927, Théâtre Sarah-Bernhardt, Paris
Singers: Hélène Sadoven (Jocasta), Stephan Belina-Skupevsky (Oedipus), Georges Lanskoy (Creon), Kapitan Zaporojetz (Tiresias), Michel d'Arial (Shepherd)
Narrator: Pierre Brasseur

Ballets

Le Pavillon d'Armide

Ballet in One Act
Music: Nicolas Tcherepnin
Book: Alexandre Benois, after Théophile Gautier's *Omphale*
Scenery and costumes: Alexandre Benois
Scene painting: Oreste Allegri, (?) Lockenberg
Choreography: Michel Fokine
Conductor: Nicolas Tcherepnin
Premiere: 18*/19 May 1909, Théâtre du Châtelet, Paris
Principal dancers: Vera Karalli (Suzanne de S./Armide), Mikhail Mordkin (Vicomte René/Renaud), Alexis Bulgakov (Marquis de S./King Hidraot), Tamara Karsavina, Alexandra Baldina, Alexandra Fedorova, Elena Smirnova (Confidantes of Armide), Vaslav Nijinsky (Armide's Favorite Slave)
Note: This ballet was first produced on 25 November 1907 at the Maryinsky Theater, St. Petersburg.

Prince Igor (*also called* The Polovtsian Dances)

Polovtsian Scenes and Dances
Music: Alexander Borodin, completed and partly orchestrated by Nikolai Rimsky-Korsakov and Alexander Glazunov
Libretto: Alexander Borodin, after a scenario by Vladimir Stasov
Scenery and costumes: Nicholas Roerich
Scene painting: Boris Anisfeld
Stage direction: Alexander Sanin
Chorus master: Ulrich Avranek

Valentin Serov, poster for Diaghilev's first Paris ballet season, 1909

Choreography: Michel Fokine
Conductor: Emile Cooper
Premiere: 18*/19 May 1909, Théâtre du Châtelet, Paris
Principal dancers: Adolph Bolm (A Polovtsian Warrior), Sophie Fedorova (A Young Polovtsian Girl), Elena Smirnova (An Oriental Slave Woman), Alexis Kosloff, Nicolas Kremnev, Leonid Leontiev, Laurent Novikov, Alexander Orlov, Georgy Rozai (Young Polovtsian Boys)
Principal singers: Elizaveta Petrenko (Konchakovna), Vasily Sharonov (Prince Igor), Dmitry Smirnov (Vladimir), Kapitan Zaporojetz (Khan Konchak), Michel d'Arial (Ovlur)
Note: In 1923 the opening dance was rechoreographed by Bronislava Nijinska.

Le Festin
Suite of Dances
Music: Mikhail Glinka (Cortège Lesghinka, Mazurka), Nikolai Rimsky-Korsakov (Cortège Lesghinka), Peter Ilitch Tchaikovsky (L'Oiseau de Feu, Trepak, Finale), Alexander Glazunov (Czardas, Grand Pas Classique Hongrois from *Raymonda*), Modest Mussorgsky (Hopak)
Scenery: Konstantin Korovin
Costumes: Léon Bakst, Alexandre Benois, Ivan Bilibin, Konstantin Korovin
Scene painting: Peter Lambin, Nikolai Charbé
Choreography: Michel Fokine (Cortège Lesghinka, Hopak, Trepak, Finale), Marius Petipa (Cortège Lesghinka, L'Oiseau de Feu, Grand Pas Classique Hongrois), Alexander Gorsky (Czardas), Nikolai Goltz, Felix Kchessinsky (Mazurka)
Conductor: Emile Cooper
Premiere: 18*/19 May 1909, Théâtre du Châtelet, Paris
Principal dancers: Vera Fokina, Alexander Monakhov (Cortège Lesghinka), Tamara Karsavina, Vaslav Nijinsky (L'Oiseau de Feu), Sophie Fedorova, Mikhail Mordkin (Czardas), Olga Fedorova, Nicolas Kremnev (Hopak), Georgy Rozai (Trepak), Vera Karalli, Mikhail Mordkin (Grand Pas Classique Hongrois)
Note: The Grand Pas Classique Hongrois was from *Raymonda*. "L'Oiseau de Feu" (also called "Firebird" and "La Princesse Enchantée") was the Bluebird pas de deux from *The Sleeping Beauty*. The music for the finale was from Tchaikovsky's Second Symphony.

Les Sylphides
Romantic Reverie in One Act
Music: Frédéric Chopin, orchestrated by Igor Stravinsky, Alexander Glazunov, Anatoly Liadov, Nikolai Sokolov, Alexander Taneyev
Scenery and costumes: Alexandre Benois
Scene painting: Stepan Yaremich
Choreography and theme: Michel Fokine
Conductor: Nicolas Tcherepnin
Premiere: 2*/4 June 1909, Théâtre du Châtelet, Paris
Principal dancers: Anna Pavlova, Tamara Karsavina, Alexandra Baldina, Vaslav Nijinsky (Poet)

Note: *Chopiniana*, the earliest version of this ballet, was produced on 10 February 1907 at the Maryinsky Theater, St. Petersburg. The music for the various sections was as follows: Overture (Prelude, op. 28, no. 7), Nocturne (op. 32, no. 2), Valse (op. 70, no. 1), Mazurka (op. 33, no. 3), Mazurka (op. 67, no. 3), Prelude (same as Overture), Valse (op. 64, no. 2), Valse (op. 18, no. 1). The formal premiere took place on 4 June 1909.

Cléopâtre

Choreographic Drama in One Act

Music: Anton Arensky, with additional music by Sergei Taneyev (Prelude), Nikolai Rimsky-Korsakov (Entrance of Cleopatra), Mikhail Glinka (Veil Dance), Alexander Glazunov (Bacchanale)

Scenery and costumes: Léon Bakst

Scene painting: Boris Anisfeld

Choreography: Michel Fokine

Conductor: Nicolas Tcherepnin

Premiere: 2*/4 June 1909, Théâtre du Châtelet, Paris

Principal dancers: Ida Rubinstein (Cleopatra), Anna Pavlova (Ta-Hor), Tamara Karsavina (A Slave of Cleopatra), Michel Fokine (Amoun), Vaslav Nijinsky (A Slave of Cleopatra), Alexis Bulgakov (High Priest)

Note: *Cléopâtre* was based on Fokine's earlier *Egyptian Nights*, produced on 16 January 1908 at the Maryinsky Theater, St. Petersburg. In 1918 the ballet was restaged with sets by Robert Delaunay, new costumes for Cleopatra and Amoun by Sonia Delaunay, and a new pas de deux by Léonide Massine.

Carnaval

Pantomime-Ballet (later "Ballet") in One Act

Music: Robert Schumann, orchestrated by Nikolai Rimsky-Korsakov, Anatoly Liadov, Nicolas Tcherepnin, and Alexander Glazunov

Scenery and costumes: Léon Bakst

Scene painting: Boris Anisfeld

Choreography: Michel Fokine

Conductor: Nicolas Tcherepnin

Premiere: 21 May 1910, Theater des Westens, Berlin

Principal dancers: Lydia Lopokova (Columbine), Michel Fokine (Harlequin), Vera Fokina (Chiarina), Bronislava Nijinska (Papillon), Alexis Bulgakov (Pierrot), Alexander Orlov (Pantalon), Fedor Scherer (Eusebius), Fedor(?) Vassiliev (Florestan), Maria Piltz (Estrella)

Note: This ballet was first produced on 20 February 1910 at the Pavlov Hall, St. Petersburg.

Schéhérazade

Choreographic Drama in One Act (later "Persian Tale in One Act")

Music: Nikolai Rimsky-Korsakov

Book: Michel Fokine and Léon Bakst, after the first tale of *The Thousand and One Nights*

Scenery and costumes: Léon Bakst

Scene painting: G. Golov

Choreography: Michel Fokine

Conductor: Nicolas Tcherepnin

Premiere: 4 June 1910, Théâtre National de l'Opéra, Paris

Principal dancers: Ida Rubinstein (Zobéide), Vaslav Nijinsky (Zobéide's Favorite Slave), Alexis Bulgakov (Shahryar, King of the Indies), Vasily Kiselev (Shah-Zeman), Sergei Ognev (Chief Eunuch), Sophie Fedorova, Vera Fokina, Elena Poliakova (Odalisques)

Giselle

Ballet-Pantomime in Two Acts

Music: Adolphe Adam

Book: Vernoy de Saint-Georges, Théophile Gautier, and Jean Coralli

Scenery and costumes: Alexandre Benois

Scene painting: Orest Allegri, Boris Anisfeld

Choreography: Marius Petipa; fugue and variation for Lydia Lopokova and Vaslav Nijinsky by Michel Fokine

Conductor: Paul Vidal

Premiere: 17*/18 June 1910, Théâtre National de l'Opéra, Paris

Principal dancers: Tamara Karsavina (Giselle), Vaslav Nijinsky (Loys), Alexis Bulgakov (Hilarion), Vasily Kiselev (Duke of Courland), (?) Iakovleva (Princess Bathilde), Raisa Matskevitch (Giselle's Mother), Elena Poliakova (Myrtha), Lydia Lopokova (A Peasant Girl), Ivan Kusov (Valet), Fedor Scherer (Bathilde's Page), Leonid Leontiev (Buffoon)

Note: This ballet was first produced in 1841 at the Paris Opéra. The fugue and variation were performed by Lopokova and Nijinsky. There were two Iakovlevas in the Imperial Ballet at this time — Alexandra Efimovna Iakovleva (I) and Olga Matveevna Iakovleva (II). It is unclear which one performed the role of Bathilde.

L'Oiseau de Feu (*also called* Firebird)

Fantastic Ballet in One Act

Music: Igor Stravinsky

Scenery: Alexander Golovin, executed by Nikolai Sapunov and Nikolai Charbé

Costumes: Alexander Golovin, with additional costumes by Léon Bakst

Choreography and book: Michel Fokine

Conductor: Gabriel Pierné

Premiere: 25 June 1910, Théâtre National de l'Opéra, Paris

Principal dancers: Tamara Karsavina (Firebird), Vera Fokina (Beautiful Tsarevna), Michel Fokine (Ivan Tsarevich), Alexis Bulgakov (Kostchei, the Immortal)

Note: Bakst designed the costumes for the Firebird and Ivan Tsarevich. The ballet was restaged at the Lyceum Theatre, London, on 25 November 1926 with new scenery and costumes by Natalia Goncharova.

Les Orientales
Choreographic Sketches
Music: Alexander Glazunov (Saracens' Dance and Pas de Deux), Christian Sinding (Oriental Dance, orchestrated by Alexander Taneyev), Anton Arensky (Torch Dance), Edvard Grieg (The Djinn, orchestrated by Igor Stravinsky)
Scenery: Konstantin Korovin, executed by Boris Anisfeld
Choreography: Michel Fokine (Oriental Dance, Torch Dance), Marius Petipa (Pas de Deux and, with Fokine, Saracens' Dance)
Conductor: Nicolas Tcherepnin
Premiere: 25 June 1910, Théâtre National de l'Opéra, Paris
Principal dancers: Vera Fokina, Alexander Orlov (Saracens' Dance), Vaslav Nijinsky (Oriental Dance, The Djinn), Ekaterina Geltzer, Alexandre Volinine (Pas de Deux), Tamara Karsavina (Torch Dance)
Note: Torch Dance (also called Assyrian Dance) was first performed in 1907 at a Maryinsky charity performance organized by Fokine. According to Bronislava Nijinska, both Oriental Dance and The Djinn (which she calls *Danse Siamoise* and *Kobold*, respectively) were mounted by Fokine for a performance at the Maryinsky Theater, St. Petersburg, on 20 February 1910. Since the Paris program does not credit the choreography of The Djinn to Fokine (or anyone else), it is possible, as régisseur Serge Grigoriev maintained, that the dance was Nijinsky's "own arrangement."

Le Spectre de la Rose
Choreographic Tableau
Music: Carl Maria von Weber, orchestrated by Hector Berlioz
Book: Jean-Louis Vaudoyer, after a poem by Théophile Gautier
Scenery and costumes: Léon Bakst
Choreography: Michel Fokine
Conductor: Nicolas Tcherepnin
Premiere: 19 April 1911, Théâtre de Monte-Carlo
Principal dancers: Tamara Karsavina (Young Girl), Vaslav Nijinsky (Spirit of the Rose)

Narcisse
Mythological Poem in One Act
Music: Nicolas Tcherepnin
Scenery, costumes, and book: Léon Bakst
Choreography: Michel Fokine
Conductor: Nicolas Tcherepnin
Premiere: 26 April 1911, Théâtre de Monte-Carlo
Principal dancers: Vaslav Nijinsky (Narcisse), Tamara Karsavina (Echo), Bronislava Nijinska (A Bacchante), Vera Fokina (A Young Boeotian Woman), Ludmila Schollar, Anna Tcherepanova (Nymphs)

Sadko — In the Underwater Kingdom

Scene 6 from the Opera

Music: Nikolai Rimsky-Korsakov

Libretto: Nikolai Rimsky-Korsakov and Vladimir Belsky

Scenery and costumes: Boris Anisfeld

Choreography: Michel Fokine

Conductor: Nicolas Tcherepnin

Premiere: 6 June 1911, Théâtre du Châtelet, Paris

Principal dancers: Margarita Frohman, Lubov Tchernicheva (Princesses), Bronislava Nijinska, Ludmila Schollar (Streams), Sophie Fedorova, Vera Fokina (Naiads), Leonid Leontiev, Alexander Orlov, Georgy Rozai, Nicolas Kremnev, Boris Romanov (Goldfish)

Principal singers: (?) Issatchenko (Sadko), Kapitan Zaporojetz (King of the Seas), Raisa(?) Stepanova-Chevtchenko (Volkhova)

Note: This ballet was restaged in August 1916 in San Sebastián, Spain, with choreography by Adolph Bolm and designs by Natalia Goncharova. The full opera premiered in Moscow in January 1898.

Petrouchka

Burlesque in Four Scenes

Music: Igor Stravinsky

Book: Igor Stravinsky and Alexandre Benois

Scenery and costumes: Alexandre Benois

Scene painting: Boris Anisfeld

Choreography: Michel Fokine

Conductor: Pierre Monteux

Premiere: 13 June 1911, Théâtre du Châtelet, Paris

Principal dancers: Vaslav Nijinsky (Petrouchka), Tamara Karsavina (Ballerina), Alexander Orlov (Moor), Enrico Cecchetti (Old Showman), Bronislava Nijinska, Alexandra Vassilievska (Street Dancers), Ludmila Schollar, Maria Reisen (Gypsies)

Note: The bear was designed by Valentin Serov.

Le Lac des Cygnes (*also called* Swan Lake)

Fantastic Ballet in Two Acts and Three Scenes

Music: Peter Ilitch Tchaikovsky

Book: Vladimir Begichev and Vasily Geltzer, adapted by Marius Petipa

Scenery: Konstantin Korovin (Act 1) and Alexander Golovin (Act 2)

Costumes: Alexander Golovin

Choreography: Marius Petipa, Lev Ivanov, with revisions by Michel Fokine

Conductor: Pierre Monteux

Premiere: 30 November 1911, Royal Opera House, London

Principal dancers: Mathilde Kchessinska (Swan Queen), Vaslav Nijinsky (Prince)

Note: This production was a two-act condensation of the version first produced in 1895 at the Maryinsky Theater, St. Petersburg, with scenery and costumes, purchased by Diaghilev, from the 1901 Bolshoi production. The choreography included a variation interpolated in Act 2 (the party scene) for Nijinsky to the Sugar Plum Fairy music from *The Nutcracker*, as well as a variation interpolated by Kchessinska into Act 1 (the lakeside scene). According to the Monte Carlo program, the waltz and dances of the Prince were by Fokine. In 1923, at the Opéra de Monte-Carlo, Diaghilev revived the ballet, again in two acts, with scenery by Korovin (Act 1) and Golovin (Act 2). The principal roles were danced by Vera Trefilova (Swan Queen), Anatole Vilzak (Prince), Serge Grigoriev (Evil Genie), and Jean Jazvinsky (Prince's Friend). In 1927 Diaghilev presented a one-act version ("Choreographic Poem in One Act") with scenery and "dresses" by Korovin.

Le Dieu Bleu

Hindu Legend in One Act

Music: Reynaldo Hahn

Book: Jean Cocteau and Frédéric de Madrazo

Scenery and costumes: Léon Bakst

Choreography: Michel Fokine

Conductor: D.-E. Inghelbrecht

Premiere: 13 May 1912, Théâtre du Châtelet, Paris

Principal dancers: Vaslav Nijinsky (Blue God), Tamara Karsavina (Young Girl), Bronislava Nijinska (Dancing Girl), Lydia Nelidova (Goddess), Max Frohman (Youth), Michel Fedorov (High Priest), Maria Piltz, Serafima Astafieva, Lubov Tchernicheva (Peacock Bearers)

Thamar

Choreographic Drama in One Act

Music: Mily Balakirev

Book: Léon Bakst, after a poem by Mikhail Lermontov

Scenery and costumes: Léon Bakst

Scene painting: Nikolai Charbé, (?) Soudoraines

Choreography: Michel Fokine

Conductor: Pierre Monteux

Premiere: 20 May 1912, Théâtre du Châtelet, Paris

Principal dancers: Tamara Karsavina (Thamar, Queen of George), Adolph Bolm (Prince)

L'Après-midi d'un Faune

Choreographic Scene (later "Choreographic Poem")

Music: Claude Debussy, after the poem by Stéphane Mallarmé

Scenery and costumes: Léon Bakst

Choreography: Vaslav Nijinsky

Conductor: Pierre Monteux

Premiere: 29 May 1912, Théâtre du Châtelet, Paris

Principal dancers: Vaslav Nijinsky (Faun), Lydia Nelidova (Chief Nymph), Bronislava Nijinska, Olga Kokhlova, Anna Tcherepanova, Henriette Maikerska, Leocadia Klementovicz, Kasimira Kopycinska (Nymphs)

Note: In 1922 the ballet was revived with Bronislava Nijinska in her brother's role as the Faun and Lubov Tchernicheva as the Chief Nymph. In addition to Henriette Maikerska and Leocadia Klementovicz (now "Russianized" as Klementovitch), who danced in the original production, the Nymphs were Vera Nemchinova, Hilda Bewicke, and Anna and Lubov Soumarokova.

Daphnis et Chloé (*also called* Daphnis and Chloe; Daphnis and Chloé)

Choreographic Symphony in Three Scenes

Music: Maurice Ravel

Scenery and costumes: Léon Bakst

Scene painting: Serge Sudeikin (Scene 1), Nikolai Charbé (Scene 2)

Choreography and book: Michel Fokine

Conductor: Pierre Monteux

Premiere: 8 June 1912, Théâtre du Châtelet, Paris

Principal dancers: Tamara Karsavina (Chloé), Margarita Frohman (Lyceion), Vaslav Nijinsky (Daphnis), Adolph Bolm (Darkon), Enrico Cecchetti (Lammon), Michel Fedorov (Bryaxis), Maria Piltz, Lubov Tchernicheva, Kasimira Kopycinska (Nymphs)

Note: In June 1914, when the ballet premiered in London, it was performed without chorus, eliciting a protest from Ravel. In 1924, when the ballet was revived in Monte Carlo, the choreography was "after Michel Fokine." A new costume for Daphnis, played by Anton Dolin, was designed by Juan Gris.

Jeux

Danced Poem

Music: Claude Debussy

Scenery and costumes: Léon Bakst

Choreography and theme: Vaslav Nijinsky

Conductor: Pierre Monteux

Premiere: 15 May 1913, Théâtre des Champs-Elysées, Paris

Principal dancers: Vaslav Nijinsky (Youth), Tamara Karsavina (First Girl), Ludmila Schollar (Second Girl)

Le Sacre du Printemps (*also called* The Rite of Spring)

Scenes of Pagan Russia in Two Acts

Music: Igor Stravinsky

Book: Igor Stravinsky and Nicholas Roerich

Scenery and costumes: Nicholas Roerich

Scene painting: Orest Allegri, Georgy Iakovlev, (?) Naoumow

Choreography: Vaslav Nijinsky

Conductor: Pierre Monteux

Premiere: 28*/29 May 1913, Théâtre des Champs-Elysées, Paris

Principal dancers: Maria Piltz (Chosen Maiden), Ludmila Guliuk (An Old Woman 300 Years Old), Alexander Vorontzov (A Wise Man)

Note: This ballet was restaged in 1920 with choreography by Léonide Massine.

La Tragédie de Salomé

Ballet by Robert d'Humières

Music: Florent Schmitt

Scenery and costumes: Serge Sudeikin

Choreography: Boris Romanov

Conductor: Pierre Monteux

Premiere: 12 June 1913, Théâtre des Champs-Elysées, Paris

Principal dancer: Tamara Karsavina (Salomé)

Note: Schmitt's score was composed for Loie Fuller's "tragic pantomime in two acts," produced in 1907 at the Théâtre des Arts, Paris.

Papillons

Ballet in One Act

Music: Robert Schumann, orchestrated by Nicolas Tcherepnin

Scenery: Mstislav Dobujinsky, executed by G. Golov

Costumes: Léon Bakst

Choreography and book: Michel Fokine

Conductor: Rhené-Baton

Premiere: 16 April 1914, Théâtre de Monte-Carlo

Principal dancers: Tamara Karsavina (First Young Girl), Lubov Tchernicheva (Second Young Girl), Michel Fokine (Pierrot), Kasimira Kopycinska, Sophie Pflanz, Alexandra Wassilewska, Ludmila Guliuk (Butterflies)

Note: *Papillons* was first produced in 1912 at the Maryinsky Theater, St. Petersburg. The choreography was "rearranged" by Adolph Bolm for the 1916–1917 American tour. Later programs state that the scenery was executed as well as designed by Dobujinsky.

La Légende de Joseph (*also called* Legend of Joseph)

Ballet in One Act

Music: Richard Strauss

Book: Count Harry Kessler and Hugo von Hofmannsthal

Scenery: José-María Sert

Costumes: Léon Bakst

Choreography: Michel Fokine

Conductor: Richard Strauss

Premiere: 14 May 1914, Théâtre National de l'Opéra, Paris

Principal dancers: Maria Kuznetsova (Potiphar's Wife), Vera Fokina (Shulamite Woman, A Dancer), Alexis Bulgakov (Potiphar), Léonide Massine (Joseph), Serge Grigoriev (A Sheik), Lubov Tchernicheva, Sophie Pflanz, Doris Faithful (Three Veiled Women), Max Frohman (An Archangel)

Le Coq d'Or (*also called* The Golden Cockerel *and* The Golden Cock)
Opera in Three Scenes
Music: Nikolai Rimsky-Korsakov
Libretto: Vladimir Belsky, after Alexander Pushkin, revised by Alexandre Benois
Scenery and costumes: Natalia Goncharova
Stage direction and choreography: Michel Fokine
Chorus Master: Nicolas Palitzine
Conductor: Pierre Monteux
Premiere: 24 May 1914, Théâtre National de l'Opéra, Paris
Principal dancers: Tamara Karsavina (Queen of Shemakhan), Alexis Bulgakov (King Dodon), Adolph Bolm (Astrologer), Louis Kowalski (General Polkan), (?) Jezierska (Amelfa), Serge Grigoriev (Guidone), Max Frohman (Afrone)
Principal singers: Aurelia Dobrovolska (Queen of Shemakhan), Vasily Petrov (King Dodon), Ivan Alchevsky (Astrologer), Alexander Belianin (General Polkan), Elizaveta Petrenko (Amelfa), Elena Nikolaeva (Golden Cockerel)

Le Rossignol (*also called* The Nightingale)
A Musical Fairy Tale in Three Acts
Music: Igor Stravinsky
Libretto: Igor Stravinsky and Stepan Mitusov, after the tale by Hans Christian Andersen
Stage direction: Alexandre Benois and Alexander Sanin
Scenery and costumes: Alexandre Benois
Scene painting: Nikolai Charbé
Chorus master: Nicolas Palitzine
Choreography: Boris Romanov
Conductor: Pierre Monteux
Premiere: 26 May 1914, Théâtre National de l'Opéra, Paris
Principal dancers: Ekaterina Fokina (Dancer), Max Frohman (Dancer with the Nightingale), Boris Romanov, Nicolas Semenov, Michel Fedorov, Louis Kowalski (Warriors), Nicolas Kremnev, Nikolai Ivanovsky, Nicolas Zverev, Alexander Gavrilov, Anatole Bourman (Young Men)
Principal singers: Aurelia Dobrovolska (Nightingale), Elizaveta Petrenko (Death), Marie Brian (Cook), Pavel Andreyev (Emperor of China), Alexander Varfolomeev (Fisherman), Nicolas Gulaev (High Priest), Alexander Belianin (High Chamberlain), Elisabeth Mamsina, Vasily Sharonov, Fedor Ernst (Ambassadors of the Emperor of China)
Note: The chorus was from the Bolshoi Opera. The first London performance took place on 18 June 1914 at the Theatre Royal, Drury Lane. Ekaterina Fokina was also known as Fokina II.

Midas

Mythological Comedy in One Scene

Music: Maximilian Steinberg

Book: Léon Bakst, after Ovid

Scenery and costumes: Mstislav Dobujinsky

Choreography: Michel Fokine

Conductor: Rhené-Baton

Premiere: 2 June 1914, Théâtre National de l'Opéra, Paris

Principal dancers: Tamara Karsavina (Oreade), Adolph Bolm (Midas), Max Frohman (Apollo), Boris Romanov (Pan), Ludmila Schollar, Sophie Pflanz, Lubov Tchernicheva

Soleil de Nuit (*also called* Midnight Sun)

Russian Games and Dances (later "Russian Scenes and Dances")

Music: Nikolai Rimsky-Korsakov

Book: Léonide Massine

Scenery and costumes: Mikhail Larionov

Choreography: Léonide Massine

Conductor: Ernest Ansermet

Premiere: 20 December 1915, Grand Théâtre, Geneva

Principal dancers: Léonide Massine (Midnight Sun), Nicolas Zverev (Bobyl, the Innocent)

Note: Vasily Kibalchich's Geneva-based Russian chorus sang at the premiere.

Las Meninas

Pavane

Music: Gabriel Fauré

Scenery: Carlo Socrate

Costumes: José-María Sert

Choreography: Léonide Massine

Conductor: Ernest Ansermet

Premiere: 21 August 1916, Teatro Victoria Eugenia, San Sebastián (Spain)

Principal dancers: Lydia Sokolova, Olga Khokhlova (Maids of Honor), Léonide Massine, Léon Woizikowski (Gentlemen)

Note: In the late 1920s the ballet was performed with scenery by Prince Alexander Schervashidze.

Kikimora

Russian Fairy Tale

Music: Anatoly Liadov

Scenery and costumes: Mikhail Larionov

Choreography: Léonide Massine

Conductor: Ernest Ansermet

Premiere: 25 August 1916, Teatro Victoria Eugenia, San Sebastián (Spain)

Principal dancers: Maria Chabelska (Kikimora), Stanislas Idzikowski (Cat)
Note: In 1917 this became part of the ballet *Contes Russes*.

Till Eulenspiegel
Comico-Dramatic Ballet
Music: Richard Strauss
Scenery and costumes: Robert Edmond Jones
Choreography and book: Vaslav Nijinsky
Conductor: Anselm Goetzl
Premiere: 23 October 1916, Manhattan Opera House, New York
Principal dancers: Vaslav Nijinsky (Till), Flora Revalles (First Chatelaine), Doris Faithful (Second Chatelaine), Sophie Pflanz (Third Chatelaine), Nicolas Kremnev (A Cloth Merchant), Lydia Sokolova (An Apple Woman), Nicolas Zverev (First Street Urchin), Alexander Gavrilov (One of the People)

Feu d'Artifice (*also called* Fireworks)
Symphonic Poem
Music: Igor Stravinsky
Scenery and lighting: Giacomo Balla
Conductor: Ernest Ansermet
Premiere: 12 April 1917, Teatro Costanzi, Rome
Note: This "ballet" had no dancers.

Le Donne di Buon Umore (*also called* Les Femmes de Bonne Humeur *and* The Good-Humoured Ladies)
Ballet in One Act (later "A Dance Comedy")
Music: Domenico Scarlatti, orchestrated by Vincenzo Tommasini
Book: Vincenzo Tommasini, after Carlo Goldoni
Scenery and costumes: Léon Bakst
Choreography: Léonide Massine
Conductor: Ernest Ansermet
Premiere: 12 April 1917, Teatro Costanzi, Rome
Principal dancers: Enrico Cecchetti (Luca), Giuseppina Cecchetti (Silvestra), Lubov Tchernicheva (Costanza), Olga Khokhlova (Felicita), Lydia Lopokova (Mariuccia), Léonide Massine (Leonardo), Stanislas Idzikowski (Battista), Léon Woizikowski (Niccolò)

Contes Russes (*also called* Children's Tales)
Three Choreographic Miniatures with Danced Interludes and an Epilogue (later "Suite of Popular Legends," "People's Play," and "Popular Tales")
Music: Anatoly Liadov

Scenery, curtains, and costumes: Mikhail Larionov
Choreography: Léonide Massine
Conductor: Ernest Ansermet
Premiere: 11 May 1917, Théâtre du Châtelet, Paris
Principal dancers: Léonide Massine, Lubov Tchernicheva, Léon Woizikowski, Maria Chabelska, Stanislas Idzikowski, Alexander Gavrilov, Dmitry Kostrovsky, Valentina Kachouba, Elena Antonova
Note: The 1917 version of *Contes Russes* consisted of the following sections: (1) Koliada-Maleda, Christmas Carol for Orchestra (Léon Woizikowski); (2) Kikimora (Maria Chabelska, Stanislas Idzikowski); (3) Lament for Orchestra (Alexander Gavrilov, Dmitry Kostrovsky); (4) Bova Korolevich (also called Bova Korolevich and the Swan Princess) (Léonide Massine, Valentina Kachouba); (5) Berceuse for Orchestra (Lubov Tchernicheva, Léon Woizikowski); (6) Baba Yaga (Stanislas Idzikowski, Elena Antonova); (7) Legend of Birds for Orchestra; (8) Danced Epilogue and Russian Dances (corps de ballet). In 1918 a Danced Prelude replaced Koliada-Maleda, and Lament of the Swan Princess replaced Lament for Orchestra. The music for these new sections, also by Liadov, was orchestrated by Arnold Bax. By 1922 the Funeral of the Dragon had replaced the Berceuse for Orchestra, and the Legend of Birds had been dropped.

Parade
Realist Ballet in One Scene
Music: Erik Satie
Book: Jean Cocteau
Scenery, curtain, and costumes: Pablo Picasso
Choreography: Léonide Massine
Conductor: Ernest Ansermet
Premiere: 18 May 1917, Théâtre du Châtelet, Paris
Principal dancers: Léonide Massine (Chinese Conjuror), Maria Chabelska (Little American Girl), Lydia Lopokova, Nicolas Zverev (Acrobats)

La Boutique Fantasque (*also called* The Fantastic Toyshop)
Ballet in One Act
Music: Gioacchino Rossini, arranged and orchestrated by Ottorino Respighi
Scenery, curtain, and costumes: André Derain
Scene painting: André Derain, Vladimir and Elizabeth Polunin
Choreography: Léonide Massine
Conductor: Henry Defosse
Premiere: 5 June 1919, Alhambra Theatre, London
Principal dancers: Enrico Cecchetti (Shopkeeper), Alexander Gavrilov (His Assistant), Jean Jazvinsky (An American), Alice Alanova (His Wife), Serge Grigoriev (A Russian Merchant), Giuseppina Cecchetti (His Wife), Lydia Sokolova, Léon Woizikowski (Tarantella Dancers), Lubov Tchernicheva (Queen of Clubs), Vera Nemchinova (Queen of Hearts), Maximilian Statkiewicz (King of Spades),

Zygmund Novak (King of Diamonds), Stanislas Idzikowski (Snob), Nicolas Zverev (A Cossack Chief), Vera Savina, Nicolas Kremnev (Dancing Poodles), Lydia Lopokova, Léonide Massine (Can-Can Dancers)

Le Tricorne (*also called* The Three-Cornered Hat)
Ballet in One Act
Music: Manuel de Falla
Book: Gregorio Martínez Sierra, after a novella by Pedro Alarcón
Scenery, curtain, and costumes: Pablo Picasso
Scene painting: Vladimir and Elizabeth Polunin (except for the curtain, which was painted by Picasso)
Choreography: Léonide Massine
Conductor: Ernest Ansermet
Premiere: 22 July 1919, Alhambra Theatre, London
Principal dancers: Léonide Massine (Miller), Tamara Karsavina (Miller's Wife), Léon Woizikowski (Corregidor), Rachel Grantzeva (Corregidor's Wife), Stanislas Idzikowski (Dandy), Nicolas Zverev, Jean Jazvinsky, Zygmund Novak, Maximilian Statkiewicz, Louis Kowalski, Michel Pavlov (Alguaciles)
Singer: Zoia Rosovska

Le Chant du Rossignol (*also called* The Song of the Nightingale)
Choreographic Poem in One Act (later "Ballet in One Act"), After Hans Christian Andersen's Fairy Tale
Music: Igor Stravinsky
Scenery, curtain, and costumes: Henri Matisse
Choreography: Léonide Massine
Conductor: Ernest Ansermet
Premiere: 2 February 1920, Théâtre National de l'Opéra, Paris
Principal dancers: Tamara Karsavina (Nightingale), Lydia Sokolova (Death), Serge Grigoriev (Emperor), Stanislas Idzikowski (Mechanical Nightingale)
Note: This one-act ballet was adapted from Stravinsky's opera *Le Rossignol*, produced by Diaghilev in 1914. In 1925 the ballet was restaged with choreography by George Balanchine. The principal roles were danced by Alicia Markova (Nightingale), Lydia Sokolova (Death), Serge Grigoriev (Emperor), George Balanchine (Mechanical Nightingale), and Nicolas Kremnev (Japanese Maestro).

Pulcinella
Ballet with Song in One Act
Music: Igor Stravinsky, after Giambattista Pergolesi
Scenery, curtain, and costumes: Pablo Picasso
Scene painting: Vladimir and Elizabeth Polunin
Choreography: Léonide Massine

Conductor: Ernest Ansermet

Premiere: 15 May 1920, Théâtre National de l'Opéra, Paris

Principal dancers: Tamara Karsavina (Pimpinella), Lubov Tchernicheva, Vera Nemchinova, Léonide Massine, Stanislas Idzikowski, Enrico Cecchetti (Doctor), Nicolas Zverev, Zygmund Novak

Principal singers: Mafalda de Voltri, Angelo Masini Pieralli, Zoia Rosovska, Romanitza, Aurelio Anglada, Gino de Vecchi

Le Astuzie Femminili (*also called* Astuce Féminine)

Opera-Ballet in Three Scenes (later "Opera-Ballet in Two Acts and Three Scenes")

Music: Domenico Cimarosa, with recitatives after Cimarosa by Ottorino Respighi

Scenery, curtain, and costumes: José-María Sert

Scene painting: Vladimir and Elizabeth Polunin

Choreography: Léonide Massine

Conductor: Ernest Ansermet

Premiere: 27 May 1920, Théâtre National de l'Opéra, Paris

Principal dancers: Tamara Karsavina, Stanislas Idzikowski (Pas de Deux), Lydia Sokolova, Léon Woizikowski (Tarantella), Vera Nemchinova, Felia Radina, Thadée Slavinsky (Pas de Trois), Leocadia Klementovicz, Alexandra Wassilewska, Hilda Bewicke, Nicolas Kremnev, Nicolas Zverev, Zygmund Novak (Pas de Six)

Principal singers: Mafalda de Voltri (Bellina), Romanitza (Ersilia), Zoia Rosovska (Leonora), Angelo Masini Pieralli (Romualdo), Aurelio Anglada (Filandro), Gino de Vecchi (Giampaolo)

Chout (Le Bouffon)

Russian Legend in Six Scenes

Music: Serge Prokofiev

Scenery, curtain, and costumes: Mikhail Larionov

Choreography: Mikhail Larionov, Thadée Slavinsky

Conductor: Serge Prokofiev

Premiere: 17 May 1921, Théâtre de la Gaîté-Lyrique, Paris

Principal dancers: Thadée Slavinsky (Buffoon), Catherine Devillier (Buffoon's Wife), Jean Jazvinsky (Merchant), Vera Nemchinova, Olga Zyrmonska (Bridesmaids)

Cuadro Flamenco

Suite of Andalusian Dances

Scenery and costumes: Pablo Picasso

Premiere: 17 May 1921, Théâtre de la Gaîté-Lyrique, Paris

Dancers: María Dalbaicín, La Rubia de Jérez, Estampillo, La Gabrielita del Garrotín, Mate El Sin Pies, La López, Rojas, El Tejero, El Moreno

Singer: La Miñarita

Guitarists: El Sevillano, El Martell

Note: The ballet consisted of nine sections: La Malagueña (La Miñarita); Tango Gitano (Rojas, El

Tejero); La Farruca (María Dalbaicín); La Jota Aragonesa (La López, El Moreno); Alegría (Estampillo); Garrotín Grotesco (La Rubia de Jérez, María Dalbaicín, Mate El Sin Pies); Garrotín Cómico (La Gabrielita del Garrotín); Sevillana (La Miñarita, La Rubia de Jérez, María Dalbaicín, La Gabrielita del Garrotín, La López, Estampillo, El Tejero, El Moreno, Rojas, Mate El Sin Pies).

The Sleeping Princess
Ballet in Five Tableaux
Music: Peter Ilitch Tchaikovsky, partly reorchestrated by Igor Stravinsky
Book: Ivan Vsevolozhsky and Marius Petipa, after Charles Perrault
Scenery and costumes: Léon Bakst
Choreography: Marius Petipa, staged by Nicholas Sergeyev, with additional dances by Bronislava Nijinska (Dance of the Marchionesses, Bluebeard, Schéhérazade, Innocent Ivan and His Brothers, and Prince Charming's variation in the Act 3 pas de deux)
Conductor: Gregor Fitelberg
Premiere: 2 November 1921, Alhambra Theatre, London
Principal dancers: Olga Spessivtzeva (Princess Aurora), Pierre Vladimirov (Prince Charming), Lydia Lopokova (Lilac Fairy/The Enchanted Princess), Carlotta Brianza (Carabosse, The Wicked Fairy), Leonard Tree (King Florestan XXIV), Vera Sudeikina (Queen), Jean Jazvinsky (Cantalbutte), Felia Doubrovska (Fairy of the Pine Woods/Sister Anne), Lydia Sokolova (Cherry Blossom Fairy/Red Riding Hood), Bronislava Nijinska (Fairy of the Humming Birds/Pierrette), Lubov Egorova (Fairy of the Song Birds), Vera Nemchinova (Carnation Fairy/Columbine), Lubov Tchernicheva (Fairy of the Mountain Ash/Countess/Ariana), Anatole Vilzak (Spanish Prince/Harlequin), Léon Woizikowski (Indian Prince), Thadée Slavinsky (Italian Prince), Errol Addison (English Prince/Puss-in-Boots), Nicolas Zverev (Pierrot), Ludmila Schollar (White Cat), Stanislas Idzikowski (Bluebird), María Dalbaicín (Schéhérazade), Michel Pavlov (Shah), Nicholas Singaevsky (His Brother), Hilda Bewicke, Ursula Moreton (Porcelain Princesses), Nicolas Kremnev (Mandarin), Léon Woizikowski, Thadée Slavinsky, Jacob(?) Kornetsky (Innocent Ivan and His Brothers)
Note: This was a revival of Petipa's *Sleeping Beauty*, first performed in 1890 at the Maryinsky Theater, St. Petersburg.

Le Mariage de la Belle au Bois Dormant (*also called* Aurora's Wedding)
Classical Ballet in One Act
Music: Peter Ilitch Tchaikovsky, partly reorchestrated by Igor Stravinsky
Scenery and costumes: Alexandre Benois (from *Le Pavillon d'Armide*), with costumes for the fairy tales by Natalia Goncharova
Choreography: Marius Petipa, with additional numbers (Blue Beard, Schéhérazade, the Buffoons, and the dances for the courtiers) by Bronislava Nijinska
Conductor: Grégor Fitelberg
Premiere: 18 May 1922, Théâtre National de l'Opéra, Paris
Principal dancers: Vera Trefilova (Princess), Pierre Vladimirov (Prince Charming), María Dalbaicín (Schéhérazade), Vera Nemchinova, Lubov Tchernicheva, Lubov Egorova, Nina Oghinska,

Felia Doubrovska, Ludmila Schollar, Stanislas Idzikowski (Bluebird)

Note: In 1927 Balanchine replaced the pas de trois for a man and two women known as "Florestan and His Sisters" with a pas de trois for a woman and two men called "Ariadne and Her Brothers."

Le Renard

Burlesque Ballet with Song

Music and libretto: Igor Stravinsky

French translation: Charles-Ferdinand Ramuz

Scenery and costumes: Mikhail Larionov

Choreography: Bronislava Nijinska

Conductor: Ernest Ansermet

Premiere: 18 May 1922, Théâtre National de l'Opéra, Paris

Principal dancers: Bronislava Nijinska (Fox), Stanislas Idzikowski (Cock), Jean Jazvinsky (Goat), Michel Fedorov (Cat)

Singers: Henri Fabert, Gaston Dubois, Armand Narçon, Charles Mahieux

Note: In 1929 this ballet was restaged with choreography by Serge Lifar.

Danses Russes

Russian Dances

Music: Frédéric Chopin (La Valse), Peter Ilitch Tchaikovsky (Trepak), Alexander Borodin (Polovtsian Dance)

Conductor: (?) Vialet

Premiere: 19 March 1923, Palais des Beaux-Arts, Monte Carlo

Principal dancers: Vera Nemchinova, Anatole Vilzak (La Valse), Nicolas Zverev (Trepak), Bronislava Nijinska (Polovtsian Dance), Vera Nemchinova, Nicolas Kremnev (La Bacchanale)

Note: The performance given on 11 April 1923 also included "The Swan Princess," to music by Anatoly Liadov, performed by Lubov Tchernicheva. The "theatrical matinees" at the Palais des Beaux-Arts were variety-style programs.

Les Noces

Russian Choreographic Scenes in Four Tableaux

Words and music: Igor Stravinsky

Scenery and costumes: Natalia Goncharova

Choreography: Bronislava Nijinska

Conductor: Ernest Ansermet

Premiere: 13 June 1923, Théâtre de la Gaîté-Lyrique, Paris

Principal dancers: Felia Doubrovska (Bride), Léon Woizikowski (Bridegroom), Lubov Tchernicheva, Ludmila Schollar, Alice Nikitina, Nicolas Zverev, Thadée Slavinsky, Nicolas Kremnev

Principal singers: Hélène Smirnova, Maria Davidova, Michel d'Arial, Georges Lanskoy

Pianists: Hélène Léon, Marcelle Meyer, Georges Auric, Edouard Flament

Le Mariage d'Aurore (Aurora's Wedding)

Divertissement

Music: Peter Ilitch Tchaikovsky (from *Le Marriage d'Aurore*), Jean-Philippe Rameau (Fanfare and March from *Hippolyte et Aricie*, Hymne au Soleil), Giovanni Paisiello (from *La Serva Padrona*), Gabriel Fauré (Pavane), Domenico Cimarosa (from *Astuce Feminine*), Jean-Baptiste Lully (from *Carnaval de Versailles*)

Scenery: Juan Gris

Costumes: Juan Gris, Alexandre Benois, José-María Sert, Natalia Goncharova

Choreography: Marius Petipa, Bronislava Nijinska, Léonide Massine, Michel Fokine

Conductor: Ernest Ansermet

Premiere: 30 June 1923, Hall of Mirrors, Palace of Versailles

Principal dancers: Ludmila Schollar, Bronislava Nijinska, Lubov Tchernicheva, Vera Nemchinova, Lydia Sokolova, Felia Doubrovska, Lubov Egorova, María Dalbaicín, Stanislas Idzikowski, Léon Woizikowski, Anatole Vilzak, Nicolas Kremnev, Nicolas Zverev, Jean Jazvinsky, Constantin Tcherkas

Principal singers: Daniel Vigneau, Maria Kuznetsova

Note: This unique work consisted ten sections: Entrée du Maître de Cérémonies (Rameau/Vigneau); Entrée des Seigneurs et Dames de la Cour (Tchaikovsky/Petipa); Entrée de la Chanteuse de l'Opéra de Sa Majesté Tsarienne (Paisiello/Kuznetsova); Entrée des Infantes d'Espagne (Fauré/Nijinska); Entrée du Ballet de la Reine de Naples (Cimarosa/Massine); Chanson de la Galanterie du "Carnaval de Versailles" (Lully/Vigneau); Entrée des Fous du Roy (Fokine); Entrée des Contes de Fées (Tchaikovsky/Petipa-Nijinska); Grand Final; Apothéose: Hymne au Soleil (Rameau/Vigneau).

Les Tentations de la Bergère, ou l'Amour Vainqueur

Ballet in One Act

Music: Michel de Montéclair, arranged and orchestrated by Henri Casadesus

Scenery, curtain, and costumes: Juan Gris

Scene painting: Vladimir and Elizabeth Polunin

Choreography: Bronislava Nijinska

Conductor: Edouard Flament

Premiere: 3 January 1924, Théâtre de Monte-Carlo

Principal dancers: Vera Nemchinova (Shepherdess), Léon Woizikowski (Shepherd), Thadée Slavinsky (Marquis), Nicolas Zverev, Anton Dolin, Jean Jazvinsky (Counts), Anatole Vilzak (King)

Les Biches (*also called* The House Party)

Ballet with Song in One Act

Music: Francis Poulenc

Scenery, curtain, and costumes: Marie Laurencin

Scene painting: Prince Alexander Schervashidze

Choreography: Bronislava Nijinska

Conductor: Edouard Flament
Premiere: 6 January 1924, Théâtre de Monte-Carlo
Principal dancers: Léon Woizikowski, Anatole Vilzak, Nicolas Kremnev, Vera Nemchinova, Bronislava Nijinska, Lubov Tchernicheva, Lydia Sokolova
Principal singers: Romanitza, (?) Fouquet, (?) Cérésol

Ballet de l'Astuce Féminine
Music: Domenico Cimarosa
Scenery and costumes: José-María Sert
Scene painting: Vladimir and Elizabeth Polunin
Choreography: Léonide Massine
Conductor: Edouard Flament
Premiere: 8 January 1924, Théâtre de Monte-Carlo
Principal dancers: Lubov Tchernicheva, Felia Doubrovska, Anatole Vilzak (Pas de Trois), Lydia Sokolova, Léon Woizikowski (Tarantella), Vera Nemchinova, Stanislas Idzikowski (Pas de Deux)
Note: In 1925 the ballet was given with a new title, *Cimarosiana*, and a new pas de quatre choreographed by Nijinska.

Les Fâcheux
Ballet in One Act
Music: Georges Auric
Book: Boris Kochno, after the comedy-ballet of Molière
Scenery, curtain, and costumes: Georges Braque
Scene painting: Prince Alexander Schervashidze
Choreography: Bronislava Nijinska
Conductor: Edouard Flament
Premiere: 19 January 1924, Théâtre de Monte-Carlo
Principal dancers: Lubov Tchernicheva (Orphise), Ludmila Schollar, Alice Nikitina (Two Gossips), Henriette Maikerska (Naiad), Léon Woizikowski (Card Player), Jean Jazvinsky (Tutor), Anatole Vilzak (Eraste), Nicolas Zverev (La Montagne), Stanislas Idzikowski (Lysandre, The Dancer), Anton Dolin (Dandy)
Note: In 1926 the ballet was staged with new choreography by Léonide Massine.

La Nuit sur le Mont Chauve
Choreographic Scene
Music: Modest Mussorgsky
Choreography: Bronislava Nijinska
Conductor: Edouard Flament
Premiere: 13 April 1924, Théâtre de Monte-Carlo
Principal dancers: Lydia Sokolova (Sorceress), Michel Fedorov (Satan), Alice Alanova, Felia

Doubrovska, Alice Nikitina, Ninette de Valois, Hélène Komarova (Spirits of Darkness), Thadée Slavinsky, Nicolas Kremnev, Nicholas Sverev (Evil Spirits), Jean Jazvinsky, Michel Pavlov, Nicholas Singaevsky (Servants of Satan)

Note: This was the ballet act of the opera *Sorochintsy Fair*.

Le Train Bleu

Danced Operetta in One Act

Music: Darius Milhaud

Book: Jean Cocteau

Scenery: Henri Laurens

Costumes: Gabrielle Chanel

Curtain: Pablo Picasso

Choreography: Bronislava Nijinska

Conductor: André Messager

Premiere: 20 June 1924, Théâtre des Champs-Elysées, Paris

Principal dancers: Bronislava Nijinska (Tennis Champion), Lydia Sokolova (Perlouse), Anton Dolin (Beau Gosse), Léon Woizikowski (Golf Player)

Le Festin

Suite of Dances

Music: Alexander Glazunov, Anton Arensky, Modest Mussorgsky, Erik Satie, Léo Delibes, Nicolas Tcherepnin

Choreography: Marius Petipa (Grand Pas Hongrois), George Balanchine (Enigme, Hopak, Variation), Léonide Massine (Dance of the Little American Girl), Michel Fokine (Armide's Buffoons)

Conductor: Marc-César Scotto

Premiere: 18 February 1925, Nouvelle Salle de Musique (Salle Ganne), Monte Carlo Casino

Principal dancers: Vera Nemchinova, Léon Woizikowski, Alexandra Danilova (Grand Pas Hongrois), Tamara Geva, George Balanchine (Enigme), Lubov Tchernicheva (Hopak), Lydia Sokolova (Dance of the Little American Girl), Alicia Markova (Variation), Léon Woizikowski (Armide's Buffoons)

Note: At some performances, Alicia Markova danced the Valse-Caprice (Balanchine after Serafima Astafieva, music by Anton Rubinstein) instead of Variation, and Anton Dolin performed Nocturne, a solo to music by Georges Auric. Eight soloists, including Vladimir Dukelsky (Vernon Duke), one of three pianists, provided the musical accompaniment for the series of programs presented at the Salle Ganne.

Les Contes de Fées

Suite of Dances

Music: Peter Ilitch Tchaikovsky

Costumes: Natalia Goncharova

Choreography: Marius Petipa (Florestan and His Sisters, Red Riding Hood, the Porcelain Princesses, Variation), Enrico Cecchetti (The Bluebird), Bronislava Nijinska (The Three Ivans)

Premiere: 25 February 1925, Nouvelle Salle de Musique (Salle Ganne), Monte Carlo Casino

Principal dancers: Alice Nikitina, Ninette de Valois, Nicolas Zverev (Florestan and His Sisters), Alicia Markova, Constantin Tcherkas (Red Riding Hood), Vera Savina, Anton Dolin (The Bluebird), (?) Soumarokova, Dorothy Coxon, Nicolas Kremnev (The Porcelain Princesses), Vera Nemchinova (Variation), Léon Woizikowski, Thadée Slavinsky, Eugene Lapitzky (The Three Ivans)

Note: This "suite of dances" consisted of the fairy tales from the last act of *The Sleeping Princess*. On another program, Nemchinova's variation is identified as "Aurora's Dance." According to the payroll sheets, there were two Soumarokovas in the company at this time — Anna and Lubov.

L'Assemblée

Suite of Dances

Music: Charles Gounod (Lovers' Dance, Shepherds' Dance), Anatoly Liadov (Le Moucheron), Alexander Scriabin (Etude), Georges Auric (Nocturne), Anton Rubinstein (Valse-Caprice, Lesghinka)

Choreography: Bronislava Nijinska, George Balanchine, and others

Premiere: 7 March 1925, Nouvelle Salle de Musique (Salle Ganne), Monte Carlo Casino

Principal dancers: Lubov Tchernicheva, Anton Dolin (Shepherds' Dance), Alexandra Danilova, Léon Woizikowski (Le Moucheron), Tamara Geva, George Balanchine (Etude), Anton Dolin (Nocturne), Alicia Markova (Valse-Caprice), Lubov Tchernicheva, Léon Woizikowski (Lesghinka)

Note: The Shepherds' Dance was from the ballet in Gounod's comic opera *Le Médecin malgré lui*, produced by Diaghilev in 1924.

Le Bal du Lac des Cygnes

Suite of Dances

Music: Peter Ilitch Tchaikovsky

Costumes: Alexander Golovin

Choreography: Marius Petipa

Premiere: 11 March 1925, Nouvelle Salle de Musique (Salle Ganne), Monte Carlo Casino

Principal dancers: Alice Nikitina, Ninette de Valois, Vera Savina (Dance of the Swans), Alicia Markova, Nicholas Efimov, Constantin Tcherkas (Adagio), Lubov Tchernicheva, Léon Woizikowski (Spanish Dance), Felia Doubrovska, Alexandra Danilova (Mazurka), Vera Nemchinova, Anton Dolin (Pas de Deux), Lydia Sokolova, Nicolas Kremnev (Czardas)

Note: This "suite of dances" consisted of the Pas de Deux (presumably the Black Swan Pas de Deux) and divertissements from Act 3 of the ballet plus the adagio and ensemble dances from Act 2. Interestingly, none of the choreography is attributed to Lev Ivanov.

Zéphire et Flore (*also called* Zephyr and Flora)

Ballet in Three Scenes

Music: Vladimir Dukelsky (Vernon Duke)

Book: Boris Kochno

Scenery and costumes: Georges Braque

Scene painting: Prince Alexander Schervashidze
Choreography: Léonide Massine
Conductor: Marc-César Scotto
Premiere: 28 April 1925, Théâtre de Monte-Carlo
Principal dancers: Alice Nikitina (Flora), Anton Dolin (Zephyr), Serge Lifar (Boreas)
Note: Masks and symbols by Oliver Messel were added in November 1925 in London. In 1926 the ballet was partly rechoreographed.

Les Matelots
Ballet in Five Scenes
Music: Georges Auric
Book: Boris Kochno
Scenery, curtain, and costumes: Pedro Pruna
Scene painting: Prince Alexander Schervashidze
Choreography: Léonide Massine
Conductor: Marc-César Scotto
Premiere: 17 June 1925, Théâtre de la Gaîté-Lyrique, Paris
Principal dancers: Vera Nemchinova (Young Girl), Lydia Sokolova (Her Friend), Léon Woizikowski (First Sailor), Thadée Slavinsky (Second Sailor), Serge Lifar (Third Sailor)

Barabau
Ballet with Chorus
Music and book: Vittorio Rieti
Scenery and costumes: Maurice Utrillo
Scene painting: Prince Alexander Schervashidze
Choreography: George Balanchine
Conductor: Roger Desormière
Premiere: 11 December 1925, Coliseum Theatre, London
Principal dancers: Léon Woizikowski (Barabau), Serge Lifar (Sergeant), Alice Nikitina, Alexandra Danilova, Tamara Geva (Servants of Barabau)

Romeo and Juliet
A Rehearsal, Without Scenery, in Two Parts
Music: Constant Lambert
Design: Night and Day curtains by Max Ernst; front curtain and stage pieces by Joan Miró
Scene painting: Prince Alexander Schervashidze
Choreography: Bronislava Nijinska, with entr'acte by George Balanchine
Conductor: Marc-César Scotto
Premiere: 4 May 1926, Théâtre de Monte-Carlo
Principal dancers: Tamara Karsavina (Juliet), Serge Lifar (Romeo), Lydia Sokolova (Nurse), Léon

Woizikowski (Pierre), Thadée Slavinsky (Maestro, Rehearsing as Tybalt), Constantin Tcherkas (Paris)

La Pastorale
Music: Georges Auric
Book: Boris Kochno
Scenery, curtain, and costumes: Pedro Pruna
Scene painting: Prince Alexander Schervashidze
Choreography: George Balanchine
Conductor: Roger Desormière
Premiere: 29 May 1926, Théâtre Sarah-Bernhardt, Paris
Principal dancers: Felia Doubrovska (Star), Tamara Geva (A Young Lady), Serge Lifar (Telegraph Boy), Thadée Slavinsky (Régisseur)

Jack in the Box
Music: Erik Satie, orchestrated by Darius Milhaud
Scenery and costumes: André Derain
Scene painting: Prince Alexander Schervashidze
Choreography: George Balanchine
Conductor: Roger Desormière
Premiere: 8 June 1926, Théâtre Sarah-Bernhardt, Paris
Principal dancers: Stanislas Idzikowski (Puppet), Alexandra Danilova (Black Dancer)
Note: The first performance of the ballet was dedicated to "the memory of Erik Satie."

The Triumph of Neptune (*also called* **Le Triomphe de Neptune**)
English Pantomime in Twelve Tableaux
Music: Lord Berners
Book: Sacheverell Sitwell
Scenery and costumes: George and Robert Cruikshank, Tofts, Honigold, and Webb, collected by B. Pollock and H. J. Webb and adapted and executed by Prince Alexander Schervashidze
Choreography: George Balanchine
Conductor: Henri Defosse
Premiere: 3 December 1926, Lyceum Theatre, London
Principal dancers: Alexandra Danilova (Fairy Queen), Serge Lifar (Tom Tug), Michel Fedorov (W. Brown), Lydia Sokolova (Goddess [Britannia]), Lubov Tchernicheva, Vera Petrova (Sylphs), Tatiana Chamié (Street Dancer), George Balanchine (Snowball), Constantin Tcherkas (Dandy), Michel Pavlov (King of the Ogres)
Note: Within six months of the premiere, Scenes 5, 8, and 9 had been deleted, along with several minor characters. Cupid, a role for Stanislas Idzikowski, was added in 1927.

La Chatte (*also called* **The Cat**)
Ballet in One Act
Music: Henri Sauguet
Book: Sobeka (Boris Kochno), after one of Aesop's fables
Scenery and costumes: Naum Gabo and Anton Pevsner
Choreography: George Balanchine
Conductor: Marc-César Scotto
Premiere: 30 April 1927, Théâtre de Monte-Carlo
Principal dancers: Olga Spessivtzeva (Cat), Serge Lifar (Young Man)

Mercure (*also called* **Mercury**)
Plastic Poses
Music: Erik Satie
Scenery and costumes: Pablo Picasso
Scene painting: Vladimir and Elizabeth Polunin
Theme and choreography: Léonide Massine
Conductor: Roger Desormière
Premiere: 2 June 1927, Théâtre Sarah-Bernhardt, Paris
Principal dancers: Léonide Massine, Vera Petrova, (?) Lissanevich
Note: This ballet was originally produced in 1924 by Comte Etienne de Beaumont's Soirées de Paris.

Le Pas d'Acier
Ballet in Two Scenes
Music: Serge Prokofiev
Book: Serge Prokofiev, Georgy Yakulov
Scenery and costumes: Georgy Yakulov
Choreography: Léonide Massine
Conductor: Roger Desormière
Premiere: 7 June 1927, Théâtre Sarah-Bernhardt, Paris
Principal dancers: Lubov Tchernicheva, Alexandra Danilova, Vera Petrova, Léonide Massine, Serge Lifar, Léon Woizikowski

Ode
Spectacle in Two Acts, for Chorus, Two Solo Voices, and Symphony Orchestra
Music: Nicolas Nabakov
Book: Boris Kochno, after Mikhail Lomonosov
Scenery and costumes: Pavel Tchelitchev
Projections: Pierre Charbonnier
Choreography: Léonide Massine
Conductor: Roger Desormière

Premiere: 6 June 1928, Théâtre Sarah-Bernhardt, Paris

Principal dancers: Serge Lifar (Student), Ira Belianina (Belline) (Nature), Felia Doubrovska, Alice Nikitina, Léonide Massine, Nicholas Efimov, Constantin Tcherkas

Apollon Musagète (*also called* Apollo)

Ballet in Two Scenes

Music and book: Igor Stravinsky

Scenery and costumes: André Bauchant

Scene painting: Prince Alexander Schervashidze

Choreography: George Balanchine

Conductor: Igor Stravinsky

Premiere: 12 June 1928, Théâtre Sarah-Bernhardt, Paris

Principal dancers: Serge Lifar (Apollo), Alice Nikitina (Terpsichore), Lubov Tchernicheva (Calliope), Felia Doubrovska (Polyhymnia), Sophie Orlova (Leto)

Note: In 1929 the ballet was given with new costumes by Gabrielle Chanel.

The Gods Go a-Begging (*also called* Les Dieux Mendiants)

Pastorale

Music: George Frederick Handel, arranged by Thomas Beecham

Book: Sobeka (Boris Kochno)

Scenery: Léon Bakst (backcloth from *Daphnis and Chloé*)

Costumes: Juan Gris (from *Les Tentations de la Bergère*)

Choreography: George Balanchine

Conductor: Thomas Beecham

Premiere: 16 July 1928, His Majesty's Theatre, London

Principal dancers: Alexandra Danilova (Serving Maid, a Goddess in Disguise), Léon Woizikowski (Shepherd, a God in Disguise), Lubov Tchernicheva, Felia Doubrovska (Two Ladies), Constantin Tcherkas (A Nobleman)

Le Bal (*also called* The Ball)

Ballet in Two Tableaux

Music: Vittorio Rieti

Book: Boris Kochno, after a story by Count Vladimir Sologub

Scenery and costumes: Giorgio de Chirico

Choreography: George Balanchine

Conductor: Marc-César Scotto

Premiere: 7 May 1929, Théâtre de Monte-Carlo

Principal dancers: Alexandra Danilova (Lady), Anton Dolin (Young Man), André Bobrow (Astrologer), Felia Doubrovska, Léon Woizikowski, George Balanchine (Spanish Entrance), Eugenia Lipkowska, Serge Lifar (Italian Entrance)

Le Fils Prodigue (*also called* **Prodigal Son**)

Ballet in Three Scenes

Music: Serge Prokofiev

Book: Boris Kochno, after the biblical parable

Scenery and costumes: Georges Rouault

Scene painting: Prince Alexander Schervashidze

Choreography: George Balanchine

Conductor: Sergei Prokofiev

Premiere: 21 May 1929, Théâtre Sarah-Bernhardt, Paris

Principal dancers: Serge Lifar (Prodigal Son), Felia Doubrovska (The Siren), Michel Fedorov (The Father), Eleanora Marra, Nathalie Branitska (The Servants), Léon Woizikowski, Anton Dolin (Confidants of the Prodigal Son) introduction

1. George Jackson, review of *The Life and Ballets of Lev Ivanov, Choreographer of The Nutcracker and Swan Lake*, by Roland John Wiley, *DanceView*, 15, no. 1 (1997–1998), p. 24.

2. See, for instance, Montesquiou's poem "La Dame Bleue," *Figaro littéraire* (Supplement), 19 June 1909, p. 2, and his article "Galas printaniers," *La Vie parisienne*, 19 June 1909, pp. 445–446; Diaghilev is quoted in Arnold L. Haskell, in collaboration with Walter Nouvel, *Diaghileff: His Artistic and Private Life* (New York: Simon and Schuster, 1935), p. 137; Rimsky-Korsakov's comment appears in V. V. Yastrebtsev, *Reminiscences of Rimsky-Korsakov*, ed. and trans. Florence Jonas, foreword by Gerald Abraham (New York: Columbia University Press, 1985), p. 90.

3. Quoted in Richard Buckle, *Diaghilev* (London: Weidenfeld and Nicolson, 1979), pp. 86–87.

4. Quoted in Tim Scholl, *From Petipa to Balanchine: Classical Revival and the Modernization of Ballet* (London: Routledge, 1994), p. 9.

5. Letter to the editor, *Peterburgskaia gazeta*, in Roland John Wiley, ed. and trans., *A Century of Russian Ballet: Documents and Accounts, 1810–1910* (Oxford: Oxford University Press, 1990), p. 421.

6. Lasar Galpern, who served as ballet master of the Habima Theater before emigrating to Germany in the 1920s and New York in the 1930s, had this to say about the origin of the sixth position: "In 1917 Kassyan Goleizovsky, the outstanding Russian choreographer, and myself simultaneously 'invented' the sixth position. A year later we both met and were amazed at the coincidence. Since that time the use of the Parallel Foot Positions spread widely, and is now accepted by many dancers and choreographers" ("The Sixth Position," in *Letters on the Theatre and the Dance* [New York: Polychrome Corporation, 1942], p. 23). Galpern, who sought in both his choreography and his writing to establish a middle ground between modern dance and ballet, identified six parallel positions and six turned-in positions, the latter being used in Russian, Ukrainian, Gypsy, and Tatar dances. Goleizovsky was an important influence on the young Balanchine.

7. Richard Buckle, *In Search of Diaghilev* (New York: Thomas Nelson and Sons, 1956). This was in addition to the informative catalogue published in connection with the exhibition. As well as editing Lydia Sokolova's memoirs *Dancing for Diaghilev* (London: John Murray, 1960), Buckle has written major biographies of Nijinsky, Diaghilev, and Balanchine. Drummond has published a memoir of the BBC programs and substantial excerpts from the transcripts; see his *Speaking of Diaghilev* (London: Faber and Faber, 1997).

one   The Diaghilev Family in Perm

This chapter was originally published as "Sem'ia Diagilevykh i kul'turnaia zhizn' Permi XIX veka" in *Sergei Diagilev i khudozhestvennaia kul'tura XIX-XX vekov* (Serge Diaghilev and nineteenth- and twentieth-century artistic culture), ed. N. V. Beliaeva et al. (Perm: Permskoe knizhnoe izdatel'stvo, 1989), pp. 4–11.

1. Local historians of nineteenth- and early twentieth-century Perm collected a fair amount of information about the history of the Diaghilev family and the activities of its individual members. In a volume of articles about the Perm region published in 1881, D. D. Smyshliaev gave an account of Dmitry Vasilievich Diaghilev; see D. D. Smyshliaev, *Sbornik statei o Permskoi gubernii* (Collection of articles about the province of Perm) (Perm, 1881), pp. 134–136, 156–157. This account was supplemented by A. A. Dmitriev, who published a history of the city in 1889, and by V. S. Verkholantsev, whose book on Perm past and present appeared on the eve of the First World War. See A. A. Dmitriev, *Ocherki po istorii gubernskogo goroda Permi, s osnovaniia poseleniia do 1845 goda s prilozheniem letopisi g. Permi s 1845 do 1890 g.* (Essays on the history of the provincial city of Perm from its settlement to 1845, with an appendix of chronicles of the city of Perm from 1845 to 1890) (Perm, 1889), pp. 218–219, 263, 267; V. S. Verkholantsev, *Gorod Permi', ego proshloe i nastoiashchee* (The city of Perm, its past and its present) (Perm: Elektro-tip. Gubernskago zemstva, 1913), pp. 75, 194, 203. Professor P. S. Bogoslovsky, who taught at the Perm Pedagogical Institute, spent many years gathering material for a museum of literature and theater. Unfortunately, the collection, which he completed in 1929, was lost during the Second World War. However, from the surviving list of exhibits one gathers that many of them were directly related to the musical and theatrical activities of the Diaghilevs. See Gosudarstvennyi arkhiv Permskoi oblasti (Perm Regional State Archives) (GAPO), fond 973, op. 1, ed. khr. 520, l. 9.

   The Perm "necrology" compiled by V. P. Golubtsov and preserved in the Bogoslovsky Collection at the Perm Regional State Archives is a unique document. Not only does it list the surnames of the townspeople buried in Perm's cemeteries during the eighteenth and early nineteenth centuries, but it contains information about many of them.

   The journal is in GAPO, fond 973, op. 1, ed. khr 696, l. 25. Its Russian name is *Irtysh, prevrashchaiushchiisia v Ipokrenu*. The property list is in GAPO, fond 247, op. 2, ed. khr. 229, l. 32.

2. GAPO, fond 673, op. 2, ed. khr. 696, l. 25.

3. Smyshliaev, *Sbornik statei*, p. 135.

4. GAPO, fond 247, op. 2, ed. khr. 229, l. 4–6.

5. Smyshliaev, *Sbornik statei*, p. 135.

6. Tsentral'nyi gosudarstvennyi arkhiv goroda Moskvy (Central State Archives of the City of Moscow) (TsGAGM), fond 10, op. 4, ed. khr. 686, l. 15–16.

7. GAPO, fond 177, op. 1, ed. khr. 632, l. 231.

8. GAPO, fond 72, op. 1, ed. khr. 235, l. 21.

9. TsGAGM, fond 10, op. 4, ed. khr. 686, l. 15–16.

10. Quoted in Ariadna Tyrkova-Williams, *Sbornik pamiati Anny Pavlovny Filosofovoi* (Collected memories of Anna Pavlovna Filosofova) (Petrograd: Golicke et Willborg, 1915), pp. 9, 12.

11. Ibid. In the 1840s and early 1850s there was probably an organ, which was later brought from Bikbarda to St. Petersburg.

12. OR IRLI (Pushkinskii dom) (Pushkin House), fond 102, op. 1, ed. khr. 77, l. 25.

13. GAPO, fond 82, op. 1, d. 36.

14. Natalia Pavlovna, a sister of Diaghilev's father, was married to Tchaikovsky's cousin, A. I. Antipov, while Alexandra Valerianovna Panaeva, the sister of Diaghilev's stepmother, was married to Tchaikovsky's nephew G. Kartsev. The composer frequented the Diaghilevs' home as a relation.

15. TsGIA, fond 789, op. 14, ed. khr. 4–SH, l. 8.

16. L. E. Iofa, *Goroda Urala* (Cities of the Urals) (Moscow: Gosudarstvennoe izdatel'stvo geograficheskoi literatury, 1951), pt. 1, p. 28.

t w o *Diaghilev's Musical Education*

This chapter is adapted from a chapter in Israel Nesteev, *Diagilev i muzykal'nyi teatr xx veka* (Diaghilev and twentieth-century music theater) (Moscow: Muzyka, 1994).

1. Quoted in Serge Lifar, *Serge Diaghilev: His Life, His Work, His Legend: An Intimate Biography* (1940; rpt. New York: Da Capo, 1976), p. v.

2. Diaghilev was born on 19 March 1872 at Gruzino, an estate in Novgorod Province, where his father was billeted. Soon thereafter the family moved to St. Petersburg and took up residence in a government-owned apartment in the barracks of the Horse Guards regiment on Shpalerny Street. When Diaghilev was ten, the family moved to Perm, where they spent the next eight years.

3. "I think that a better Tatiana than . . . Panaeva would be impossible to imagine," asserted Nadezhda F. von Meck in a letter to Tchaikovsky dated 12 January 1879 (*Perepiska s N. F. fon-Mekk/P. I. Chaikovskii* [Correspondence between N. F. von Meck and P. I. Tchaikovsky], ed. V. A. Zdanov and N. T. Zhegin [Moscow: Academia, 1935], vol. 2, p. 24).

4. Quoted in Lifar, *Serge Diaghilev*, p. 21.

5. Ibid., p. 14.

6. Ariadna Tyrkova-Williams, *Anna Pavlovna Filosofova i ee vremia* (Anna Pavlovna Filosofova and Her Times) (Petrograd: Skl. izdatel'stvo M. O. Vol'f, 1915), p. 10.

7. Quoted in *Sergei Diagilev i russkoe iskusstvo* (Serge Diaghilev and Russian art), ed. I. S. Zil'bershtein and V. A. Samkov (Moscow: Iskusstvo, 1982), vol. 2, p. 339.

8. Diaghilev's letters to his stepmother and other family members are in the Diaghilev Family Archive, fond 102, Pushkin House, Russian Academy of Sciences (St. Petersburg).

9. Aleksandr Benua [Benois], "O Diagileve" (About Diaghilev), in *Diagilev i russkoe iskusstvo*, vol. 2, p. 221.

10. Dmitry Filosofov, unpublished "Memoirs," Diaghilev Family Archive.

11. Diaghilev's love for Tchaikovsky's creations originated in their longstanding acquaintance. While still a youngster, he was taken by his aunt and introduced to the composer at his home in Klin. Diaghilev later recalled the journey to visit his dear "Uncle Petya" in his "Notes autobiographiques." Both the Russian original and Boris Kochno's French translation of these notes are in the Fonds Kochno, Pièce 122, Bibliothèque de l'Opéra (Paris).

12. Benua, "O Diagileve," p. 223.

13. Dmitry Filosofov, *Staroe i novoe: sbornik statei po voprosam iskusstva i literatury* (Old and new: a collection of essays on questions of art and literature) (Moscow: Tip. T-va I. D. Sytina, 1912).

14. Quoted in *Diagilev i russkoe iskusstvo*, vol. 2, pp. 469–470.

15. This letter, dated 18 February 1892, is published in its entirety in *Diagilev i russkoe iskusstvo*, vol. 2, pp. 7–16.

16. *Diagilev i russkoe iskusstvo*, vol. 2, p. 14.

17. Ibid., p. 226.

18. Pascal Dagnan-Bouveret was a French painter connected with the symbolist movement.

19. When Tchaikovsky lay dying in October 1893, Diaghilev, who lived nearby, stopped by the composer's apartment several times a day and kept his friends up to date on the state of Tchaikovsky's health. "We are all totally shocked by Tchaikovsky's death," he wrote to his stepmother on 11 October 1893. "I sobbed through the whole requiem. It was particularly awful since we had just seen him conducting, and he was in great form."

20. A. N. Benua [Benois], *Vozniknovenie Mira iskusstva* (The emergence of the World of Art) (Moscow: Komitet populiarizatsii khudozhestvennykh, 1928), p. 9.

21. Boris Kochno, *Diaghilev and the Ballets Russes*, trans. Adrienne Foulke (New York: Harper and Row, 1970), p. 280. The notes are in the Fonds Kochno, Pièce 122.

22. V. V. Yastrebtsev, *Reminiscences of Rimsky-Korsakov*, ed. and trans. Florence Jonas, introd. Gerald Abraham (New York: Columbia University Press, 1985), p. 90.

23. Ibid., p. 91.

24. Fond 361, op. 4, d. 181.

three *Early Writings of Serge Diaghilev*

1. I. S. Zil'bershtein and V. A. Samkov, eds., *Sergei Diagilev i russkoe iskusstvo* (Serge Diaghilev and Russian art), 2 vols. (Moscow: Iskusstvo, 1982). For a sensitive and insightful review, see N. V. Davydova, "Fundamental'nyi iskusstvovedcheskii trud," in N. V. Beliaeva et al., eds., *Sergei Diagilev i khudozhestvennaia kul'tura XIX-XX vekov* (Serge Diaghilev and nineteenth- and twentieth-century artistic culture) (Perm: Permskoe knizhnoe izdatel'stvo, 1989), pp. 176–183. Mention should also be made of Zil'bershtein's and Samkov's exhaustive collections of letters, diaries, and memoirs concerned with the painter Valentin Serov: *Valentin Serov v vospominaniiakh, dnevnikakh i perepiske sovremennikov* (Valentin Serov in the memoirs, diaries, and letters of contemporaries), 2 vols. (Leningrad: Khudozhnik RSFSR, 1971), and *Valentin Serov v perepiske, dokumentakh i interv'iu* (Valentin Serov in letters, documents, and interviews), 2 vols. (Leningrad: Khudozhnik RSFSR, 1985–1989).

2. N. Zaretsky, "Sergei Diaghilev," in September sale catalogue no. 18 of Rossica Gmbh (Berlin: Rossica Gmbh, 1929), p. iv.

3. S. Diaghilev, "Osnovy khudozhestvennoi kritiki" (Principles of art criticism), *Mir iskusstva*, no. 9 (1899), p. 55.

4. S. P. Diaghilev and V. P. Gorlenko, *D. G. Levitsky (1735–1822)*, *Russkaia zhivopis' v XVIII veke*

(Russian painting in the eighteenth century), vol. 1 (St. Petersburg: Evdokimov, 1902). This was the only monograph in the series on early Russian portrait painters Diaghilev had intended to compile, although his expertise was reflected in the eight-volume catalogue of the Exhibition of Historic Russian Portraits, for which he wrote the preface: Baron N. N. Vrangel', comp., *Katalog istoriko-khudozhestvennoi vystavki russkikh portretov* (St. Petersburg: Department for the Preparation of State Papers, 1905).

5. M. G. Etkind, *Aleksandr Nikolaevich Benua, 1870–1960* (Leningrad: Iskusstvo, 1965), p. 30.

6. The entire letter was first published in Zil'bershtein and Samkov, *Diagilev i russkoe iskusstvo*, vol. 2, pp. 7–16. This extract is from pp. 9, 10, 14, and 16. Diaghilev's letter to Tolstoy of 28 January 1892 appears on page 15. At the time of writing, Diaghilev and his cousin and companion Dmitry Vladimirovich Filosofov (1872–1940) were law students at St. Petersburg University. Enthusiasts of both Tolstoy and Dostoevsky, Diaghilev and Filosofov had not yet declared their allegiance to the new trends of symbolism and decadence. However, only a few years later, their essays in Diaghilev's journal *Mir iskusstva* (World of art) reflected a marked orientation away from the thematic tendentiousness of the realists and toward the formal aesthetic of the fin de siècle, and neither Diaghilev nor Filosofov accepted the dogmatic principles that Tolstoy summarized in his treatise *What Is Art?* (1897).

7. Diaghilev and Filosofov visited Tolstoy on the formal pretext of contributing funds to the latter's campaign for the starving.

8. Diaghilev refers to Ivan and Petr Raevsky, who were the sons of the owner of an adjacent estate, and to Ilya Lvovich Tolstoy (1866–1933).

9. Tat'iana L'vovna Tolstaia (1864–1950) was Tolstoy's oldest daughter.

10. Diaghilev's article "Peredvizhnaia vystavka" was published in *Novosti i birzhevaia gazeta* (News and stock exchange gazette) (St. Petersburg) on 5 and 9 March 1897, and reprinted in Zil'bershtein and Samkov, *Diagilev i russkoe iskusstvo*, vol. 1, pp. 67–69. The subject of the review is the twenty-fifth Exhibition of the Society of the Wanderers that opened at the Society for the Encouragement of the Arts, St. Petersburg, in March 1897. The Society of Wandering Exhibitions, or Wanderers (*peredvizhniki*; sometimes translated Travelers), founded in 1870, maintained that art should emphasize the moral and social problems of contemporary Russia rather than the retrospective subject matter of the academy. Ilya Efimovich Repin (1844–1930) was perhaps the most prominent member of the group.

11. The entire letter was first published in Zil'bershtein and Samkov, *Diagilev i russkoe iskusstvo*, vol. 2, pp. 18–19. Princess Maria Klavdievna Tenisheva (1867–1928), founder of the artistic retreat Talashkino, near Smolensk, was a collector, patron, and artist in her own right. With the industrialist Savva Mamontov, she helped subsidize the first volumes of *Mir iskusstva*. Diaghilev is referring to his Exhibition of German, English, and Scottish Watercolorists, which opened at the Stieglitz Museum, St. Petersburg, in March 1897. The exhibition showed works by Arnold Böcklin, Frank Brangwyn, Franz von Lenbach, Adolf von Menzel, James Paterson, James McNeill Whistler, and others.

12. Diaghilev refers to the exhibition of Russian and Western European drawings and watercol-

ors from Princess Tenisheva's collection that opened at the Society for the Encouragement of the Arts, St. Petersburg, in January 1897.

13. Diaghilev refers to the annual exhibition of the Society of Russian Watercolorists, St. Petersburg.

14. Nikolai Nikolaevich Karazin (1842–1908) was a watercolorist and graphic illustrator whose work was in the exhibition.

15. Prince Viacheslav Nikolaevich Tenishev (1843–1903) was a railroad engineer and ethnographer.

16. Shura was the familiar name of the painter, designer, and art historian Alexandre Benois (1870–1960). A shorter version of the letter was first published in M. G. Etkind, *Aleksandr Nikolaevich Benua, 1870–1960* (Leningrad: Iskusstvo, 1965), p. 167; the entire text is reprinted in Zil'bershtein and Samkov, *Diagilev i russkoe iskusstvo*, vol. 2, pp. 21–22.

17. Diaghilev refers to his and Benois's friend Valter (Valechka) Fedorovich Nuvel (Walter Nouvel, 1871–1949), the "president" of the Nevsky Pickwickians.

18. The industrialist and collector Alexander Nikolaevich Ratkov was related to Diaghilev through the marriage of his cousin Zinaida Filosofova.

19. Diaghilev uses the pronoun "you" in the second personal plural, indicating that "you" here means the aforementioned group and not just Benois.

20. A shorter version of this letter was first published in Aleksandr Benua [Benois], *Vozniknovenie Mira iskusstva* (The emergence of the World of Art) (Leningrad: Komitet populiarizatsii khudozhestvennykh izdanii, 1928), pp. 24–25; the entire text is reprinted in Zil'bershtein and Samkov, *Diagilev i russkoe iskusstvo*, vol. 2, p. 28. Kostia is the artist Konstantin Andreevich Somov (1869–1939), Diaghilev's close friend at this time.

21. A reference to the journal *Mir iskusstva*, published between November 1898 and December 1904.

22. Diaghilev opened his Exhibition of Russian and Finnish Artists at the Stieglitz Institute, St. Petersburg, in January 1898.

23. Princess Maria Tenisheva. See above, note 11.

24. Anders Zorn (1860–1920), Frits Thaulow (1847–1906), and Albert Edelfelt (1854–1905) all contributed to the Exhibition of Russian and Finnish Artists.

25. The symbolist painter Mikhail Alexandrovich Vrubel (1856–1910) contributed to all the early World of Art exhibitions.

26. Anna Karlovna Benois (née Kind, 1869–1952) was Benois's wife.

27. The painter and sculptor Artemy Lavrentevich Ober (1843–1917).

28. This interview is reprinted in Zil'bershtein and Samkov, *Diagilev i russkoe iskusstvo*, vol. 1, p. 76. Diaghilev expressed similar sentiments in a letter of 29 May 1897 to Apollinary Vasnetsov, published in V. P. Lapshin, *Soiuz russkikh khdozhnikov* (The union of Russian artists) (Leningrad: Khudozhnik RSFSR, 1974), pp. 18–19; a partial English translation is in John E. Bowlt, *The Silver Age: Russian Art of the Early Twentieth Century and the "World of Art" Group* (Newtonville, Mass.: Oriental Research Partners, 1979), pp. 156–157.

29. See "The Wandering Exhibition" above.

30. During one of the sittings for the portrait he was making of Nicholas II in 1900, Valentin Serov broached the question of a subsidy for *Mir iskusstva*. The emperor responded with an annual guarantee of 15,000 rubles for three years from his private funds. Baron Vladimir Vladimirovich Fon Mekk (von Meck, 1877–1932), member of a family of railroad tycoons, was a fashion and interior designer who contributed to the organization and layout of the Contemporary Art enterprise in St. Petersburg in 1902 (see note 41, below). Von Meck was also a patron of the arts, collecting modern Russian painting and Japanese engravings. This letter, one of a group from Diaghilev to von Meck located in the Manuscript Department of the Tretiakov Gallery, Moscow, was first published by Natalia Priimak in *Sergei Diagilev i khudozhestvennaia kul'tura XIX-XX vekov* (Serge Diaghilev and nineteenth- and twentieth-century artistic culture), ed. N. V. Beliaeva et al. (Perm: Permskoe knizhnoe izdatel'stvo, 1989), pp. 132–133.

31. The salon painter Genrikh Ippolitovich Semiradsky (1843–1902), the marine painter Ivan Konstantinovich Aivazovsky (1817–1900), and the protorealist Pavel Andreevich Fedotov (1815–1852) enjoyed great popularity with the Russian public at this time. Among his many photographic albums, the critic Fedor Ilich Bulgakov (1852–1908) published *Al'bom russkoi zhivopisi: Kartiny G. I. Semiradskogo* (An album of Russian painting: The pictures of G. I. Semiradsky) (St. Petersburg: Suvorin, 1890), *Novye kartiny professora I. K. Aivazovskogo* (New pictures by Professor I. K. Aivazovsky) (St. Petersburg: Suvorin, 1891), and *Pavel Andreevich Fedotov i ego proizvedeniia khudozhestvennye i literaturnye* (Pavel Andreevich Fedotov and his artistic and literary works) (St. Petersburg: Suvorin, 1893). In spite of Diaghilev's dismissal, Bulgakov should also be remembered for his albums on Ernest Meissonnier (1897) and Adolf von Menzel (1897).

32. The landscape artist Isaak Ilich Levitan (1860–1900) had died five days before Diaghilev wrote this letter. Diaghilev was particularly interested in Levitan's work, ensuring that his paintings were reproduced and discussed on the pages of *Mir iskusstva* and represented at the World of Art exhibitions. Diaghilev also arranged for the publication of a special folio of twenty-six heliogravures of Levitan's works (*Isaak Levitan. 26 geliograviur*) that were printed in Berlin and published by *Mir iskusstva* in St. Petersburg in 1901. The folio appeared shortly after the Levitan exhibition that Diaghilev included in the third World of Art exhibition at the Academy of Arts, St. Petersburg, in January–February 1901.

33. Diaghilev published only one monograph in the projected series, his catalogue of Dmitry Levitsky's portraits.

34. Diaghilev's discussion of Delibes is part of his essay entitled "V teatre" that appeared in installments in *Mir iskusstva* in 1902 (nos. 9–10, pp. 31–34, and no. 12, pp. 60–62), and is reprinted in Zil'bershtein and Samkov, *Diagilev i russkoe iskusstvo*, vol. 1, pp. 148–150.

35. In 1901 Prince Sergei Volkonsky, then director of the Imperial Theaters, entrusted Diaghilev with a special production of *Sylvia*. Benois was the chief designer, working in collaboration with Konstantin Korovin, Léon Bakst, Evgeny Lancéray, and Valentin Serov, but because of a disagreement between Diaghilev and Volkonsky, the ballet was not produced. *Zabava Pitiatia* is an opera by Mikhail Mikhailovich Ivanov (1849–1927).

36. Vera Trefilova (1875–1943) was in fact among the most talented of the company's young generation of ballerinas.

37. Marie Petipa (1857–1930), the daughter of the ballet master Marius Petipa, continued to dance until 1907, even though by contract she was supposed to have retired in 1895.

38. This letter was first published in *Iz arkhiva A. P. Chekhova: Publiaktsii* (From the archive of A. P. Chekhov: Publications) (Moscow: State Lenin Library, 1980), p. 206; it is reprinted in Zil'bershtein and Samkov, *Diagilev i russkoe iskusstvo*, vol. 2, p. 80. Chekhov was living mainly in Yalta at this time. Among the lead articles in *Mir iskusstva*, no. 11 (1902) was Dmitry Filosofov's essay on *The Seagull* ("Teatral'nye zametki. 2 'Chaika,'" pp. 47–50).

39. Diaghilev presumably refers to the World of Art exhibition that opened in Moscow in November 1902.

40. The journal *Novyi put'* was predominantly religious and philosophical. Edited by Dmitry Merezhkovsky and Filosofov, it was published in St. Petersburg in 1903–1904.

41. Diaghilev's article "Sovremennoe iskusstvo" (Contemporary art) was published in *Mir iskusstva*, no. 3 (March 1903), pp. 22–24, and is reprinted in Zil'bershtein and Samkov, *Diagilev i russkoe iskusstvo*, vol. 1, pp. 164–167. In the summer of 1902 Prince Sergei Alexandrovich Shcherbatov (ca. 1875–1962) and Baron Vladimir von Meck (see note 30, above) bought premises on Bolshaia Morskaia Street in St. Petersburg and, with the help of the artist Igor Emmanuilovich Grabar (1871–1960) and the engineer Sergei Filippovich Sobin, renovated the inside to create the store that opened as Contemporary Art that fall. The primary aim of Contemporary Art was to present and publicize new principles of interior design, furniture, jewelry, and clothing for the bourgeois home. Many World of Art figures were involved in the enterprise: Grabar designed the entrance, Benois and Evgeny Lancéray a dining room (or living room, according to some sources), Léon Bakst a boudoir, Konstantin Korovin a tearoom, and Alexander Golovin a *teremok*—or chamber—in the *style russe*, while many contemporary European artists (including Pierre Bonnard, Maurice Denis, René Lalique, Félix Valloton, and Edouard Vuillard) contributed decorative items. Contemporary Art also hosted exhibitions of works by Somov and Nicholas Roerich, and a survey of Japanese engravings. During its brief active life of little more than a year, the enterprise received mixed press, was undermined by financial mismanagement, and attracted few clients, so that, as Benois noted, "only one chair was sold" ("Russkoe sovremennoe iskusstvo" [Russian contemporary art], *Rech'*, 9 Mar. 1912, p. 3).

42. Viktor Mikhailovich Vasnetsov (1848–1925), Vrubel (see note 25, above), Elena Dmitrievna Polenova (1850–98), and Sergei Vasilievich Maliutin (1858–1937) were all committed to the neonationalist revival of the arts and crafts.

43. Diaghilev's article "Gibel' bogov" was published in March 1903 in *Mir iskusstva* (no. 3, pp. 29–30, and no. 4, pp. 35–38), and is reprinted in Zil'bershtein and Samkov, *Diagilev i russkoe iskusstvo*, vol. 1, pp. 167–173. This excerpt is from pp. 167–169. The production of *Götterdämmerung* was put on at the Maryinsky Theater in St. Petersburg in January 1903.

44. Felia Litvinne (1861–1936), the dramatic soprano.

45. This letter was first published in Zil'bershtein and Samkov, *Diagilev i russkoe iskusstvo*, vol. 2,

p. 90. For Princess Tenisheva, see note 11, above. Diaghilev refers to the Church of the Holy Spirit that was decorated by Nicholas Roerich for Princess Tenisheva's estate at Talashkino.

46. Diaghilev refers to a philanthropic exhibition of Talashkino wares that opened in February 1904 in St. Petersburg to benefit soldiers wounded in the Russo-Japanese War.

47. Throughout 1904 Diaghilev traveled extensively in Russia and Europe, searching for portraits in forgotten palaces and estates and borrowing from collections in Paris, Vienna, Berlin, Amsterdam, Weimar, and Geneva. The result was his spectacular Exhibition of Historic Russian Portraits, which, with a generous subsidy from Nicholas II, opened at the Tauride Palace, St. Petersburg, in March 1905. With a complement of 4,000 canvases, including thirty-five portraits of Peter the Great, forty-four of Catherine the Great, and thirty-two of Alexander I, with long forgotten works by Vladimir Borovikovsky, Dmitry Levitsky, and Fedor Rokotov, and with a scholarly catalogue in eight separate books compiled by Baron Nikolai Vrangel and introduced by Diaghilev, the exhibition was itself a historic event. Between March and May, when it closed, the exhibition was visited by 45,000 people, and its philanthropic mission—to benefit the widows and orphans of those who had fallen in the Russo-Japanese War—was profitable to the tune of 60,000 rubles. The Tauride Palace exhibition was a grand visual record of Russia's imperial history. Open during the tragic events of the first Russian revolution, the exhibition summarized a majestic and noble brilliance that had already passed. Diaghilev himself was acutely aware of this conflict between past and present, as he indicated in a moving speech at a Moscow banquet held in honor of the exhibition (reprinted as the next excerpt).

48. Princess Ekaterina Konstantinovna Sviatopolk-Chetvertinskaia was Tenisheva's close friend and confidante.

49. On 24 March 1905 a banquet was given at the Metropole Hotel, Moscow, in recognition of Diaghilev's services to art, in the wake of his Exhibition of Historic Russian Portraits and just as the last two numbers of his journal Mir iskusstva were being published (still dated 1904). Among the guests at the banquet were Valentin Serov, Konstantin Korovin, Savva Mamontov, the poet Valery Bryusov, the businessman and collector Ivan Morozov, the artist Ilya Ostroukhov, the architect Fedor Shekhtel', and the businessman and collector Sergei Shchukin. The text of Diaghilev's speech, "V chas itogov," was published in Vesy no. 4 (1905), pp. 45–46, and is reprinted in Zil'bershtein and Samkov, Diagilev i russkoe iskusstvo, vol. 1, pp. 193–194. An English translation can be found in Arnold Haskell, with Walter Nouvel, Diaghileff: His Artistic and Private Life (London: Gollancz, 1935), pp. 135–137; portions are translated in Bowlt, Silver Age, pp. 168–169, and Richard Buckle, Diaghilev (London: Weidenfeld and Nicolson, 1979), p. 87.

50. The English painter George Dawe (1781–1829) was commissioned by Alexander I to paint 332 portraits of heroes of the War of 1812, forming the so-called Military Gallery at the Hermitage.

51. Diaghilev wrote this letter at a critical moment in Russian social and political history—the aftermath of Russia's ignominious defeat in the Russo-Japanese War and during the civil disturbances of the 1905 revolution that were especially manifest in St. Petersburg and

Moscow. The brutal reprisals undertaken by the authorities against the strikes and demonstrations resulted in bloodshed, mass arrests, and Petr Stolypin's stern reactionary policies of the ensuing years. Inevitably, the 1905 revolution caused damage to public and private property; stores were raided and houses vandalized, and Diaghilev feared for the well-being of the paintings in his Exhibition of Historic Russian Portraits. An abridged version of this letter was published in A. D. Alekseev et al., eds., *Russkaia khudozhestvennaia kul'tura kontsa XIX-nachala XX veka* (Russian artistic culture in the late nineteenth and early twentieth centuries) (Moscow: Nauka, 1968), book 1, p. 140; the entire text is reprinted in Zil'bershtein and Samkov, *Sergei Diagilev*, vol. 2, p. 95.

52. See note 4, above.

53. Diaghilev refers to the suite of poets and philosophers that surrounded Dmitry Merezhkovsky and his wife, Zinaida Gippius, with whom Filosofov lived in St. Petersburg and Paris. For Diaghilev, Filosofov's choice of them over him was an act of unspoken disloyalty and one more emotional discord that hastened the end of his World of Art period. The neologistic verb "to Herzenize" refers to the radical thinker Alexander Herzen (1812–1870), who spent most of his life outside Russia.

f o u r Diaghilev's "Complicated Questions"

Joan Acocella thanks Sally Banes, Joseph Frank, Elizabeth Souritz, and, above all, Nathan and Rena Krishtul for their help.

1. A. N. Benua [Benois], *Vozniknovenie Mira iskusstva* (The emergence of the World of Art) (Leningrad: Komitet populiarizatsii khudozhestvennykh izdanii, 1928), p. 41. "Our Supposed Decline" and "The Eternal Conflict" appeared in Mir iskusstva, vol. 1, nos. 1–2, November 1898; "The Search for Beauty" and "Principles of Art Criticism" in vol. 1, nos. 3–4, February 1899. Other writings to consult on the subject of Diaghilev's manifesto are Joan Acocella, "The Reception of Diaghilev's Ballets Russes by Artists and Intellectuals in Paris and London, 1909–1914" (Ph.D. diss., Rutgers University, 1984); John E. Bowlt, *The Silver Age: Russian Art of the Early Twentieth Century and the "World of Art" Group* (Newtonville, Mass.: Oriental Research Partners, 1979); Arnold L. Haskell, in collaboration with Walter Nouvel, *Diaghileff: His Artistic and Private Life* (New York: Simon and Schuster, 1935); Janet Kennedy, *The "Mir iskusstva" Group and Russian Art, 1898–1912* (New York: Garland, 1977); Serge Lifar, *Serge Diaghilev: His Life, His Work, His Legend: An Intimate Biography* (1940; rpt. New York: Da Capo, 1976). Further bibliography is given in Kennedy, who also helpfully tracks down the sources of the ideas expressed in the manifesto. For Filosofov, see Haskell, *Diaghileff*, p. 86.

2. D. S. Mirsky, *A History of Russian Literature*, ed. Francis J. Whitfield (New York: Knopf, 1949), p. 410. The Wanderers (*peredvizhniki*, sometimes translated Travelers), founded in 1870, grew out of a revolt at the Imperial Academy of Arts in St. Petersburg in 1863. They maintained that art should address the moral and social problems of contemporary Russia rather than the idealized subject matter dictated by the academy.

3. Kennedy, *"Mir Iskusstva" Group*, p. 110.

4. Ibid., p. 64; Mirsky, *History of Russian Literature*, pp. 410–411.

5. The reign of Alexander III (1881–1894)—that is, the period immediately preceding that of *Mir iskusstva*—was known as the "era of small deeds" because, compared with the turbulent, utopian-minded 1860s and 1870s, it was a time of political repression and artistic introversion.

6. Diaghilev is quoting loosely from Gautier's introduction to Baudelaire's *Les Fleurs du mal* (Paris: Michel Lévy, 1869): "Le poète des *Fleurs du mal* aimait ce qu'on appelle improprement le style de décadence, et qui n'est autre chose que l'art arrivé à ce point de maturité extrême que déterminent à leurs soleils obliques les civilisations qui vieillissent" (p. 16).

7. Led by Lodovico, Agostino, and Annibale Carracci, who founded its academy, the Bolognese school of painting flourished in the late sixteenth century.

8. Turgenev's novel *Fathers and Sons* (1862) was the classic portrait of the mutual incomprehension prevailing between the radicals of the mid-century and their parents' generation.

9. *The Barque of Dante*, first exhibited in 1822, established Delacroix as the leader of the French romantic school. Baron Antoine-Jean Gros, the neoclassical painter, actually praised Delacroix's picture. The quotation from the art critic Eugène Delécluze is taken in part from his review of the Salon of 1822 in *Le Moniteur universel*, 3 May 1822.

10. Both quotations are from Zola's *Mes haines* (1866), a collection of his critical writings.

11. These are the opening sentences of Baudelaire's 1857 essay "Further Notes on Edgar Poe."

12. In his 1865 essay "Pushkin and Belinsky," a work typical of the literary thought of the 1860s, the utilitarian critic Dmitry Ivanovich Pisarev denounced Pushkin's work for its failure to contribute to the cause of social justice. In 1880 Dostoevsky gave a famous speech proclaiming Pushkin a prophetic symbol of Russian national destiny. In an essay of 1896 the religious philosopher Dmitry Sergeevich Merezhkovsky, who was to be a contributor to *Mir iskusstva*, annexed Pushkin to the metaphysical idealism of the 1890s.

13. John Everett Millais's *Christ in the House of His Parents*, first shown at the Royal Academy exhibition of 1880, disgusted many critics. Dickens's review, entitled "New Lamps for Old," appeared in his journal *Household Words* on 15 June 1850. Ruskin, in his two letters to the *Times* (13 and 30 May 1851), actually criticized and counseled the Pre-Raphaelites as much as he defended them.

14. These remarks on Whistler's *Nocturne in Black and Gold: The Falling Rocket* appeared in the 18 June 1877 installment of Ruskin's newsletter *Fors Clavigera*. (Sir Coutts Lindsay was the director of the gallery.) Whistler thereupon sued for libel. This famous trial (1878) in some measure epitomized the quarrel the realist and antirealist aesthetics of the late nineteenth century. Diaghilev's translation has been replaced here by Ruskin's actual statement, which is too well known to appear in any wording other than the original.

15. Count Antoine de la Rochefoucauld was a minor symbolist painter and a patron of the Salon de la Rose + Croix (Paris), which exhibited the more mystical artists of the movement. The French writer Pierre Louÿs (1875–1925) was the author of prose poems

and novels (e.g., *Aphrodite*, which Diaghilev mentions in "Principles of Art Criticism") popular for their exquisite style and licentious content. In both cases—van Gogh and La Rochefoucauld, Mallarmé and Louÿs—Diaghilev is pairing a major with a minor artist.

16. Jacques-Louis David, *The Coronation of Josephine* (1805–1807).

17. Edward John Poynter (English, 1836–1919), Lawrence Alma-Tadema (Dutch-born, English school, 1836–1912), Adolphe William Bouguereau (French, 1825–1905), Alexandre Cabanel (French, 1823–1889), Jules-Joseph Le Febvre (French, 1836–1911), and Genrikh Ippolitovich Semiradsky (Russian, 1843–1902) all painted in the academic classical style of the late nineteenth century.

18. Jules Bastien-Lepage (1848–1884) and Pierre Puvis de Chavannes (1824–1889) were French painters, realist and symbolist, respectively.

19. Stefan Bakalovich (1857–1947), Polish academic classical painter.

20. Diaghilev is paraphrasing Zola, who defined a work of art as "un coin de la création vu à travers un tempérament" in "Mon salon," included in *Mes haines*.

21. Mozart's *Don Giovanni* and Gluck's *Orpheus and Eurydice*.

22. In his famous 1892 *Degeneration*, as well as in other books, Max Nordau (Hungarian, 1849–1923) discussed and deplored what he viewed as the decline of European culture at the turn of the nineteenth century. It is not clear which of Nordau's books Diaghilev is referring to here, what "Village Honor" is, who Oné is, or whether his or her name has been correctly transliterated.

23. *The Autobiography of Benvenuto Cellini*, chap. 90.

24. The critics Hippolyte Taine (1828–1893) and Ferdinand Brunetière (1849–1906) both belonged to the French positivist school, which attempted to apply the methods of the natural sciences to the study of literature and art.

25. Vasily Ivanovich Surikov (1848–1916), a member of the Wanderers. His works were marked by a return to the dynamic forcefulness and Byzantine colors of medieval Russian painting as well as by old Russian subject matter. Stenka Razin, a Don Cossack leader, headed a peasant rebellion in 1670. He was celebrated in song and story as a symbol of populist virtue.

26. Pushkin, "The Hero" (1830).

27. *Thus Spake Zarathustra*, pt. 1, "On the Gift-Giving Virtue."

28. Both quotations are from Dostoevsky, *The Brothers Karamazov*, pt. 2, bk. 5, chap. 5, "The Grand Inquisitor."

f i v e *Isadora Duncan and Prewar Russian Dancemakers*

1. Isadora Duncan, *My Life* (Garden City, N. Y.: Garden City Publishing, 1927), p. 164. Bakst made two drawings of Duncan—a portrait, now in the Museum of Private Collections, Moscow, which is reproduced in Cynthia Splatt, *Life into Art: Isadora Duncan and Her World*, ed. Dorée Duncan, Carol Pratl, and Cynthia Splatt, foreword by Agnes de Mille (New York: Norton, 1993), p. 70, and in Irina Pruzhan, *Léon Bakst*, trans. Arthur Shkarovski-Raffé (New York: Viking, 1987), pl. 160; and "Isadora Duncan Dancing," a movement study now in the

Ashmolean Museum, Oxford, that was published in *Birzhevye vedomosti* in December 1907. It is reproduced in Pruzhan (pl. 155); in Valerian Svetlov, *Le Ballet contemporain*, trans. M. D. Calvocoressi (St. Petersburg: Golicke et Willborg, 1912), p. 60; and in Larissa Salmina-Haskell, *Russian Paintings and Drawings in the Ashmolean Museum* (Oxford: Ashmolean Museum, 1989), p. 22. Diaghilev is quoted in W. A. Propert, *The Russian Ballet 1921–1929*, preface by Jacques-Emile Blanche (London: John Lane, 1931), p. 88.

2. On Isadora in Grecian dress, see *Moskovskie vedomosti*, 12 Dec. 1903, p. 5; Sergei Rafalovich, "Novoe v iskusstve baleta" (Something new in the art of ballet), *Birzhevye vedomosti*, 8 Feb. 1903, p. 3.

3. Maximilian Voloshin, "Aisedora Dunkan" (Isadora Duncan), *Rus'*, 7 May 1904, p. 2. A shorter version appeared the same year in the journal *Vesy*, no. 5.

4. S[ergei] S[oloviev], "Aisedora Dunkan v Moskve" (Isadora Duncan in Moscow), *Vesy* 2 (1905), and "Mune Siulli i Aisedora Dunkan" (Mounet-Sully and Isadora Duncan), *Tsvety i Ladan* (Flowers and incense) (Moscow, 1907), pp. 108–110; Andrei Bely, "Lug zelenyi" (The green meadow), *Vesy* 8 (1905); Fedor Sologub, "Mechta Don Kikhota" (Don Quixote's dream), *Zolotoe runo* 1 (1908), pp. 79–80. The Soloviev article and poem are reproduced in *Aisedora: gastroli v Rossii* (Isadora: tours in Russia) (ed. T. S. Kasatkina, introd. Elizabeth Souritz [Moscow: ART, 1992]) on pages 84–87 and 382–384; the Bely and Sologub articles on pages 89 and 121–126, respectively. On the Bloks, see Lubov Blok, *Klassicheskii tanets: istoriia i sovremennost'* (Classical dance: history and today) (Moscow: Iskusstvo, 1987), pp. 343–344. For the correspondence between Blok and Soloviev, see, for example, Soloviev to Blok, 22 Jan. 1905; Blok to Soloviev, 23 Jan. 1905; Soloviev to Blok, 25 Jan. 1905; Blok to Soloviev, 26 Feb. 1905, in *Aleksandr Blok: novye materialy i issledovaniia* (Alexander Blok: new materials and research), ed. V. R. Sherbin, in the series *Literaturnoe nasledstvo* 92, no. 1 (Moscow: Nauka, 1980), pp. 384, 386, 387–388, and 395, respectively. For Bely's letters, see p. 387, note 7.

5. Valery Bryusov, "Nenuzhnaia pravda" (Unnecessary truth), *Mir iskusstva*, no. 4 (1902), pp. 67–74.

6. Aleksandr Benua [Benois], "Muzyka i plastika" (Music and plastique), in *Aisedora*, p. 72. The article was published in *Slovo* on 23 December 1904.

7. See Vasily Rosanov, "Tantsy nevinnosti" (Dances of innocence), in *Aisedora*, p. 131. This article was originally published in 1909 in *Russkoe slovo*; Konstantin Stanislavsky, *Moia zhizn' v iskusstve* (My life in art), in *Sobranie sochinenii* (Collected works), ed. M. N. Kedrov (Moscow: Iskusstvo, 1954–1961), vol. 1, pp. 332–333; *My Life in Art*, trans. J. J. Robbins (1924; rpt. New York: Routledge/Theatre Arts Books, 1994), p. 505; diary quotes from *Sobranie sochinenii*, vol. 5, p. 255; vol. 6, pp. 378, 380. The English translation quoted here is from Natalia René, "Isadora Duncan and Constantin Stanislavsky," *Dance Magazine*, July 1963, p. 42.

8. Alisa Koonen, *Stranitsy zhizni* (Pages of a life) (Moscow: Iskusstvo, 1975), pp. 42–43.

9. Lubov Gurevich, "Dve novye postanovki Khudozhestvennogo teatra" (Two new productions of the Art Theater), *Slovo*, 30 Apr. 1908, p. 2.

10. Nikolai Kurov, "Vecher antichnykh tantsev" (Evening of ancient dances), *Teatr*, 21–22 Oct. 1911, p. 6.

11. Alexei Sidorov, *Sovremennyi tanets* (The modern dance) (Moscow: Pervina, 1922), p. 41.

12. For Ludmila Alexeeva, Inna Chernetskaia, and Vera Maya, see Elizabeth Souritz, "Der 'Plastische' und 'Rythmo-Plastische' Tanz im Russland der Zehner und Zwanziger Jahre," in *Ausdruckstanz: Eine mitteleuropaische Bewegung der ersten Halfte des 20. Jahrhunderts,* ed. Gunhild Oberzaucher-Schüller (Wilhelmshaven: Florian Noetzel Verlag, 1992), pp. 405–420; for Nikolai Posniakov, see Elizabeth Souritz, "Moscow's Island of Dance, 1934–1941," *Dance Chronicle* 17, no. 1 (1994), pp. 1–92.

13. "Spectator" [Fedor Troziner], "Novoe v balete" (Something new in ballet), *Peterburgskaia gazeta,* 20 Jan. 1902, p. 5.

14. S. Grigorov, *Baletnoe iskusstvo i S. V. Fedorova 2ia* (Ballet art and S[ofia] V. Fedorova II) (Moscow: Trud, 1914), p. 43; for the description of the dance in the 1920s, see Vera Krasovskaya, *Russkii baletnyi teatr nachala XX veka* (Russian ballet theater in the early twentieth century) (Leningrad: Iskusstvo, 1971–1972), vol. 1, p. 132.

15. "Kin," "25 let v balete: beseda s A. A. Gorskim" (Twenty-five years in ballet: a conversation with A. A. Gorsky), *Rannee utro,* 1 June 1914, p. 7.

16. This account of the action is based on Gorsky's libretto at the Bakhrushin Theater Museum, Moscow (fond 77, ed. khr. 56, l. 68–69).

17. Quoted in S. Ya., "Nashi besedy: Vera Karalli ob Aisedore Dunkan" (Our conversations: Vera Karalli on Isadora Duncan), *Teatr,* 20 Jan. 1908, p. 17.

18. This manuscript is from the personal archive of the late Natalia Chernova, the Moscow dance historian.

19. I am indebted to the film historian Vladimir Kremen for information about Karalli's screen career.

20. Krasovskaya, *Russkii baletnyi,* vol. 1, p. 274.

21. See, for instance, Kay Bardsley, "Isadora Duncan and the Russian Ballet," *Proceedings of the Society of Dance History Scholars* (1988), p. 129.

22. Diaghilev, quoted in Propert, *Russian Ballet,* p. 88; Arnold L. Haskell, *Balletomania: The Story of an Obsession* (London: Gollancz, 1934), p. 136; Michel Fokine, *Memoirs of a Ballet Master,* trans. Vitale Fokine, ed. Anatole Chujoy (Boston: Little, Brown, 1961), p. 72; Krasovskaya, *Russkii baletnyi,* vol. 1, p. 164. The two copies of the *Daphnis* libretto in the Maryinsky archives are undated.

23. Quoted in M[ikhail] V[asilevich] Borisoglebskii, ed., *Proshloe baletnogo odeleniia peterburgskogo teatralnogo uchilishcha: Materialy po istorii russkogo baleta* (The past of the ballet section of the Petersburg theatrical school: documents for the history of Russian ballet) (Leningrad: Leningrad State Choreographic School, 1939), vol. 2, p. 114n.

24. Russian scholars have established that the premiere of *The Dying Swan* was not in 1905, as Fokine claimed, but on 22 December 1907. The solo was first danced at a Maryinsky charity performance to "benefit newborn children and poor mothers"; "Teatral. Noch Terpsikhory (u M. M. Fokina) [Theater: Night of Terpsichore (with M. M. Fokine)]," *Peterburgskaia gazeta,* 21 Jan. 1908, p. 13.

25. Blok, *Klassicheskii tanets,* pp. 330–331.

26. Galina Dobrovolskaia, "Mikhail Fokin i ego 'Umiraiushchii lebed'" (Michel Fokine and his "Dying Swan"), in *M. Fokin: "Umiraiushchii lebed'*," ed. Yury Slonimsky (Leningrad: Muzyka, 1961), p. 15.

27. Bardsley, "Isadora Duncan and the Russian Ballet," p. 127; Nikolai Shebuev, "Dunkan," in *Aisedora*, p. 43. Shebuev's article, written under the pseudonym "N. Georgevich," was published in the *Peterburgskaia gazeta* on 14 December 1904.

28. A. Potemkin, "U A. P. Pavlovoi" (At A[nna] P[avlovna] Pavlova's), *Birzhevye vedomosti* (evening edition), 10 Jan. 1913, p. 5; Pavlova's comment to Anna Duncan is in Fredrika Blair, *Isadora: Portrait of the Artist as a Woman* (New York: McGraw-Hill, 1986), p. 117; Belyaev, quoted in Krasovskaya, *Russkii baletyni*, vol. 2, p. 269.

29. Valerian Svetlov, "Balet," *Peterburgskaia gazeta*, 27 Feb. 1909, p. 4.

30. Cyril W. Beaumont, *Michel Fokine and His Ballets* (London: C. W. Beaumont, 1945), p. 97; André Levinson, *Ballet Old and New*, trans. Susan Cook Summer (New York: Dance Horizons, 1982), p. 89. This text is identical to the review published by Levinson after the Russian premiere ("Balet 'Les Préludes' g. Fokina" [Monsieur Fokine's ballet "Les Préludes"], *Rech'*, 2 Apr. 1913, p. 4).

s i x   Firebird and the Idea of Russianness

1. I use the terms *orientalist* and *orientalism* in this essay to mean artistic constructions and representations of the East, in particular of the Middle East, Central Asia, and South Asia. As John M. Mackenzie points out, the term *orientalism* has a long and complex history, ranging from its politically oppressive use in British imperial policy in eighteenth-century India to its descriptive use of Asian motifs in Western art history (*Orientalism: History, Theory, and the Arts* [Manchester: Manchester University Press, 1995], pp. xii-xviii). In the literature on ballet, the term has often been used without political resonance simply to refer to use of Eastern motifs in the West. As the present essay should make clear, my use of the term has been influenced by Edward Said's pioneering work on the subject, most notably in *Orientalism* (New York: Pantheon, 1978). However, the case in Russia—because it straddles East and West—is more complicated than Said allows. For discussions of the ballets of the 1910s, see, for instance, Lynn Garafola, *Diaghilev's Ballets Russes* (New York: Oxford University Press, 1989), pp. 287 and 17; Martin Battersby, "Diaghilev's Influence on Fashion and Decoration," in Charles Spencer, *The World of Sergei Diaghilev*, with contributions by Philip Dyer and Martin Battersby (London: Paul Elek; Chicago: Henry Regnery, 1974), p. 149; Charles Spencer, *Leon Bakst and the Ballets Russes*, rev. ed. (London: Academy Editions, 1995), pp. 77–79; and Richard Taruskin, *Stravinsky and the Russian Traditions* (Berkeley: University of California Press, 1996), vol. 1, pp. 490–497.

2. Garafola, *Diaghilev's Ballets Russes*, p. 16. I have borrowed the term *russki* as a shorthand for the Russian folkloric ballets from Joan Acocella, "The Reception of Diaghilev's Ballets Russes by Artists and Intellectuals in Paris and London, 1909–1914" (Ph.D. diss., Rutgers University, 1984), p. 241. Garafola discusses the way Fokine was dismissed by such critics as Gordon

Craig and André Levinson for what she terms his "orientalist extravaganzas" (*Diaghilev's Ballets Russes*, pp. 43, 46–47).

3. Garafola, *Diaghilev's Ballets Russes*, p. 16; Spencer, *Bakst*, p. 78.

4. In coining the term "bodily canon" to denote a set of standards for appropriate images of the body, as well as behaviors, stances, shapes, postures, and gestures, I refer to Mikhail Bakhtin's discussions of how the medieval, folkloric, grotesque body came into conflict with Renaissance values (deriving from classical notions of beauty) regarding the human form. (Mikhail Bakhtin, *Rabelais and His World*, trans. Helene Iswolsky [Bloomington: Indiana University Press, 1984; rpt. of 1968 MIT Press ed.], pp. 19–30).

5. Prince Peter Lieven, *The Birth of Ballets-Russes*, trans. L. Zarine (London: Allen and Unwin, 1936; rpt. New York: Dover, 1973), pp. 106–107; Igor Stravinsky and Robert Craft, *Expositions and Developments* (Garden City, N.Y.: Doubleday, 1962), p. 147.

6. Richard Taruskin, "From Firebird to *The Rite*: Folk Elements in Stravinsky's Scores," *Ballet Review* 10, no. 2 (Summer 1982), p. 74 (also see Taruskin, *Stravinsky*, vol. 1, p. 558); Taruskin, *Stravinsky*, vol. 1, pp. 556–557.

7. See Eric Hobsbawm, "Introduction: Inventing Traditions," in Eric Hobsbawm and Terence Ranger, eds., *The Invention of Tradition* (Cambridge: Cambridge University Press, 1983), p. 1; and Benedict Anderson, *Imagined Communities* (London: Verso, 1983), pp. 15–16. Garafola notes that Diaghilev's ballets appealed to various Eastern European émigrés, including Jews, Poles, and Romanians, who lived in Paris. She writes: "In the stateless cosmopolitans who figured so prominently in Diaghilev's public, one finds an analogue to the supranationalist sensibility of his exotic fare" (*Diaghilev's Ballets Russes*, p. 285). But perhaps another interpretation here is that rather than *transcending* nationalism, these works evoking "the Slavic East" gave each group license to create its own nationalist imagined community.

8. Alexandre Benois, who perhaps initiated the idea of a new Russian fairy-tale ballet (to supersede *The Little Humpbacked Horse*), remembers, "The working out of these elements [of the libretto] was undertaken by a sort of conference in which Tcherepnine (who was supposed to be writing the music), Fokine, the painters Steletzky, Golovine, and I took part" (Alexandre Benois, *Reminiscences of the Russian Ballet* [London: Putnam, 1941; rpt. New York: Da Capo, 1977], p. 304). However, according to Stravinsky, even more changes took place in the scenario after he received the music commission: "Fokine is usually credited as the librettist of *The Firebird*, but I remember that all of us, and especially Bakst, who was Diaghilev's principal adviser, contributed ideas to the plan of the scenario" (Stravinsky and Craft, *Expositions*, p. 146). The symbolist writer Aleksei Remizov, known for his grotesque, comic diableries based on pagan Russian rites, was called in to consult on Kostchei's retinue and other aspects of Russian folklore. See Lieven, *Birth of Ballets-Russes*, pp. 106–107, and Michael Green, ed. and trans., *The Russian Symbolist Theatre* (Ann Arbor: Ardis, 1986) pp. 311–312. (See also Taruskin, *Stravinsky*, vol. 1, p. 558.) In 1926, the ballet was restaged with new costumes and decor by Natalia Goncharova. For the libretto, see Cyril W. Beaumont, *Complete Book of Ballets* (London: Putnam, 1937), p. 712, who mentions "The Tale of Ivan Tsarevich," "The Bird of Light and the Grey Wolf," and a story about Kostchei. Also

see Simon Karlinsky, "A Cultural Educator of Genius," in Nancy Van Norman Baer, ed., *The Art of Enchantment: Diaghilev's Ballets Russes, 1909–1929* (San Francisco: Fine Arts Museums/Universe Books, 1988), p. 21; and Garafola, *Diaghilev's Ballets Russes*, p. 29. The most detailed archaeology of the plot is set out in Taruskin, *Stravinsky*, vol. 1, pp. 556–574.

9. We have already seen that Lieven spoke of the "jumbled" quality of the plot. The critic André Levinson considered the pas de deux "annoyingly silly," and while complimenting the design, he complained that the ballet "has nothing in common with real folk art and even the plot of the folk tale was presented in the scenario in an insipid, confused way" (*Ballet Old and New*, trans. Susan Cook Summer [New York: Dance Horizons, 1982], pp. 14, 16). According to Buckle, "Benois thought *The Firebird* too short; Stravinsky thought it too long. Benois considered that Diaghilev's stipulation that the ballet should last no more than an hour restricted Fokine, made the action too precipitate and prevented the development of the principal characters. Stravinsky disliked the padding and atmospheric linking passages that a story ballet necessitated" (Richard Buckle, *Diaghilev* [New York: Atheneum, 1979], p. 175).

10. Michel Fokine, *Memoirs of a Ballet Master*, trans. Vitale Fokine and ed. Anatole Chujoy (Boston: Little, Brown, 1961), p. 167.

11. Dale Harris, "Diaghilev's Ballets Russes and the Vogue for Orientalism," in Baer, *Art of Enchantment*, pp. 84–95. See also Nicoletta Misler, "Siamese Dancing and the Ballets Russes" (in Baer, *Art of Enchantment*, pp. 78–83), who discusses the influence of the ballet troupe of the Royal Siamese Court, which performed in St. Petersburg in 1900, on both Bakst and Fokine. The orientalist trend in Diaghilev's productions had begun earlier than *Schéhérazade*, with *Cléopâtre* (1909), and continued with other works, including *Les Orientales* (1910), *Le Dieu Bleu* and *Thamar* (both 1912), *La Tragédie de Salomé* (1913), and *Le Coq d'Or* (1914). Taruskin cites Benois's quest for this mystical Russian liturgical quality (*Stravinsky*, vol. 1, p. 556).

12. In "Prince Ivan, the Firebird, and the Gray Wolf," the Firebird's incessant golden-apple-eating creates a nuisance in the kingdom of Ivan's father, and she has to be stopped; this sparks a complex series of travels and adventures that eventually leads to Ivan's finding and marrying his princess. In "The Firebird and Princess Vasilisa," the king's huntsman picks up the Firebird's feather on the road, an act that leads to all sorts of dilemmas but eventually results in his marrying the beautiful princess and becoming king of the realm. (See A. N. Afanaseyev, *Russian Fairy Tales*, 2d ed. [New York: Pantheon, 1973].) Vladimir Propp analyzed the dramatis personae of the fairy tale and their functions, which he sees as constant across all tales despite surface variety. According to Propp, the donor—who gives the hero a magical agent that will lead to his success—may be either friendly or unfriendly. Hostile donors are (like the Firebird in the ballet) "personages who unwillingly furnish the hero with something," either a magical object or a living creature who will serve him, often after a skirmish and a proposal for an exchange (*Morphology of the Folktale* [1928], ed. Svatava Pirkova-Jakobson, trans. Laurence Scott, 2d ed. [Austin: University of Texas Press, 1968], pp. 39–50). See Taruskin, *Stravinsky*, vol. 1, pp. 568–569.

13. Taruskin points out that, according to Afanaseyev, the mythological Firebird is "one of the

countless avatars in Russian folkore of the ancient sun-god of the pagan Slavs [Yarilo]" (Stravinsky, vol. 1, p. 568). I am basing my analysis of *Firebird* on my viewings of two revivals of Fokine's choreography: the American Ballet Theatre version and the version danced by the Royal Ballet in Paul Czinner's film *The Royal Ballet* (1959), featuring Margot Fonteyn as the Firebird. This version, with costumes and decor by Goncharova, unfortunately omits the dance of the maidens with the golden apples.

14. Fokine, *Memoirs*, pp. 167–168.

15. Garafola, *Diaghilev's Ballets Russes*, p. 36.

16. Taruskin, *Stravinsky*, vol. 1, pp. 617, 622, 624; see pp. 589–602 for an analysis of Kostchei's and the Firebird's musical motifs.

17. Although Levinson simply disparages the pas de deux, without seeing in it an alternative interpretation of the sort I am advancing (on the contrary, he thinks there is a mistake), he hints that there is a conflict between the plot and the performance: "She wants to break loose, fly off, but his strong hand holds her fast. Whether it was a difficulty with the musical rhythm or the technical inadequacy of the *danseuse*, the impression created was just the opposite, and was annoyingly silly. It looked as though Ivan Tsarevich were attempting in vain to hoist the Firebird into the air, to force her to leave the ground and fly while she, meanwhile, was foiling his plan" (*Ballet Old*, p. 14).

18. Igor Stravinsky and Robert Craft, *Memories and Commentaries* (London: Faber and Faber, 1960), p. 33.

19. See Nancy Reynolds and Susan Reimer-Torn, *Dance Classics: A Viewer's Guide to the Best-Loved Ballets and Modern Dances* (Pennington, N.J.: A Cappella 1991), p. 98. Taruskin points out that the princesses' khorovod (round-dance) "is not really a khorovod but rather a wedding song—more specifically, a song to be sung at a *devichnik*, the wedding eve bridal shower at which the bride's girlfriends plait her hair" (*Stravinsky*, vol. 1, p. 627). Thus Ivan has arrived just in time to become the Tsarevna's awaited bridegroom.

20. Boris Kochno, *Diaghilev and the Ballets Russes*, trans. Adrienne Foulke (New York: Harper and Row, 1970), p. 53. In Maurice Béjart's 1970 version of the ballet, the Firebird is a male figure.

21. See Joanna Hubbs, *Mother Russia: The Feminine Myth in Russian Culture* (Bloomington: Indiana University Press, 1988), pp. 27–34.

22. Fokine, *Memoirs*, p. 171.

23. See Cyril W. Beaumont, *Michel Fokine and His Ballets* (New York: Dance Horizons, 1981), p. 66, who calls Ivan the "deliverer" of Kostchei's realm. Fokine writes that the death of Kostchei represents "the triumph of good over evil" (*Memoirs*, p. 169); Garafola, *Diaghilev's Ballets Russes*, p. 29.

24. *Le Figaro*, 24 June 1910, quoted in Beaumont, *Fokine*, p. 67.

25. For an overview of orientalism on the eighteenth- and nineteenth-century Western European theatrical stage, see Mackenzie, *Orientalism*, pp. 176–197. Also see Joellen Meglin, "Representations and Realities: Analyzing Gender Symbols in the Romantic Ballet" (Ph.D. diss., Temple University, 1995), for a discussion of a crucial nineteenth-century harem bal-

let by Filippo Taglioni, *La Révolte au sérail* (chap. 5); and Judith Chazin-Bennahum, *Dance in the Shadow of the Guillotine* (Carbondale: Southern Illinois University Press, 1988), for descriptions of two eighteenth-century harem ballets (pp. 139–142 and 193).

26. Fokine, *Memoirs*, p. 165; indeed, the ballet almost could be read as a paean to Prince Alexander Bariatinsky, who in 1859 vanquished a legendary leader of Muslim resistance in the Caucasus. See Paul Dukes, *A History of Russia* (Durham: Duke University Press, 1990) p. 167.

27. Vladimir Stasov, "Proiskhozhdenie russkikh bylin [Provenance of the Russian epics]," *Vestnik Evropy* no. 3 (1868), p. 218, quoted in Taruskin, *Stravinsky*, vol. 1, p. 622.

28. For instance, Sharon Carnicke has recently analyzed the importance of yoga and its associated Hindu philosophy to the development of Stanislavsky's system beginning in 1906 ("'The Life of the Human Spirit': Stanislavsky's Eastern Self," American Society for Theatre Research annual conference, Pasadena, Nov. 1996); Alexander Shevchenko, "Neoprimitivism: Its Theory, Its Potentials, Its Achievements, 1913," in John E. Bowlt, ed. and trans., *Russian Art of the Avant-Garde: Theory and Criticism 1902–1934* (New York: Viking, 1976), p. 49.

s e v e n *Fernand Léger and the Ballets Russes*

1. In nearly all of the literature on Léger's involvement with the Ballets Suédois, scholars have endeavored to identify the artist's views on performance and theater. See Marie-Thérèse Audige Genin, "Fernand Léger et le décor de théâtre, l'oeuvre dessiné" (Mémoire, Ecole du Louvre, Paris, 1975); Melissa McQuillan, "Painters and the Ballet, 1917–1926: An Aspect of the Relationship Between Art and Theatre" (Ph.D. diss., New York University, 1979), esp. pp. 524–536 and 614–628; Laura Rosenstock, "Léger: 'The Creation of the World,'" in *"Primitivism" in Twentieth-Century Art: Affinity of the Tribal and the Modern*, ed. William Rubin (New York: Museum of Modern Art, 1984), pp. 474–484; Richard Brender, "Reinventing Africa in Their Own Image: The Ballets Suédois 'Ballet Nègre,' *La Création du Monde*," *Dance Chronicle* 9, no. 1 (1986); Sylvie Manouas, "Fernand Léger et le ballet *La Création du Monde*," Maîtrise, Université de Paris, 1989; Giovanni Lista, "De 'l'objet-spectacle' au 'théâtre du peuple,'" in *Fernand Léger* (Villeneuve d'Ascq: Musée d'Art Moderne, 1990), pp. 59–86; Erik Naslund, *Fernand Léger & Svenska Baletten, ur dansmuseets samlingar* (Stockholm: Bukowskis Auktioner, 1990); Christian Derouet, ed., *Léger och Norden* (Stockholm: Moderna Museet, 1992–1993); Jennifer Krasinsky, "The Recreation of the World: Fernand Léger and the Birth of the Mechanized Primitive" (M.A. thesis, Courtauld Institute of Art, 1993); Hartwig Fischer, "Un Art plus complet: Léger et le ballet," in *Fernand Léger: Le Rythme de la vie moderne, 1911–1924*, ed. Dorothy Kosinski (Basel: Kunstmuseum, 1994), pp. 239–242; and *Fernand Léger et le spectacle*, ed. Brigitte Hédel-Samson (Biot: Musée national Fernand Léger, 1995).

My own work on this subject has spotlighted Léger's non-easel painting projects and has sought to integrate them with his evolving oeuvre and his overall philosophy of art. See my "Léger Reexamined," *Art History* 7, no. 3 (Sept. 1984), pp. 349–359; "Fernand Léger and the Ballets Suédois: The Pursuit of Collaborative Ideals in Performance," in *Actes du 25ème Congrès International d'Histoire de l'Art* (1985), vol. 2, pp. 161–172; "Fernand Léger and the

Ballets Suédois," *Die Maler und das Theater im 20. Jahrhunderts,* ed. Erika Billeter and Denis Bablet (Frankfurt: Schirn Kunsthalle, 1986); "Fernand Léger and the Ballets Suédois: The Convergence of Avant-Garde Ambitions and Collaborative Ideals," in *Paris Modern: The Swedish Ballet 1920–1925,* ed. Nancy Van Norman Baer (San Francisco: Fine Arts Museums of San Francisco, 1995), pp. 86–107; and my forthcoming dissertation on Léger's collaborative projects of the 1920s for Yale University.

2. This largely unpublished correspondence, a part of the Fernand Léger Archives (private collection, France), consists of nearly three hundred letters from Léger to Lohy. See Judi Freeman, "'Chère Janot': Fernand Léger and His Wartime Correspondence, 1914–1917," *Apollo* 142, no. 404 (Oct. 1995), pp. 40–43. Eight of the letters from this correspondence have been published in *Fernand Léger: Sa Vie, son oeuvre, son rêve* (Milan: Edizioni Apollinaire, 1971), and Georges Bauquier, *Fernand Léger, vivre dans le vrai* (Paris: A. Maeght, 1987), pp. 70–74.

3. "I am selling . . .": Léger, letter to Louis Poughon, from Champagne, 13 Feb. 1917, in Christian Derouet, ed., "Fernand Léger: Une correspondance de guerre à Louis Poughon, 1914–1918," *Les Cahiers du Musée national d'art moderne,* hors-série (1990), p. 77 (hereafter Derouet). One of these drawings was "La Rue Mazel," sold at Sotheby's, London, on 1 March 1980 as part of the sale of Léonide Massine's collection. Léger, letter to Charlotte Mare, from Champagne, 25 Feb. 1917, André Mare Archives, Musée national d'art moderne, Centre Georges Pompidou, Paris. Unless otherwise stated, all letters from Léger to André and Charlotte Mare are in this archive. Léger, letter to Jeanne Lohy, from Champagne, 17 Feb. 1917.

4. Léger, letter to Jeanne Lohy, from Champagne, 6 Jan. 1917.

5. Léger was on leave at least six times: 19–26 August 1915, late January–early February 1916, late August 1916, December 1916, July 1917, and June 1918.

6. For excellent studies of Goncharova and Larionov's careers, with detailed discussions of their post-1914 activities, see *Nathalie Gontcharova et Michel Larionov* (Paris: Musée national d'art moderne, Centre Georges Pompidou, 1995), and Anthony Parton, *Mikhail Larionov and the Russian Avant-Garde* (London: Thames and Hudson, 1993).

7. See Tatiana Loguine, *Gontcharova et Larionov: Cinquante ans à Saint Germain-des-Près* (Paris: Klincksieck, 1971), p. 200.

8. Léonide Massine, *My Life in Ballet,* ed. Phyllis Hartnoll and Robert Rubens (London: Macmillan, 1968), p. 74.

9. Léger's lecture heretofore has been erroneously dated June 1914, based on its subsequent publication in *Les Soirées de Paris* 3, no. 25 (June 1914), pp. 340–356, but this ignores Apollinaire's account of the talk in "Une conférence de Fernand Léger," *Paris-Journal* (14 May 1914); see Kosinski, *Fernand Léger: Le Rythme de la vie moderne,* p. 67. For Apollinaire's comments see Guillaume Apollinaire, "Le futurisme et les Ballets Russes," *Paris-Journal,* 24 May 1914, quoted in *Nathalie Gontcharova,* p. 233.

10. Léger, letter to Mikhail Larionov, from Argonne, 13 Jan. 1916, reproduced in Waldemar George, *Larionov* (Paris: Bibliothèque des Arts, 1966), p. 119; "I would like . . .": Léger, letter

to Louis Poughon, from Argonne, 29 Jan. 1916, in Derouet, p. 57; Léger, letters to Jeanne Lohy, from Argonne, 20, 22, and 27 Mar. 1916. The location of Léger's enclosure of Larionov is unknown.

11. Marie Wassilieff, "Mémoires," unpublished mss., 1929, p. 102, collection of Andrei Nakov, Paris. Wassilieff drew in the margins an image she captioned "Fernand Léger prenant mon fils sous sa protection."

12. See Léger, letter to Jeanne Lohy, from Argonne, 5 June 1916.

13. Guillaume Apollinaire, "A Lecture by Fernand Léger," *Paris-Journal*, 13 May 1914, in *Apollinaire on Art: Essays and Reviews, 1902–1918*, ed. LeRoy C. Breunig, trans. Susan Suleiman (New York: Viking, 1972), p. 382.

14. See Boris Kochno, *Diaghilev and the Ballets Russes*, trans. Adrienne Foulke (New York: Harper and Row, 1970), p. 119. For Cocteau's letter, see Francis Steegmuller, *Cocteau: A Biography* (Boston: Little, Brown, 1970), p. 158. Billy Klüver discovered the photographs and reconstructed the events of the day. See Billy Klüver, "A Day with Picasso," *Art in America* 74, no. 9 (Sept. 1986), p. 161, and *Un jour avec Picasso: Le 12 août 1916*, trans. Edith Ochs (Paris: Hazan, 1994), pp. 76–77. For a thorough discussion of Picasso's work on *Parade*, see Deborah Menaker Rothschild, *Picasso's Parade: From Street to Stage* (New York: Drawing Center, 1991).

15. Léger, letters to Jeanne Lohy, from Argonne, 8 and 10 Aug. 1916.

16. Léger, letter to Louis Poughon, from Argonne, 22 Jan. 191[6] [misprinted date of 1915 in published version], in Derouet, p. 53.

17. "Le Cubisme aux armées," *Mercure de France*, 16 Mar. 1916, pp. 378–79, in Derouet, p. 97, n. 3, and trans. in Eric Michaud, "Art, War, Competition: The Three Battles of Fernand Léger," in *Fernand Léger: The Rhythm of Modern Life*, p. 58.

18. Léger, letter to Jeanne Lohy, from Argonne, 22 Mar. 1916; Léger, letter to Jeanne Lohy, from Argonne, 30 Apr. 1916.

19. See Léger, letter to Jeanne Lohy, from Argonne, 11 Apr. 1916.

20. Cocteau, quoted in Steegmuller, *Cocteau*, p. 165; *SIC* 1, no. 11 (Nov. 1916), n.p.

21. Léger, letter to Louis Poughon, from Argonne, 25 Apr. 1917.

22. Guillaume Apollinaire, program notes to *Parade*, 18 May 1917, p. 69.

23. With the notable exception of *Léger och Norden*, especially the essays by Steinar Gjessing, "Hellesen, Léger och Norden" (pp. 109–118), and Christian Derouet, "Fernand Léger och Norden" (particularly pp. 11–12).

24. Léger, postcard to Ragnar Hoppe, from London, postmarked 2 Dec. 1919, in Ragnar Hoppe Collection, Lund Universitet Bibliotek, Lund, Sweden.

25. Vladimir Polunin, *The Continental Method of Scene Painting* (London: C. W. Beaumont, 1927), pp. 61–62.

26. Léger, letter to Léonce Rosenberg, from Vernon, 11 July 1919 ("The Annals of Cubism" Archive, the Museum of Modern Art, New York).

27. Many of these studies have been labeled as studies for an unknown *Sketch de revue*. In her very useful thesis "Fernand Léger et le décor de théâtre," Marie-Thérèse Audige Genin

identifies eight pieces as part of the body of work she relates to the *Sketch de revue*, based in part on Douglas Cooper's 1949 identification of the decor design. In addition to those reproduced here, these include: (1) *Femme portant un manteau*, ink and pencil on paper, 26 x 20 cm, Galerie d'art moderne, Basel (labeled by the Musée national Fernand Léger, Biot, as "maquette pour le ballet suédois"); (2) *Femme vue de face*, gouache, ink, and pencil on paper, 26.7 x 20.5 cm, private collection (exhibited at the Espace Pierre Cardin, Paris, *Théâtre de Fernand Léger*, 1971–1972); (3) *Femme vue de face*, pencil on paper, 21 x 14 cm, Galerie d'art moderne, Basel (labeled by the Musée national Fernand Léger, Biot, as "maquette pour le ballet suédois"); (4) *Femme vue de face*, pencil on paper, 24 x 17 cm, Galerie d'art moderne, Basel (labeled by the Musée national Fernand Léger, Biot, as "maquette pour le ballet suédois") (pp. 42–44). See Douglas Cooper, *Fernand Léger et le nouvel espace* (London: Lund, Humphries, 1949), p. 158

In a recent study, Giovanni Lista speculates that these sketches (which he states belonged to Jeanne Léger until she sold them in 1945) may have been Léger's preparatory studies for a Ballets Suédois work, eventually realized in 1924 under the title *Within the Quota* with decors and costumes designed by Gerald Murphy. If this is so, then I would propose that because of their earlier dating, the sketches may have been prepared by Léger around 1919 as a proposal for a ballet on an urban theme and were later resuscitated as part of the early thinking on *Within the Quota*. See Giovanni Lista, "Léger scénographe et cinéaste," in *Fernand Léger et le spectacle*, p. 39.

28. Such a parallel might also be found in Larionov's illustrations to Vladimir Mayakovsky's *Sointse* (1923) and a number of Léger's standing creatures in *La Création du monde*. See Parton, *Mikhail Larionov*, p. 194.

29. Léonide Massine, letter to Alfred H. Barr, Jr., from Neuilly-sur-Seine, France, 20 May 1959. "In reply to your kind letter of May 14th, I wish to confirm that the title *La Sortie des Ballets Russes (Exit the Ballets Russes)* was given to the painting by Léger." Information from file on Léger's *Exit the Ballets Russes*, Museum of Modern Art, New York. My thanks to Judith Cousins for sharing this material with me in 1982. The painting, along with the two drawings, was included in an exhibition of works from Massine's collection presented in Italy in 1917. For more about Léger as a scenic artist (with the Ballets Suédois), see my articles cited above in note 1.

e i g h t   *Classicism and Neoclassicism*

1. For more on this issue, see the introduction to *André Levinson on Dance: Writings from Paris in the Twenties*, ed. and introd. Joan Acocella and Lynn Garafola (Hanover, N.H.: Wesleyan University Press/University Press of New England, 1991).

2. For the Benois design, see Lynn Garafola, "Diaghilev's Unruly Dance Family," in *Diaghilev: Creator of the Ballets Russes*, ed. Ann Kodicek (London: Lund Humphries, 1996), p. 54; for *The Sleeping Beauty*, see John Warrack, *Tchaikovsky* (New York: Scribner's, 1973), pp. 226–227.

3. André Levinson, "A Crisis in the Ballets Russes," *Theatre Arts Monthly*, Nov. 1926, reprinted in *André Levinson on Dance*, p. 65; Bronislava Nijinska, *Early Memoirs*, trans. and ed. Irina Nijinska

and Jean Rawlinson, introd. Anna Kisselgoff (New York: Holt, Rinehart and Winston, 1981), p. 445; Michel Fokine, "The New Russian Ballet," *Times*, 6 July 1914, p. 6. The entire letter is reprinted in Cyril W. Beaumont, *Michel Fokine and His Ballets* (London: C. W. Beaumont, 1935), app. A(b), pp. 144–147.

4. Léonide Massine, *My Life in Ballet*, ed. Phyllis Hartnoll and Robert Rubens (New York: St. Martin's Press, 1968), p. 95.

5. Vicente García-Márquez, *Massine: A Biography* (New York: Knopf, 1995), p. 153. The author later suggests (p. 201) that Massine's classes in London with Nicholas Legat in 1926 led to the development of a "new classicism" in his work that was manifested in *Ode* and other later ballets outside the scope of this chapter, especially the symphonic ballets of the 1930s, though again those ballets were not, strictly speaking, neoclassical.

6. A. V. Coton, *A Prejudice for Ballet* (London: Methuen, 1938), p. 87; Cyril W. Beaumont, *The Diaghilev Ballet in London* (London: Putnam, 1940), p. 287.

7. S. L. Grigoriev, *The Diaghilev Ballet 1909–1929*, trans. and ed. Vera Bowen (London: Constable, 1953), p. 178.

8. W. A. Propert, *The Russian Ballet 1921–1929* (London: John Lane, 1931), p. 50.

9. Ibid., pp. 53–54.

10. George Balanchine, "The Dance Element in Stravinsky's Music," *Dance Index* 6, nos. 10–12 (1947), pp. 254–255.

11. Coton, *Prejudice for Ballet*, p. 227.

n i n e Bringing Les Noces to the Stage

1. Eric Walter White, *Stravinsky: The Composer and His Works*, 2d ed. (Berkeley: University of California Press, 1979), p. 251. For more on *Les Noces* and its text, see Stephen Jay Weinstock, "Independence Versus Interdependence in Stravinsky's Theatrical Collaborations: The Evolution of the Original Production of *The Wedding*" (Ph.D. diss., University of California, Berkeley, 1981); Roberta Reeder and Arthur Comegno, "Stravinsky's *Les Noces*," *Dance Research Journal* 18, no. 2 (Winter 1986–1987), pp. 30–61; Margarita Mazo, "Stravinsky's *Les Noces* and Russian Village Wedding Ritual," *Journal of the American Musicological Society* 43, no. 1 (Spring 1990), pp. 99–142. For a more detailed discussion of the issues broached here, see Drue Fergison, "*Les Noces*: A Microhistory of the Paris 1923 Production" (Ph.D. diss., Duke University, 1995). Readers are urged to consult Richard Taruskin's landmark study *Stravinsky and the Russian Traditions: A Biography of the Works Through Mavra* (Berkeley: University of California Press, 1996), vol. 2, pp. 1319–1440, for an illuminating discussion of the ballet's Russian background and sources as well as a brilliant analysis of its structure, prosody, melodic borrowings, and tonal organization. For more on Ramuz's collaboration with Stravinsky, see his *Souvenirs sur Igor Strawinsky* (Lausanne: Mermod, 1929). For Kireyevsky's collection, see Pavel Vasileyvich Kireyevsky, *Pesni, sobrannïye P. V. Kireyevskim. Novaya seriya. Izdanï Obshchestvom Lyubiteley Rossiyskoy Slovesnosti pri Imperatorskom Moskvskom Universitete* (Songs collected by P. V. Kireyevsky: New series; published by the Society of Lovers of the Russian Literature of the Imperial Moscow University), vol. 1: *Pesni obryadovïye*

(Ritual songs), ed. V. F. Miller and M. N. Speranksy (Moscow: Pechatnya A. I. Snegiryovoy, 1911).

2. The full extent to which Stravinsky was directly influenced by folk music sources and procedures in *Les Noces* has only recently come to light. In his *Autobiography*, Stravinsky denied that he was trying to imitate the sounds of popular fetes of this kind, which he had neither seen nor heard. "I had composed my music without borrowing anything from folk music with the exception of the theme of a factory song which I used several times in the last scene, with different words. . . . All the other themes, airs, and melodies were of my own invention" (Igor Stravinsky, *An Autobiography* [New York: Norton, 1936], pp. 105–106). Nevertheless, a number of direct and indirect musical links to folk music and ritual in *Les Noces*, refuting the composer's claims, have been pointed out by Dmitri Pokrovsky and others. See "An Interview with Dmitri Pokrovsky" and Richard Taruskin's "Stravinsky and Russia: Why the Memory Hole?" in the Brooklyn Academy of Music program for "The Russian Stravinsky" series of concerts, 1994; Richard Taruskin, "Russian Folk Melodies in *The Rite of Spring*," *Journal of the American Musicological Society* 33, no. 3 (Fall 1980), pp. 501–543; and Frederick W. Sternfeld, "Some Russian Folk Songs in Stravinsky's *Petrouchka*," *Music Library Association—Notes* 2, no. 2 (Mar. 1945), pp. 95–107.

3. Igor Stravinsky and Robert Craft, *Expositions and Developments* (Berkeley: University of California Press, 1962), p. 69. For more on the Swiss period, see Jean-Pierre Pastori's *Soleil du nuit: La Renaissance des Ballets Russes* (Lausanne: Luce Wilquin, 1993). On Ansermet and Stravinsky, see White, *Stravinsky*, pp. 55–56, 242–243. White gives a fuller account of this meeting, in which Ansermet took Stravinsky to Maxim's in Geneva to hear Rácz play. Stravinsky was immediately captivated by the cimbalom and bought one for himself. For a translation of the original account, from which White quotes, see Yvonne Rácz-Barblan, "Remembering Igor Stravinsky," *Hungarian Book Review* 14, no. 2 (May–Aug. 1972), pp. 44–45. Rácz-Barblan quoted her husband's 1956 radio broadcast. Stravinsky's cimbalom is at the Paul Sacher Stiftung, Basel, Switzerland. On Kibalchich: interview with Madame Denise Stravinsky (widow of the late Theodore Stravinsky), Geneva, 5 May 1993. In 1917 Kibalchich conducted the premiere of Stravinsky's *Four Russian Peasant Songs* in Geneva (White, *Stravinsky*, p. 247).

4. Igor Stravinsky and Robert Craft, *Expositions and Developments*, p. 118.

5. Nathalie Gontcharova, "The Creation of *Les Noces*," *Ballet and Opera* 8, no. 3 (Sept. 1949), p. 23; Nathalie Gontcharova, "The Metamorphoses of the Ballet *Les Noces*," *Leonardo* 12, no. 2 (Spring 1979), pp. 139, 140. This is a translation of part of an article originally published in *Russkiy Arkhiv* (Belgrade), nos. 20–21 (1932).

6. Bronislava Nijinska, "Creation of *Les Noces*," trans. Jean M. Serafetinides and Irina Nijinska, *Dance Magazine*, Dec. 1974, pp. 59, 61.

7. For an overview of the ballet's collaborative relationships, see Stephen Jay Weinstock's "The Evolution of *Les Noces*," *Dance Magazine*, Apr. 1981, pp. 70–75; for a more detailed discussion, see his "Independence Versus Interdependence," pp. 217–278, and Nancy Van Norman Baer's *Bronislava Nijinska: A Dancer's Legacy* (San Francisco: Fine Arts Museums of San Francisco,

1986), pp. 32–36. The way Nijinska's vision immediately crystallized suggests that her artistic identity had been significantly marked by her years in postrevolutionary Russia.

8. In this connection Goncharova made the following observation: "I began to realize that the visual presentation of a ballet on the stage, 'decors and costumes,' need not be directly related to the music; that the music was in closer liaison with the movement (the choreography) than with the decors; and that costume was closely related with movement and subject" ("Creation," p. 25).

9. The contracts for the 1919 and 1920 seasons are in Réserve, Pièce 8/2–3, 8, and Fonds Rouché, Pièce 60/2, BN-Opéra; those for the 1922 season are in Réserve, Pièce 8/4, BN-Opéra, and AJ13/1292, Archives Nationales. Ansermet's telegram from Stravinsky is in the Fonds Kochno, Pièce 1, BN-Opéra.

10. "Are you sure Bronia and you would be ready?" Diaghilev wired Stravinsky on 23 April 1922 (Stravinsky Collection, Film 40, Box 29, Paul Sacher Stiftung). The following day Stravinsky wired back: "Certain Bronia will never be able to mount *Noces* in one month" (Fonds Kochno, Pièce 96). Corroborating this is the rehearsal schedule for the week of 7–16 April in Diaghilev's black book (Fonds Kochno, Pièce 154). For *Mavra*, see the letter to Stravinsky from Chester's Otto Kling, 24 Apr. 1922, in Vera Stravinsky and Robert Craft, *Stravinsky in Pictures and Documents* (New York: Simon and Schuster, 1978), p. 157, and Stravinsky's telegram to Diaghilev, 24 Apr. 1922 (Fonds Kochno, Pièce 96).

11. Kling to Stravinsky, 25 Apr. 1922, Stravinsky Collection, Paul Sacher Stiftung. See also V. Stravinsky and Craft, *Stravinsky in Pictures and Documents*, pp. 156–157. The relevant documents for the legal wrangling are in the Fonds Kochno and in the Paul Sacher Stiftung's Stravinsky Collection. See also V. Stravinsky and Craft, *Stravinsky in Pictures and Documents*, pp. 150–158.

12. Fonds Kochno, Pièce 154.

13. Arnold L. Haskell, in collaboration with Walter Nouvel, *Diaghileff: His Artistic and Private Life* (New York: Simon and Schuster, 1935), p. 127. Vera Stravinsky's diaries indicate that she attended at least four performances, some of which were probably with Stravinsky (*Dearest Bubushkin: The Correspondence of Vera and Igor Stravinsky, 1921–1954, with Excerpts from Vera Stravinsky's Diaries, 1922–1971*, ed. Robert Craft, trans. Lucia Davidova [New York: Thames and Hudson, 1985], p. 18). Goncharova, in company with Larionov, also attended every performance (Archimandrite Seraphin Rodionov, "Souvenirs et visages spirituels," in *Gontcharova et Larionov: Cinquante ans à Saint Germain-des-Prés*, ed. Tatiana Loguine [Paris: Klincksieck, 1971], p. 217). Lynn Garafola, in her discussion of *Les Noces*, quotes Irina Nijinska, the choreographer's daughter, as telling her that "Nijinska attended the premiere with Diaghilev, who was miffed by the enthusiasm expressed by Cocteau and other artists for Tairov's modernism" (*Diaghilev's Ballets Russes* [New York: Oxford University Press, 1989], pp. 435–436, n. 66).

14. For 27 March rehearsal date, see V. Stravinsky and Craft, *Stravinsky in Pictures and Documents*, p. 158; Stravinsky to Nijinska, 27 Mar. 1923, Nijinska Archives. I am grateful to Gibbs Raetz for permission to cite this document and to Penka Kouneva for translating it for me; on Sudeikina's arrival, see V. Stravinsky, *Dearest Bubushkin*, p. 18; Craft makes this assertion in *Igor*

and *Vera Stravinsky: A Photograph Album, 1921 to 1971*, with Vera Stravinsky and Rita McCaffrey (New York: Thames and Hudson, 1982), p. 56; interview with Vera Rosenstein, Gers, France, Mar. 1993 and Oct. 1994. A Russian raised in Paris, Rosenstein was the daughter of the company physician. She had studied both Dalcroze eurhythmics and ballet before joining the Ballets Russes in the early 1920s. In later life, her creative pursuits turned to the visual arts.

15. Serge Lifar, *Serge Diaghilev: His Life, His Work, His Legend: An Intimate Biography* (New York: Putnam's, 1940), p. 255.

16. Charles M. Joseph, for instance, argues that the spacing of Stravinsky's hands on the keyboard may have determined the "Petrouchka chord" (*Stravinsky and the Piano* [Ann Arbor: UMI Research Press, 1983]). For more on the important issue of Stravinsky's physicality, see Roger Shattuck, "The Devil's Dance: Stravinsky's Corporal Imagination," in Shattuck, *The Innocent Eye: On Modern Literature and the Arts* (New York: Farrar, Straus, and Giroux, 1984), pp. 263–276; Jann Pasler, "Stravinsky's Visualization of Music," *Dance Magazine*, Apr. 1981, pp. 66–69; and Robert Craft, "*The Rite*: Counterpoint and Choreography," *Musical Times*, Apr. 1988, pp. 171–176. Stravinsky was interviewed in "A Propos de Noces," *L'Excelsior*, 13 June 1923. This notice, and the reviews cited below, come from the *Noces* press clipping books at the Bibliothèque de l'Opéra (C9763, Don 26017) and Bibliothèque de l'Arsenal (4–Ro12546), and the *Noces* clipping file, Fonds Montpensier, BN-Musique.

17. Lifar, *Serge Diaghilev*, p. 258, and *Ma Vie: From Kiev to Kiev*, trans. James Holman Mason (London: Hutchinson, 1965), pp. 31–32. The payroll sheets kept by Serge Grigoriev, Diaghilev's longtime régisseur, are at the Harvard Theatre Collection, along with many of the contracts with dancers that were formerly in the collection of the Stravinsky-Diaghilev Foundation.

18. Lydia Sokolova, *Dancing for Diaghilev: The Memoirs of Lydia Sokolova*, ed. Richard Buckle (London: John Murray, 1960), p. 206.

19. Quoted in Géa Augsbourg, Paul Budry, and Romain Goldron, *Ernest Ansermet: Une vie en images* (Paris and Neuchâtel: Delachaux et Niestlé, 1965), p. 38.

20. Lifar, *Serge Diaghilev*, pp. 258–259. For another account, see S. L. Grigoriev, *The Diaghilev Ballet, 1909–1929*, ed. and trans. Vera Bowen (Harmondsworth: Penguin, 1960), p. 192.

21. Grigoriev, *Diaghilev Ballet*, p. 192.

22. Jacques Brindejont-Offenbach, "Chez la Princesse Edmond de Polignac: Une Répétition des *Noces* de Stravinsky," *Le Gaulois*, 12 June 1923.

23. Lifar, *Serge Diaghilev*, pp. 259–260.

24. For more on the theater, see Nicole Wild, *Dictionnaire des théâtres parisiens au XIXe siècle: Les Théâtres et la musique*, pref. Jean Mongrédien (Paris: Aux Amateurs de Livres, 1989), pp. 172–174; Geneviève Latour and Florence Claval, eds., *Les Théâtres de Paris* (Paris: Délégation à l'Action Artistique de la Ville de Paris/Bibliothèque Historique de la Ville de Paris/Association de la Régie Théâtrale, 1991), p. 110; Pierre Andrieu, ed., *Souvenirs des frères Isola: Cinquante ans de vie parisienne* (Paris: Flammarion, 1943), pp. 111–133; René Dumesnil, *Le Monde des musiciens*, 2d ed. (Paris: G. Crès, 1924), pp. 123–124. Gérard d'Houville, "Mes Spectacles. Les Ballets Russes de Serge de Diaghilew," *Le Gaulois*, 23 June 1923.

25. Mikhail Astorov, letter to Serge Diaghilev, 18 Aug. 1923, Serge Lifar Collection. Astorov was the president of the Central Committee on Patronage of Russian University Youth Abroad, which received a portion of the receipts. I would like to thank Penka Kouneva for her translation of this letter.

26. Grigoriev, *Diaghilev Ballet*, pp. 192–193; Lifar, *Serge Diaghilev*, p. 260.

27. Emile Vuillermoz, "Premières. Ballets Russes: *Noces*, d'Igor Strawinsky," *L'Excelsior*, 18 June 1923.

28. Raymond Charpentier, "Les Ballets Russes à la Gaîté-Lyrique. 'Noces.' Ballet de M. Igor Stravinski," *Comoedia*, 16 June 1923.

29. Roland Manuel, "La Quinzine Musicale. Les Ballets Russes à la Gaîté-Lyrique-Les 'Noces,' d'Igor Stravinsky," *L'Eclair*, 25 June 1923.

30. André Levinson, "Les Ballets Russes à la Gaîté-Lyrique. 'Noces.' Ballet de M. Igor Stravinski. Le décor, la chorégraphie," *Comoedia*, 16 June 1923.

31. André Levinson, "La Danse. Où sont les 'Ballets russes,'" *Comoedia*, 18 June 1923.

32. This review, from the Nijinska Archives, is in the choreographer's clipping book of the period. I would like to thank Penka Kouneva for translating it.

t e n Diaghilev and Stravinsky

1. For various exchanges between Stravinsky and Diaghilev, see Robert Craft's reprint of some of their letters in *Stravinsky: Selected Correspondence*, vol. 2 (New York: Knopf, 1984), pp. 3–45.

2. Tony Palmer, well known for his many documentaries on musicians (Benjamin Britten, William Walton, Maria Callas, Yehudi Menuhin, André Previn, and others) was kind enough to share with me his thoughts on the making of his film. Palmer interviewed more than fifty individuals, many of them associated with Diaghilev. Some footage in Palmer's film actually includes unused footage from other television documentaries, such as *Portrait of Stravinsky*, made by CBS in 1965. The Paul Sacher Stiftung transcribed all of Palmer's interviews, and it is from these transcriptions as well as Palmer's excised footage (transferred to videotape) that the "cut" segments are quoted. The Paul Sacher Stiftung also contains many of Stravinsky's letters; unless otherwise noted, all unpublished letters quoted in this chapter are located there.

3. Simon Volkov in his recent *St. Petersburg: A Cultural History* ([New York: Free Press, 1995], p. 315) is the last to repeat the mistaken notion that Stravinsky was Diaghilev's second choice. Richard Taruskin, in his monumental *Stravinsky and the Russian Traditions* (Berkeley: University of California Press, 1996), demonstrates that it was Nicholas Tcherepnin who received the initial commission from Diaghilev. Liadov was his second choice, and when this commission fell through, Diaghilev seems to have considered Alexander Glazunov and possibly Nikolai Sokolov—all before Stravinsky's name was added to the list. For Taruskin's reconstruction of this chronology, see vol. 1, pp. 574–579.

4. Igor Stravinsky, *An Autobiography* (1936; New York: Norton, 1962), pp. 27–29; Michel Fokine, *Memoirs of a Ballet Master*, trans. Vitale Fokine, ed. Anatole Chujoy (Boston: Little, Brown, 1961), p. 161.

5. Several of the actual sketches are reprinted in my *Stravinsky and the Piano* (Ann Arbor: UMI Research Press, 1983), pp. 255–269. I have also discussed and reproduced some of the *Firebird* sketches in "Stravinsky Manuscripts in the Pierpont Morgan Library and the Library of Congress," *Journal of Musicology* 1, no. 3 (1982), pp. 327–337.

6. See Robert Craft, "Diaghilev," *The Moment of Existence: Music, Literature, and the Arts, 1990–1995* (Nashville: Vanderbilt University Press, 1996), p. 210.

7. In an unpublished letter to Stravinsky (23 February 1960), Robbins wrote, "It has been my life's dream to do this work." A few weeks later, Stravinsky explained to the manager of the Royal Theater: "I am very sorry not to be able to help you in this, especially as I am a very sincere admirer of Jerome Robbins, and I would be happy to know him staging *Sacre*, but we must accept the fact that the rewriting for a smaller ensemble is already a 45 year old headache without result." Stravinsky went on to remark that when Diaghilev did *Sacre* in London they had to remove some boxes in order to expand the pit and thus accommodate all the instruments.

8. Igor Stravinsky, *The Rite of Spring Sketches: 1911–1913* (London: Boosey and Hawkes, 1969).

9. Nicolas Nabokov (who remained one of Stravinsky's closest friends throughout his life) writes colorfully of Diaghilev and music in "Diaghilev in Paris," in his *Old Friends and New Music* (Boston: Little, Brown, 1951), pp. 69–89; letter from Diaghilev to Stravinsky, 16 November 1916, in Robert Craft, ed., *Stravinsky: Selected Correspondence*, vol. 1 (New York: Knopf, 1982), p. 29.

10. Quoted in Craft, *Stravinsky: Selected Letters*, vol. 2, p. 43.

11. Arthur Rubinstein, *My Many Years* (New York: Knopf, 1980), p. 173. Rubinstein's remembrances of Diaghilev and Stravinsky are numerous, as the pianist was often in their company during the 1920s.

12. Léonie Rosenstiel, *Nadia Boulanger: A Life in Music* (New York: Norton, 1982), p. 263.

13. S. L. Grigoriev, *The Diaghilev Ballet 1909–1929*, trans. and ed. Vera Bowen (London: Constable, 1953), p. 258. The tepid reception of Markevitch's Piano Concerto was a great disappointment to Diaghilev, "so terrible," wrote Grigoriev, "that [Diaghilev's] illness immediately took a turn for the worse."

14. The director told me that of all the interviewees with whom he spoke, Markevitch was the only one who came prepared with what Palmer characterized as a "canned speech."

15. See Minna Lederman, *Stravinsky in the Theatre* (New York: Da Capo, 1975), pp. 128–129.

16. Serge Lifar, *Ma Vie: From Kiev to Kiev*, trans. James Holman Mason (Cleveland: World, 1970), p. 30. In an article published in the 1930s Ninette de Valois mentions that the pianola was used during rehearsals of *Les Noces*. "We always had to rehearse with a pianola. Nijinska had a score with the ballet worked out on it. I have heard it said her work on this particular score was a masterpiece, but I never had the privilege of seeing it" ("Modern Choreography," pt. 2, *Dancing Times*, Feb. 1933, p. 550).

17. See Francis Mason, *I Remember Balanchine* (New York: Doubleday, 1991), p. 15.

18. Stravinsky, *Autobiography*, p. 101.

19. For those interested in a fuller description of Stravinsky's use of the instrument, see Rex

Lawson, "Stravinsky and the Pianola," in *Confronting Stravinsky*, ed. Jann Pasler (Berkeley: University of California Press, 1986), pp. 284–301. Lawson has also played and recorded several of Stravinsky's original Pleyela rolls (including *Sacre* and *Petrouchka*) on compact disc for Music Masters Classics (01612–67138–2). These amazing documents are probably as close as one can get to these works as they sounded in the Ballets Russes rehearsal hall.

20. Directed by Richard Leacock and Rolf Liebermann, the documentary was produced by Norddeutscher Rundfunk Television.

21. Stravinsky, *Autobiography*, p. 148.

22. Part of the letter is published in Vera Stravinsky and Robert Craft, *Stravinsky in Pictures and Documents* (New York: Simon and Schuster, 1978), p. 285. Stravinsky had, in fact, been a fan of Nijinska's dancing as early as 1912 when she performed the role of the ballerina doll in *Petrouchka*. In an interview with the *St. Petersburg Gazette*, dating from October 1912, Stravinsky commented that Nijinska was "extremely talented, a fascinating ballerina, fully the equal of her brother."

23. The letter is dated 20 October 1928. A few days after that, on 26 October, Stravinsky writes again to Païchadze: "Tell Ida that the program of the Monte Carlo winter season is posted everywhere around here and on it is emblazoned 'Le Baiser de la Fée' of Yegor Stravinsky, music to a tale by Anderson [sic]. . . . In the first place my name is well enough known not to call me Yegor, and secondly I am alone the author of the libretto of my ballet, and not Andersen of whom not even a hint has remained."

24. Vera Sudeikina's relationships with her husband Serge as well as with Diaghilev, Kochno, and Stravinsky are richly explored and illustrated in *The Salon Album of Vera Sudeikin-Stravinsky*, ed. and trans. by John E. Bowlt (Princeton: Princeton University Press, 1995).

25. See Christopher Isherwood, *Diaries: 1939–1960*, vol. 1 (London: Harper Collins, 1996), p. 764.

e l e v e n *Adolph Bolm in America*

1. Diaghilev, quoted in Tamara Geva, *Split Seconds: A Remembrance* (New York: Harper and Row, 1972), p. 349; on the American tours, see Lynn Garafola, *Diaghilev's Ballets Russes* (New York: Oxford University Press, 1989), pp. 205–206; Edward L. Bernays, *Biography of an Idea: Memoirs of Public Relations Counsel Edward L. Bernays* (New York: Simon and Schuster, 1965), p. 125.

2. The drawing of these parallels relies on Lynn Garafola's analysis of the Diaghilev repertory in *Diaghilev's Ballets Russes*, in which she delineates concerns she labels modernism, neoprimitivism, period modernism, lifestyle modernism, retrospective classicism, and choreographic neoclassicism.

3. Biographical information drawn from Rosalind K. Shaffer, "Outline on Biography of Adolph Bolm," n.d., typescript in Box 1, Biographical Material folder, Adolph Bolm Collection, George Arents Research Library, Syracuse University (hereafter cited as Bolm Collection); M. Borisoglebekii, *Materialy po istorii russkago baleta* (Materials for the history of Russian ballet) 2 vols. (Leningrad, 1939); John Dougherty, "Perspective on Adolph Bolm,"

pt. 1, *Dance Magazine*, Jan. 1963, p. 44. For a more detailed discussion of Bolm's tours, see Keith Money, *Anna Pavlova: Her Life and Art* (New York: Knopf, 1982), p. 78.

4. Michel Fokine, *Memoirs of a Ballet Master*, trans. Vitale Fokine, ed. Anatole Chujoy (Boston: Little, Brown, 1961), pp. 147–148.

5. See Box 5, Writings by Bolm folder, in Bolm Collection.

6. Lynn Garafola has pointed out that, unlike Nijinsky's androgynous and plastic persona, Bolm had a "transgressive force"; he was a hyper-masculine presence who "ranged the stage like a force of nature . . . the barbarian untamed by civilization" (*Diaghilev's Ballets Russes*, p. 33). See also p. 179.

7. "Adolph Bolm Gives His Exotic Dances," *New York Times*, 21 Aug. 1917, in Adol'f Rudol'fovich Bolm Reserve Clippings (hereafter cited as Bolm Reserve Clippings), Dance Collection, New York Public Library for the Performing Arts (hereafter cited as DC-NYPLPA); Merle Armitage, *Dance Memoranda*, ed. Edwin Corle (New York: Duell, Sloan and Pearce, 1947), p. 46.

8. Adolph Bolm, in collaboration with Vera Caspary, "Dancer's Days: American Adventures— Experiments on Broadway," [ca. 1926], typescript in Box 4, Told by AB for Young folder, Bolm Collection; publicity brochure, "Adolph Bolm's Choreo Dramas Comedies Ballets- Intimes," n.d., in Bolm Reserve Clippings, DC-NYPLPA.

9. F. R. G., "Bolm Ballet with Damrosch Symphony," *Musical America*, 28 Feb. 1920, in Bolm Reserve Clippings, DC-NYPLPA.

10. Adolph Bolm, "How I Arrange My Ballets and Dances," n.d., typescript in Box 4, By Bolm folder, Bolm Collection. In January 1919 Bolm also choreographed "Spanish Choreographic Episode," a dance-pantomime to music of Albéniz, depicting a monk who is captivated by the charms of a dancing girl. It was performed as a prologue at the Rivoli Theater in New York.

11. John Martin, *Ruth Page: An Intimate Biography* (New York: Marcel Dekker, 1977), p. 33. Rosalind K. Schaffer, "Outline for Biography of Adolph Bolm," Box 1, Biographical Materials Ms. folder, Bolm Collection. Bolm had arranged for Prokofiev to receive the commission for *The Love for Three Oranges* at the Chicago Opera, and he also introduced Roerich to New York intellectual and cultural life by arranging an exhibition of his paintings.

12. Bolm, "Dancer's Days."

13. Gilbert Seldes, "A Personal Preface," in *The Seven Lively Arts* (New York: Sagamore Press, 1957), p. 2.

14. The action was printed as notes on the published score. See George Herriman and John Alden Carpenter, *Krazy Kat: A Jazz-Pantomime*, annotated and illustrated piano score, 1922, in Box 5, Musical Scores folder, Bolm Collection.

15. Seldes, *Seven Lively Arts*, p. 241.

16. In his preface, Seldes acknowledged the debt: "In a way, the Krazy Kat ballet demonstrated both the essence and the eccentricity of what I was going to be doing for several years. . . . My theme was to be that entertainment of a high order existed in places not usually associated with Art. . . . Obviously the appearance of a comic strip character in an art-form as

remote and chic as ballet (years before Agnes de Mille and *Oklahoma!* showed us that we were all balletomanes) gave me an opportunity to back into my subject. It was as if the ballet had thrown a cloak of dignity around Krazy Kat" ("Personal Preface," *Seven Lively Arts,* p. 3). Robert Edmond Jones designed "The Krazy Kat's Ball," produced by John Murray Anderson and set to Carpenter's score, in the *Greenwich Village Follies* of 1922. See John Murray Anderson, *Out Without My Rubbers: The Memoir of John Murray Anderson,* as told to and written by Hugh Abercrombie Anderson (New York: Library Publishers, 1954), and Robert Baral, *Revue: A Nostalgic Reprise of the Great Broadway Period* (New York: Fleet, 1962), p. 125. On the interest in popular culture, see Garafola, *Diaghilev's Ballets Russes,* pp. 76–78, 99–105. Garafola makes a distinction between the genuine futurist fascination with popular culture and the "slumming" of the French upper classes abetted by Cocteau. Simeon Strunsky, in the *New York Evening Post,* denounced "the intellectualist rush to be elemental and almost vulgar, which has recently elevated Krazy Kat and Miss Fanny Brice to very near the top-most rank in American art." Quoted in Michael Kammen, *The Lively Arts: Gilbert Seldes and the Transformation of Cultural Criticism in the United States* (New York: Oxford University Press, 1996), p. 87.

17. Diaghilev entered into negotiations with Otto Kahn and impressario Morris Gest to produce Carpenter's ballet *Skyscrapers: A Ballet of Modern American Life.* Carpenter was the only American composer with whom Diaghilev ever considered working. He wrote to Kochno that Carpenter's score "is American de Falla, with appropriate folklore." The ballet was considered as part of a proposed American tour that never materialized. Quoted in Boris Kochno, *Diaghilev and the Ballets Russes,* trans. Adrienne Foulke (New York: Harper and Row, 1970), p. 223. The ballet was eventually produced at the Metropolitan Opera on 19 February 1926, with choreography by Sammy Lee and designs by Robert Edmond Jones. See Gilbert Chase, "John Alden Carpenter," *The New Grove Dictionary of American Music,* vol. 1, ed. H. Wiley Hitchcock and Stanley Sadie (London: Macmillan, 1986), 359. John Dizikes, *Opera in America: A Cultural History* (New Haven: Yale University Press, 1993), p. 413; Ann Barzel, "Dance in Chicago—An Early History," *American Dance* 2, no. 1 (1986), p. 28.

18. Bolm, "Dancer's Days."

19. Edward C. Moore, *Forty Years of Opera in Chicago* (New York: Horace Liveright, 1930), p. 271. "Never since," he added, "has it come within miles of touching that level." For the "striking success" quote, see p. 256.

20. Alfred V. Frankenstein, "Program at Goodman Theater Displays Modern Music Trend," *Chicago Daily Maroon,* 13 Nov. 1925, Scrapbook 3, Bolm Collection.

21. Biographical information on Remisoff drawn from Oliver M. Sayler, *The Russian Theatre* (New York: Brentano's, 1922), p. 319; "Stage Settings at Arts Club," unidentified Chicago newspaper, n.d., Scrapbook 3, Bolm Collection; and "Remisoff Designer for Bolm Ballet," *Rockford Gazette,* 29 Dec. 1924, Scrapbook 3, Bolm Collection.

22. "Nicholas Remisoff, Interpreter of Russia," *Chicago Post,* 15 Dec. 1925, Scrapbook 3, Bolm Collection; Edward Moore, "First Program of Allied Arts Fine Success," *Chicago Tribune,* 28 Nov. 1926, Scrapbook 3, Bolm Collection; O. L. Hall, unidentified newspaper clipping, 14 Nov. 1924, Scrapbook 3, Bolm Collection.

23. "Undoubtedly one of the most fantastic . . .": George M. Seaberg, "Allied Arts Inaugurates Fine Schedule," *North Side Citizen*, Jan. 1925, Scrapbook 3, Bolm Collection; "suggestive of Chinese art . . .": Olin Downes, "Music," *New York Times*, 28 Mar. 1927, Scrapbook 3, Bolm Collection.

24. "Amusing and unbeautiful": untitled article, *Chicago Journal of Commerce*, 28 Dec. 1925, Scrapbook 3, Bolm Collection; "the backing of authoritative surroundings . . .": James Weber Linn, "Lights and Darks," unidentified Chicago newspaper, 10 Nov. 1925, Scrapbook 3, Bolm Collection; "right to the surname . . .": "Bolm and De Lamarter," *Chicago American*, 9 Nov. 1925, Scrapbook 3, Bolm Collection.

25. "Not of the moonlit gardens . . .": "Allied Arts Too 'Arty'; Ballet Is Target of Critics," *Chicago Post*, 24 Dec. 1925, Scrapbook 3, Bolm Collection; on *Bourgeois Gentilhomme*, see Felix Borowski, *Christian Science Monitor*, 21 Nov. 1925, Scrapbook 3, Bolm Collection, and Borowski, "The Lighter Vein of Modern Music and Modern Dance," *Boston Evening Transcript*, 12 Nov. 1925, Scrapbook 3, Bolm Collection; Alfred V. Frankenstein, "Program at Goodman Theater Displays Modern Music Trend," *Chicago Daily Maroon*, 13 Nov. 1925, Scrapbook 3, Bolm Collection.

26. "Allied Arts Too 'Arty'"; Frankenstein, "Program at Goodman Theater."

27. Unidentified article, *Chicago Topics*, n.d., Scrapbook 3, Bolm Collection; "Allied Arts Too 'Arty.'"

28. Felix Borowski, "Arts in Fusion," *Christian Science Monitor*, 6 Nov. 1926, Scrapbook 3, Bolm Collection; Samuel Putnam, "America and the Undiscovered Dance," *Chicago Evening Post Magazine*, n.d., Scrapbook 3, Bolm Collection.

29. Garafola, *Diaghilev's Ballets Russes*, pp. 137–139; Chicago Allied Arts, Eighth Street Theatre, 24–31 Oct. 1926, [program], Box 3, Dance Programs folder, Bolm Collection.

30. "Music Invokes Aid of Dance Fantasies," *Musical America*, 12 Mar. 1927, p. 40; "new attempt . . .": "Society Sponsors Bolm Ballet," unidentified New York newspaper, 13 Mar. 1927, Scrapbook 3, Bolm Collection; Putnam, "America and the Undiscovered Dance"; Putnam, "The New Ballet: A Theatrical Art," *The Drama* 17, no. 3 (Dec. 1926), Scrapbook 3, Bolm Collection; Hazel Moore, "Allied Arts Gives First of Season's Notable Programs," *Chicago Daily Tribune*, 25 Oct. 1926, Scrapbook 3, Bolm Collection. Some critics saw mysticism as a cover for eroticism. Samuel Chotzinoff wrote that Bolm and Page made "artistic passes at each other" ("Music," *New York World*, 28 Mar. 1927); for an anonymous writer in the *New Yorker*, it was "a few minutes of amatory hokum" (9 Apr. 1927); Richard L. Stokes wrote that "it was certainly visual though scarcely mystic. It was an exhibit of erotic excitation which left little to the imagination" ("Realm of Music," *New York Evening World*, 28 Mar. 1927); Olga Samaroff worried that the ballet "at times came near a stifling sultriness" ("Music," *New York Post*, 29 Mar. 1927). All in Scrapbook 3, Bolm Collection.

31. Eugene Stinson, "New Ballets Given by Chicago Society," *Musical America*, 13 Nov. 1926, Scrapbook 3, Bolm Collection.

32. "'Christmas Carol' Scenes in Pantomime by Bolm," *Chicago Herald Examiner*, 19 Dec. 1926,

Scrapbook 3, Bolm Collection; Karleton Hackett, "Allied Arts at the Eighth Street Theater," *Chicago Evening Post*, 27 Dec. 1926, Scrapbook 3, Bolm Collection.

33. Bolm, "How I Arrange My Ballets"; Eugene Stinson, "Opera, Ballet and Concert," *Chicago Daily Journal*, 27 Dec. 1926, Scrapbook 3, Bolm Collection; Olin Downes, "Music," *New York Times*, 28 Mar. 1927, Scrapbook 3, Bolm Collection.

34. Unidentified article, 21 Oct. 1925, Scrapbook 3, Bolm Collection.

35. The Larionov designs commissioned by Bolm for "The Adventures of Karaguez" were exhibited at the Everson Museum of Art, Syracuse, 9–26 Feb. 1978. Larionov had designed a marionette show on the same theme in 1924. See *Mikhail Larionov Designs for the Ballet "The Adventures of Karaguez,"* Everson Museum of Art, 1978.

36. Frederick Jacobi, "The New Apollo," *Modern Music* 5, no. 4 (May–June 1928), p. 11.

37. The ballet is described in "Joining Music and the Dance," unidentified clipping in Bolm Reserve Clippings, DC-NYPLPA, and Jacobi, "The New Apollo," pp. 11–15 (quotes from this source).

38. Bolm, "How I Arrange My Ballets"; [John Martin], "The Dance: Four Ballets—Music Afield," *New York Times*, n.d., Scrapbook 3, Bolm Collection.

39. Quoted in John Dougherty, "Perspective on Adolph Bolm," pt. 2, *Dance Magazine*, Feb. 1963, p. 58.

40. *Ballet Mécanique*, the first ballet Bolm created in Hollywood, had a score by Soviet composer Alexander Mosolov and was clearly inspired by Diaghilev's production of *Le Pas d'Acier* (1927). It was created for Warner Brothers' *The Mad Genius* (1931), a thinly disguised portrait of the Diaghilev-Nijinsky relationship, starring John Barrymore. Although most of the ballet was cut from the film, Bolm successfully restaged versions of it at the Hollywood Bowl, the San Francisco Ballet, and Ballet Theatre.

t w e l v e *Reconfiguring the Sexes*

1. Lucy Hughes-Hallett, *Cleopatra: Histories, Dreams and Distortions* (New York: Harper and Row, 1990), p. 233.

2. Alexandre Benois, *Reminiscences of the Russian Ballet*, trans. Mary Britnieva (London: Putnam, 1941), p. 296.

3. Ibid., p. 315.

4. Prince Pieter Lieven, *The Birth of Ballets-Russes*, foreword by Catherine Lieven Ritter (London: Allen and Unwin, 1936), p. 260.

5. Although Diaghilev gave *Les Sylphides* a new title, the ballet itself, as *Chopiniana*, was first given at a Maryinsky charity performance.

6. H[oward] H[annay], "Zephyr and Flora," *The Observer*, 25 Nov. 1925, p. 11.

7. Apollinaire spoke of the connection between "feminine art" and the "serpentine" in one of his art chronicles of the period: "C'est cela même, la peinture féminine est serpentine et c'est peut-être cette grande artiste de la ligne et des couleurs, la Loïe Fuller, qui fut le précurseur de l'art féminin d'aujourd'hui quand elle inventa cette chose géniale où se

mêlient la peinture, la danse, le dessin et la coquetterie et que l'on apella très justement: la danse serpentine" (Guillaume Apollinaire, "Chronique d'art: Les Peintresses," *Le Petit Bleu*, 5 Apr. 1912, in *Chroniques d'art 1902–1918*, ed. L. C. Breunig [Paris: Gallimard, 1960], p. 302).

8. Lydia Lopokova to John Maynard Keynes, 12 May 1924, John Maynard Keynes Papers, King's College (Cambridge).

9. "Starved to Be a Saint; To Be Gilded to Be a Goddess?" *The Sketch*, 31 May 1911, in Ida Rubinstein clipping file, Mander and Mitchenson Theatre Collection (Beckenham Junction, Kent).

10. Herbert Farjeon, "Seen on the Stage," *Vogue* (British edition), 11 July 1928, p. 80. At least one Ballets Russes dancer complained (although not publicly) about the influence of such iconography on the style of male dancing generally. Stanislas Idzikowski, a Polish dancer who joined the company in 1914, told Karsavina that he had left it in 1926 when the style of male dancing underwent a change: "I could not demean myself . . . by wiggling my posterior" (Stanislas Idzikowski, interviewed by John Gruen, 2 Aug. 1974, pp. 116–117, Oral History Archive, Dance Collection, New York Public Library for the Performing Arts).

f o u r t e e n   Diaghilev and Lincoln Kirstein

1. In his book of essays on artists, *The Art Presence* (New York: Horizon, 1982), Sanford Schwartz uses "aristocrat of life and culture" as the title for his review of Kirstein's book *Elie Nadelman*. Although he intends the "aristocrat" to refer to the majority of the artists Kirstein champions, Schwartz observes that Kirstein's writings about art are so personal that his characterizations apply as much to himself as to the artists he defends; Lincoln Kirstein, *The New York City Ballet* (New York: Knopf, 1973), p. 13.

2. In 1982 Kirstein told *New York Times* art critic John Russell: "London was everything I liked best. . . . [My father] was crazy about England, and about English ways. [He] raised me on King Arthur, Robin Hood, David Balfour, David Copperfield and Rudyard Kipling's *Kim*. . . . Later, I was dressed by Anderson and Sheppard, the best tailor in London." At fifteen, Kirstein met John Maynard Keynes, E. M. Forster, Lytton Strachey, and the Sitwells (and began going regularly to Diaghilev's Ballets Russes). See "Lincoln Kirstein: A Life in Art," *New York Times Magazine*, 20 June 1982, p. 27. In his memoir *Mosaic* (New York: Farrar, Straus and Giroux, 1994), Kirstein writes of his "real blood tribe" (p. 256) and, within the context of a discussion of anti-Semitism, includes a suggestive remark from Cocteau (p. 58): "Un juif connaît un autre juif comme un pédéraste connaît un autre" (Kirstein was Jewish). In 1941 Kirstein married Fidelma Cadmus, an artist and dance student and the sister of the artist Paul Cadmus, whose work Kirstein supported and championed. Cadmus, a "blood" brother, was a realist in tempera, possessing the kind of mastery of craft and technique that Kirstein esteemed. In 1934 Cadmus had caused a furor with his Works Progress Administration–sponsored painting *The Fleet's In*, which depicted a male soliciting another male. (The picture, which is in the collection of the Naval Historical Center, Washington, D.C., is reproduced in Lincoln Kirstein, *Movement and Metaphor* [New York: Praeger, 1970], p. 236.)

3. Kirstein reminisced that as a young man, "I seemed to be able to do anything I wanted, simply because I knew everybody. I mean, I knew anybody I *wanted* to know" (W. MacNeil Lowry, "Conversations with Lincoln Kirstein," pt. 2, *New Yorker*, 22 Dec. 1986, p. 53). And so it was to continue throughout his life.

4. Kirstein, quoted in Lowry, "Conversations," pt. 2, p. 50. Kirstein's earliest commissions were an oil portrait by Martin Mower, his painting instructor, and a bronze portrait bust by Isamu Noguchi, both in 1927. In ensuing years, he commissioned a number of other portraits of himself by such artists as Gaston Lachaise (1932), Pavel Tchelitchev (1937), Lucian Freud (1950), Jamie Wyeth (1962), and Michael Leonard (1984). Somewhat disingenuously, he expressed the notion that his art collection, which comprised pieces from premedieval times to the present, and included Eastern, Western, and primitive pieces, was so self-revelatory that his essay-catalogue of it could serve as his autobiography: *Quarry: A Collection in Lieu of Memoirs* (Pasadena: Twelvetrees Press, 1986). Over the years, usually without publicity, in addition to his continuing commissions Kirstein backed a number of artists both with outright financial support and by helping to arrange exhibitions of their work. Diaghilev, quoted in Arnold L. Haskell, in collaboration with Walter Nouvel, *Diaghileff: His Artistic and Private Life* (New York: Simon and Schuster, 1935), p. 60. Kirstein quotes this passage in a slightly different translation in *Movement and Metaphor*, p. 182.

5. Kirstein, *Mosaic*, p. 127; Lincoln Kirstein, "For John Martin: Entries from an Early Diary," *Dance Perspectives* 54 (Summer 1973), p. 24 (italics added); W. MacNeil Lowry, "Conversations with Lincoln Kirstein," pt. 1, *New Yorker*, 15 Dec. 1986, p. 45; "Conversations," pt. 2, p. 59.

6. His failure to make Diaghilev's acquaintance is the subject of an entire scene in *Flesh Is Heir*, Kirstein's thinly disguised autobiography written in 1930 and published in 1932 (rpt. Carbondale, Ill.: Southern Illinois University Press, 1975). First, the young male protagonist explains to his female companion who Diaghilev is: "Some people call him the wickedest man in Europe. . . . He had the imagination to put the ballet across. . . . He never has any money and yet from year to year he goes on and gives the ballet and commissions painters and musicians." She concludes that he is "one of those men who devours people's talent." "Not at all, he makes them use it in the best way" (pp. 193–196). Later, following a debate as to whether they should have introduced themselves to Diaghilev earlier in the day, he reproaches her: "I suppose you know you've lost a chance to meet one of the greatest—the greatest men in our century" (p. 202); Kirstein to Tate, 8 May 1933, reprinted in Mitzi Berger Hamovitch, ed., *The Hound and Horn Letters* (Athens, Ga.: University of Georgia Press, 1982), pp. 185–186; Kirstein, *Movement and Metaphor*, p. 182. In an early draft of the acknowledgments, the author included Diaghilev's "spry ghost" among his inspirations, an indication that the impresario was still a living presence for him.

7. Kirstein, *New York City Ballet*, p. 13; Kirstein, *Mosaic*, p. 214.

8. Kirstein, *Mosaic*, pp. 214–215 (italics added).

9. Lincoln Kirstein, "The Diaghilev Period," *Hound and Horn* 3, no. 4 (July–Sept. 1930), pp. 468–501, reprinted in Lincoln Kirstein, *Ballet: Bias and Belief*, introduction by Nancy Reynolds

(New York: Dance Horizons, 1983), pp. 3–25 (quote pp. 4, 5, 16). *Hound and Horn* was the literary magazine Kirstein founded with Varian Fry in 1927. In existence until 1934, when Kirstein abandoned it to concentrate more fully on ballet, the magazine was celebrated for its literary daring, especially for its support of American authors.

10. Ibid., pp. 22, 20, 21.

11. Kirstein, "For John Martin," pp. 9 ("the main progressive line") and 24. Wheeler later became publications director of the Museum of Modern Art.

12. Ibid., p. 43. Much later, Kirstein wrote suggestively, as if continuing the thought: "This remained, even through later years, as my chief impression of him: never wholly discouraged, often depressed, absent as a tangible personality when not in actual labor onstage or in rehearsal" (*Mosaic*, p. 244).

13. Kirstein to Austin, 16 July 1933, in Francis Mason, ed., *I Remember Balanchine* (New York: Doubleday, 1991), pp. 115, 119. The letter is in the collection of the Wadsworth Atheneum.

14. Lowry, "Conversations," pt. 2, p. 58.

15. "Bayreuth, a world wholly, profoundly, dedicated to the realization of the unreal, made a deep and lasting impression, and the seriousness involved in the current festival's operations convinced me that not only was such activity the aim of my life, but that it was also, however remote, a realizable possibility" (Kirstein, *Mosaic*, p. 65); Kirstein, *Flesh Is Heir*, p. 193. Les Ballets 1933, the brainchild of Edward James, lasted only a few months, but it provided Balanchine with his first opportunity to create an independent repertory. The six ballets he choreographed were *Mozartiana* (Tchaikovsky/Christian Bérard, designer); *Les Songes* (Darius Milhaud/André Derain); *Les Sept Péchés Capitaux* (also called *Anna, Anna*, or *The Seven Capital Sins*) (Kurt Weill–Berthold Brecht/Caspar Neher); *Fastes* (Henri Sauguet/André Derain); *L'Errante* (Schubert/Pavel Tchelitchev); *Les Valses de Beethoven* (Beethoven/Emilio Terry). In Kirstein's opinion, one program offered "too much Balanchine for one evening, but two out of three knock-outs, not bad." He liked *Mozartiana* and *Les Sept Péchés Capitaux* but was less fond of *Les Songes* ("Entries from an Early Diary," p. 11).

16. Kirstein commissioned the decors from Franklin Watkins; the music was by Liszt.

17. Lincoln Kirstein, "Ballet: Record and Augury," *Theatre Arts*, Sept. 1940, pp. 650–659. Of his original intentions for Ballet Caravan, Kirstein wrote: "I made Cocteau's philosophy mine: theatrical, indeed all, lyric magic does not derive from the exotic, fantastic, or strange, but from a 'rehabilitation of the commonplace'" (Kirstein, *Thirty Years: The New York City Ballet* [New York: Knopf, 1978], p. 72). Although the idea may have been provocatively realized in Cocteau's ballet *Parade*, it proved a sterile philosophy for an entire repertory.

18. Kirstein, always a penetrating analyst of Balanchine's work, wrote: "The ballet presents unwinnable games for a dozen dancers and ceremonial competitions between them. . . . Its syntax is the undeformed, uninverted grammar, with shades of courtly behavior and echoes of antique measure. . . . Blocks of units in triads and quartets shift like chess pieces or players in musical chairs. Dancers are manipulated as irreplaceable spare parts, substituting or alternating on strict beats. Here 'production' consists of execution alone. . . . The

innovation of *Agon* lay in its naked strength, bare authority, and self-discipline in constructs of stressed extreme movement. Behind its active physical presence there was inherent a philosophy; *Agon* was by no means 'pure' ballet, 'about' dancing only. It was an existential metaphor for tension and anxiety" (*Movement and Metaphor*, pp. 242–243). From 1954 to 1969 Jerome Robbins was busy elsewhere.

19. Lowry, "Conversations," pt. 1, p. 45; on Balanchine, see, for instance, Nathan Milstein, "My Friend George Balanchine," *Ballet Review* 18, no. 3 (Fall 1990), pp. 23–34, and no. 4 (Winter 1990), pp. 82–90; Bernard Taper, *Balanchine*, 2d rev. ed. (Berkeley: University of California Press, 1996); and *I Remember Balanchine*. Perhaps the posthumous publication of Kirstein's voluminous diaries and other notes will yield up some of these secrets; Lincoln Kirstein, "A Ballet Master's Belief," in *Portrait of Mr. B* (New York: Ballet Society/Viking, 1984), p. 15.

20. The Ford Foundation gave an even larger grant (four million dollars) to the School of American Ballet (SAB), both to enlarge its scholarship program—thereby enabling it to attract students from all over the country—and to provide local scholarships to other schools on the recommendation of evaluators sent by SAB or the New York City Ballet. Although Ford's aim was ostensibly to upgrade teaching standards throughout the United States, by concentrating the money in the hands of Balanchine-Kirstein enterprises it seemed tacitly to endorse not only SAB's administrative apparatus but Balanchine's artistic policies. This latter point was the subject of much heated criticism at the time. The man considered the impetus behind the grants was W. McNeil Lowry, then a vice president at the Ford Foundation, who became a lifelong Kirstein friend and supporter.

21. Lowry, "Conversations," pt. 1, p. 46.

22. Kirstein, *Mosaic*, p. 249.

23. Lincoln Kirstein, "The Curse of Isadora," *New York Times*, 23 Nov. 1986, sec. 2, pp. 1 et seq. In this highly polemical piece, Kirstein excoriated "postmodern" and "post-postmodern" dance as an "etiolated exercise." *Lincoln Kirstein: A First Bibliography*, compiled by Harvey Simmonds, Louis H. Silverstein, and Nancy Lassalle (New York: Eakins Press, 1978), runs to more than 150 pages, and Kirstein continued to write and publish virtually until his death in 1996. His last two books—*Mosaic* and *Tchelitchev*—both appeared in 1994, when the author was eighty-seven years old. In addition to dance, Kirstein wrote on politics, history, literature, drama, music, film, photography, architecture, sculpture, painting, drawing, and the general cultural scene. A partial list of Kirstein's many other activities would start with his cofounding in 1928 of the Harvard Society for Contemporary Art, and the several exhibitions at the Museum of Modern Art for which he served as curator, cataloguer, and consultant. Over the years, he held positions with the City Center of Music and Drama, WPA Federal Dance Theater, American National Theater and Academy (ANTA), American Shakespeare Festival Theater Academy, and Pro Musica Antiqua, whose twelfth-century *Play of Daniel*, which he produced, became a fixture in the New York cultural landscape for twenty years.

24. Kirstein, *Movement and Metaphor*, pp. 17, v.

25. Lincoln Kirstein, *Dance: A Short History of Classic Theatrical Dancing* (New York, 1935; rpt. New York: Dance Horizons, 1969), p. 283; Kirstein, *Movement and Metaphor*, p. 199; Kirstein, *Nijinsky Dancing* (New York: Knopf, 1975), pp. 145 and 42.

26. George Balanchine, "The Dance Element in Stravinsky's Music," *Dance Index* 6 (1947), p. 254.

27. Lowry, "Conversations," pt. 1, p. 80; Kirstein, *Blast at Ballet: A Corrective for the American Audience* (1937), reprinted in *Ballet: Bias and Belief*, p. 168.

bibliography

Archives

Archives Nationales (Paris)

Ashmolean Museum (Oxford)

Gabriel Astruc Papers, Dance Collection, New York Public Library

Bakhrushin State Central Theater Museum (Moscow)

Adolph Bolm Papers, George Arents Research Library, Syracuse University

Central State Historical Archives (Leningrad)

Tatiana Chamié Collection, Dance Collection, New York Public Library

Jean Cocteau Papers, George Arents Research Library, Syracuse University

Covent Garden Archives (London)

Serge Diaghilev Correspondence, Dance Collection, New York Public Library

Serge Diaghilev Papers, Dance Collection, New York Public Library

Roger Pryor Dodge Collection, Dance Collection, New York Public Library

Fine Arts Museums of San Francisco

Fundación "Archivo Manuel de Falla" (Granada)

Harvard Theatre Collection (Cambridge)

Institute of Russian Literature, Academy of Sciences (St. Petersburg)

Otto Kahn Papers, Princeton University

John Maynard Keynes Papers, King's College (Cambridge)

Boris Kochno Papers, Bibliothèque de l'Opéra (Paris)

Serge Lifar Collection, Wadsworth Atheneum (Hartford)

Serge Lifar Papers, Archives de la Ville de Lausanne

Metropolitan Opera Archives (New York)

Musée des Arts Décoratifs (Paris)

Musée Picasso (Paris)

Museum of Modern Art (New York)

Music Division, Library of Congress (Washington, D.C.)

Ruth Page Collection, Dance Collection, New York Public Library

Joseph Paget-Fredericks Collection, Bancroft Library, University of California, Berkeley

Palace Archives (Monaco)

Performing Arts Library and Museum (San Francisco)

Pierpont Morgan Library (New York)

Max Rabinoff Papers, Rare Book and Manuscript Library, Columbia University

Rondel Collection, Département des Arts du Spectacle, Bibliothèque Nationale (Paris)

Royal Ballet School Archives (White Lodge, England)

Alexander Shervashidze Papers, Bakhmeteff Archive, Rare Book and Manuscript Library, Columbia University

Société des Bains de Mer (Monte Carlo)

State Museum of Theater and Music (St. Petersburg)

State Russian Museum (St. Petersburg)

Stravinsky Papers, Paul Sacher Stiftung (Basel)

Theatre Museum (London)

Robert L. B. Tobin Collection, Marion Koogler McNay Art Museum (San Antonio)

Tretiakov Gallery (Moscow)

George Verdak Collection (Indianapolis)

Victoria and Albert Museum (London)

Books

Acton, Harold. *Memoirs of an Aesthete.* London: Methuen, 1948.

Alexandre, Arsène, and Jean Cocteau. *The Decorative Art of Leon Bakst.* Trans. Harry Melvill. London, 1913. Rpt. New York: Dover, 1972.

André Levinson on Dance: Writings from Paris in the Twenties. Ed. and introd. Joan Acocella and Lynn Garafola. Hanover, N.H.: Wesleyan University Press/University Press of New England, 1991.

Armitage, Merle. *Dance Memoranda.* Ed. Edwin Corle. New York: Duell, Sloan and Pearce, 1947.

Art of Extravagance, The/Overdadets konst: Kostymer frain Diaghilews Ryska Baletten i Paris. Ed. Erik Naslund. Stockholm: Dansmuseet, 1996.

Arvey, Verna. *Choreographic Music: Music for the Dance.* New York: Dutton, 1941.

Aschengreen, Erik. *Jean Cocteau and the Dance.* Trans. Patricia McAndrew and Per Avsum. Copenhagen: Gyldendal, 1986.

Astruc, Gabriel. *Le Pavillon des fantômes.* Paris: Grasset, 1929.

Au Temps du Boeuf sur le Toit, 1918–1928. Introd. Georges Bernier. Paris: Artcurial, 1981.

Axsom, Richard H. *Parade: Cubism as Theater.* New York: Garland, 1979.

Bablet, Denis. *Esthétique générale du décor de théâtre de 1870 à 1914.* Paris: Centre national de la recherche scientifique, 1965.

Baer, Nancy Van Norman. *Bronislava Nijinska: A Dancer's Legacy.* San Francisco: Fine Arts Museums of San Francisco, 1986.

Baer, Nancy Van Norman, ed. *The Art of Enchantment: Diaghilev's Ballets Russes, 1909–1979.* San Francisco: Fine Arts Museums of San Francisco, 1988.

—————. *Paris Modern: The Swedish Ballet, 1920–1925.* San Francisco: Fine Arts Museums of San Francisco, 1995.

Ballet: Bias and Belief; "Three Pamphlets Collected" and Other Dance Writings of Lincoln Kirstein. Ed. and introd. Nancy Reynolds. New York: Dance Horizons, 1983.

Ballets Russes de Serge de Diaghilew, Les. Ed. Henry Prunières. Special number of *La Revue Musicale,* 1 Dec. 1930.

Banes, Sally. *Dancing Women: Female Bodies on Stage*. London: Routledge, 1998.

Barbier, George. *Designs on the Dances of Vaslav Nijinsky*. Foreword by Francis de Miomandre. Trans. C. W. Beaumont. London: C. W. Beaumont, 1913.

Barbier, George, and Jean-Louis Vaudoyer. *Album dédié à Tamara Karsavina*. Paris: Pierre Conrad, 1914.

Bartlett, Rosamund. *Wagner and Russia*. Cambridge: Cambridge University Press, 1995.

Beaton, Cecil. *Ballet*. Garden City, N.Y.: Doubleday, 1951.

Beaumont, Cyril W. *Bookseller at the Ballet, Memoirs 1891 to 1929, Incorporating the Diaghilev Ballet in London*. London: C. W. Beaumont, 1975.

———. *Complete Book of Ballets*. London: Putnam, 1937.

———. *Michel Fokine and His Ballets*. London: C. W. Beaumont, 1935.

Beecham, Thomas. *A Mingled Chime: An Autobiography*. New York: Putnam, 1943.

Bennett, Arnold. *Paris Nights and Other Impressions of Places and People*. New York: George H. Doran, 1913.

Benois, Alexandre. *Memoirs*. 2 vols. Trans. Moura Budberg. London: Chatto and Windus, 1964.

———. *Reminiscences of the Russian Ballet*. Trans. Mary Britnieva. London: Putnam, 1941.

Berg, Shelley C. *Le Sacre du Printemps: Seven Productions from Nijinsky to Martha Graham*. Ann Arbor, Mich.: UMI Research Press, 1988.

Bernays, Edward L. *Biography of an Idea: Memoirs of Public Relations Counsel Edward L. Bernays*. New York: Simon and Schuster, 1965.

Beyssac, Michèle. *La Vie culturelle de l'émigration russe en France: Chronique (1920–1930)*. Paris: Presses Universitaires de France, 1971.

Blanche, Jacques-Emile. *Portraits of a Lifetime: The Late Victorian Era; The Edwardian Pageant, 1870–1914*. Ed. and trans. Walter Clement. Introd. Harley Granville Barker. London: Dent, 1937.

Blok, L. D. *Klassicheskii tanets: istoriia i sovremennost'* (Classical dance: history and modernity). Ed. Vadim Gaevsky and Elizabeth Souritz. Moscow: Iskusstvo, 1987.

Borisoglebskii, M., ed. *Materialy po istorii russkogo baleta* (Materials for a history of Russian ballet). Vol. 2. Leningrad: Leningrad State Choreographic Academy, 1939.

Bowlt, John E. *The Silver Age: Russian Art of the Early Twentieth Century and the "World of Art" Group*. Newtonville, Mass.: Oriental Research Partners, 1979.

Bowlt, John E., ed. and trans. *Russian Art of the Avant-Garde: Theory and Criticism*. Rev. ed. New York: Thames and Hudson, 1988.

———. *Russian Stage Design: Scenic Innovation, 1904–1930; From the Collection of Mr. and Mrs. Nikita D. Lobanov-Rostovsky*. Jackson: Mississippi Museum of Art, 1982.

Brillarelli, Livia. *Cecchetti: A Ballet Dynasty*. Toronto: Dance Collection/ Danse Educational Publications, 1995.

Brody, Elaine. *Paris: The Musical Kaleidoscope, 1870–1925*. New York: George Braziller, 1987.

Buckle, Richard. *Diaghilev*. London: Weidenfeld and Nicolson 1979.

———. *George Balanchine, Ballet Master*. In collaboration with John Taras. New York: Random House, 1988.

———. *In Search of Diaghilev*. New York: Thomas Nelson, 1956.

———. *Nijinsky*. New York: Simon and Schuster, 1971.

———. *Nijinsky on Stage*. London: Studio Vista, 1971.

Burt, Ramsay. *The Male Dancer*. London: Routledge, 1995.

Calvocoressi, M. D. *Musicians Gallery: Music and Ballet in Paris and London*. London: Faber and Faber, 1933.

Carrieri, Raffaele. *La Danza in Italia, 1500–1900*. Milan: Domus, 1946.

Chadd, David, and John Cage. *The Diaghilev Ballet in England*. Foreword by Richard Buckle. Catalogue for an exhibition at the Sainsbury Centre for Visual Arts, University of East Anglia, 11 Oct.–20 Nov. 1979.

Chamot, Mary. *Goncharova: Stage Designs and Paintings*. London: Oresko Books, 1979.

———. *Gontcharova*. Trans. Helen Gerebzow. Paris: Bibliothèque des Arts, 1972.

Charles-Roux, Edmonde. *Chanel: Her Life, Her World and the Woman Behind the Legend She Herself Created*. Trans. Nancy Amphoux. New York: Knopf, 1975.

Chisholm, Anne. *Nancy Cunard: A Biography*. Harmondsworth, Middlesex: Penguin, 1981.

Choreography by George Balanchine: A Catalogue of Work. Ed. Leslie George Katz, Nancy Lassalle, and Harvey Simmonds. New York: Eakins Press, 1983.

Cochran, Charles B. *I Had Almost Forgotten*. Preface A. P. Herbert. London: Hutchinson, 1932.

Cocteau, Jean. *A Call to Order*. Trans. Rollo H. Myers. London: Faber and Faber, 1926.

———. *Dessins*. Paris: Stock, 1923.

Cocteau, Jean, Georges Auric, Georges Braque, and Louis Laloy. *Théâtre Serge de Diaghilew: Les Fâcheux*. Paris: Editions des Quatre Chemins, 1924.

Cocteau, Jean, Marie Laurencin, Darius Milhaud, and Francis Poulenc. *Théâtre Serge de Diaghilew: Les Biches*. Paris: Editions des Quatre Chemins, 1924.

Cogniat, Raymond. *Cinquante ans de spectacles en France: Les Décorateurs de théâtre*. Paris: Librairie Théâtrale, 1955.

Collection des plus beaux numéros de Comoedia Illustré et des programmes consacrés aux ballets et galas russes. Paris: de Brunoff, 1922.

Cooper, Douglas. *Picasso Theatre*. New York: Abrams, 1987.

Cossart, Michael de. *The Food of Love: Princesse Edmond de Polignac (1865–1943) and Her Salon*. London: Hamish Hamilton, 1978.

Craig, Gordon. *Gordon Craig on Movement and Dance*. Ed. and introd. Arnold Rood. New York: Dance Horizons, 1977.

Danilova, Alexandra. *Choura: The Memoirs of Alexandra Danilova*. New York: Knopf, 1986.

Decter, Jacqueline. *Nicholas Roerich: The Life and Art of a Russian Master*. Rochester, Vt.: Park Street Press, 1989.

Designs of Leon Bakst for The Sleeping Princess, The. Preface by André Levinson. London: Benn Brothers, 1923.

Détaille, Georges, and Gérard Mulys. *Les Ballets de Monte-Carlo, 1911–1944*. Preface by Jean Cocteau. Paris: Editions Arc-en-Ciel, 1954.

Devereux, Tony. "Alexandre Benois and the Russian Revolution." *Dance Research* 15, no. 1 (Summer 1997), pp. 58–78.

Diaghilev: Creator of the Ballets Russes. Ed. Ann Kodicek. London: Barbican Art Gallery/Lund Humphries, 1996.

Diaghilev, S. P. Preface to *Katalog Istoriko-khudozhestvennoi vystavki russkikh portretov* (Catalogue of the exhibition of historic Russian portraits). Comp. Baron N. N. Vrangel'. St. Petersburg: Department for the Preparation of State Papers, 1905.

Diaghilev, S. P., ed. *Exposition de l'Art Russe*. Paris: Moreau, 1906.

Diaghilev, S. P., and V. P. Gorlenko. *D. G. Levitsky (1735–1822), Russkaia zhivopis' v XVIII veke* (Russian painting in the eighteenth century), vol. 1. St. Petersburg: Evdokimov, 1902.

Diaghilev-Lifar Library, The. Auction catalogue. Monte Carlo: Sotheby Parke Bernet Monaco, 28 Nov.–1 Dec. 1975.

di Milia, Gabriella. *Mir iskusstva–Il Mondo dell'arte: Artisti russi dal 1898 al 1934*. Naples: Società Napoletana, 1982.

Divoire, Fernand. *Découvertes sur la danse*. Paris: Editions G. Crès, 1924.

Dolin, Anton. *Autobiography: A Volume of Autobiography and Reminiscence*. London: Oldbourne, 1960.

———. *Last Words: A Final Autobiography*. Ed. Kay Hunter. Foreword by John Gilpin. London: Century Publishing, 1985.

———. *The Sleeping Ballerina: The Story of Olga Spessivtzeva*. Foreword by Dame Marie Rambert. London: Frederick Muller, 1966.

Drummond, John. *Speaking of Diaghilev*. London: Faber and Faber, 1997.

Duke, Vernon. *Passport to Paris*. Boston: Little, Brown, 1955.

Duncan, Isadora. *My Life*. New York: Boni and Liveright, 1927.

Dunning, Jennifer, et al. *L'Après-midi d'un Faune: Vaslav Nijinsky—1912. Thirty-Three Photographs by Baron Adolf de Meyer*. Introd. Richard Buckle. New York: Dance Horizons, 1983.

Engelstein, Laura. *The Keys to Happiness: Sex and the Search for Modernity in Fin-de-Siècle Russia*. Ithaca: Cornell University Press, 1992.

Fitzgerald, Michael C. *Making Modernism: Picasso and the Creation of the Market for Twentieth-Century Art*. New York: Farrar, Straus and Giroux, 1995.

Fitzgerald, Zelda. *Save Me the Waltz*. Introd. Harry T. Moore. London: Jonathan Cape, 1968.

Flanner, Janet. *Paris Was Yesterday, 1925–1939*. Ed. Irving Drutman. New York: Popular Library, n.d.

Fokine, Michel. *Memoirs of a Ballet Master*. Trans. Vitale Fokine. Ed. Anatole Chujoy. Boston: Little, Brown, 1961.

———. *Protiv techeniia: Vospominaniia baletmeistera, stat'i, pis'ma* (Against the tide: Memoirs of a ballet master, articles, and letters). Ed. and introd. Yuri Slonimsky. Leningrad: Iskusstvo, 1962.

Gale, Joseph. *I Sang for Diaghilev: Michel Pavloff's Merry Life*. New York: Dance Horizons, 1982.

Garafola, Lynn. *Diaghilev's Ballets Russes*. New York: Oxford University Press, 1989.

Garafola, Lynn, ed. and trans. *The Diaries of Marius Petipa. Studies in Dance History* 3, no. 1 (Spring 1992).

García-Márquez, Vicente. *Massine: A Biography*. New York: Knopf, 1995.

García-Márquez, Vicente, ed., with Lynn Garafola. *España y los Ballets Russes*. Catalogue of an exhibition held at the Auditorio Manuel de Falla, Granada, 17 June–2 July 1989.

Genné, Beth. *The Making of a Choreographer: Ninette de Valois and Bar aux Folies-Bergère. Studies in Dance History*, no. 12. N.p.: Society of Dance History Scholars, 1996.

Georges-Michel, Michel. *Ballets Russes: Histoire anecdotique suivie du Poème de Shéhérazade*. Paris: Editions du Monde Nouveau, 1923.

Geva, Tamara. *Split Seconds: A Remembrance by Tamara Geva*. New York: Harper and Row, 1972.

Gofman, I. *Alexander Golovin*. Moscow: Iskusstvo, 1981.

Golub, Spencer. *Evreinov: The Theatre of Paradox and Transformation*. Ann Arbor, Mich.: UMI Research Press, 1984.

Gontcharova, Nathalie, Michel Larionov, and Pierre Vorms. *Les Ballets Russes: Serge Diaghilew et la décoration théâtrale*. Rev. ed. Belves Dordogne: Pierre Vorms, 1955.

Goossens, Eugene. *Overture and Beginners: A Musical Autobiography*. London: Methuen, 1951.

Green, Martin. *Children of the Sun: A Narrative of "Decadence" in England After 1918*. New York: Basic, 1976.

Gregor, Joseph, and René Fülop-Miller. *Das russische Theater*. Vienna: Amalthea-Verlag, 1928.

Grigoriev, S. L. *The Diaghilev Ballet, 1909–1979*. Trans. and ed. Vera Bowen. London: Constable, 1953.

Guest, Ivor. *Ballet in Leicester Square: The Alhambra and the Empire 1860–1915*. London: Dance Books, 1992.

Hager, Bengt. *Ballets Suédois (The Swedish Ballet)*. Trans. Ruth Sharman. New York: Abrams, 1990.

Hanson, Lawrence, and Elisabeth Hanson. *Prokofiev: A Biography in Three Movements*. New York: Random House, 1964.

Haskell, Arnold L. *Balletomania: The Story of an Obsession*. London: Gollancz, 1934.

————. *Diaghileff: His Artistic and Private Life*. In collaboration with Walter Nouvel. London: Gollancz, 1935.

Healy, Robyn, and Michael Lloyd. *From Studio to Stage: Costumes and Designs from the Russian Ballet in the Australian National Gallery*. Canberra: Australian National Gallery, 1990.

Hodson, Millicent. *Nijinsky's Crime Against Grace: Reconstruction Score of the Original Choreography for Le Sacre du Printemps*. Stuyvesant, N.Y.: Pendragon, 1996.

Horwitz, Dawn Lille. *Michel Fokine*. Foreword by Don McDonagh. Boston: Twayne, 1985.

Hugo, Jean. *Avant d'oublier, 1918–1931*. Paris: Fayard, 1976.

Jeschke, Claudia, Ursel Berger, and Birgit Zeidler, eds. *Die Ballets Russes und die Künste*. Berlin: Vorlag Vorwerk, 1997.

José María Sert (1874–1945). Madrid: Ministerio de Cultura, [1987].

Jullian, Philippe. *Robert de Montesquiou: A Fin-de-Siècle Prince*. Trans. John Haylock and Francis King. London: Secker and Warburg, 1965.

Kahane, Martine, and Nicole Wild. *Les Ballets Russes à l'Opéra*. Paris: Hazan/Bibliothèque Nationale, 1992.

Kahnweiler, Daniel-Henry. *Juan Gris: His Life and Work*. Trans. Douglas Cooper. Rev. ed. New York: Abrams, 1969.

Karsavina, Tamara. *Theatre Street: The Reminiscences of Tamara Karsavina*. Foreword by J. M. Barrie. London: Heinemann, 1930.

Kean, Beverly Whitney. *All the Empty Palaces: The Merchant Patrons of Modern Art in Pre-Revolutionary Russia*. New York: Universe, 1983.

Kennedy, Janet. *The "Mir Iskusstva" Group and Russian Art, 1898–1912*. New York: Garland, 1977.

Kessler, Count Harry. *In the Twenties: The Diaries of Count Harry Kessler*. Trans. Charles Kessler. Introd. Otto Friedrich. New York: Holt, Rinehart and Winston, 1971.

Keynes, Geoffrey. *The Gates of Memory*. London: Oxford University Press, 1983.

Kirstein, Lincoln. *Dance: A Short History of Classic Theatrical Dancing*. New York: Putnam, 1935.

———. *Mosaic: Memoirs*. New York: Farrar, Straus and Giroux, 1994.

———. *Movement and Metaphor*. New York: Praeger, 1970.

———. *The New York City Ballet*. New York: Knopf, 1973.

———. *Nijinsky Dancing*. New York: Knopf, 1975.

———. *Tchelitchew*. Santa Fe, N.M.: Twelvetrees Press, 1994.

Klüver, Billy, and Julie Martin. *Kiki's Paris: Artists and Lovers 1900–1930*. New York: Abrams, 1989.

Kochno, Boris. *Diaghilev and the Ballets Russes*. Trans. Adrienne Foulke. New York: Harper and Row, 1970.

Kopelson, Kevin. *The Queer Afterlife of Vaslav Nijinsky*. Stanford: Stanford University Press, 1997.

Koritz, Amy. *Gendering Bodies/Performing Art: Dance and Literature in Early Twentieth-Century British Culture*. Ann Arbor: University of Michigan Press, 1995.

Krasovskaia [Krasovskaya], Vera. *Russkii baletnyi teatr nachala XX veka* (Russian ballet theater in the early twentieth century). 2 vols. Leningrad: Iskusstvo, 1971–1972.

Krasovskaya, Vera. *Nijinsky*. Trans. John E. Bowlt. New York: Schirmer, 1979.

Kschessinska, Mathilde (Princess Romanovsky-Krassinsky). *Dancing in Petersburg: The Memoirs of Kschessinska*. Trans. Arnold Haskell. Garden City, N.Y., 1961. Rpt. New York: Da Capo, 1977.

Kyasht, Lydia. *Romantic Recollections*. Ed. Erica Beale. London: Brentano, 1929.

Lambert, Constant. *Music Ho! A Study of Music in Decline*. Introd. Arthur Hutchings. New York: October House, 1967.

Lepape, Claude, and Thierry Defert. *From the Ballets Russes to Vogue: The Art of Georges Lepape*. Trans. Jane Brenton. New York: Vendome, 1984.

Levinson, André. *Bakst: The Story of the Artist's Life*. 1923. Rpt. New York: Blom, 1971.

———. *Ballet Old and New*. Trans. Susan Cook Summer. New York: Dance Horizons, 1982.

———. *La Danse au théâtre: Esthétique et actualité mêlées*. Paris: Bloud et Gay, 1924.

———. *La Danse d'aujourd'hui: Etudes, notes, portraits*. Paris: Duchartre et Van Buggenhoudt, 1929.

———. *Serge Lifar: Destin d'un danseur*. Paris: Grasset, 1934.

———. *Les Visages de la danse*. Paris: Grasset, 1933.

Lieven, Prince Peter. *The Birth of Ballets-Russes*. Trans. L. Zarine. London: George Allen and Unwin, 1936.

Lifar, Serge. *Ma Vie: From Kiev to Kiev*. Trans. James Holman Mason. New York: World, 1970.

———. *Les Mémoires d'Icare*. Preface by Irène Lidova. Monaco: Editions Sauret, 1993.

———. *Serge Diaghilev: His Life, His Work, His Legend. An Intimate Biography*. 1940. Rpt. New York: Da Capo, 1976.

Lista, Giovanni. *Loïe Fuller: Danseuse de la Belle Epoque*. Paris: Stock, 1994.

Lockspeiser, Edward. *Debussy: His Life and Mind*. 2 vols. Cambridge: Cambridge University Press, 1978.

Lydia and Maynard: The Letters of Lydia Lopokova and John Maynard Keynes. Ed. Polly Hill and Richard Keynes. London: André Deutsch, 1989.

Lydia Lopokova. Ed. Milo Keynes. London: Weidenfeld and Nicolson, 1983.

Macdonald, Nesta. *Diaghilev Observed by Critics in England and the United States, 1911–1929*. New York: Dance Horizons, 1975.

————. "A Nijinsky Costume in the Theatre Museum: A Case of Mistaken Identity." *Dance Research* 13, no. 1 (Summer 1995), pp. 104–106.

Magriel, Paul, ed. *Nijinsky, Pavlova, Duncan: Three Lives in Dance*. New York: Da Capo, 1977.

Maré, Rolf de. *Les Ballets Suédois dans l'art contemporain*. Paris: Editions du Trianon, 1931.

Markevitch, Igor. *Etre et avoir été: Mémoires*. Paris: Gallimard, 1980.

Markova, Alicia. *Markova Remembers*. Boston: Little, Brown, 1986.

Massine, Léonide. *My Life in Ballet*. Ed. Phyllis Hartnoll and Robert Rubens. London: Macmillan, 1968.

Matz, Mary Jane. *The Many Lives of Otto Kahn*. New York: Macmillan, 1963.

Mayer, Charles S. *Bakst Centenary, 1876–1976*. London: Fine Art Society, 1976.

Menaker Rothschild, Deborah. *Picasso's "Parade": From Street to Stage*. London: Sotheby's, 1991.

Migel, Parmenia. *Pablo Picasso: Designs for The Three-Cornered Hat (Le Tricorne)*. New York: Dover/Stravinsky-Diaghilev Foundation, 1978.

Milhaud, Darius. *Notes Without Music: An Autobiography*. New York: Knopf, 1953.

Money, Keith. *Anna Pavlova: Her Life and Art*. New York: Knopf, 1982.

Montenegro, Robert. *Vaslav Nijinsky: An Artistic Interpretation of His Work in Black, White and Gold*. Introd. Cyril W. Beaumont. London: C. W. Beaumont, 1913.

Monteux, Doris G. *It's All in the Music*. New York: Farrar, Straus and Giroux, 1965.

Moto-Bio—*The Russian Art of Movement: Dance, Gesture, and Gymnastics, 1910–1930*. Ed. John Bowlt and Natalia Chernova. *Experiment* 2 (1996).

Nabokov, Nicolas. *Old Friends and New Music*. London: Hamish Hamilton, 1951.

Nathalie Gontcharova/Michel Larionov. Ed. Jessica Boissel. Paris: Editions du Centre Pompidou, 1995.

Nectoux, Jean-Michel, ed. *Afternoon of a Faun: Mallarmé, Debussy, Nijinsky*. New York: Vendome, 1989.

Nest'ev [Nesteev], I. V. *Diagilev i muzykal'nyi teatr XX veka* (Diaghilev and twentieth-century music theater). Moscow: Muzyka, 1994.

Nijinska, Bronislava. *Early Memoirs*. Trans. and ed. Irina Nijinska and Jean Rawlinson. Introd. Anna Kisselgoff. New York: Holt, Rinehart and Winston, 1981.

Nijinsky, Romola. *Nijinsky*. Foreword by Paul Claudel. New York: Simon and Schuster, 1934.

Nijinsky, Tamara. *Nijinsky and Romola*. London: Bachman and Turner, 1991.

Nijinsky, Vaslav. *The Diary of Vaslav Nijinsky*. Ed. Romola Nijinsky. Berkeley: University of California Press, 1968.

————. *The Diary of Vaslav Nijinsky*. Trans. Kyril FitzLyon. Ed. Joan Acocella. New York: Farrar, Straus, and Giroux, 1999.

Nikitina, Alice. *Nikitina by Herself*. Trans. Baroness Budberg. London: Alan Wingate, 1959.

Nineteen Thirteen: Le Théâtre des Champs-Elysées. Ed. Jean-Michel Nectoux. Les Dossiers du Musée d'Orsay, no. 13. Paris: Editions de la Réunion des Musées Nationaux, 1987.

Oliver Messel. Ed. Roger Pinkham. London: Victoria and Albert Museum, 1983.

Orenstein, Arbie. *Ravel: Man and Musician*. New York: Columbia University Press, 1975.

Ostwald, Peter. *Vaslav Nijinsky: A Leap into Madness*. New York: Lyle Stuart, 1991.

Painter, George D. *Marcel Proust: A Biography*. 2 vols. Harmondsmith, Middlesex: Penguin, 1977.

Parnakh, Valentin. *Gontcharova et Larionow: L'Art décoratif théâtral moderne*. Paris: La Cible, 1919.

Parton, Anthony. *Mikhail Larionov and the Russian Avant-Garde*. London: Thames and Hudson, 1993.

Pasler, Jann, ed. *Confronting Stravinsky*. Berkeley: University of California Press, 1986.

Pastori, Jean-Pierre. *Soleil de Nuit: La Renaissance des Ballets Russes*. Lausanne: Luce Wilquin Editrice, 1993.

Pozharskaya, M. N. *The Russian Seasons in Paris: Sketches of the Scenery and Costumes, 1908–1929*. Trans. V. S. Friedman. Moscow: Iskusstvo Art Publishers, 1988.

Pritchard, Jane, ed. *Rambert: A Celebration*. Introd. Mary Clarke and Clement Crisp. London: Rambert Dance Company, 1996.

Proujan, Irina. *Léon Bakst: Esquisses de décor et de costumes, arts graphiques, peintures*. Trans. Denis Dabbadie. Leningrad: Editions d'art Aurora, 1986.

Prokofiev, Serge. *Prokofiev by Prokofiev: A Composer's Memoir*. Trans. Guy Daniels. Garden City, N.Y.: Doubleday, 1979.

Propert, W. A. *The Russian Ballet, 1921–1929*. Preface by Jacques-Emile Blanche. London: John Lane, 1931.

———. *The Russian Ballet in Western Europe, 1909–1920*. London: John Lane, 1921.

Racster, Olga. *The Master of the Russian Ballet: The Memoirs of Cav. Enrico Cecchetti*. Introd. Anna Pavlova. London: Hutchinson, [1922].

Rambert, Marie. *Quicksilver: An Autobiography*. London: Macmillan, 1972.

Richardson, John. *A Life of Picasso*. With the collaboration of Marilyn McCully. New York: Random House, 1991.

Richardson, William. *Zolotoe runo and Russian Modernism: 1905–1910*. Ann Arbor, Mich.: Ardis, 1986.

Ries, Frank W. D. *The Dance Theatre of Jean Cocteau*. Ann Arbor, Mich.: UMI Research Press, 1986.

Roslavleva, Natalia. *Era of the Russian Ballet, 1770–1965*. Foreword by Ninette de Valois. London: Gollancz, 1966.

Rudnitsky, Konstantin. *Meyerhold the Director*. Trans. George Petrov. Ed. Sydney Schultze. Introd. Ellendea Proffer. Ann Arbor, Mich.: Ardis, 1981.

Salmina-Haskell, Larissa. *Russian Paintings and Drawings in the Ashmolean Museum*. Oxford: Ashmolean Museum, 1989.

Sasportes, José. *Pensare la danza: Da Mallarmé a Cocteau*. Trans. Lavinia Cavalletti. Bologna: Il Mulino, 1989.

Scholl, Tim. *From Petipa to Balanchine: Classical Revival and the Modernization of Ballet*. London: Routledge, 1994.

Schouvaloff, Alexander. *The Art of Ballets Russes: The Serge Lifar Collection of Theater Designs, Costumes, and Paintings at the Wadsworth Atheneum, Hartford, Connecticut*. New Haven: Yale University Press/Wadsworth Atheneum, 1997.

———. *Léon Bakst: The Theatre Art*. London: Sotheby's, 1991.

Schouvaloff, Alexander, and Victor Borovsky. *Stravinsky on Stage*. London: Stainer and Bell, 1982.

Senelick, Laurence, ed. *Wandering Stars: Russian Emigré Theatre, 1905–1940*. Iowa City: University of Iowa Press, 1992.

Sergei Diagilev i khudozhestvennaia kul'tura XIX-XX vekov (Serge Diaghilev and nineteenth- and twentieth-century artistic culture). Ed. N. V. Beliaeva et al. Perm: Permskoe knizhnoe izdatel'stvo, 1989.

Serge Lifar: Une Vie pour la danse. Introd. Marie-Claude Jequier. Lausanne: Musée Historique de l'Ancien-Evêché, 1986.

Serge Lifar Collection of Ballet Set and Costume Designs, The. Hartford, Conn.: Wadsworth Atheneum, 1965.

Sert, Misia. *Two or Three Muses: The Memoirs of Misia Sert.* Trans. Moura Budberg. London: Museum Press, 1953.

Shead, Richard. *Ballets Russes.* London: Quarto, 1989.

———. *Constant Lambert.* With a memoir by Anthony Powell. London: Simon, 1973.

———. *Music in the Twenties.* London: Duckworth, 1976.

Silver, Kenneth E. *Esprit de Corps: The Art of the Parisian Avant-Garde and the First World War, 1914–1925.* Princeton: Princeton University Press, 1989.

Sitwell, Edith. *Children's Tales From the Russian Ballet.* London: Leonard Parsons, 1920.

Sitwell, Osbert. *Great Morning: An Autobiography.* London: Reprint Society, 1948.

———. *Laughter in the Next Room.* London: Reprint Society, 1950.

Sokolova, Lydia. *Dancing for Diaghilev.* Ed. Richard Buckle. London: John Murray, 1960.

Souhami, Diana. *Bakst: The Rothschild Panels of* The Sleeping Beauty. London: Philip Wilson, 1992.

Souritz, Elizabeth. *Soviet Choreographers in the 1920s.* Trans. Lynn Visson. Ed. Sally Banes. Durham, N.C.: Duke University Press, 1990.

Spalding, Frances. *Roger Fry: Art and Life.* Berkeley: University of California Press, 1980.

Spencer, Charles. *Leon Bakst.* London: Academy, 1973.

Spencer, Charles, and Philip Dyer. *The World of Serge Diaghilev.* Chicago: Henry Regnery, 1974.

Stanciu-Reiss, Françoise, and Jean-Michel Pourvoyeur. *Ecrits sur Nijinsky.* Paris: Editions Chiron, 1992.

Steegmuller, Francis. *Cocteau: A Biography.* Boston: Little, Brown, 1970.

Stravinsky, Igor. *Stravinsky: An Autobiography.* New York: Simon and Schuster, 1936.

———. *Stravinsky: Selected Correspondence.* Ed. Robert Craft. 3 vols. New York: Knopf, 1982–1985.

Stravinsky, Igor, and Robert Craft. *Conversations with Igor Stravinsky.* London: Faber and Faber, 1959.

———. *Expositions and Developments.* Berkeley: University of California Press, 1981.

———. *Memories and Commentaries.* Garden City, N.Y.: Doubleday, 1960.

Stravinsky, Vera, and Robert Craft. *Stravinsky in Pictures and Documents.* London: Hutchinson, 1979.

Svetlov, Valerian. *Anna Pavlova.* Trans. A. Grey. 1922. Rpt. New York: Dover, 1974.

———. *Le Ballet contemporain.* With the collaboration of Leon Bakst. Trans. M. D. Calvocoressi. Paris: de Brunoff, 1912.

Taper, Bernard. *Balanchine: A Biography.* 2d rev. ed. Berkeley: University of California Press, 1996.

Taruskin, Richard. *Stravinsky and the Russian Traditions: A Biography of the Works Through Mavra.* 2 vols. Berkeley: University of California Press, 1996.

Terry, Ellen. *The Russian Ballet.* London: Sidgwick and Jackson, 1913.

Tikanova, Nina. *La Jeune Fille en bleu.* Lausanne: Editions L'Age d'Homme, 1991.

Tompkins, Calvin. *Living Well Is the Best Revenge.* New York: Dutton, 1982.

Turi, Anna-Maria. *Nijinsky: L'Invention de la danse.* Trans. Marie-José Hoyet. Paris: Editions du Félin, 1987.

Tyler, Parker. *The Divine Comedy of Pavel Tchelitchew.* New York: Fleet, 1967.

Valois, Ninette de. *Come Dance with Me: A Memoir, 1898–1956.* London: Dance Books, 1973.

———. *Invitation to the Ballet.* London: John Lane, 1937.

Van Vechten, Carl. *The Dance Writings of Carl Van Vechten.* Ed. and introd. Paul Padgette. New York: Dance Horizons, 1974.

Veroli, Patrizia. *Milloss.* Lucca: Libreria Musicale Italiana Editrice, 1996.

Volkov, Solomon. *Balanchine's Tchaikovsky.* Trans. Antonina W. Bouis. New York: Simon and Schuster, 1985.

Wachtel, Andrew, ed. *Petrushka: Sources and Contexts.* Evanston, Ill.: Northwestern University Press, 1998.

Walker, Kathrine Sorley. *De Basil's Ballets Russes.* London: Hutchinson, 1982.

———. *Ninette de Valois: Idealist Without Illusions.* With contributions by Dame Ninette. London: Hamish Hamilton, 1987.

White, Eric Walter. *Stravinsky: The Composer and His Works.* Berkeley: University of California Press, 1979.

Whitworth, Geoffrey. *The Art of Nijinsky.* 1913. Rpt. New York: Benjamin Blom, 1972.

Wiley, Roland John. *A Century of Russian Ballet: Documents and Eyewitness Accounts, 1810–1910.* Oxford: Oxford University Press, 1990.

———. *Tchaikovsky's Ballets: Swan Lake, Sleeping Beauty, Nutcracker.* Oxford: Oxford University Press, 1985.

Wolff, Stephane. *L'Opéra au Palais Garnier (1875–1962).* Introd. Alain Gueullette. Paris: Slatkine, 1983.

Wolkonsky, Prince Serge. *My Reminiscences.* Trans. A. E. Chamot. 2 vols. London: Hutchinson, 1925.

Yastrebtsev, V. V. *Reminiscences of Rimsky-Korsakov.* Ed. and trans. Florence Jonas. Introd. Gerald Abraham. New York: Columbia University Press, 1985.

Zil'bershtein, I. S., and V. A. Samkov, eds. *Sergei Diagilev i russkoe iskusstvo* (Serge Diaghilev and Russian art). 2 vols. Moscow: Iskusstvo, 1982.

Articles

Acocella, Joan. "Photo Call with Nijinsky: The Circle and the Center." *Ballet Review* 14, no. 4 (Winter 1987), pp. 49–71.

Archer, Kenneth, and Millicent Hodson. "Nijinsky for the 90s—Till Eulenspiegel Is Coming Back." *Dance Now* (Spring 1992), pp. 10–20.

Bentivoglio, Leonetta. "Danza e futurismo in Italia (1913–1933)." *La Danza italiana* 1 (Autumn 1984), pp. 61–82.

Bowlt, John E. "Constructivism and Russian Stage Design." *Performing Arts Journal* 1, no. 3 (Winter 1977), pp. 62–84.

———. "Nikolai Ryabushinsky: Playboy of the Eastern World." *Apollo* (Dec. 1973), pp. 486–493.

Celli, Vincenzo. "Enrico Cecchetti." *Dance Index* 5, no. 7 (1946), pp. 158–179.

Chujoy, Anatole. "Russian Balletomania." *Dance Index*, 7, no. 3 (Mar. 1948), pp. 45–71.

Cohen, Barbara Naomi. "The Borrowed Art of Gertrude Hoffmann." *Dance Data* 2 (n.d.), pp. 2–11.

Crisp, Clement, ed. "*Giselle* Revived: The Benois Notebooks." *Dance Research* 13, no. 2 (Autumn 1995), pp. 47–61.

Fagiolo Dell'Arco, Maurizio. "Balla's Prophecies." *Art International* 12, no. 6 (Summer 1968), pp. 63–68.

Fraser, John. "The Diaghilev Ballet in Europe: Footnotes to Nijinsky, Part Two." *Dance Chronicle* 5, no. 2 (1982), pp. 156–166.

———. "The Diaghilev Ballet in South America: Footnotes to Nijinsky, Part One." *Dance Chronicle* 5, no. 1 (1982), pp. 11–23.

Garafola, Lynn. "Diaghilev in Perm." *Ballet Review* 24, no. 2 (Summer 1996), pp. 78–82.

———. "Forgotten Interlude: Eurhythmic Dancers at the Paris Opéra." *Dance Research* 13, no. 1 (Summer 1995), pp. 59–83.

———. "Soloists Abroad: The Pre-War Careers of Natalia Trouhanova and Ida Rubinstein." *Experiment* 2 (1996), pp. 9–39.

Goldman, Debra. "Mothers and Fathers: A View of Isadora and Fokine." *Ballet Review* 6, no. 4 (1977–1978), pp. 33–43.

Goncharova, Natalia. "The Creation of 'Les Noces.'" *Ballet and Opera*, Sept. 1949, pp. 23–26.

———. "The Metamorphoses of the Ballet 'Les Noces.'" *Leonardo* 12, no. 2 (Spring 1979), pp. 137–143.

Gordon, Mel. "Meyerhold's Biomechanics." *Drama Review* 18, no. 3 (Sept. 1974), pp. 73–88.

Guest, Ann Hutchinson. "Nijinsky's *Faune*." *Choreography and Dance* 1, no. 3 (1991), pp. 3–34. This article is in the issue "A Revival of Nijinsky's Original *L'Après-midi d'un Faune*," edited by Jill Beck.

Hammer, Martin, and Christina Lodder. "A Constructivist *Pas de Deux*: Naum Gabo and Sergei Diaghilev." *Experiment* 2 (1996), pp. 81–99.

Hodson, Millicent. "Nijinsky's Choreographic Method: Visual Sources from Roerich for *Le Sacre du Printemps*." *Dance Research Journal* 18, no. 2 (Winter 1986–1987), pp. 7–15.

Horwitz, Dawn Lille. "A Ballet Class with Michel Fokine." *Dance Chronicle* 3, no. 1 (1979), pp. 36–45.

Iavorskaia, N. A. "Les Relations artistiques entre Paris et Moscou dans les années 1917–1930." In *Paris-Moscou, 1900–1930*. Paris: Centre National d'Art et de Culture Georges Pompidou, 1979.

Jones, Robert Edmond. "Nijinsky and *Till Eulenspiegel*." *Dance Index* 4, no. 4 (Apr. 1945), pp. 44–54.

Karlinsky, Simon. "Stravinsky and Russian Pre-Literate Theater." *Nineteenth Century Music* 6, no. 3 (Spring 1983), pp. 232–240.

Kettering, Karen. "The Rose-Colored Specter: Natalia Danko's Nijinsky." *Experiment* 2 (1996), pp. 127–141.

Kirstein, Lincoln. "The Diaghilev Period." *Hound and Horn* 3, no. 4 (July–Sept. 1930), pp. 468–501. Reprinted in *Ballet: Bias and Belief; "Three Pamphlets Collected" and Other Dance Writings of Lincoln Kirstein*. Ed. and introd. Nancy Reynolds. New York: Dance Horizons, 1983.

Martin, Marianne W. "The Ballet *Parade*: A Dialogue Between Cubism and Futurism." *Art Quarterly*, Spring 1978, pp. 85–111.

Mazo, Margarita. "Stravinsky's *Les Noces* and Russian Village Wedding Ritual." *Journal of the American Musicological Society* 43, no. 1 (Spring 1990), pp. 99–142.

Moon, Michael. "Flaming Closets." In *Bodies of the Text: Dance as Theory, Literature as Dance*. Ed. Ellen W. Goellner and Jacqueline Shea Murphy. New Brunswick: Rutgers University Press, 1995, pp. 57–78.

Nijinska, Bronislava. "Creation of *Les Noces*." Trans. and introd. Jean M. Serafetinides and Irina Nijinska. *Dance Magazine*, Dec. 1974, pp. 58–61.

———. "On Movement and the School of Movement." Introd. Joan Ross Acocella and Lynn Garafola. *Ballet Review* 13, no. 4 (Winter 1986), pp. 75–81.

———. "Reflections About the Production of *Les Biches* and *Hamlet* in Markova-Dolin Ballets." Trans. Lydia Lopokova. *Dancing Times*, Feb. 1937, pp. 617–620.

Piccione, Carmela. "Gli italiani e i Ballets Russes." *La Danza Italiana* 7 (Spring 1989), pp. 121–144.

Polignac, Princesse Edmond de. "Memoirs of the Late Princess Edmond de Polignac. *Horizon*, Aug. 1945, pp. 110–141.

Pudelek, Janina. "Fokine in Warsaw, 1908–1914." *Dance Chronicle* 15, no. 1 (1992), pp. 59–71.

Rabinowitz, Stanley. "Against the Grain: Akim Volynskii and the Russian Ballet." *Dance Research* 14, no. 1 (Summer 1996), pp. 3–41.

Reeder, Roberta, and Arthur Comegno. "Stravinsky's *Les Noces*." *Dance Research Journal* 18, no. 2 (Winter 1986–1987), pp. 30–61.

Ricco, Edward. "The Sitwells at the Ballet." *Ballet Review* 6, no. 1 (1977–1978), pp. 58–117.

Richardson, Philip J. S. "A Chronology of the Ballet in England, 1910–1945." In *The Ballet Annual: A Record and Yearbook of the Ballet*. Ed. Arnold Haskell. London: Adam and Charles Black, 1947, pp. 115–131.

Riviere, Jacques. "Le Sacre du Printemps." *La Nouvelle Revue Française*, Nov. 1913, pp. 706–730.

Sayers, Lesley-Anne. "Sergei Diaghilev's 'Soviet' Ballet: *Le Pas d'Acier* and Its Relationship to Russian Constructivism." *Experiment* 2 (1996), pp. 101–125.

Sharp, Jane A. "Redrawing the Margins of Russian Vanguard Art: Natalia Goncharova's Trial for Pornography in 1910." In *Sexuality and the Body in Russian Culture*. Ed. Jane T. Costlow, Stephanie Sandler, Judith Vowles. Stanford: Stanford University Press, 1993, pp. 97–123.

Silver, Kenneth E. "Jean Cocteau and the *Image d'Epinal*: An Essay on Realism and Naivete." In *Jean Cocteau and the French Scene*. Ed. Alexandra Anderson and Carol Saltus. New York: Abbeville, 1984.

Singleton, Suzanne. "Performances of the Russian Ballet in South Carolina, 1912, 1916, and 1922." *South Carolina Historical Magazine* 93 (July–Oct. 19982), pp. 231–239.

Slonimsky, Yuri. "Balanchine: The Early Years." Trans. John Andrews. Ed. Francis Mason. *Ballet Review* 5, no. 3 (1975–1976), pp. 1–64.

Svetlov, Valerian. "The Diaghileff Ballet in Paris." Pt. 1. *Dancing Times*, Dec. 1929, pp. 263–274.

———. "The Diaghileff Ballet in Paris." Pt. 2. *Dancing Times*, Jan. 1930, pp. 460–463.

———. "The Diaghileff Ballet in Paris." Pt. 3. *Dancing Times*, Feb. 1930, pp. 569–574.

———. "The Old and the New." *Dancing Times,* July 1929, pp. 326–331.

Telyakovsky, V. A. "Balletomanes." Trans. Nina Dimitrievich. *Dance Research* 13, no. 2 (Autumn 1995), pp. 77–88.

———. "Memoirs." Trans. Nina Dimitrievich. Pt. 1. Preface by Clement Crisp. *Dance Research* 8, no. 1 (Summer 1990), pp. 37–46.

———. "Memoirs." Trans. Nina Dimitrievich. Pt. 2. *Dance Research* 9, no. 1 (Spring 1991), pp. 26–39.

———. "Memoirs." Trans. Nina Dimitrievich. [Pt. 3] *Dance Research* 12, no. 1 (Summer 1994), pp. 41–47.

Testa, Alberto. "Diaghilev in Italia." *La Danza Italiana* 2 (Spring 1985), pp. 73–84.

Tripp, Susan B. "Bakst." *Johns Hopkins Magazine,* June 1984, pp. 12–22.

Valois, Ninette de. "The Future of the Ballet." *Dancing Times,* Feb. 1926, pp. 589–593.

———. "Modern Choregraphy." Pt. 2. *Dancing Times,* Feb. 1933, pp. 549–552.

———. "Modern Choregraphy." Pt. 4. *Dancing Times,* Apr. 1933, pp. 9–11.

Veroli, Patrizia. "Cangiullo e Diaghilev." *Terzo occhio* 65 (Dec. 1992), pp. 9–11.

Wiley, Roland John. "Alexandre Benois' Commentaries." Pts. 1–7. *Dancing Times,* Oct. 1980–Apr. 1981.

Wollen, Peter. "Fashion/Orientalism/The Body." *New Formations* 1 (Spring 1987), pp. 5–33.

Theses and Dissertations

Acocella, Joan Ross. "The Reception of Diaghilev's Ballets Russes by Artists and Intellectuals in Paris and London, 1909–1914." Ph.D. diss., Rutgers University, 1984.

Baldwin, Frances. "Critical Response in England to the Work of Designers for Diaghilev's Russian Ballet, 1911–1929." M.A. thesis, Courtauld Institute of Art, 1980.

Block, Alice. "Isadora Duncan and Vaslav Nijinsky: Dancing on the Brink." Ph.D. diss., Temple University, 1991.

Bullard, Truman C. "The First Performance of Igor Stravinsky's *Sacre du Printemps.*" Ph.D. diss., Eastman School of Music, 1971.

Carbonneau Levy, Suzanne. "The Russians Are Coming: Russian Dancers in the United States, 1910–1933." Ph.D. diss., New York University, 1990.

DeBold, Conrad II. "*Parade* and 'Le Spectacle Interieur': The Role of Jean Cocteau in an Avant-Garde Ballet." Ph.D. diss., Emory University, 1982.

Fergison, Drue. "*Les Noces:* A Microhistory of the Paris 1923 Production." Ph.D. diss., Duke University, 1995.

Grover, Stuart R. "Savva Mamontov and the Mamontov Circle: 1870–1905; Art Patronage and the Rise of Nationalism in Russian Art." Ph.D. diss., University of Wisconsin, 1971.

Hodson, Millicent Kaye. "Nijinsky's New Dance: Rediscovery of Ritual Design in *Le Sacre du Printemps.*" Ph.D. diss., University of California, Berkeley, 1985.

Horwitz, Dawn Lille. "Michel Fokine in America, 1919–1942." Ph.D. diss., New York University, 1982.

McQuillan, Melissa A. "Painters and the Ballet, 1917–1926: An Aspect of the Relationship Between Art and Theatre." Ph.D. diss., New York University, 1979.

Mayer, Charles Steven. "The Theatrical Designs of Leon Bakst." Ph.D. diss., Columbia University, 1977.

Pasler, Jann Corinne. "Debussy, Stravinsky, and the Ballets Russes: The Emergence of a New Musical Logic." Ph.D. diss., University of Chicago, 1981.

Ries, Frank W. D. "Jean Cocteau and the Ballet." Ph.D. diss., Indiana University, 1980.

Weinstock, Stephen Jay. "Independence Versus Interdependence in Stravinsky's Theatrical Collaborations: The Evolution of the Original Production of *The Wedding*." Ph.D. diss., University of California, Berkeley, 1981.

Joan Acocella, dance critic for the *New Yorker* and author of *Mark Morris*, is the editor of the 1999 *Diary of Vaslav Nijinsky*, the first complete English edition.

Nancy Van Norman Baer was curator of the Theater and Dance Collection at the Fine Arts Museums of San Francisco. Among the exhibitions and catalogues she produced before her untimely death are *Bronislava Nijinska: A Dancer's Legacy*, *The Art of Enchantment: Diaghilev's Ballets Russes, 1909–1929*, *Theatre in Revolution: Russian Avant-Garde Stage Design, 1913–1935*, and *Paris Modern: The Swedish Ballet, 1920–1925*.

Sally Banes is the Marian Hannah Winter Professor of Theatre History and Dance Studies at the University of Wisconsin. Her most recent book is *Dancing Women: Female Bodies on Stage*.

John E. Bowlt is professor of Russian art and literature at the University of Southern California, Los Angeles, where he also directs the Institute of Modern Russian Culture. A specialist in symbolism and the avant-garde, he is the author of *The Silver Age: Russian Art of the Early Twentieth Century and the "World of Art" Group* and editor, most recently, of *The Salon Album of Vera Stravinsky*. He has published widely on many aspects of Russian art, theater, and dance.

Suzanne Carbonneau is a dance historian and critic whose writings have appeared in the *Washington Post* and other publications. She teaches in the Institute of the Arts at George Mason University.

Evgenia Egorova grew up near the Diaghilev family estate of Bikbarda in the aftermath of the Russian Revolution. She heads the regional research section of the Perm State Art Gallery.

Drue Fergison is assistant professor of Interdisciplinary Studies at Saint Mary's University in Minnesota.

Judi Freeman is an independent curator specializing in art of the late nineteenth and twentieth centuries. She has organized a number of significant exhibitions on key figures and phases in twentieth-century art and has written extensively on Fernand Léger.

Lynn Garafola is the author of *Diaghilev's Ballets Russes* and editor, most recently, of *Rethinking the Sylph: New Perspectives on the Romantic Ballet*, *José Limon: An Unfinished Memoir*, and *Dance for a City: Fifty Years of the New York City Ballet*. She is the former editor of the series Studies in Dance History.

Charles M. Joseph is William R. Kenan Professor of Liberal Arts at Skidmore College. He is the author of *Stravinsky and the Piano* and a forthcoming book on Stravinsky's collaborations with Balanchine.

Israel Nesteev, the late Russian musicologist, is the author of books about Prokofiev, Bartók, Hanns Eisler, Puccini, and popular Soviet song. His last book, published in 1994, was *Diaghilev and Twentieth-Century Music Theater*.

Nancy Reynolds is a former member of the New York City Ballet, the author of *Repertory in Review: Forty Years of the New York City Ballet*, and director of research for the George Balanchine Foundation.

Elizabeth Souritz is the head of the Dance Section of the Moscow Institute of the History of the Arts. She is the author of *Soviet Choreographers in the 1920s*.

David Vaughan is the archivist of the Cunningham Dance Foundation. He is the author of *Merce Cunningham: 50 Years* and *Frederick Ashton and His Ballets*, and a member of the editorial board of the *International Encyclopedia of Dance*.

Color Plates

Pls. 1, 2, 5, 6: State Russian Museum, St. Petersburg

Pl. 3: Dagestan Museum of Fine Arts, Makhachkala, Russia

Pl. 4: *Zolotoe runo*, no. 4 (1906)

Pls. 13, 15, 16: The Fine Arts Museums of San Francisco, Theater and Dance Collection, Gift of Mrs. Adolph B. Spreckels

Pl. 7: The Fine Arts Museums of San Francisco, Theater and Dance Collection, Gift of Mrs. Adolph B. Spreckels. © 1999 Artists Rights Society (ARS), New York/ADAGP, Paris.

Pl. 8: Private collection, San Francisco. © 1999 Artists Rights Society (ARS), New York/ADAGP, Paris.

Pls. 9, 12, 14, 18, 27: Marion Koogler McNay Art Museum, San Antonio, Robert L. B. Tobin Collection

Pl. 10: Dance Collection, New York Public Library for the Performing Arts

Pl. 11: *Collection des plus beaux numéros de Comoedia Illustré et des programmes consacrés aux ballets et galas russes* (Paris: de Brunoff, 1922)

Pl. 17: Courtesy of Sotheby's, London

Pl. 19: Oil on canvas, 53¾ × 39½ in. (136.5 × 100.3 cm), The Museum of Modern Art, New York, Gift of Mr. and Mrs. Peter A. Rübel (partly by exchange). Photo © 1998 The Museum of Modern Art, New York. © 1999 Artists Rights Society (ARS), New York/ADAGP, Paris.

Pl. 20: The Fine Arts Museums of San Francisco, Theater and Dance Collection, Gift of Mrs. Adolph B. Spreckels. © 1999 Estate of Pablo Picasso/Artists Rights Society (ARS), New York.

Pl. 21: Ballets Russes souvenir program, Paris, 1923. © 1999 Estate of Pablo Picasso/Artists Rights Society (ARS), New York.

Pl. 22: Private collection, New York. © 1999 Estate of Pablo Picasso/Artists Rights Society (ARS), New York.

Pl. 23: Ballets Russes souvenir program, Paris, May–June 1922

Pl. 24: Ballets Russes souvenir program, Paris, May–June 1922. © 1999 Artists Rights Society (ARS), New York/ADAGP, Paris.

Pl. 25: Musée Picasso, Paris. © 1999 Estate of Pablo Picasso/Artists Rights Society (ARS), New York.

Pl. 26: Bakhrushin State Central Theater Museum, Moscow

Pl. 28: Jean Cocteau et al., *Théâtre de Serge Diaghilew: Les Biches* (Paris: Editions des Quatre Chemins, 1924). © 1999 Artists Rights Society (ARS), New York/ADAGP, Paris.

Pl. 29: Ballets Russes souvenir program, Monte Carlo, 1926. © 1999 Artists Rights Society (ARS), New York/ADAGP, Paris.

Pl. 30: Theatre Museum, London

Pl. 31: Ballets Russes souvenir program, Paris, 1929

Pl. 32: The Fine Arts Museums of San Francisco, Theater and Dance Collection, Gift of Jane Daggett Dillenberger and John Dillenberger

Black and White Prints

Page 3: Copyright © Sotheby's, 1984

9: Photo by Elliott and Fry. Roger Pryor Dodge Collection, Dance Collection, New York Public Library for the Performing Arts

10: Serge Diaghilev, 1916. Photo by Jan de Strelecki. Dance Collection, New York Public Library for the Performing Arts

14: Prints and Photographs Division, Library of Congress, Washington, D.C.

17: A. S. Terekhin, *Perm': Ocherk arkhitektury* (Perm: Permskoe knizhnoe izdatel'stvo, 1980), n.p.

21: Private collection, St. Petersburg

24: *Mir iskusstva*, no. 7 (1901), p. 17

25: Private collection, New York

26: Natalia Roslavleva, *Era of the Russian Ballet* (New York: Dutton, 1966), p. 161

28: Rambert Dance Company Archives, London

29, 30: Prints and Photographs Division, Library of Congress

35, 36: Music Collection, New York Public Library for the Performing Arts

47: Photo by Sergei Mikhailovich Prokudin-Gorskii. Prints and Photographs Division, Library of Congress.

54: *Mir iskusstva*, nos. 5–6 (1902), cover

55: *Mir iskusstva*, nos. 21–22 (1899), cover. The Bancroft Library, University of California, Berkeley.

58: Collection of Herbert Schimmel, New York

59: Central State Archive of Cinema and Photo Documents, St. Petersburg

60: *Zolotoe runo* 4 (1906), p. 12

61: *Mir iskusstva*, no. 4 (1901), p. 103. The Bancroft Library, University of California, Berkeley.

65: *Sergei Diagilev i russkoe iskusstvo*, ed. I. S. Zil'bershtein and V. A. Samkov (Moscow: Iskusstvo, 1982), vol. 1, pl. 38

66–67: S. P. Diaghilev and V. P. Gorlenko, *D. G. Levitsky (1735–1822), Russkaia zhivopis' v XVIII veke* (Russian painting in the eighteenth century), vol. 1 (St. Petersburg: Evdokimov, 1902).

72: *Mir iskusstva*, nos. 23–24 (1899), cover. The Bancroft Library, University of California, Berkeley.

73: *Mir iskusstva* (1899). The Bancroft Library.

74: *Mir iskusstva*, no. 5 (1901), p. 207. The Bancroft Library.

77: *Mir iskusstva*, nos. 1–2 (1898), p. 1. The Bancroft Library.

84: *Mir iskusstva*, no. 7 (1902), p. 4. The Bancroft Library. © 1999 Artists Rights Society (ARS), New York/ADAGP, Paris.

86, 87: *Mir iskusstva*, nos. 3–4 (1899), p. 54. The Bancroft Library.

88: *Mir iskusstva*, nos. 8–9 (1901), p. 69. The Bancroft Library.

92 (top): *Mir iskusstva*, no. 1 (1901), p. 27. The Bancroft Library.

92 (bottom): *Mir iskusstva*, nos. 16–17 (1899), p. 92. The Bancroft Library.

93: *Mir iskusstva*, nos. 5–6 (1900), p. 69. The Bancroft Library.

98: *The Dance of Isadora Duncan* (Paris, 1952)

100, 101: Anna Duncan Collection, the Dansmuseet, Stockholm

103: Photos by the Dover Street Studios. *The Sketch* [Supplement], 27 July 1910, p. 5.

104: Bakhrushin State Central Theater Museum, Moscow

107: Private collection, Moscow

108: Ballets Russes souvenir program, New York, 1916

110: Photo by Boissonas. In Valerian Svelov, *Le Ballet contemporain* (St. Petersburg: Golicke et Willborg, 1912), p. 81.

111: Ballets Russes souvenir program, New York, 1916

112: Photo by Claude Harris. *The Sketch*, 14 Oct. 1914.

113: Photo by Auguste Bert. In *Collection des plus beaux numéros de Comoedia Illustré et des programmes consacrés aux ballets et galas russes* (Paris: de Brunoff, 1922).

115: Photo by Saul Bransburg. *Illustrated London News*, 4 July 1914, p. 24.

118: *Collection des plus beaux numéros de Comoedia Illustré*

119: Ballets Russes souvenir program, 1909

120: Svetlov, *Ballet contemporain*, p. 18

121: Photo by E. O. Hoppé. *The Graphic*, 20 July 1912, p. 97.

122: A. N. Afanaseyev, *Tale of Ivan Tsarevich, the Firebird, and the Gray Wolf* (St. Petersburg: Izdanie Ekspeditsii zagotovleniia gosudarstvennykh bumag, 1901), p. 2. Photo by Joseph Zehavi. The Pierpont Morgan Library, New York. PML 86045+.

125: Ballet Society Archives, New York

126, 129, 132: Photo by Auguste Bert. In *Collection des plus beaux numéros de Comoedia Illustré*.

138: Photo by J. Perret

139: Marion Koogler McNay Art Museum, San Antonio, Robert L. B. Tobin Collection

140, 141, 142: Private collection, New York

146, 147: Collection Pierre Alechinsky

148: Location unknown, formerly in the collection of Lucien Lefebvre-Foinet, Paris. © 1999 Artists Rights Society (ARS), New York/ADAGP, Paris.

149: Private collection, Paris. © 1999 Artists Rights Society (ARS), New York/ADAGP, Paris.

150 (top), 151 (top): Dansmuseet, Stockholm

Page 150 (bottom): Private collection, England

151 (bottom): Ballets Russes souvenir program, Paris, May–June 1920

154: Svetlov, *Ballet contemporain*, p. 56. © 1999 Artists Rights Society (ARS), New York/ ADAGP, Paris.

155: Photo by Auguste Bert. *Le Théâtre*, Aug. 1909, vol. 1, p. 13.

156: Roger Pryor Dodge Collection, Dance Collection, New York Public Library for the Performing Arts

157: Photo by Stage Photo Company. Dance Collection, New York Public Library for the Performing Arts.

158: Private collection, New York

159: Photo by Lipnitzki. Copyright © Lipnitzki-Violet.

161: Photo by Henry Manuel. In W. A. Propert, *The Russian Ballet, 1921–1929* (London: John Lane, 1931), pl. 24.

162: Photo by Man Ray. Stravinsky-Diaghilev Foundation, New York. © 1999 Man Ray Trust/Artists Rights Society (ARS), New York/ADAGP, Paris.

163: Photo by Manuel Frères. Ballet Society Archives, New York.

164: Propert, *Russian Ballet*, pl. 36

168: Ballets Russes souvenir program, Paris, 1921. © 1999 Estate of Pablo Picasso/Artists Rights Society (ARS), New York.

169: Private collection, Switzerland

170, 171: Michel Larionov, *Diaghilev et les Ballets Russes* (Paris: Bibliothèque des Arts, 1970)

173: Bakhrushin State Central Theater Museum, Moscow

174: Fine Arts Museums of San Francisco, Theater and Dance Collection, Gift of Arne Ekstrom in memory of Parmenia Migel Ekstrom

175: Photo by James Abbé. In Propert, *Russian Ballet*, pl. 7.

177: Jean Cocteau, *Dessins* (Paris: Stock, 1924). © 1999 Artists Rights Society (ARS), New York/ADAGP, Paris.

182: National Photo. Prints and Photographs Division, Library of Congress.

184: *The Sketch* (Supplement), 23 July 1913

187: Ballets Russes souvenir program, Paris, 1923

190, 192, 195: Sammlung Igor Stravinsky, Paul Sacher Stiftung, Basel

198, 199: Photo by Vladimir Dimitriev. Ballets Russes souvenir program, Paris, 1929.

202: Photo by Claude Harris. Ballets Russes souvenir program, Monte Carlo, 1926.

203: © 1998 Artists Rights Society (ARS), New York/ADAGP, Paris

205: Anton Dolin, *Markova: Her Life and Art* (London: W. H. Allen, 1953), p. 64

208: Photo by Vera Sudeikina. Sammlung Igor Stravinsky, Paul Sacher Siftung, Basel.

210: Division of Recorded Sound, Library of Congress

212: Stravinsky-Diaghilev Foundation, New York

214: Private collection, New York

221: Photo by Wayne Albee. Adolph Bolm Papers, Syracuse University Library, Department of Special Collections.

222, 225, 234, 238, 243: Adolph Bolm Papers

224: Photo by Washington Photo Company. Adolph Bolm Papers.

226: Photo by Maurice Goldberg. Adolph Bolm Papers.

227: Photo by Mishkin. Adolph Bolm Papers.

228: Photo by Dagnerre Studio. Adolph Bolm Papers.

230, 231: *Krazy Kat* (musical score) (New York: Schirmer, 1922)

246, 247, 249: Photo by Baron de Meyer. Roger Pryor Dodge Collection, Dance Collection, New York Public Library for the Performing Arts.

248: Photo by George Hoyningen-Huene. In William A. Ewing, *Dance and Photography* (New York: Holt, 1987), pl. 89.

250: *Yearbook of the Imperial Theaters,* 1903–1904 season, p. 113

251: *Le Théâtre,* May 1909, vol. 1, n.p.

252: George Barbier, *Designs on the Dances of Vaslav Nijinsky* (London: C. W. Beaumont, 1913), n.p.

253: Photo by L. Roosen. Roger Pryor Dodge Collection, Dance Collection, New York Public Library for the Performing Arts.

254: Photo by Gerschel. Roger Pryor Dodge Collection.

256: Marion Koogler McNay Art Museum, San Antonio, Robert L. B. Tobin Collection

257: Stravinsky-Diaghilev Foundation, New York

260: Photo by Sasha. In Propert, *Russian Ballet,* pl. 27.

263: Barbier, *Designs on the Dances of Nijinsky*

264: Ballets Russes souvenir program, Paris, 1919–1920. © 1999 Estate of Pablo Picasso/Artists Rights Society (ARS), New York.

265: Private collection, New York

267: Stravinsky-Diaghilev Foundation, New York

270: Punch, 8 Nov. 1911, p. 335

271: Punch, 24 Jan. 1912, p. 61

272: *The Sketch,* 2 July 1913, p. 408

273: Punch, 27 Aug. 1913, p. 197

274: Rhythm 1, no. 1 (Summer 1911), p. 15

275: Douglas Blair Turnbaugh, "Duncan Grant and the Bloomsbury Group," pl. 36, no. 68, DBT 11, © Douglas Blair Turnbaugh, Collection of Douglas Blair Turnbaugh, New York

276: Yale Center for British Art, Paul Mellon Collection

277: Edith Sitwell, *Children's Tales (From the Russian Ballet)* (London: Leonard Parsons, 1920), p. 73.

278: *The Dancing Times,* July 1919, frontispiece

279: *Current Opinion,* Oct. 1919, p. 232

280: *The Sketch,* 28 Dec. 1921, p. 497

281: Kings College, Cambridge

282: Library of Congress

283: Max Beerbohm, *Things Old and New* (London: Heinemann, 1923), pl. 12

Page numbers in bold refer to illustrations.

Nijinsky, Kyra, 204

Nijinsky, Romola, 197, 297

Nijinsky, Vaslav, **9, 195,
310;** *L'Après-midi d'un Faune,*
246, 254, 255, **263;**
Carnaval, **247;** choreography of, 157–158, 196,
254–255, 309; *Cléopâtre,*
249; and Diaghilev, 8,
246; *Don Giovanni,* **251;**
feminized image of,
263–264, 379n7; *Firebird,*
119; *Giselle,* **156;** *Jeux,* 254,
255; Kirstein on, 309;
Narcisse, **275;** *Le Sacre du
Printemps,* 158, 196, 254–
55; *Schéhérazade,* **249,** 250,
252; *Le Spectre de la Rose,*
253; and Stravinsky, 194–
197, 206; *Till Eulenspiegel,*
308

Nijinsky Dancing (Kirstein),
308, 309, **310**

Nikitina, Alice, 163, 197,
266, **285, 286**

Noces, Les, 165, 167–187; costuming, 170, 184–185,
371n8; folkloric sources,
167–168, 170, 370n2;
fusion of styles, 170, 171,
183, 185–187; Goncha-
rova, 138, 170–171, **172,**
174, **187,** 371n8, pl. **14;**
Nijinska, 158, 170–171,
174–175, 184, 186, 258,
370n7; and the pianola,
207, 209; premiere and
reviews, 183–187, **284;**
production difficulties,
172–174, 371n10;
rehearsals, 176–179, 180;
reviews, 183–186, **284;**
revival of, 7; Stravinsky,
167–170, 172, 370n2

Nouvel, Walter (Valechka),
27, 28, 29, 30, 51, 52,
352n17, pl. **5**

Novyi put, 58, 354n40

Nuit, La, 112

Nur and Anitra, 106

Nureyev, Rudolf, 8

Nutcracker, The (Balanchine),
302

objective criticism,
Diaghilev on, 89, 358n24

Oboukhoff, Anatole, 8

Ode, **159,** 160, 165, **265,** 266

Orientales, Les, 119

orientalism: in Diaghilev's
ballets, 117–120, 123,
362n4, 363n11; in *Firebird*
(*see* Russian identity, in
Firebird); popularity of, 2,
117, 131; and Russian
artists, 133–134, 365n28;
use of term, 361n1

Orpheus, 199, 301, **304**

Orpheus and Eurydice, 298

Otero, José, 227, 235

Oukrainsky, Serge, 230

"Our Supposed Decline"
(Diaghilev), 74, 76–84

Page, Ruth, 227, 236, 238,
241, 242

Panaeva-Kartseva,
Alexandra, 19, 24–25,
30, 41, 349nn3,14

pantomime, 102–103, 109,
194, 225, 227, 228, 234

Parade, 4, 136, 143, 145,
150, **151,** 165

parallel position, 5–6, 158,
347n6

Parnassus on Montmartre, 240

Pas d'Acier, Le, 159, 379n40

pas de deux: abandoned, 5,

254; *Bluebird,* **119,** 154;
Firebird, **119,** 123–124,
125–127, **126,** 364n17;
neoclassic, 258, 259

Pastorale, La, 160–161, 165,
259, **289**

Pavillon d'Armide, Le, 109, 154,
249, pl. **7**

Pavley, Andreas, 230

Pavlova, Anna, 97, 109, 110–
112, 221, 250–251, **282**

peasant images, 119–120,
137, 171, 233

Péri, La, 119, pl. **11**

Perm, **14,** 19–21

Petipa, Marie, 57, 354n37

Petipa, Marius, 5, 6, 104,
158, 159

Petrouchka, **9,** 119, 154, 192,
222, 252, 255, pl. **8**

Petrouchka (Bolm), 227

"Petrouchka" (Gross), **118**

Pevsner, Anton, **286**

Phèdre, **173,** 174, 371n13

pianolas, 206, 207–210,
374nn16, 19

Picasso, Pablo, 213, pls. **21,
22, 25;** *Dancers,* **264;** and
Léger, 141–143, 144, 148,
150; *Parade,* 4, 136, 143,
151, pl. **20;** portrait of
Stravinsky, 168; *Le Tricorne,*
8, 147, 148, 257

Pierrot Lunaire, 237

Pisarev, Dmitry, 80, 357n12

*Plastic Poem. See Visual
Mysticism*

plastique dance, 102–104,
107, 114

pointe work, 114, 158, 252,
254, 258, 259. *See also*
ballerina, classical

Polignac, Princesse Edmond
de, 181, **182,** 203